PEACE AND WAR

Cross-Cultural Perspectives

PEACE AND WAR

Cross-Cultural Perspectives

Edited by

Mary LeCron Foster and Robert A. Rubinstein

Transaction Books
New Brunswick (U.S.A.) and Oxford (U.K.)

Library of Congress Catalog Number: 85-20122
ISBN: 0-88738-069-7 (cloth), 0-88738-619-9 (paper)
Printed in the United States of America

Library of Congress Cataloging in Publication Data

Main entry under title:

Peace and war.

1. War—Addresses, essays, lectures. 2. Peace—Addresses, essays, lectures. 3. Sociology, Military—Addresses, essays, lectures. 4. Ethnology—Addresses, essays, lectures. I. Foster, Mary LeCron, 1914- II. Rubinstein, Robert A.
U21.2.P34 1985 303.6′6 85-20122
ISBN 0-88738-069-7
ISBN 0-88738-619-9 (pbk.)

Contents

Acknowledgments

The four days of symposia from which this book results were the contribution of the American Anthropological Association to the 11th International Congress of Anthropological and Ethnological Sciences. A small grant from the Association made possible our initial organizational work for these symposia. This support and the endorsement of the symposia by the Association were instrumental in helping us to gain further support for the program.

A Ford Foundation grant helped to pay the expenses of many of he symposia participants, and made possible the participation of many of the nonanthropologists and non-North American anthropologists. Further, we are grateful to the Foundation for permission to use the small surplus from the initial grant to support the publication of this book.

A small grant from the Wenner-Gren Foundation for Anthropological Research helped to facilitate the process of editing these papers and bringing them to their present form. Moreover the support and encouragement of the Foundation's Director of Research, Lita Osmundsen, have been invaluable throughout every stage of this project.

Without this help the Vancouver symposia would have been much less fruitful than they turned out to be, and this book would have been much longer in preparation. For all of this help, and for the help of the many colleagues, anthropologists and others, who suggested participants for the symposia, we are very grateful.

Preface

Anthropologists often say that their intensive fieldwork, the descriptive and comparative analyses resulting from that fieldwork, and the theories concerning the nature of culture and society that they develop from the analyses, provide unique insights into the nature of human problems. Unfortunately, these insights seldom reach those who must deal with global problems on a day-to-day basis. There are various reasons for this, some of which are discussed in this volume.

Motivated by a concern that anthropological insights which might be of value in finding solutions to the world's most pressing problems were available only to the initiated, we organized a series of symposium panels on peace and war, held at the Eleventh Congress of the International Union of Anthropological and Ethnological Sciences (IUAES) in Vancouver, British Columbia, Canada, in August 1983. Our hope was to stimulate further anthropological involvement with this topic and to encourage anthropologists to increase their role as policy consultants on a national and an international scale.

Because many of the participants had little experience in addressing a constituency broader than their own peers, yet were interested in exploring how their work could have a broader impact on policy, we invited a group of experts on war and peace policy and research from other areas of social science to join us in Vancouver and help us to broaden our perspective.

Our discussions began with a two-day pre-Congress workshop at Harrison Hot Springs, British Columbia. Most participants attended both this session and the two-day series of symposia at the Congress proper. The preliminary, less formal, discussions gave us the opportunity not only to think theoretically about a selection of papers delivered within the workshop setting, but to begin to think of steps in the process of enhancing the policymaking potential of anthropology.

Out of these discussions emerged the decision to give our efforts a more permanent character by proposing the establishment of a commission on peace studies as one of a series of already established IUAES commissions on global problems. Such a commission would provide a forum for research and discussion of peace and war-related issues on a worldwide scale.

In Vancouver, we formalized our proposal and presented it to the Executive Council of the IUAES, which voted unanimously to include a

Commission on the Study of Peace as one of its ongoing activities. The Commission has since set up a series of international committees to pursue the goals outlined in the commission proposal.

The traditional focus of social and cultural anthropology, or ethnology, is a relatively small, easily bounded geographical area with a fairly homogeneous population which can be studied over time in such a way as to isolate shared belief systems, social institutions, ritualized activities, methods of production, and social and environmental interaction of various kinds. The passage of time may or may not be taken into account. Formerly, it was usually ignored, and societies were studied as if isolated in time and space. At present, outside influences are increasingly viewed as fundamental to the understanding of any society, and all societies are viewed as dynamic, constantly changing entities, influenced by, and influencing the world around them.

Focusing on different aspects of conflict, the papers in this volume build from the role of the individual in his or her society, through the dynamics of specific conflict situations, to discussions of the global nature of modern militarism, finally discussing more specifically a role for anthropology in policy formation leading toward a more peace-oriented future.

Mary LeCron Foster

Robert A. Rubinstein

Introduction

Mary LeCron Foster and Robert A. Rubinstein

With the dawn of the nuclear age, the gap between our ability to resolve technical problems and our knowledge about how to solve social problems took on new and ominous dimensions. The problems that beset us in the nuclear era, although triggered by technological advances, are largely social; we must organize our international relations to cope with the military implications of this destructive force. To date, attempts at designing such international relations have relied primarily on physical science expertise. In the face of the broadening scope of nuclear-related technology there are signs of increasing reliance on physical science knowledge, often to the exclusion of social considerations. Yet, instead of increasing our reliance on physical science, it seems to us especially prudent and important to strengthen the role played by the systematic understanding of human behavior in attempts at devising new methods of furthering international understanding and cooperation.

As science and its product, technology, have become our twin gods, we have neglected the behavioral knowledge necessary to control the threat of destruction that our technological advances have created.

Anthropology is the behavioral science that has delved most deeply into the question of how diverse societies solve their social problems. Anthropologists, almost uniquely, also appreciate the degree to which members of human societies are affected by the cultural milieu into which they have been born and in which they are raised. It is customary to take for granted the subtle chains of belief and institutionalized values that govern our daily reactions to social and physical phenomena. It is especially easy to overlook the fact that these are *not universal* to the human condition.

The nuclear confrontation that threatens us today, and the dangers to global survival that it entails, force us to realize that we must change the fundamental premises of what constitutes power among and within groups of individuals if we are to avoid the prevailing deadly pattern of threat, counterthreat, and escalation.

Never has there been a period in which human wisdom is more needed, nor a period when the right decisions must be made if humanity is to survive. Yet policy is too frequently shaped by unexamined ideological assumptions that were more appropriate to a past technological era, or by assumptions that conflict in unrecognized ways with those of other peoples with whom we disagree, or by assumptions so rigidly fixed that alternative ways of devising strategies for reaching agreements never come to mind. Knowledge of how other societies cope with problems of inter- or intra-group conflict often suggest helpful new methods for conflict resolution. Wisdom in resolving social problems is best derived from knowledge of possibilities and past experiences.

Anthropologists have gathered data on a wide range of cultural solutions to human problems, and they share theoretical insights that make anthropology a potentially useful policy tool. Unfortunately, anthropologists have said little on the subject of peace and war. During and immediately after World War II, Margaret Mead and Gregory Bateson worked on the topic, and later Mead (1962, 1965) proposed that anthropology engage in war-related research with a view to making policy recommendations. Since 1965, a handful of books as well as scattered articles written by anthropologists have dealt with aspects of peace/war issues (e.g., Fried et al., 1967; Nettleship et al., 1975; Simonis et al., 1983; Ferguson, 1984). The predominant focus of these works has been on war, mainly among nonliterate people, and few have sought to contribute to contemporary policy discussions for building peace. Moreover, despite this sporadic interest, war and peace research has never become a central topic for discussion in anthropology. Contributors to this book feel strongly that anthropologists must move toward policy involvement, applying their knowledge of the dynamics of human conflict to the problem of securing a peaceful world.

Both anthropological and social-psychological research show that individuals learn at a very early age the value systems reflected in the institutions and rituals practiced by their societies. This institutionalization is what many anthropologists mean by the term "culture." A child's reality, as an adult's, is a cultural reality; the child's caretakers reflect their cultural heritage in every gesture, every word, every social encounter, every prohibition or approbation, and every organization of the child's time, space, and human interactions. All societies provide means both to encourage and discourage conflict. It is a psychobiological universal that frustration can lead to aggression. Hence, to be viable, a society must provide an acceptable means of directing the anger that stems from frustration. Warfare is, in many societies, an acceptable outlet. It is not, however, innate or inevitable. Human groups can and do exist without warfare.

To have warfare, military institutions must be created and warfare and warriors glorified. To be sustained, martial institutions must be reinforced by the periodic elevation of competitors to the status of enemies of society. The papers in this volume show that because warfare requires institutionalization and social reinforcement, its causes are multiple, covert, and culturally generated. Groups create institutions, and the interaction between individual and group tends to maintain and reinforce the belief systems that the institutions represent. Military power and its dangers have increased steadily, in part because of the transformation from state to nation-state in the process of world industrialization (Gellner, 1983; Worsley, 1984), coupling technological advances with the fusion of diverse ethnic and religious groups into larger political units. Often these powers have also elevated belief systems to national loyalties that often crosscut internal ethnic and religious differences. Since groups create institutions, the interaction between individual and group tends to maintain and reinforce the belief systems that the institutions represent. On the level of the nation-state, with technological advances in communication systems, this reinforcement and perpetuation achieve great power.

Although the papers in this volume focus principally on the cultural factors that give rise to or support war, several authors explicitly recognize the underlying psychobiological imperatives that require solutions for the aggressive and other drives, of which warfare is but one among a variety of possible solutions (Clark, Frank, Foster). None of the contributors believes war to be a human biological necessity.

The papers in this volume have been grouped into labeled sections in order to point out convergences of salient points in the authors' arguments. By so doing, we have tried to build from an initial focus on the individual and the meaning of conflict in his or her particular cultural environment, through the dynamics of particular conflicts, to more specific considerations of the potential role of anthropology in confronting peace/war issues. That these papers can be fitted together in other equally enlightening combinations highlights both the nascent state of anthropological studies of peace and the richness of the anthropological data that can be brought to bear on those studies.

Part I, The Individual, Community and Conflict, discusses the interplay between psychobiological and cultural universals as they are reflected in social institutions. Goldschmidt selects anthropological data from a variety of social groups in order to demonstrate how individual role gratification is encoded into particular military institutions. Lomnitz provides a case study showing the way in which the lack of socially approved outlets for masculine self-realization leads to the formation of urban street gangs which gain power and self-esteem through intimidation and threat. This is a socially disruptive expression of Mexican adherence to an ideal of *machismo.*

Huyghe, like Goldschmidt and Lomnitz, focuses on means of establishing male role gratification. He describes the ritual channeling of the masculine need for power among a group of New Guinea head-hunters and the way in which a variety of social institutions work together to support and perpetuate the practice and the associated belief systems. Although this form of warfare seems particularly abhorrent to Westerners, it demonstrates that there seems to be no universal norm by which degrees of cultural pathology can be measured. Our periodic mass killings would quite possibly seem far less moral to New Guinean tribal peoples than the selective or sporadic taking of a few heads.

Although many anthropologists find modern warfare morally reprehensible, Greenhouse shows clearly that for many American (and in her example, Christian) fundamentalists the question of the morality of wartime killing does not arise. Their enculturation toward militarism is as unquestioned as is that of Huyghe's New Guinea headhunters. In both cases war is fought because of belief in some higher good, and not because of personal aggressiveness or anger—in fact local conflict is studiously avoided. For the Americans described by Greenhouse there is no moral opposition between peace and war because both are supported by a transcending belief in the need for order, discipline, and faith.

Randall provides a chilling picture of the barrenness, uniformity, and lack of personal creativity of American peacetime military service abroad. It provides little personal satisfaction for soldiers and their dependents, except the security of an enduring job with monetary compensation and some possibility of moving up the hierarchical ladder through faithful service. Randall speculates that the lack of personal self-realization that such a rigidly organized and hierarchically determined life provides may be, in truth, a cultural pathology.

In trying to better understand the causes of war it is necessary to ask what individual and group satisfactions war provides, and for what innate drives it provides an outlet. This question is explored in the papers by Foster and Clark. Their analyses suggest that if war is to be abolished because its cultural utility is diminished or eliminated, other institutions providing alternative outlets for the same drives must be substituted.

Conflict between groups tends to develop its own internal dynamic. The papers in Part II, The Dynamics of Conflict, explore this tendency in specific situations. This dynamic is often perpetuated by the perception of those who are different from oneself as inferior, evil, and hence to be feared, or by conflicting claims for possession of resources. Often both factors are involved. Exclusive possession of a particular religious "truth" or other cherished ideology frequently justifies dominance over, or elimination of, those who do not share it.

Furst provides us with a microcosmic, ethnohistorical account of land disputes among lineages in ancient Mexico. Battles were fought and claims justified by appeal to contrasting origin myths. Doughty's theme is also ethnic, revolving around the right of one Peruvian group to control the productive lives of another. Gonzalez shows that ethnic differences can also be exploited, though misunderstood, in planning modern military strategy. Gamst meticulously describes the history of the interplay among ethnicity, control of resources, and technological means in the unending struggles among peoples in the Horn of Africa. Kehoe's dicussion of the history of the spread of Christianity nicely illustrates the fact that a pacifist ideology can be made to serve military purposes.

Part III, Social Scientists React, includes some strongly expressed arguments against the military practices and policies of today's superpowers by a varied group of social scientists: Frank, a psychiatrist well known for his insightful analyses of war and its causes (Frank, 1967); Nader, a social and legal anthropologist; Melman, a specialist in the social aspects of industrial engineering and a pioneer in advocacy of industrial conversion from military to nonmilitary uses; Sarkesian, a professor of military history; and Tishkov, a Soviet ethnologist. These papers form an interesting group because they are examples of the advocacy positions that stem from exposure to and identification with a variety of disciplinary sources. Social scientists often fail to speak out on issues that they are particularly well suited to address. Well-reasoned protest can play a useful role.

Part IV, Conflict and the Nation-State, is also concerned with more general political and social issues rather than the more particularized conflict dynamics that was the focus of Part II. Brucan discusses the connections between the ideologies and the institutions of modern nation-states. He argues that by broadening the scope of a given ideology in the service of social control, today's nation-states have overcome some of the earlier conflicts between social classes and ethnic units. However the expansion of nationalist ideology increases the power of the state at the cost of cultural diversity (see also Gellner, 1983:39). Ideology and the drive for power become inextricably interwoven, creating an intolerable international situation which can be overcome only by the shifting of ideological priorities toward the goal of world peace.

Brucan's paper sets the stage for the major theme of the papers in this section: that there is a great need to discover ideological commonalities among the world's communities and to focus on interdependencies rather than differences, in both research and policy recommendations. As much of the dependency is economic, these papers emphasize the fact that durable peace will be impossible to achieve if the world is polarized between the haves and the have-nots.

Like Brucan, Cohen takes a social-evolutionary perspective. Both are interested in the processes of nationalization, competing ideologies, and the struggle for power. Cohen reviews the history of industrialization of the world's societies, arguing that industrialization decreases rather than increases war-proneness, and that a primary international goal should be the development of industry and technology in the Third World. Pinxten futhers this argument by stressing that military use of economic resources for "deterrence" saps the strength of social and economic development efforts (cf. Melman, this volume).

Silverberg emphasizes the need to integrate social resources and, like Cohen, is optimistic about the trend and the outcome. He uses anthropological data to support the view that worldwide social integration is not just desirable but also likely. Although complex societies are characterized by an internal organization of social and ideological diversity, most individuals have multiple interests and social identifications which work for integration of the whole because of crosscutting social networks. The spread of such networks across national boundaries bodes well for ultimate ideological and social integration and world security.

Worsley challenges widespread assumptions about the nature of international affairs with the assertion that, in reality, politics is always ultimately about ideas, whether political, religious, or economic. Since "political realism," based on the threat of force, leads toward nuclear destruction, it is clearly failing. This dangerous situation can be averted only by a search for alternative conceptions of the goals of international relations.

If the dangers of nuclear disaster are to be avoided, new approaches to international relations must be explored. International security can best be achieved if nations forgo the temptation to denounce one another as evil or demonic and attempt instead to resolve common problems by establishing common goals.

War has no single cause; neither can peace be achieved through a single act. Causality derives from a multitude of interconnected factors. To avoid mass slaughter in the interests of securing the power of one's own group, it is essential to begin to view other societies as aggregates of human beings who have evolved solutions different from our own to human problems which we all share, rather than as adversaries. A correlate need is to understand ourselves and the underlying reasons for our own propensity for international confrontation. The contributors to this volume believe that anthropology can make a significant contribution to the achievement of both of these goals.

To this end, the papers in Part V, Anthropology and Policy, address the question of anthropology as a policy science. To date, anthropology's greatest policy contributions probably have been in the fields of health care and development programs in Third World countries. Here, planners, those carrying out the plans, and those affected by the planning, have been in immediate contact with one another. In contrast, in international planning there is little or no direct contact between policymakers and those most affected by their plans. Despite this difference, anthropology can provide insights into the nature of the intersection of belief systems and social institutions, as well as into factors underlying change and stability, can add a valuable dimension to both national and international planning.

Mandelbaum believes in the virtual inevitability of a nuclear disaster, a disaster that will thrust the world into a second stage of the nuclear age in which we will be forced into a reorganization of values and priorities. Governments should foresee such an eventuality and start preparing to cope with it. In this task anthropology can make a significant contribution. Maday points out why, to date, anthropology has not been notably successful as a policy science. Brucan calls attention to still further limitations to the effectiveness of social science, including anthropology, and calls for a methodological revolution. The new methodology would study social systems from the top down, rather than moving from the particular to the global. He also calls for increased objectivity. Although total objectivity is undoubtedly impossible, there is little doubt that social scientists in all countries need to expand their own ideological flexibility if they are to be as effective as the international crisis requires.

Beeman provides an example of the kind of ideological inflexibility that too often guides foreign policy decisions and makes them counterproductive. He argues that in the Iran/American hostage crisis, "principles of belief" served as rationalizations for actions already undertaken and blocked actions that were potentially more promising for reaching an agreement. Rubinstein examines the structure of the policymaking process in order to provide insight into the factors that determine whether strategies are open-ended and flexible, or of the rigid and entrenched type, as criticized also by Beeman. He explores ways in which policymakers can increase the likelihood of choosing strategies that allow for a greater number of possible options, providing a greater possibility for reaching satisfactory agreements. Such an approach would take account of a wider variety of information, including not only the cultural premises from which an adversary's strategies are derived but also one's own cultural biases that may be impeding progress.

The goal of this book is to encourage anthropologists to explore the potential of their own discipline in the task of increasing internal and external stability, as well as to give nonanthropologists some understanding of the kind of insights that anthropology can provide. This book is an invitation. It does not answer the questions: Why war? and, How do we achieve peace? Rather, by displaying the range of questions and a part of the value anthropology holds for better answering these questions, we hope that anthropologists and other behavioral scientists will begin to treat the study of peace as a legitimate and central topic of inquiry. We see this book as a beginning because it builds toward the prospect of a broadened role for anthropology in helping to improve policy strategy in the task of creating a more stable world.

References

Ferguson, R. Brian. 1984. *Warfare, Culture, and Environment.* New York: Academic Press.

Frank, Jerome D. 1967. *Sanity and Survival: Psychological Aspects of War and Peace.* New York: Vintage Books.

Fried, Morton; Harris, Marvin; and Murphy, Robert, eds. 1967. *War: The Anthropology of Armed Conflict and Aggression.* Garden City, N.Y.: Natural History Press.

Gellner, Ernest. 1983. *Nations and Nationalism.* Ithaca, N.Y.: Cornell University Press.

Mead, Margaret. 1962. "The Participation of Anthropologists in Research Relevant to Peace." Manuscript prepared for the Center for Research in Conflict Resolution and the American Anthropological Association.

Mead, Margaret, and Metraux, Rhoda. 1965. "The Anthropology of Human Conflict." In *The Nature of Conflict,* edited by Elton B. McNeil. Englewood Cliffs, N.J.: Prentice-Hall.

Nettleship, Martin A.; Givens, R. Dale; and Nettleship, A. 1975. *War: Its Causes and Correlates.* The Hague: Mouton.

Simonis, Yvan, ed. 1983. *Guerres et Stratègies* (special issue of *Anthropologie et Societes,* 7(1)). Quebec: Department of Anthropology, University of Laval.

Worsley, Peter. 1984. *The Three Worlds: Culture and World Development.* London: Weidenfeld and Nicolson.

PART I

THE INDIVIDUAL, COMMUNITY, AND CONFLICT

1

Personal Motivation and Institutionalized Conflict

Walter Goldschmidt

If anthropology is to contribute to the understanding of warfare, it must adopt a more dynamic approach. In particular, it must take cognizance of personal motivation and examine the interplay between individual interests and the social order (see also Huyghe, this volume). We have by now become well enough aware that individuals are shaped by their culture and live their lives in the context of a social system, but in learning this lesson, we have failed to examine the way tradition and structure are themselves shaped by human interests. To the social anthropologist, the individual is lost in structure, emerging, where he must, merely as a social role; to the cultural anthropologist the individual is baked in a "cake of custom," following the dictates of established and sacred tradition; to the psychological anthropologist he or she is stamped in the mold of traditional upbringing. Such treatment of the individual runs counter to our common sense notions about human behavior, to our perception of ourselves as actors in the human scene and, I think, to ethnographic realities as well.

In this essay I propose the concept of the human career as the focal element in the dynamic relationship between individual and community. By career I mean the trajectory of the individual life as it operates in pursuit of satisfaction. In order to understand what this means, it will be necessary to give the briefest possible summary of a theoretical treatise I am currently working on, a manuscript that I have been calling *Dynamic Anthropology* or, alternately, *Purpose and Progress in Social Life* (Goldschmidt, 1982). In it I argue that human motivation for self-gratification is the prime mover in the formulation of social structure. This self-gratification is not hedonism, however, for it is concerned not only with physical needs and desires or with what are often identified as social needs, but more importantly with the gratification of what I call the symbolic self.

The character of the human career, as with virtually all things human beings do, is set by the cultural definition of the situation, and basic career activities relate to the needs for social maintenance. We must, however, emphasize the *symbolic* aspect of career activities. The transition into humanity was accomplished by the formulation of a symbolic world, a superimposed system of understandings, of meanings and of sentiments that were shared by a population by virtue of systematic communication. Ever since, humans have lived in a symbolic as well as a real world. Language structures the cognitive elements of the symbolic world; ritual the emotional ones. There are three things that must be said about this symbolic world: first, it is a *structured* system that defines the whole relevant universe, second, each individual is a part of that systematic universe (and to him or herself, the most important part), and third, this symbolic world does not replace the world of physical reality, which remains with all its force and effect on human life, even though that physical world is interpreted and understood in terms of the symbolic world.

It is also necessary to appreciate the role of values, for everything in this world of understanding is given emotional valence. The world is not merely a cognitive system, it is also a system of sentiments. It is for the communication and coordination of sentiment that ritual and the arts were created, just as language communicates cognitive structure. (There has been debate over whether Neanderthal people had the power of speech, but there is no doubt that they had ritual.) When we stop to realize that the understandings and sentiments that constitute the symbolic world are acquired by each individual in the process of maturation, with all the attendant pains and pleasures, satisfactions and disappointments that such learning engenders, we should have no difficulty understanding the universality of values.

The most important thing each person learns in this process is what he himself or she herself is. This symbolic self, like everything else in the symbolic world derives from consensus. But far more than with other things, it is excruciatingly important. It is, of course, also emotionally laden. The process of self definition is never completed; it is in a lifelong process of reinterpretation.

I use the word "career" because I think its connotation most accurately reflects my meaning. In particular, I consider as central to the pursuit of career the kinds of work in which individuals engage. In tribal societies these tend to be standardized for each sex, though often with variants or secondary elements. But career is not the work itself, but rather performance, and it is not limited to the work activity, but involves all the other activities that go into the formation of what we may call reputation, including such matters as sexual prowess, fecundity, style, and the like. There is another attribute implicit in the concept: namely, that career performance varies; it is an element in social differentiation, and it is this potential for variance that makes it so important to the individual.

Social Gratification and Careers

It need not be said to a community of anthropologists that symbolic worlds differ from one place to another, and that it follows from this that what gives self-gratification and a positive valence to the self will also vary. A society that is successfully coping with its environment transforms the work necessary to daily life into ego-gratifying behavior. In shorthand terms, career performance is ecologically relevant. Let me make this point by brief reference to some of the anthropological classics.

- The immolation of the self into the clan and community of the Pueblo Indians, best caught in the Hopi phrase, "The Hopi way," and its relevance to enforced close collaboration that this environment demands (Thompson and Joseph, 1944).
- Trobriand garden magic (and hence personal power) evidenced by the public display of yam piles as an inspiration to horticultural production (Malinowski, 1935).
- Hunting ability, with its combination of physical skill, energy, and knowledge, among the Mbuti (Turnbull, 1965), the Andamanese (Radcliffe-Brown, 1933), and indeed I suspect everywhere hunting peoples are found.
- The close collaboration established among herdsmen in East Africa through their initiation into age sets so that they can collectively protect the herds against raids and successfully rob the kraals of others (e.g. Peristiany, 1939).

Here I must pause, for I have failed to make another point. The prosecution of career involves, in varying degrees and in diverse ways, collaboration with others. In one sense, ego gratification may be viewed as a lonely pursuit, for few others besides the self care about that self, but in another and more important way it involves structured relations with others—units of essential social collaboration. Indeed, it is this need for collaboration that, in my view, produces social structure.

- The inculcation of the young male Sioux into aggressive exploits and personal independence (Erikson, 1963), which are later reinforced by the initiatory experience in the vision quest, with its acquisition of power through personal deprivation and physical hardship, which together shape the buffalo hunter *cum* warrior necessary to the fluid territoriality of the American Plains.

The Military Career in Tribal Societies

Finally, we come to the consideration of militarism in relation to career. From the standpoint of the individual, career relates to the activities that give personal satisfaction, but from the standpoint of society, career performance is the engagement in tasks necessary for the maintenance of the community. One such task may be the service of protection against the outside or the exploitation of neighboring peoples through military aggression (or, perhaps more usually, both). In small-scale societies, the military role is often a universal aspect of male careers; in complex societies it may be regarded as a special cadre. Between these extremes are situations as described for the Iroquois, where warfare was a kind of freebooting activity engaged in by self-selected men interested in its rewards, yet nevertheless also in the service of the League's interest (Morgan, 1954:68).

The career aspects of military activity are exemplified by the following classic cases. Robert Lowie (1935:215) sums it up for the Crow in a paragraph:

> Social standing and chieftainship, we have seen, were dependent on military prowess; and that was the only road to distinction. Value was set on other qualities, such as liberality, aptness at story-telling, success as a doctor. But the property a man distributed was largely the booty he had gained in raids, and any accomplishments, prized as they might be, were merely decorative frills, not substitutes for the substance of a reputation, a man's record as a warrior. I know of at least one Crow of the old school whose intelligence would have made him a shining light wherever store was set by sheer capacity of the legal type, but who enjoyed no prestige whatsoever among his people [because] he had gained no honors in war and had tried to doctor this deficiency when publicly reciting his achievements. War was not the concern of a class nor even of the male sex, but all of the whole population, from cradle to grave.

And Grinnell (1923:7) for the Cheyenne does the same:

> From their earliest days boys were taught to long for the approbation of their elders, and this approbation was most readily to be earned by success in war. The applause of their public was the highest reward they knew.

Among East African pastoralists, the military career is closely associated with the economics of cattle production. For example P. T. W. Baxter (1977:77– 78), writing of the Boran, says:

> To be a stock herder and to be a warrior then are not separable occupations, because being the former involves being the latter. A herder must not only

guide the stock in his charge to good and safe pastures but he must also protect them from predators and raiders . . .

A herder's life is on the job training to be a warrior; in its daily course it provides many of the features that modern armies go to great expense to simulate for infantry or cavalry training. For a man whose life follows an ordinary course, to be a warrior is simply a routine feature of late youth and early manhood, it is not a specialized occupation simply because it is one which every male follows for the specially marked period of his life when he is an active herder. During warriorhood, features of the male role, such as valour and aggressive virility, are accentuated and others, such as oratorical skills, wisdom, and gentleness are subdued because they are appropriate to elderhood. The rigorous life that herders are forced to lead, particularly in the distant camps with the dry stock, is the ideal training ground for war in that it develops stamina, self-reliance, self-knowledge, and bush skills such as an eye for ground and for cover. The shared tasks, hardships and dangers of camp life generate intense spirits of mutual obligation, loyalty and trust. Herders in the camps share windbreaks, sleeping-hides and rations. They herd together and mess together; the milk and blood is shared equally among camp members on the basis of equal work deserving equal shares.

The rewards of warriorhood in terms of social gratification are equally explicit. Baxter (1977:82–83), again:

During warriorhood a man should acquire at least one trophy and, in the past, a man who did not do so was not welcomed as a son- in-law. A man who did kill was given gifts of stock, *sarma*, lavished with sexual favors by the wives of elders (whose attitude to him was therefore ambiguous), and allowed to wear ear rings, special necklaces and heavy iron armlets *arbora* and, crucially, a successful warrior was allowed to grow a male hair tuft, *guutu diira*, from the top of his head. This tuft was quite explicitly associated symbolically with an erect penis. . . . Successful warriors were acclaimed wherever they went and their exploits everywhere praised. A young man who had earned the right to "make his head" by erecting a *guutu* was everyone's darling. . . . Men who had killed were honored at the ceremonies which marked the entry of their generation-set into political adulthood, at their retirement into ritual elderhood, and at their mortuary ceremonies. At each, their exploits were loudly proclaimed and honored. Military glory was never extinguished.

Gregory Bateson (1958:138–41) has similar comments regarding the Iatmul, though it is by no means clear that head-hunting has the same economic rationale.

In the business of head-hunting, the masculine ethos no doubt reached its most complex expression; and though at the present time the ethos of head-hunting cannot be satisfactorily observed, there is enough left of the old system to give the investigator some impression of what that system implied.

> Two main motives informed this system, the personal pride of the individual and his pride and satisfaction in the prosperity and strength of his community. These two motives were closely tangled together. On the purely personal side, the successful homicide was entitled to special ornaments and paints and to the wearing of a flying fox skin as a pubic apron; while the apron of stripped *Dracaena* leaves was the reproach of the man who had never killed. The homicide was the hero of the most elaborate *naven* and the proud giver of feasts. . . . Lastly, he was admired by the women; and even today the women occasionally make scornful remarks about the calico loincloths worn by the young men who should strictly still be wearing *Dracaena* aprons like those which were given them when they were little boys being initiated.
>
> Running through this plexus of cultural details we can clearly see the general position of head-hunting as the main source of the pride of the village, while associated with the pride is prosperity, fertility and the male sexual act; while on the opposite side of the picture but still a part of the same ethos, we can see the association of shame, mourning, and *ngglambe.*
>
> Closely linked with these emphases upon pride and shame is the development of the spectacular side of head-hunting. Every victory was celebrated by great dances and ceremonial which involved the whole village. The killer was the hero of these and he was at the same time the host at the feasts which accompany them. Even the vanquished assented to the beauty of the dances. . . .

Militarism and Motivation

But you will say, we have known all this. Yet militarism is not a universal cultural element. You will not find it among the Mbuti or the San. You will not find it in the peasant villages of Taitou nor indeed, in peasant villages generally, for central governments that are strong enough to do so, stamp out any incipient military career unless they can be coopted to the purposes of nationalism.

We are not concerned, however, with why some tribal peoples engage in militaristic pursuits and others do not. That important issue is far too complex and the factors too variant to be dealt with here. What we are interested in, however, is the relationship between the institution of war and the motivations of the citizenry. The essential point is that this constitutes a feedback loop, the old term for which is *vicious cycle.* If a society is to have the advantages of having military personnel, the motivations for warriorhood must be established. It is a matter of great significance that these must be *created.* Man is not naturally aggressive (pace Lorenz) any more than he is naturally given to mutuality (pace Prince Kropotkin). Humanity has the capacity for aggressive behavior that can be institutionalized through social supports. Once this motivation for warriorhood is institutionalized, however, it takes on a life of its own. The image of Frankenstein's monster comes to mind.

Warfare, even on the tribal level, is not a pretty thing to see. It is not merely that people are maimed and die that makes it an ugly affair, but that it excites the human capacity for viciousness. We anthropologists have for good intellectual and moral reasons looked away from this aspect of tribal life, as anyone dealing with the comparative ethnography of warfare will testify (e.g., Otterbein, 1970:11). We have been aided and abetted in this by the fact that most of us have arrived a generation or more after these activities have been stamped out of native life. Even those who have dealt with warfare have disregarded its structural, political, and social importance, as when Grinnell (1924:1) makes it appear largely a product of indirect Western influence or when Heider (1970) stresses the game and a ceremonial aspect of Dani warfare. Go back to the firsthand accounts of tribal fighting, and you will be reminded that it is not a pretty business; read the account of Asmat head-hunting by Father Zegwaard (1959) for an examination of what the inspiration to killing does to human behavior. We are reminded of Mai Lai.

And this is a major point: it is not that people are naturally aggressive, and most particularly it is not that *primitive* people are naturally aggressive. It is that the military career draws upon those qualities of which we are all capable, ennobles them, and therefore reinforces them.

Tribal peoples are themselves not totally unaware of the effects of military careers on their own stability. The Iatmul, according to Gregory Bateson (1958:224–27), recognized two kinds of careers: those for men of action and those for men of knowledge—jocks and eggheads, if you will. Each kin group needed both sets of talents if it were to survive the constant feuding. The Boran were aware that their militarism constituted an inherent danger; that those aggressive and virile warriors that their culture inspired were a threat to what they called the Peace of Boran (Baxter 1977:83–84).

> Boran need that Peace not only between themselves but also at large, to be able to graze their flocks and herds. . . . Warriorhood and aggressive virility . . . are restricted to prescribed stages of a man's life after which they become increasingly inappropriate. . . . The opposition of youth and age is clearly signified in a number of ways. . . . When a generation set becomes responsible for the nation, each of its members puts up a phallic *Kalaacha*, which is a symbol of firm but responsible manliness, but when they retire each removes his and puts it to rest dangling in a milk pot. An elder . . . should be cool and not even speak or look in anger, let alone strike out in the heat of passion. One sign of the cool passivity of such elders is that they should not carry spears.

Breaking the Cycle

Human beings are neither genetic nor sociological robots, but complexly motivated and highly dynamic personages whose generalized aims are channeled by their sociocultural environment into particular forms, and who in turn, help to channel the aims of others in their community. If the community is to continue, individual aims must be channeled to the performance of essential tasks, of which protection against outside threats may be one, in which case militaristic values have their place. Institutions involving human careers show great inertia; the values and motives laid down in childhood not only persist as individual motives, but as presuppositions for the values and incentives that in turn are transferred to the next generation. Individuals may escape this cycle, but unless they do so collectively, the social ambiance is not thereby altered.

It is in this context that Homer Barnett's story of the destruction of bobotism in the Ajimaroe District of New Guinea is so fascinating (Barnett, 1959). Here an institution of elaborate indebtednesses involving cloths called *kain timor* had grown so burdensome, even for those who were advantaged by it, that, at the sudden outburst of a District Officer, the whole system suddenly collapsed by agreement of those who were profiting from it.

Let us see how Barnett (1016-17) describes the event:

> Repeatedly the District Officer inveighed against the nuisance and tried to get the people to turn their attention to economic production, to more food and cash crops, to health standards and to education. Finally, one day in March of 1954 at an open meeting called to investigate a row of kain timor debts, he lost his patience and exclaimed, "Why don't you get rid of the useless things!" He expected no answer, but he got one immediately. A man in the group—a bobot—apparently sensing that the moment had arrived, spoke up and said, "All right, we will." There was no opposition. On the contrary, the crowd murmured its approval. . . . Realizing that he might have evoked expression of a widespread sentiment he paid visits to other hamlets, related what had happened at the first, and made a plea for the general abandonment of kain timor. The suggestion was so well received that he called a meeting of all the important men in the area, along with the Indonesian schoolteachers and pastors and a priest. Because it was crucial to everything else, his specific question was: What is to be done about the marriage payment? The first person to speak was the richest and most powerful man in the district, who argued for the abolition of kain timor. The District Officer suggested that cotton yardage and guilders in limited amounts be substituted. There was no dissent and everyone agreed to have all kain timor out of circulation in six months.

Unfortunately there is no super District Officer to make the same outburst regarding the kain timor that burdens the modern world.

Alternatives to Militarism

When we recognize that militarism has a career aspect, and that this career element is a factor in the perpetuation and growth of armed conflict, we can perceive the manner in which these aspirations can be deflected and rechanneled to other pursuits. There is considerable evidence that such rechanneling from military confrontation to economic rivalry has repeatedly taken place in tribal societies. From the standpoint of the individual, this means that the self is increasingly measured by access to property, whether for the purposes of consumption or of display. Helen Codere demonstrated that the Kwakiutl potlatch had the effect of transforming conflict from the arena of warfare to that of economic rivalry, aptly captured in the title of her classic monograph, *Fighting with Property* (Codere, 1950). Harold Driver and I showed that the White Deerskin Dance of the Hupa was a similar transformation, that the origins of the ceremony lay in a preexisting war dance but that it had become a demonstration of economic strength (Goldschmidt and Driver, 1940).

As we all know, head-hunting and very small scale internecine rivalry are endemic in New Guinea and Melanesia generally. But there is evidence for the local transformation of such military activity into the economic rivalry of the Big-Man complex. There is some suggestion that the Ajimaroe reduction of internecine warfare by colonial powers resulted in the rechanneling of careers from militaristic operations to economic rivalry (Barnett, 1959). The same appears to have been the case among the Siuai of Bougainville (Oliver, 1955:411).

Timothy Earle (1982) has made a comparison of Melanesian groups to show that the use of valuables relates to the development of political structure. Comparing the Tsembaga Maring of the highland fringe of New Guinea, the Melpa and Mae Enga, also of the highlands, and the Trobriand Islanders, he shows the expansion in the social use of valuables. From one standpoint, however, we see not only the expansion of areas of internal harmony, but career shifts, with increasing emphasis on economic accumulation and the relative decline of military exploits. Indeed the ritualized exchanges of the Trobriands and their neighbors functioned in a way that enabled these diverse groups to engage in economically useful trade to establish a kind of *pax kula* in the area (Malinowski, 1922). I am not sufficiently versed in the literature of this region to go beyond these speculative statements, but they suggest the relationship between economic and military rivalry as alternative career patterns.

The Military Career in America

When we turn our attention to the modern world, we naturally find things more complex. What is the military career in modern America? (For some interesting answers see Sarkesian and Randall, this volume.)

First we must examine the general character of careers in the modern world. The task aspects of career relate us to our occupations; we are doctor or lawyer or professor or skilled worker. When we leave work, however, we drive to our houses and families into residential communities made up of diverse occupations into a community undifferentiated on the basis of task, but very much differentiated in terms of the level of success that we have achieved in the workaday aspects of our careers.

Overwhelmingly in modern America, the task aspect of our career operates in the context of large bureaucratic organizations, public or private (just as among the Boran it operates within the *gada* system or among the Kwakiutl within the *numaym*). In any bureaucracy, achievement is measured by rank, and rewards are meted out in the common coin of salary or wages. Success generally involves task competence and bureaucratic entrepreneurship. Bureaucratic entrepreneurship involves the constant build-up of one's own area of activity, and success is most readily achieved with growth, whether on the campus, in financial institutions, or at the Pentagon.

Success in a modern military career does not involve the virtues that characterize those of the Cheyenne or Boran; it involves bureaucratic virtues. As I write these pages, I have before me a sixteen-page special section of the *Los Angeles Times* (1983) devoted to the military-industrial complex first publicly identified by Eisenhower in his valedictory address. The basic theme of its several articles is the public vested interest in the continuation of the military enterprise, not merely by the soldiery of our nation, but by a significant and politically powerful fraction of our society. This is not merely the vested interest of industrial monopolists, but of each and every individual whose career, and therefore whose sense of self, rests on the continuing growth of these activities.

L'Envoi

In this essay there can be no conclusions. Its purpose has been to give some thoughts to the dynamics of warfare in terms of human motivation, based on a different way of looking at anthropological data. We see that military prowess can become a central element in individual careers through the establishment of rewards for such exploits, and that even with unsophisticated weaponry it can pose a threat to social order. The glory and the sex (to borrow from the thinking of both Freud and the Boran) have been eliminated from the military career in the modern world. But the pursuit of military aims has been written into the career of millions of people who work for the military establishment and for the massive industrial establishment that supplies its arsenal.

References

Barnett, Homer. 1959. "Peace and Progress in New Guinea." *American Anthropologist* 61(6):1013–19.

Bateson, Gregory. 1958. *Naven.* 2nd ed. Stanford, Cal.: Stanford University Press.

Baxter, P.T.W. 1977. "Boran Age-sets and Warfare." In *Warfare among East African Herders*, edited by Katsuyoshi Fukui and David Turton, pp. 69–95. Kyoto: National Museum of Ethnology, Osaka.

Codere, Helen. 1950. *Fighting with Property* (American Ethnological Society Monograph 18). New York: J.J. Augustine.

Earle, Timothy. 1982. "The Ecology and Politics of Primitive Valuables." In *Culture and Ecology: Eclectic Perspectives*, edited by John Kennedy and Robert Edgerton, pp. 65–83. Washington D.C.: American Anthroplogical Association.

Erikson, Erik H. 1963. *Childhood and Society.* 2nd ed. New York: W.W. Norton.

Goldschmidt, Walter. 1982. "Dynamic Anthropology." Manuscript.

Goldschmidt, Walter, and Driver, Harold. 1940. "The Hupa White Deerskin Dance." *University of California Publication in American Archaeology and Ethnography* 35(8):103–31.

Grinnell, George Bird. 1924. *The Cheyenne Indians.* New Haven, Conn.: Yale University Press.

Heider, Karl G. 1970. *The Dugum Dani.* Chicago: Aldine.

Lowie, Robert H. 1935. *The Crow Indians.* New York: Farrar and Rinehart.

Malinowski, Bronislaw. 1922. *Argonauts of the Western Pacific.* London: Routledge & Kegan Paul.

Malinowski, Bronislaw. 1935. *Coral Gardens and Their Magic.* London: George Allen & Unwin.

Morgan, Lewis H. 1954. *League of the Ho-De-No Sau-Ne or Iroquois.* New Haven, Conn.: HRAF Press.

Oliver, Douglas L. 1955. *A Solomon Island Society.* Cambridge, Mass.: Harvard University Press.

Otterbein, Keith F. 1970. *The Evolution of War.* New Haven, Conn.: HRAF Press.

Peristiany, J.G. 1939. *The Social Institutions of the Kipsigis.* London: Routledge & Kegan Paul.

Radcliffe-Brown, A.R. 1933. *The Andaman Islanders.* 2nd ed. Cambridge, England: Cambridge University Press.

"Servants or Masters: Revisiting the Military-industrial Complex." 1983. *Los Angeles Times* (July 10): Part 6.

Thompson, Laura, and Joseph, Alice. 1944. *The Hopi Way.* Chicago, Ill.: University of Chicago Press.
Turnbull, Colin. 1965. *Wayward Servants: The Two Worlds of the African Pygmies.* Garden City, N.Y.: Natural History Press.
Zegwaard, Gerard A. 1959. "Headhunting Practices of the Asmat of Netherlands New Guinea." *American Anthropologist* 61(6):1020–41.

2

The Uses of Fear: *Porro* Gangs in Mexico

Larissa Lomnitz

Delinquent youth gangs have become a standard problem of modern cities. In this paper I discuss a peculiar urban phenomenon of modern Mexico, the *porros*. Originating in the cheering sections at University football games in the 1950s, these groups eventually became fighting gangs for hire. Their use in politics is illuminating in several important ways: it affords an unexpected insight into some other urban phenomena (student movements, agents provocateurs, and political demonstrations), and it illustrates class relations and the use and misuse of symbols for political control (Karmen, 1975, Marx, 1974:403).

I am also interested in another aspect of the *porro* phenomenon, namely the fact that *porros* belong to the informal sector. In an earlier paper (Lomnitz, 1982) I proposed a model of the social structure of urban Mexico based on three variables: types of resources (capital, power, work, etc.), direction of the exchange (horizontal or vertical), and form of articulation (formal vs. informal). This leads to the emergence of four sectors at the macro level: the Public Sector, the Private Sector, the Formal Labor Sector, and the Informal Sector. In this model, the *porros* occupy the position of an informal police force: they use coercion as a means of social control, but they carry no badges and they have no formal connection with the Public Sector, as do the police. In this paper the *porros* are discussed as an example of informal articulation, and I show how this affects the character, permanence and security of the groups, or of their members. *Porros* are in the business of fearmongering (O'Donnell, 1977). They consider themselves patriotic Mexicans and they willingly side with the regime. Some of them have similar functions to those of a formal police, yet their informal articulation within the social structure means that their activities cannot be publicly acknowledged or legitimated.

Porros as a University Phenomenon

In an earlier paper (Lomnitz, 1977) I proposed a model of the National University of Mexico as made up of four superposed universities, each of which offers a different type of education leading to a distinctive life career. Thus one finds four major types of students: the academics, the professionals, the politicos and the *porros*. In each case, regardless of the formal curricular content, the student follows a track which eventually leads to a functional specialization within the system, and more particularly within the state apparatus.

Thus, the *academics* tend to join the university faculty while the *professionals* become members of the Private Sector or of the Public Sector in a technical capacity. The National University of Mexico increasingly provides the technical staff of the public administration. The *politicos* tend to become activists and leaders in the official party or in opposition groups. The university has become a laboratory or training school for politicians, where the elements of conflict management, ideological infighting, and compromise are taught on a practical level. Lastly, the *porros* represent in some ways a dead-end track but a most significant one, since it expresses the need to control the ideology of the emerging bureaucratic class which is based on the state universities (Graciarena, 1971:99–104). This new class tends to dominate society precisely on the strength of its ability to handle specialized knowedge and symbols (Konrad and Szelenyi, 1979; Gouldner, 1979; Weber, 1979; Gramsci, 1980).

In this model of the university as composed of four distinctive tracks, the *porros* specialize in fearmongering as a means of social control, or alternatively they use confusion of symbols to prevent the rise of strong opposition movements among the student body. This role is consequential because of the key political role of the student body in Mexico (Basañez, 1981).[1]

Historical Background

In the postwar years, and particularly after 1950, American cultural influences became pervasive among Mexican urban youth. This showed in their artistic or musical tastes, their manner of dress and their preferences. American football suddenly became popular among high school and college students. The big game between the National University and the Polytechnic attracted large crowds of young people who sided with one or the other of the traditional rivals. Organized cheering sections were a regular feature of these sports events.

A professional cheerleader at the National University, nicknamed Palillo ("Toothpick"), was a registered student at the School of Psychology for many years. He acted as middleman on behalf of students in the cheering sections, for whom he obtained sports jackets with the school colors, study tours, parties and exemptions from certain academic requirements. Palillo's influence became notorious and soon he achieved recognition by the university administration as a mediator in disputes involving certain student groups (*Revista Caballero*, 1973).

Typically the members of these groups were of lower-class origins and affected distinctive forms of dress and speech. Membership was all-male and accepted forms of behavior included wild celebrations, fights among members of rival cheering sections, and other shows of school spirit. At a later stage these sporting toughs were conveniently cast in the role of mediators by the university administration in their dealings with disaffected student groups (Guitian-Bernicer, 1975).

Eventually some groups of *porros* evolved into organized fighting gangs whose connection with sports events become increasingly tenacious. Whenever students attempted to organize politically the *porros* appeared as provocateurs, disrupting meetings and attempting to keep student participation as low as possible. Intimidation and open violence were used against the predominantly middle-class student body. Members of the college football teams and wrestling teams were participating in these actions during the 1960s.

The National University of Mexico system includes a chain of ten high schools scattered over the urban area. Similarly, the National Polytechnical Institute (the other major college, at the opposite end of town) has a system of technical high schools. Each has more than two hundred thousand students. The *porros* were mostly high school students from lower-income groups, often based on neighborhood street gangs.

During the 1960s the post of principal at some of the high schools became an embattled position. Contenders for the post began to use *porros* in order to create trouble for the incumbent principal. In Mexico, the one cardinal sin of politics is to lose control; an accepted form of discrediting an office holder is to create conflict and turmoil, thus showing that he or she is incapable of maintaining stability. Quite often, leaders of opposition groups within the university who had ambition for a particular position in the administration would fan student unrest for personal gain, and the university administration would counter these threats by using *porros* of their own. It should be recalled that the university campus is out of bounds to police, and that the university administration has no campus police or other formal means of coercion (*Revista Caballero*, 1973; Rivera, 1977:12–15).

At this time the *porro* groups underwent an important qualitative change, as their leaders put up their services for sale or for hire. Mexico is a country which produces a lot of rumors. Persistent rumor had it that the president of the university, Dr.Ignacio Chávez, was overthrown in 1966 by *porros* hired by an important government official. The fact remains that around 1966 there was increasing evidence of an attempt on the part of the state apparatus to control the university on an ideological level (Segovia, 1970). There was an upsurge of critical, Marxist, student movements at the time; these groups were vocally opposing the model of economic development the administration was holding up to the country. Coincidentally, organized *porros* began to disrupt the meetings and to attempt to terrorize the student body.

The peak of *porro* activity was reached during the 1968 student movement, which cannot be discussed extensively here. It appears that the movement was heavily attacked and later infiltrated by *porros,* and that their confusing presence became a major factor which determined the eventual breakdown of the movement (Guitian-Bernicer, 1975:40)). Finally, in 1971, there was a public confrontation between the remnants of the movement and *porros* organized as a paramilitary force (*halcones*); this last street battle caused a number of casualties among the students (Ortiz, 1971).

During the 1970s there was an active campaign to get the *porros* out of the university. At present, very little *porro* activity remains on the main campus. But other forms of *porrismo* have appeared, as *porros* have learned to blend in with the new activism. They use ultraleftist tactics in order to generate confusion among the student body. Groups whose membership includes many former *porros* are adept at leftist symbolism (e.g., Che Guevara hats), attitudes and slogans. Verbal violence, wild denunciations and threats proffered during student meetings have replaced earlier methods of physical aggression. The repetitious and monotonous leftist oratory has produced boredom and political passivity among the student body.

Organization

In the incipient stage, a *porra* is merely a group of boys who get along and who are tough street fighters. Then a charismatic leader appears and the structure of the group changes. The leader issues orders and commands obedience; eventually he acts as a broker, receiving money and directions from someone and sharing the proceeds with his followers.

Under the leader one finds several levels of command, according to personal closeness. The gang leader usually has two or three lieutenants who are very close to him, almost like brothers. Then there are two or three *golpeadores* ("hit-men"), who stick close to the leader and remain at his personal command. Then there is a group of boys called *borregos* ("sheep"), who may number ten or more. A fully grown *porra* may have twenty to thirty full-time members, not including groupies (girls) and hangers-on. The leader acts like a charismatic father of all, and at the same time he is the negotiator on their behalf.

Middle-class students who make up the majority in the high schools and the university tend to be ambivalent about *porros*. They are scared of them yet they admire their courage and their panache. I notice that people go to see movies such as *The Godfather* with the same kind of ambivalent feelings: most of us would never dream of killing anyone, yet we watch a gangster kill a dozen people and we cheer. At some level, middle-class boys easily identify with gang violence. The *porros* stand for the ultimate masculinity.[2]

Male symbolism of the *porro* does not exclude other cultural values. The *porro* is a rebel of the low-income urban neighborhoods; while the middle-class kids merely dream of girls, cars and success, he flaunts all these things in their faces. But he is also a Mexican nationalist and he believes in the Virgin of Guadalupe. He reveres his mother, and he lays down his life for his friends.

Male friendship among *porros* is of a violent, exacerbated kind. There is much talk of *porros* being homosexuals; however that may be, there is certainly a homosexual component in their emotional attitude to male friendship, particularly during adolescence. (For a discussion of the relationship between homosexuality and manliness, see Huyghe, this volume.) The cultural complex known in Mexico as *machismo* includes the ideal of male friendship as a dominant value that takes precedence over any attachment to girls.

Violence against women is part of standard *porro* behavior. In the group there is much bragging about sexual exploits and about rape. In high schools one hears that *porros* will occasionally gang-rape a girl. I have found no actual evidence of this, but certainly the idea of sexual aggression and of flaunting the use of women is a part of *machismo*. The emotional ambivalence between homosexuality and heterosexuality is resolved through aggressive displays.

Power is respected, admired and sought. The *porro* submits to power by accepting money and orders from powerful individuals. Thus he himself obtains the power to cause the downfall of important officials, to humble his teachers and to be admired and envied by his middle-class peers. The use of alcohol and drugs complements power as a stimulant in the life of the youthful rebel.

There are ten *escuelas preparatorias* (high schools of the university system), and in each of them at least one *porro* may be active; altogether around one thousand *porros*, which is not many in terms of the total size of the student body. Yet these *porros* can mobilize much larger numbers when it comes to carrying out an action, because gang members live in neighborhoods where they can enlist brothers, cousins and whole street gangs which are normally removed from university affairs. Some *porro* leaders can move armies of toughs overnight from one end of the city to the other. This seems to be what happened on June 10, 1971 at the final confrontation between radical students and *halcones*. The *halcones* seemed to have been kids belonging to neighborhood social networks; they were easy to mobilize, whether to organize massive street demonstrations or to disrupt them.

In order to describe gang behavior, I distinguish between times of peace and times of war. In peace times the *porros* are tolerated; their members are registered students, and until recently they could remain registered indefinitely without attending lectures. They were called *fósiles* ("fossils") for this reason. Some were students for twenty years; finally an ordinance was issued which now prevents students from registering more than 50 percent beyond the normal length of a course leading to a degree. But in the 1960s there were some high school students in their twenties. Eventually they could transfer as a group into the university proper, taking advantage of the automatic pass which allows high school graduates belonging to the university system to register in college.

Peacetime Behavior

In peacetime the *porros* are petty delinquents. They hang round the high schools without bothering to attend classes. In twos or threes they stop students and relieve them of their money and watches; if there is resistance, they beat them up. They sell protection to the small businesses that cater to students in the neighborhood of the school: *taquerias* and coffee shops or candy stores. The protection is against themselves and other *porros*. They can walk into a protected shop, order what they want and walk out without paying. They also steal university property, but not all the time.

In high schools, the *porros* make themselves popular with the students because they are very good at organizing parties. They go to the principal and they tell him, "Look, we know that the students deserve a nice party and we need some money to hire a band and, you know, this is good for the school spirit," and so on. Alcohol and sex were very much a part of the *porro* scene in the 1960s; then drugs also came in.

Members of *porro* groups also managed to recruit sympathetic peers from the student body, by organizing parties, trips to Acapulco, and intervening whenever some kid was in trouble. They would go to a student and say, "Hey look, you are having a problem with this teacher, let us fix it." Then they would approach the teacher and say, "Listen, I hear that you are being very hard on my buddy, why don't you give him a break?"

I have interviewed some teachers who were on the faculty during the late 1960s and they were still terrified when recounting their experiences. The *porros* once made an example of a particular teacher who had opposed them openly. They smashed his small VW car with a huge rock, destroying the body and the engine. The car had cost all of the teacher's life savings. After such a deed, when *porros* approached a teacher with a request on behalf of a particular student, they expected to find an understanding ear.

Wartime Behavior

Every six years, before a presidential candidate is selected, Mexico is beset by political conflict. Because of the importance attributed to political stability (Reyna, 1974), potential candidates who occupy cabinet posts find themselves harassed by strikes or displays of public unrest that are designed to give the responsible official a "black eye." In political slang this is called "burning" someone and it is done at all levels of the hierarchy.

During the 1960s the *porros* frequently appeared in the streets, as organizers, as demonstrators, or as counterforces to break up street meetings or marches. In the 1968 movement, which lasted for several months, some *porros* fought the student groups while others joined them and even went to jail. Some *porro* leaders served jail sentences and emerged as ideologically purified figures in the eyes of the students. According to informants, some of these ideological conversions may have been sincere while others were merely convenient, as these "heroes of 1968" could more easily infiltrate the student organizations. The emergence of groups of radicalized working-class kids can be very confusing to ideologically Marxist middle-class students because they generate guilt feelings about their own class origins. As a rule, middle-class student organizations appear to be reluctant to denounce these new-left groups. The resulting confusion of symbols has contributed to the depolitization of the student body after 1968.

When President Echeverría came to power in 1970, he attempted to win over the disaffected intellectual community. He appropriated the language of the 1968 movement, and some of its prominent leaders were invited to join the administration. The last big street action involving the *porros* was the 1971 confrontation; afterwards they were suppressed as a political force, although gangs still exist and are mobilized at times.

Some gangs moved into the drug trade, others joined the police, and many just met an early death or succeeded in disengaging themselves from the *porros*. In general, however, while a political career is closed to them, they can become bodyguards to officials or political persons. Most of them ended up in the same low-income track from which they had originated: low-level security jobs, petty crime, alcoholism, jail, death on the street.

The option of joining one of the various police forces is an interesting one because it recalls *A Clockwork Orange* by Anthony Burgess. There are two sides of violence, the legal and the illegal, and people easily switch sides like children playing at cops and robbers. This phenomenon affords an insight into the urban society of the low-income neighborhoods. In the kind of class warfare which goes on within the city, the *porros* attempt to escape the fate of the poor by identifying with the powerful. When one fails he has the final option of becoming an agent of the power of the state.

Discussion

Porros are soldiers in class warfare and in generational warfare. The high schools and universities represent an opportunity for young men from low-income neighborhoods to overpower their elders and their social superiors.

Mexico is a highly organized nation. Power is based on militancy in a group, and every group has a leader and followers (see Lomnitz, 1982; Cordova, 1979:3–15). The state itself can be envisioned as a conglomerate of groups competing among themselves for power. Politics is the struggle of leaders attempting to reach certain positions. Some attempt to rise by just doing their jobs and keeping clear of controversy. But, sooner or later, everybody has to fight off rivals or neutralize enemies. In the framework of this dynamics of power, the *porro* groups have been cast in the role of mercenaries (Lomnitz, 1977).

Political warfare in Mexico is designed to discredit public officials, to weaken their positions and to "burn" them, by showing them up as incompetent and unable to preserve stability in their institution or department. Thus, if the Secretary of Education seems a likely candidate for office, there will be all kinds of movements within the educational system. Sections of the Teachers' Union will march to Mexico City to present demands, students will go on strike, and so on. Unless trouble spots are rapidly controlled, the unrest will spread and higher authority will have to intervene, sometimes by relieving the occupant of his office. A mishap of this sort represents a permanent blemish that usually cuts short the person's political career. *Porros,* though not always successful, are specialists in creating and quelling trouble.

I believe that violence does not work in the long run. The 1968 student movement showed the country that large groups of ideologically motivated people cannot be repressed by violence. The tactics of *porro* warfare changed accordingly as ideological control became more important than physical violence. One way of achieving ideological control is to produce fear, so students won't congregate at meetings, but this works only for a while. A more effective approach seems to bc to coopt them and to create a confusion of symbols.

Right after the 1968 movement, the National University had a president who was a Marxist sociologist. He was overthrown by a labor strike supported by students who claimed to be leftists. Their leaders wore green berets like Che Guevara. Eventually it became known that they had been *porros.* That produced confusion, skepticism and eventually, political passivity among the student body. Leftist groups lost their mass appeal as students became reluctant to let themselves get beaten up in the streets for suspect causes.

Porros are used and then dropped by the political system. They have no formal contracts, no security. There has been talk of *porros* being organized as paramilitary forces, but this merely means that the gangs have been given sticks and special training. Once they are seen in action, they must be dismissed and ignored. In the last analysis, the *porros* are the final victims of their own violence. It is the ironic or perhaps tragic feature of a life career which, in attempting to bypass the normal channels of upward mobility, ends up even further down the social ladder.

The example of the *porros* shows how traditional male friendship patterns and symbols of masculinity can be manipulated and used to create a climate of fear and violence within a social system. Such types of male gangs have also preceded the takeover of totalitarian, war-oriented regimes and, furthermore, have been used by such regimes to maintain the civil population in a state of constant fear.

Notes

1. The methodology used in this paper is eclectic. For obvious reasons, the traditional field methods of anthropology were of limited use. Sources of information were mostly former members of *porro* groups, including two former gang leaders, former students who had had contact with *porros* during the 1960s, faculty members and administrators, particularly from high schools, and members of the university administration whose jobs involved frequent dealings with *porros.* I had access to unpublished reports and documents, including one account written from jail by a *porro* leader. An important B.A. thesis (Guitian-Bernicer1975) describes the family life as well as the in-group life of a sample of forty-five *porros.* These sources were complemented by press items and news comments on *porro* activities which I collected over the period of 1970–1980. Altogether the amount of information which I have been able to collect is as extensive as could be obtained without actually being a member of a *porro* group.
2. A similar phenomenon is found among Japanese gangs as described by DeVos and Mizushima, 1967:289–325. See also the relationship of masculinity and university football games in Dundes, 1978.

References

Basañez, Miguel. 1981. *La Lucha por la Hegemonia en Mexico, 1968–1980*. Mexico: Siglo XXI.
Córdova, Arnaldo. 1979. "El Desafio de la Izquierda Méxicana." *Nexos* 18 (June):3–15.
De Vos, George and Mizushima, K. 1967. "Organization and Social Functions of Japanese Gangs: Historical Development and Modern Parallels." In *Aspects of Social Change in Modern Japan*, edited by R.P. Dore, pp.289–325.
Dundes, A. 1978. "Into the End Zone for a Touchdown: A Psychoanalytic Consideration of American Football." *Western Folklore* 37:75–88.
Gouldner, Alvin. 1979. *The Future of Intellectuals and the Rise of the New Class*. New York: Continuum.
Graciarena, Jorge. 1979. "Las Ciencias Sociales, la Crítica Intelectual y el Estado Technocrático: Una Discusión del Caso Latinoamericano." In *Las Ciencias Sociales en Amèrica Latina*, edited by G. Boils Morales and A. Murga Frasscinetti, pp. 94–116. Mexico: UNAM.
Gramsci, A. 1980. *Selections from Prison. Notes*. London: Lawrence & Wishart.
Guitian–Bernicer, Carolyn Cira. 1975. *Las Porras: Estudio de Caso de un Grupo de Presiòn Universitario*. Tésis profesional, Facultad de Ciencias Politicas y Sociales, UNAM.
Karmen, A.1975. "Agents Provocateurs in the Contemporary U.S. New Left Movements." In *Criminology: A Radical Perspective*. Pacific Palisades, Cal.: Goodyear.
Konrad, G. and Szelenyi, I. 1979. *The Intellectual on the Road to Class Power*. New York: Harcourt Brace Jovanovich.
Lomnitz, Larissa. 1977. "Conflict and Mediation in a Latin American University." *Journal of Interamerican Studies and World Affairs* 19 (3):315–38.
_____. 1982. "Horizontal and Vertical Relations and the Social Structure of Urban Mexico." *Latin American Research Review*. 17 (2):51–74.
Marx, Gary.1974. "Thoughts on a Neglected Category of Social Movement Participants: The Agent Provocateur and the Informant," *American Journal of Sociology* 80 (2):402–42.
O'Donnell, Guillermo. 1977. "Corporation and the Question of the State." In *Authoritarianism and Corporatism in Latin America*, edited by J.Malloy, pp. 47–87. Pittsburg, Pa.: University of Pittsburgh Press.
Ortiz, Orlando. 1971. *Jueves de Corpus*. Mexico: Ed. Diogenes.
Revista Caballero. 1973. "La Violencia Universitaria." October (80):110–16.
Reyna, José Luis. 1974. "Control Político, Estabilidad y Desarrollo en México." *Cuadernos Del Ces* 3.
Rivera, Miguel Angel. 1977. "Los *Porros*. Violencia Mercenaria en la Enseñanza Superior." *Revista Proceso* 26(21):12–15.
Segovia, Rafael. 1970. "The Mexican University Strike of 1966." In *Political Power in Latin America. Seven Confrontations*, edited by R.R.Fagen and W.A.Cornelius, Jr. Englewood Cliffs, N.J.: Prentice–Hall.
Weber, Max. 1979. *Economiá y Sociedad*. (German edition, 1922). Mexico: FCE.

3

Toward a Structural Model of Violence: Male Initiation Rituals and Tribal Warfare

Bernard Huyghe

The extent of resource expenditure for the national defense leads to the conclusion that most governments and their critics regard war as inevitable. Much popular writing ascribes aggressive "drives" and warfare, to biological "instincts" and ecological "fight for resources," or, in a word, to nature. I will demonstrate that war is at first a cultural institution (see also Foster, this volume), and that its permanency is ensured by psychic configurations that imply some sort of collective neurosis (see Nader and Frank, this volume, for similar views).

Aggression is natural, and famine, for example, may trigger it, but that does not automatically lead to war.[1] A cultural symbolic and ideological dimension is needed to organize spontaneous aggression against an exterior group. Warring cultures tend to deflect in-group aggression to the exterior.

While war has unmistakable ritual features in tribal societies, these tend to be rationalized in Western societies, where war becomes a political decision, taken coolly, in terms of well-defined interests, by unaggressive men. The cultural phenomenon called "war" has two dimensions: First, it is launched by a ruling class (e.g. political, military, religious) pursuing its own interests. Second, ordinary people lend themselves to this, despite its suicidal quality, and the suffering, oppression and absurdity involved. War as a cultural configuration is only meaningful on some symbolic-unconscious level.

Drawing on my symbolic and medical anthropological research on psychosomatic disease (Huyghe, 1983a, 1983b), I hold that there are two separate levels of symbolism which structure human behavior. These are cultural and psychodynamic. But to demonstrate the existence of a cultural order says nothing about the ability of its members to conform to it. To understand conformity we need to uncover its underlying psychodynamic configurations. This task may illustrate what symbolic anthropology and ethnopsychiatry can offer in the search for peace. My contribution to this task is a cultural symbolic model of reciprocity and violence (Huyghe, 1982), based on an analysis of the gender-identity structures and emotions of men.

My chief ethnographic source, Herdt's (1981) analysis of male gender-identity among the Sambia, a New Guinea Highland warrior tribe, lends itself especially well to comparison between cultural symbolic structure and psychoanalytic personality structure with regard to aggression and war. It includes a scrupulous ethnographic description and cultural analysis and sheds ample light on experiences, relationships, dreams, and emotions.

Among the Sambia, boys and young men have ritualized homosexual experiences before marriage and postmarital heterosexual experiences thereafter. Paradoxically, this homosexual period is believed necessary to turn soft and weak boys into virile and aggressive warriors. I first present Sambia idioms about masculinity and war, then compare Sambian psychoanalytic symbolism in cultural and individual behavior.

War and Masculinity in Sambian Culture

For the Sambia, the ideal man is the war leader: strong, aggressive and virile. By adolescence, youths are expected to be accomplished killers both in hunting and in war. Masculine pride and social esteem require this and pervade all social relations and institutions, forming the foundation for warfare, economic production and religious life. A myth of male parthenogenesis, telling how mankind was created by homosexual fellatio, bolsters this conceptualization.

Men consider themselves to be superior to women in physique, personality and social position. This gives them political and social power over women, younger males, and children. Women, and any man not "masculine" enough according to the valued criteria, are despised and derided as vulnerable, unmanly, weak and soft. Masculinity derives its public force from the suppression of women in public affairs, and the censuring of feminine qualities in men's private conversations and activities.

This sexual antagonism (quite common in New Guinea) permeates all facets of social life. Not only are there different spheres of interest, with different roles and economic activities for the sexes, but the whole cosmological and natural world is correspondingly segregated. The forest is a masculine realm of hunting and ritual, while the garden is chiefly a feminine zone (Herdt, 1981:74). Especially striking is the spatial distribution of houses. The men's clubhouse is situated at the higher end of a sloping ridge, while at the opposite end of the hamlet the women's menstrual hut is built slightly below the ridge. Men say: "Women belong down below, men on top." Men avoid female zones as polluted, especially the neighborhood of the menstrual hut. Women must not walk above or near the men's clubhouse nor look inside. Neither women nor young male initiates are free to move about as they wish. The mere neighborhood of a women is considered polluting to males. Footpaths are likewise sexually segregated: lower paths used by women and higher by men. There is also a linguistic opposition between hard, vertically growing male crops (e.g. sugarcane), and soft, horizontally growing female crops (e.g. soft potato). Hard tubers sustain strength and endurance on long-distance guerrilla raids, and in initiation ordeals. Soft tubers, which men may not plant, weed or dig, are only "stomach food," and become "only feces."

Men and women are housed together in family groups, but this only exacerbates sexual tension. A man, as head of the house, occupies the innermost "male" living space opposite the door, while female spaces are nearest the door. Men's and women's spaces are outlined by planks across the floor. Women may never step up or over the hearth or into the male space. Shaming or physical punishment by men follows infractions. Relations between the sexes are harsh even by New Guinea standards; women are represented as polluting inferiors whom a man should always distrust. Men must spit after pronouncing female-related terms such as vagina, menstrual blood or vaginal fluid, else they become polluted by swallowing their own saliva. Women are always treated as sexual and economic property. If a woman "initiates" adultery, it is unmanly for a man to refuse, and the woman bears moral responsibility. Rather than beat the adulterous man, a husband will beat his wife. Not surprisingly then, the couple's relation is difficult, awkward, quarrelsome and full of tension, suspicion, jealousy and anxiety. Nor is it surprising that suicides by women are more than triple the number by men, especially near marriage, or within a few months after it.

To ensure male supremacy a heavy price is paid in interpersonal tension, psychological conflict, and political suppression. Young boys of seven to ten years are forcibly separated from their mothers, submitted to prolonged and elaborate initiation, and withheld from feminine contact till marriage, some ten to fifteen years later. Initiates live in the men's house and must not speak to, look or be looked at, or have physical contact with women. Meanwhile, homosexual fellatio is forcibly imposed on younger initiates, to make them strong and masculine. The vital substance par excellence is semen, as babies, except for their blood which comes from the mother, are made from it. To grow into male adulthood, boys should drink semen regularly.

In the past, war was the constant test of this masculinity. War raids were sometimes launched expressly as the third stage in initiation. These often inflicted wide-scale destruction, with villages burned to the ground and all inhabitants killed. Yet through such destruction was Sambia manhood achieved.

Herdt seems to feel that such masculinization was made necessary by the constant war situation, but I would say rather that all these aspects are parts of a wider cybernetic system, continually structuring and being structured by culture. My question is to determine if and how this cultural cycle could be redirected in such a way as to make it less conflictual and traumatogenic.

The Structure of Sambian Culture

In order to determine to what extent a given means is significantly directed toward a given end, Devisch's spatio-temporal premises, or cultural metaphors are useful. In exploring the concept of bodiliness, Devisch discovered that the semantic polarization which he had described for the Yaka of Zaire (1981) seemed to share a common spatio-temporal logic with other cultures. He considered this spatio-temporal logic to be the structuring device in a variety of symbolic domains. This logic is polarized around two basic options: 1) verticality, linearity and asymmetry, and linear progressive time, to which correspond sociocultural practices of boundary tracing, hierarchy and cumulative inequality; and 2) a premise of horizontality, circularity, symmetry, and circular time, to which correspond sociocultural practices of reciprocity, equality and cyclical recurrence (Devisch, 1983:410).

There is no doubt that Sambian male cultural ideology and practices are informed by a premise of verticality, linearity and hierarchy. Sambia repeatedly assert that masculinity is an artificial achievement, never completely acquired (Herdt, 1981:160,245,286). Sambia men must demonstrate again and again their masculine strength through warfare, hunting, and sexual prowess, else they be classified as rubbishmen (*wusaatu*): unmanly weaklings or dejected nonpersons. On the contrary, the war leader (*aamooluku*) has phallic traits expected of all males as they move linearly toward ever greater achievements. "Men are society's movers" (Herdt, 1981:220). Women's activities, on the contrary, are temporally more circular, centering chiefly around their biological and life-reproducing capacities. Adult males must rise above others hierarchically (i.e. vertically) while women and younger males occupy a more egalitarian, horizontal world. The male vertical movement is also illustrated in the spatial house and path arrangements mentioned above. By initiation time, relations between the boys begin to be defined exclusively in terms of political dominance and inequality, as an introduction to the male hierarchical ladder.[2] Every level of political dominance is directly related to the use of physical violence (cf. Weber, 1947:155; Radcliffe-Brown, 1940:xiv). Initiates are soundly thrashed and nose bled, and otherwise physically punished, in order to make them "strong" and "angry" because of what has been done to them. Later they can "pay back" that anger by beating and otherwise traumatizing younger initiates. In such a cultural context there easily develops a convention of resorting to violence for territorial expansion, ostentatious male display, and the resolution of disputes.

According to Mauss (1950), reciprocity or exchange is the most fundamental structuring principle of sociocultural reality. In the male world of the Umeda, another New Guinea Highland tribe (Gell, 1975), the unfolding of reciprocal practice goes from symmetrical reciprocity (equality relations) of young age-mate boys, through the complementary unequal reciprocity of bachelors, to the relative autonomy of the adult married man, or the father and warrior (Huyghe, 1982:26ff.). Being superior implies confrontation and use of physical violence towards another, but this is only understandable where superiority is culturally assumed. This is equally true of the Sambia who also themselves create the hostile world against which they must then defend themselves.

The point has been made that warfare may be related to a male supremacist complex (Divale and Harris, 1979; Clastres, 1977a, 1977b), but it is important to see that this relation is made possible because the cultural logic of violence is only an extreme form of the logic inherent in male supremacy. I have suggested (Huyghe, 1982:27) that Sambia may be situated at one end of a continuum which goes from societies with moderate sexual polarization, and accordingly, moderate masculine supremacy, and war an occasional occurrence, to societies with extreme polarization, almost estrangement, between the sexes, and exacerbated masculine supremacy, in which warfare is almost continuous.

World peace is not endangered by tribal warring groups, but by our own industrialized society, fractioned along national and ideological lines. It is therefore tempting to effect cross-cultural comparison on the ground of these structural spatio-temporal premises. La Barre (1980:203ff.) remarks that in American and most European societies, in contrast to those of the Sambia or, for example, the Plains Indians, the warrior is only episodically and temporarily the social cynosure. A notable exception was Imperialist and Nazi Germany, the world's chief warmonger till now (LaBarre, 1980:210). From the nineteenth century, German history has been completely permeated by military values and a philosophy of force, and in the last world war, economic, social, and sexual values were all bent to the service of the soldier. The most disquieting element is that such values are culturally contagious.

Two French sociologists show that many of the structural traits cited above are found in French masculine ideology and practices, though apparently with far greater individual variability. In modern idioms represented by advertising, comics, and so forth, men appear to be virile, nonfeminine (Falconnet and Lefaucheur, 1975:22). Women must preserve femininity, but men must prove virility. Femininity is a natural state, but masculinity is never totally acquired; it must be manifested ever again. A man's life is essentially a struggle for power: economic power, intellectual power, power over women and other men, with aggression in this a fundamental value. Moreover, the words *man, male, masculine, virile,* convey high moral and social value associated with aggression, while equivalent feminine words evoke only physical and natural qualities. Men acknowledge that virility is not absolutely indispensable in an evolved and comfortable society, but in times of crisis, it becomes vital to national survival. Virility is also associated with command and hierarchy: to pull the community out of a difficult situation, a chief is needed, who imposes his ideas, can make decisive choices and can lead the masses according to the community's interests. The military system only carries to an extreme what governs everyday social relations. It reveals and renders visible the latent image of a society based on power.

From the very beginning French boys are urged "not to be like girls": "a boy does not weep" (Falconnet and Lefaucheur, 1975:140). (Here again femininity is the "natural" pole, masculinity "cultural"). Parents urge their sons to defend themselves ("life is a struggle"). Girls should not soil or tear their clothes, but mothers are anxious that a son not be too timid. Toys are sexually differentiated. Boys' toys are frequently inspired by war and military life. Even when not, they appeal to values of aggression, adventure, competition, conquest, action and domination by force or by technique. School replicates male ideology: different playtime behaviors are appropriate for girls and boys, classbooks offer images of traditional sex roles in the family, with confident, sturdy, bold and fearless boys, opposed to fragile, shy and anxious girls. Outside school hours, boys about eight to twelve years of age typically form gangs which must have a leader and fight against other gangs. (For gang behavior in another culture, see Lomnitz, this volume.) Boy Scout and other youth movements also propagate the cult of virility, of hierarchy, and of male solidarity. Scout chiefs are often virile role models. As in Sambia, peers and age mates play an important role promoting virility.

While overt homosexuality is disapproved of in Western societies, a man should prefer the company of other men to the company of women (Falconnet and Lefaucheur, 1975:99). Military service comes as a consecration of virility. Typical sayings are "As long as one has not done his military duty, one is not a man." "One does not marry as long as one has not done his military service"; "Military service will make a man out of you, it will form you" (Falconnet and Lefaucheur, 1975:156). These are more than metaphors: nowadays even being invalided out of service may be experienced as shameful.

Falconnet and Lefaucheur (1975) analyze male ideology as necessary for a capitalistic social and economic system based on concurrence and competition. For me this is a Marxist bias. Male chauvinism and war exist in tribal and noncapitalist cultures, such as the Sambia, as well as in so-called anticapitalistic movements and countries. This ideology is often implicit. Also it is risky to view France, or indeed any Western culture as a homogenous cultural group (see Roheim, 1967:435). Differences among social groups and classes may be very great. However, there is striking cross-cultural correspondence in the spatio-temporal logic of vertical hierarchization of male idioms, and in the linear and progressive accumulation of goods and prestige.

Woman's role in the implementation of masculine mythology is also worth mentioning. Femininity and masculinity define each other continuously in dialectical interaction in every culture. Among the Sambia, women expect manly men and mock the weakling, and mothers reward masculinity in their boys' behavior (Herdt, 1981:122, 203, 215). In the West women sometimes reinforce "viriloid" values in stressing the male power of the state. Thus, just before the military takeover in 1973, Chilene women demonstrated in front of army barracks and threw corn at the soldiers, to notify them that they were "chickens" not to overthrow the democratic regime (Macchiocchi, 1975:255). Contrary examples may come to mind, but this illustrates that a "phallic" kind of feminism, modelled on masculine power and values, is not helpful in promoting peace.

Western masculine folklore sometimes tends to represent woman as trickster (Falconnet and Lefaucheur, 1975:74). This fear of being deceived by women is also present in the Sambia and heightened to an almost paranoid dimension. Men are never quite certain of being the true genitor of an infant and later fear that feminine pollutions could change a son into a daughter. Old women may trick men by seduction in order to obtain regenerating semen. In some men the fear of semen depletion borders on an obsession in which they believe that their wives are "eating" their biological strength and thus gradually killing them (Herdt, 1981:250).

A Sambia paradox occurs in the fundamental opposition between masculinity and nature. Natural species (e.g. pandanus tree, cassowary) are seen as intrinsically female, and femininity is conceived of as naturally more efficacious and biologically more powerful than masculinity. Masculine atrophy is the consequence of relations with women, erotic activity threatens masculine vitality. More generally in New Guinea, men recognize that they are inferior to women in reproductive capacity, therefore they redundantly assert their supremacy and their masculinity by artificial means, viz. in rituals. This paradox extends especially into warriorhood: in fight, and in the action of killing the other, the warrior affirms himself as the only existing, autonomous man. But this movement turns against itself; as in procreation, it also represents an assertion of man's inevitable death and replacement by a new generation. According to Clastres (1977b:89–98), a warrior has no choice; he is condemned to desire war, and because of this cultural logic he is as intimately associated with death as the woman and mother is with life. His ultimate exchange is eternal glory for the eternity of death. This puts him in something of a double bind.

To understand this paradox in cultural terms one can turn to the analysis of the key metaphors and symbols used in initiatory ritual. I have shown elsewhere that in the Umeda, male autonomy and supremacy is symbolically brought about by the use of palm-heart fringes in the making of ritual masks. This autogenerative substance is symbolically a signifier of bipolar unity, of androgynic autoprocreation, encompassing conception and death, birth and parturition (Huyghe, 1982:24). Devisch (1983) stresses that such bipolar symbolic mediation in ritual creates a new, procreative identity. This gives unity and continuity to Umeda culture, while allowing a certain degree of ambiguity (Huyghe 1982:25ff). Also among the Umeda, masculine strength finds its limit in active heterosexuality and in contact with women.

Among the Sambia one finds comparable symbols in first-stage initiation (Herdt 1981:229ff.). One is a brilliant red ritual object called *Kwolyi-Mutnyi*, ceremonially struck against an initiate's chest to generate great bodily potency. The myth states that long ago, the object was created spontaneously from the blood of a slain Sambia warrior. Fundamentally, however, this is an androgynous object. The most potent of its contents is a female bone awl, encapsulating the notion of powerful femaleness hidden in the core of men's power. One brush with this artifact can confer prodigious masculinity and the potential to produce many children. The ritual brushing of the chest also stresses the body as the locus of cultural identity.

Homosexual activities leading to semen ingestion also have an androgynous dimension, as will be seen in the discussion of the psychodynamics of Sambia male personality. Since semen is the substance of life, it is a strengthening factor in a girl's as well as a boy's ontogeny. She marries before, but coitus is not permitted until menarche. In the meantime a girl and her husband may engage in fellatio, strengthening the girl's body with orally ingested semen and providing her with future breastmilk.

Symbolically, the Androgyne seems always to provide cultural mediation between the sexes. Between generations, it seems to negate the difference. This phenomenon is also psychobiological. Freud postulated an innate bisexual disposition most clearly visible in the analysis of psychoneurotics (Freud, 1962:168ff., 1971:58, 1979a:94). The Androgyne appears also in Indo-European mythology, especially in the Upanishads and in Plato's banquet. Freud saw this as an illustration of the tendency of biological substance to reunite by way of the sexual instinct (Freud, 1963:74). For Devereux (1982a:6) however, the bisexual elements in Greek myths refer to the reluctance of humanity to accept sexuality and the duality of the sexes.

The Sambia illustrate how cultural signification is manifested in male supremacy and autonomy leading to war, but this does not explain the anxieties, brutality, hatred and grimness ever present in Sambia life as Herdt describes it. A Westerner may find it hard to understand how such a fierce warriorship emerges from years of sustained, and enjoyed, homosexual relationships. I completely agree with Herdt (1981:253) that it is not enough to demonstrate a cultural and ideological universe of custom, and take for granted that men will conform to it, even if that means being "drafted into manhood screaming all the way."

The Integration of Anthropology and Psychoanalysis

My medical and symbolic anthropological research into psychosomatic symptoms related to problems of cultural and individual identification (individuation) in adolescence, uncovered two separate symbolic systems: cultural and individual-psychodynamic. In Durkheimian terms, cultural symbolism excludes individual variables, leaving no room for an anthropology that, while giving accurate accounts of custom and sociocultural structure, would also account for the feelings and experiences of the people living in those structures. To understand the dynamics of culture, we can no longer afford to ignore the psychological dimension.

To date, no efforts to provide syncretisms between anthropology and psychoanalysis, have been generally accepted (Bastide, 1972:215). Apparently there are two reasons for this. First, in psychoanalytical anthropology a symbol always remains the creation of individuals as the actualization of their common phantasms (see Roheim, 1972a:288), and second, in the culturalist perspective of such linguistically inspired authors as Foucault (1966) and Ortigues and Ortigues (1966) psychoanalytical symbols are incorporated in a more general semantic science, integrating sociocultural and psychic elements into a single meaning system. For Devereux (1972), psychoanalysis and anthropology are mutually irreducible, with a complementary relationship between them of the Heisenberg-Bohr type. This means that what is causal in one discipline becomes instrumental in the other. This complementarism constitutes a reasoned bridge between the human and the exact sciences, for it is impossible to unite two different causalities, the psychical and the social, in one theoretical construction. Similarly Bastide (1972:249) postulates two separate sources of symbolism: social and libidinal, with continuous interpenetration of the two levels. Indeed, although there is some degree of isomorphism between anthropological (semantic) and psychoanalytical interpretations (Huyghe 1983a:16), the epistemological irreducibility still remains such that a single item can offer different significations when seen from a psychoanalytical or a sociocultural perspective (Bastide, 1972:249). I do not completely agree with Bastide (1972:244) in assuming that psychodynamic dream symbolism makes use of social symbols, while social "objects," considered outside the dream, cannot be the reflection of the nuclear psychical complexes. The workings of the Freudian unconscious are certainly not limited to the dream world, and phenomena of affective transference are primordial in social relations, both on an individual and a collective level (Freud, 1963:115). Analysis of Sambia data shows that psychodynamic configuration is at least as important as is cultural symbolism and social structure in the implementation of a sociocultural phenomenon such as war.

In my view, two separate but complementary analyses are needed to understand the interrelation of the elements and pave the way for positive action. Bastide (1972:272) suggested that psychosomatic medicine may be the basis of a socioanalytical science, in which the psychoanalytical and the social would become two variables whose correlations could be studied. Indeed, through my research concerning anorexia nervosa, I have become convinced that cultural-symbolic elaboration is always to a certain extent supplemented by a psychodynamic elaboration, and vice versa (Huyghe 1983b:5).

The two kinds of interpretation serve different purposes: a purely psychoanalytical interpretation of ritual practice (Roheim, 1972b) is justified in assuming that the psychic events involved in ritual may be the same as in certain neurotic patients, if it is acknowledged that there is another level of cultural symbolic significance that is not present in neurotic symptoms or dreams, and that a purely cultural-semantic analysis of a process is valid if confronted afterwards with the psychoanalytical findings.

Psychoanalytic Interpretation of Sambia Masculinization

The nuclear family is the residential unit in Sambia, a pattern rare in the New Guinea Highlands. Marriage is a male-dominated complementary relationship, to which the age difference between husband and wife contributes. Children are reared in the house with the parents. While boys are removed by first-stage initiation and placed in the men's house, girls reside with their parents until marriage. Small boys and girls form play groups with relative freedom, quite carefree in the security of the garden-ringed village, assisting or accompanying women in their domestic chores, and this becomes a source of lifelong friendship among age mates. Soon, however, boys play only with boys, both from choice and parental guidance, and after male initiation boys strictly avoid girls (Herdt, 1981).

Sexual repression in children parallels socialization practices in Western countries: children are best kept ignorant of all erotic matters, heterosexual activity should be hidden from them and should ideally occur in the forest, although it occasionally occurs within houses after children are asleep. Adults are always careful to cover their genitals, and to avoid any direct reference to them or to intercourse in heterosexual company. Boys, unlike girls, are allowed to go about naked till they are three or four years of age and, unlike girls, are teased and (playfully) taunted about their genitals. All sex play between boys and girls is forbidden. This seems to succeed, as most boys deny any knowledge of semen or erotic intercourse until they are initiated. There is little doubt that sexual repression in creating guilt helps to inculcate obedience and subordination, and to shift sexual energy towards aggression (cf. Reich, 1972:149ff.).

Breastfeeding is prolonged (Herdt, 1981:209) for Sambia children beyond the second, and even the third year. A man's earliest memory may be of suckling at his mother's breasts. Older children are permitted to cry for the breast when frightened. While the mother is travelling or gardening throughout the day, the child is warmly suspended against her back. It sleeps with its mother, who gradually begins to feed it solid foods that she has masticated, mouth to mouth. Thus there is a prolonged, luxuriant mother-infant symbiosis, contrasted to a cool and distant relationship with the father. There is stringent postpartum avoidance between mother and father, as violations are believed to harm baby and wife, and potentially bring humiliation and shame to all. Men are prohibited both from watching their wives breastfeed and from sexual intercourse with them for twenty months or more. Herdt (1981:211) suggests that the postpartum taboo defends a man against his envy of the infant's situation, but I think rather (and it will become clear below) that it augments his resentment and anti-Oedipal feelings towards his infant son. Moreover, a child has relatively free access to its mother and her breast until coitus resumes. It is thus the father who interrupts this luxurious symbiosis. Sambia childhood is fraught with familial conflict: hostile silence, bickering or open fighting between the parents, conflicts in which the father always wins. A father repeatedly broadcasts a traumatic and humiliating message to his infant son: "I am a man, but you are something different." However, a mother may ambivalently identify a son with his father if he is overly aggressive.

Key factors, then, in Sambia socialization are: exceptionally close maternal attachment, prolonged orality, and physical and psychological distance from one's father. Gradually a father begins to spend more time with his boy, and to separate him from his mother, and to masculinize him. Adult men are openly hostile to undisciplined boys, taunting them till they cry. Men often say that their little son is a carrier of feminine pollution, perceiving him as an open vessel containing female contaminants with feminine personality traits of irrationality, suggestibility and cowardice. A boy must be wiped clean of these by characteristically painful means, or the pollution will weaken and eventually kill him. Ritual pain and trauma are a requirements of the hard-won path to manhood.

Physical aggression of adult men and older bachelors toward young initiates is the most conspicuous characteristic of the first two stages of initiation. The boys are deliberately frightened and made distraught, to set "the right mood" for ritual instruction, which amounts almost to brainwashing. To become masculine is to follow orders and observe rules. Measures intended to remove external and internal contamination by women are categorized by Herdt as "stretching" and "egestive" rites. The former is a thrashing technique in which sticks, switches or bristly objects are hit or rubbed against the group of boys' bodies until the skin flakes away and bleeds. Egestive rites are cane swallowing (with canes penetrating a foot or more), inducing vomiting and defecation, and nose bleeding to remove contaminated blood. Cane swallowing was abandoned because men themselves considered it to be excessively dangerous and too painful. Nose bleeding (sharp grasses are thrust up the nose until blood flows) is at present the most painful ritual act. Herdt (1981:224) writes: "It is secret; so when first performed on boys by surprise, it turns into a forcible, violent assault that is probably close to authentic physical and psychological trauma . . . men always perceptually focus on the actual bloodflow, which they prefer in abundance . . . men greet the expurgation with a collective war-cry." Men consider that they are doing boys a favor in introducing them into the male world and purifying them of their mother's "bad talk" and "bad blood." Nose bleeding is also intended to teach the initiates not to fear the spilling of blood during warfare, nor to fear seeing their age mates' blood spilled. They are told, "If the enemy kills your mate, you must be strong and kill him as revenge." (Herdt, 1981:226). In punishing boys for their insubordination, men project all their faults onto women. It is women, not men, who punish children, and they particularly scold and curse boys. This ritual nose bleeding undoubtedly induces intense castration fears in seven- to ten-year-old boys.

The nose is an object of many Sambia cultural practices, a very well known phallic symbol. Although Herdt does not use the word, castration fear is omnipresent in Sambia men's talk, myth and dreams. They are unkind to women, but this stems from their truly great anxieties. Women are pictured as so relentlessly dangerous to masculine health that this fear becomes psychologically embedded and morally interferes with normal eroticism. The most dreaded feature of a women is her vagina. The cliche: "Women have that vagina, something truly no good" is constantly heard (Herdt, 1981:161). Men utterly detest to say the word *laaku* (vagina), preferring the euphemism, "that thing below." Fervent spitting follows the uttering of this and related words. Menstrual blood evokes feelings of nausea and disgust in men. Disgust and fear of a woman's vagina, especially if bleeding, emphasizes the woman as a castrated and castrating being (see Freud, 1979a:206, 1979b:315; Roheim, 1970:228). Indeed, men end up discounting other vicissitudes of life as of little account compared to their draining encounters with ogress females (Herdt, 1981:243).

As all initial heterosexual activity may be anxiety provoking, males avoid it as long as possible. Heterosexual coitus leaves men shaking, trembling and anxious. There is little touching in coitus, and foreplay is minimal, denying women erotic pleasure. To avoid the 'truly bad smell' of their wives' vaginas men must spit after intercourse and keep tree bark in their mouths and spearmint leaves in their noses during intercourse, and afterwards induce a nosebleed and rub stinging nettles on their hands to remove contaminants. Mythic lore clearly indicates that a vulva is perceived and feared as a wound caused by castration by the mythic father (Numboolyu).

A case history illustrates this castration complex and its related attitude to women: Nilutwo dreamt that he was unable to ejaculate because his dream partner had no pubic hair and a cold and blood-colored vagina. On the contrary, her breasts were swollen and big. This is an example of the primitive fantasy: if she has no penis (bleeding vagina), I have none too (I cannot ejaculate) (Roheim, 1972a:239, 262). This dream occurred while the dreamer was lying next to a former fight leader, prone to violence, and in the dream the woman also had phallic characteristics: her swollen breasts, for a general equivalence is made between penis and breast (nipple).

Nilutwo was reared almost alone by his mother, a strong thrice-married widow, who saw to his premature initiation. His father "acting crazy and violent" had died early. Women generally disparaged him as a weak man, although he was a cassowary hunter, a rather privileged position. Nilutwo suffered from repetitive nightmares. His most frequent dream of copulating with "a women he knows" is associated with erotic desire towards forbidden women, such as his sister-in-law, as well as toward old women. These are wet dreams, usually associated with anxiety. He perceived them as a manifestation of his special relationship to female hamlet spirits, the cassowary familiars par excellence—in other words, to phallic women, such as his own mother. Cassowaries are identified with masculinized women. Sometimes Nilutwo dreamt that he was chased by giant snakes or evil ghosts, clearly male symbols reawakening castration fears. Such male dreams are common: of bloody streams of water, huts that leak red fluids, and particularly of stagnant, surging blood-filled bogs that threaten to engulf the dreamer. A man starts up trembling from such nightmares. Men are also prone to panicky, phobialike reactions when confronted with red blotches (such as betel-nut juice or blood), or with snakes and lizards. Castration fear is also seen in the terrible anxiety of semen depletion. Semen is here *pars pro toto*, and represents the fear of losing the good object.

Characteristically, castration is denied. Men compensate by secretly thrusting sharp canes up their noses, painfully simulating menstruation, thus denying the vagina as a castration wound; that is, they too bleed and purify themselves, yet are masculine, with penises. This typically compensating defense mechanism may be compared with subincision (see Roheim, 1970:227–28, 276). Roheim conceives Central Australian society as built on this defense mechanism as an inversion of castration anxiety. By simulating feminine functions, men render themselves far more seductive to young males (Roheim, 1970:219ff). In Sambia society, the denial of castration is represented by assertive warriorhood and of feminine qualities in men.

Homosexual cathexis is a consequence. According to Freud (1979a:206), attachment to the mother, narcissism and fear of castration (the latter including also "retiring in favor of the father"; that is, a renunciation to all rivalry with him for the mother, or homosexual submission) are the chief etiological factors in homosexuality. In Sambia society the introduction of homosexual fellatio to novices involves a dramatic cutting of the boys' childhood pubic aprons—a symbolically castrative act. Boys are to keep homosexual practices a secret, under penalty of castration and murder. They are commanded to "suck the penis" if they wish to grow big and live a long life, an experience so traumatic that a boy may later use the third person singular when speaking of it. It is also associated with anxieties of becoming pregnant and of getting feminine bodily traits. Fellatio ideally occurs often, almost daily, and becomes a whole way of life. Fellatio insemination is likened to maternal breastfeeding, and semen to mother's milk.

Fellatio thus becomes a substitute for the desire, even in older children, to cling to the breast. This reminder of maternal security attaches positive affects to relations with men, and promotes male solidarity. The ritual bamboo flute, overtly likened to the phallus, becomes a substitute mother and wife (Herdt, 1981:283). The physical fantasy that the penis is an equivalent for the breast is not unique to the Sambia: Roheim (1972a:254, 258) mentions it in Indo-European folklore, and Devereux (1982b:464) finds it in his psychotherapy of a Plains Indian. One should also mention that Sambia men drink milk sap from the aerial roots of the pandanus tree to replenish semen lost through the insemination of boys and women. These roots are said to be the same as the breasts of a woman, while in ritual these roots are described as penises.

I agree with Herdt that despite homosexual behavior most Sambia men have no homosexual identity. Such activities start only at seven to ten years of age (that is after the resolution of the Oedipal complex), and most Sambia men become exclusively heterosexual after their wives' menarche. But a few men continue to prefer homosexual fellatio over heterosexual fellatio or coitus, even when disparaged for doing so. In other words, psychological involvement in homosexual contact is much stronger than just the acting out of social roles.

Herdt (1981:174n) says: "There is evidence from individual case studies to suggest that, sometimes, all male/male body contact is eroticized." Bachelors are sometimes passionately fond of particular boys, and there is undoubtedly a strong, homosexual cathexis even when this is not, or no longer, acted out. This cathexis has a clearly compensatory character. As already mentioned, youths must become strong and angry because of the aggression and bad treatment imposed on them. Besides retaliation directed toward younger initiates, they are urged to channel that anger and relax their tight penises by engaging in homosexual fellatio. I think this is a reactive formation against the normal and understandable hostile and aggressive impulses (and indeed Oedipal impulses) felt by the youths in such circumstances. The hierarchical structure allows no expression of this to older men, so these impulses must be transformed into affectionate feelings and social feelings of identification (cf. Freud, 1979a:207).

One way to cope with aggression is to identify with the aggressor (Roheim, 1967:70). Moreover, the pleasure principle is fundamentally an economy principle tending to reduce the excitation in the psychic structures to as low and constant a level as possible (Freud, 1963:9,79). The more the psychic energy of frustration is released through erotic gratification, the more easily will it be accepted. Where the bachelor's penis replaces the mother's breast, infantile dependence is shifted from the mother to the hierarchically superior male, and a greater than normal amount of libidinal energy will thus become attached to male solidarity and to the aggressive doings of men. This is a good illustration of Roheim's (1972a:156, 1972b:19ff.) theory that a culture is constituted as a defense mechanism and a reaction formation against certain libidinal tensions and traumatisms, depending on the specific infantile situations present in it.

Such a pattern is not unique to Sambia culture (Herdt, 1981:18). In youth movements and armies in the West, a more covert form of homosexual cathexis certainly plays a role (Freud, 1963:114ff., 1979b:198; Falconnet and Lefaucheur, 1975:155). At times, homosexual activities have been overtly practiced in armies: one may recall the famous "sacred companies," composed of homosexual couples in Ancient Greece (Devereux, 1980:158n). Such homosexuality, as well as that of the Sambia, is in fact an epiphenomenon with regard to the male supremacist complex. Some degree of homosexual cathexis is fundamental for male solidarity (Freud, 1979b:198), but need not be acted out. Enactment is a cultural choice, needing strong heterosexual repression and homosexual seduction.

While aggression may be partly derived and relaxed through homosexual activity, enough remains to be turned toward the outside; that is, toward the enemy and toward women. Sambia youths are urged to keep their wives in their place and adopt a fierce warrior's posture toward enemies. The least provocation or motive unleashes war raids. Male in-group eruptions of violence and hatred do also occur.

Another aspect concerns culpability and fears as a consequence of repressive socialization. Men project the hardships of initiation, and even the institution of war on women. According to myth (Herdt, 1981:351), "Namboolyu's wife, Chenchi, killed her first male child. Why? That pregnancy was very painful. Because she killed the first male child, we men now fight war. Because she killed the child, we now have initiations and we ceremonially beat our male children." Elements of a castration complex are present, as well as a typical inversion of culpability: the (male) wish to kill or castrate the male infant is projected onto the mother.

Oedipal hostility appears to be completely repressed; the principle enemy is not the group of elder men (including one's father), but one's mother and wife. However, since most men become exclusively heterosexual again after marriage, the strong Oedipal rivalry must not be entirely deflected through homosexual attachment. Fear of mother-son incest motivates men to separate the two (Herdt 1981:147). They also fancy that boys will have promiscuous sex if allowed to look at women. In the male parthenogenesis myth, incest is constantly hinted at, for instance, "My wife is my property, I can't let my son copulate with my own sexual partner." Herdt (1981:275) says that this myth implies that women are such lascivious creatures that even maternal care would succumb to wanton eroticism. To avoid incest, fighting, and patricide, Numboolyu (the Father) gave his sons secret fellatio.

This myth contains strong anti-Oedipal factors in telling how the father institutes repressive initiation for fear of incest. That the child witnesses the aging and approaching death of a generation can generate unconscious feelings of hostility in the adult (Rosolato, 1975:66ff.). Devereux (1977:162ff.) holds that anti-Oedipal elements are one of the mechanisms in the unfolding of the Oedipus complex. On the conscious everyday level these facts are entirely negated: in the hostile attitude toward women and in the idioms of male solidarity that dominate the whole fabric of society. Sambia men stress particularly the affectionate bond between father and son. They say that when they die, their wife only pretends to wail and then gets another man. True sorrow is only felt by sons. Expression of incest in myth often induces near-hysterical laughter, demonstrating the Oedipal wishes and tensions present in Sambia culture. As Freud (1976:201) wrote: "Owing to the introduction of the proscribed idea by means of an auditory perception, the cathectic energy used for the inhibition has now suddenly become superfluous and has been lifted, and is therefore now ready to be discharged by laughter." The amount of laughter is then a good measure of the energy needed to repress these ideas.

It seems to me that Herdt distinguishes too little between cognitive processes (and logic) and affective processes. Although he describes psychological reactions, affects and dreams accurately, his conclusion is too greatly in agreement with Sambia cultural logic: that young boys are not really masculine and thus need to be masculinized in a society that needs strong and fierce warriors to cope with the continuous threat of war. Drawing chiefly on the psychiatric writings of Stoller, Herdt (1981:312) argues that in a boy (not specifically in Sambia) prolonged and exclusive maternal caring induces a primary sense of existence whose feminine qualities are a deep part of the earliest subjectivity that impels character structure and adult behavior. Boys should therefore disassociate themselves from their mothers if they are to become separate masculine individuals (Herdt, 1981:313). Thus a warring culture needs to brainwash a youth's "primary feminine identity" and replace it with a secondary male identity (Herdt, 1981:308). While girls must indviduate from their mothers, as their core gender identity is feminine, it is less difficult to do so. This is almost exactly what the Sambia themselves say: "Men have it hard, women have it easy." (Herdt, 1981:168, 245) My work on anorexia nervosa brought me to quite a contrary conclusion: that girls may have even greater problems with their gender identity (Huyghe, 1983b). From the psychological point of view it is girls, not boys, who must shift from the mother to the father as an object of desire. In the earliest symbiotic phase there is undifferentiation, and identification with the mother comes only later (see Devereux, 1982a:103).

While Herdt (1981:323) recognizes Oedipal factors in the Sambia, he does not know what to make of it. He follows contemporary shifts in Oedipal theory that suggest that before the Oedipal phase, sensing one's existence in terms of maleness or femaleness is fundamental. In such a view the Oedipal phase becomes only an incident *de parcours*, while the core gender identity remains what it was from the beginning. I cannot accept this. A person becomes genderized precisely through the unfolding of the Oedipal phase. In the Sambia this takes place at the moment when the father begins to take part in the education of his sons. Moreover Oedipality is not a theory, even less a hypothesis; it is a fact that clinical observations covering more than eighty years have demonstrated for normal people and in non-Western groups. Freud postulated such concepts and processes as libido, ego, id, superego, now forming the theoretical corpus of psychoanalysis, to account for these facts. The theory must remain "fact" as long as no other theory provides a better explanation (Mitscherlich, 1970:111). Herdt has not paid enough attention to the psychological inversion and negation of Oedipal rivalry in Sambia. Defense mechanisms derive amazing aggressive energy from the Sambia Oedipal situation. It is projected onto enemies, inversed and projected onto women, and finally, transformed into affection through the enacting of ritual homosexuality. Also, on the sociocultural level, masculinization of boys is needed, not necessarily because they would be too feminine in the face of war, but chiefly to create a repressive and alienating sociocultural order that ensures the absolute power (including erotic power) of males over women and inferiors. The underlying cultural logic entails confrontation and war.

Some Psychological Notes on War

In his fine psychoanalytic study of aggression, Mitscherlich (1970:159) denies that a death impulse (*thanatos*) underlies aggression, countering Freud (1971:15) who held for a noneroticized thirst for destruction. The Sambia data show that while war is entailed in a cultural logic and/or an economic-political power structure, individual aggressive affects necessary for war are artificially aroused, so other developmental possibilities must exist. Notwithstanding the pseudoscientific pretensions of much popular literature, primates and proto- and prehistoric people appear to be rather peace loving. While man, like other animals, may be aggressively aroused, this does not necessarily imply the in-species destruction or self-destruction of war. Man is a cultral being, and human potentialities are subjected to differential cultural adaptation, implemented through socialization. By influencing the affective economy, socialization can repress or stimulate potentialities present in humans and attach positive or negative values and feelings to certain behavior types. Through a demand for unquestioning obedience, associated to values of fidelity and virility, aggression becomes ritualized into a virtue (Mitscherlich, 1970:31). Symbols used to justify conflict, such as "national honor," "the sacred soil of the fatherland," "the defense of liberty," "fight against capitalistic exploitation," mobilize not only aggressive, but destructive tendencies. They are not values worth defending, but symbols used (by both sides) to arouse aggression (Mitscherlich, 1970:16-20). Mitscherlich (1970:23) sees accurately that young warriors tend to forget about the good cause in a conflict, to think only of satisfying an intense excitation with sexual background, and to become blind to rational argument. Logical arguments are of no avail against affective interests, and in war are only put forward to justify the sanction of this excitation (Freud, 1963:251ff.).

From a psychoanalytical point of view, the core of the problem is the fundamental ambivalence, on the level of internal dynamics, between love, hatred and aggression, which has its source in the child/parent relation. The investment of objects with love or hate can change from one to the other. Thus, through further socialization of school, initiation, or military drill and the like, libidinal value can attach to destructive behavior, as in the sexual perversion called sadism, destruction and aggression become pleasurable. On the other hand, the aggressive and destructive behavior conceals a self-destructive, masochistic and erotically loaded desire. A blind and absolute submission to military chiefs takes on the character of a sexual slavery, or of an infantile state of submission amounting to a complete abolishment of conscience and repression of culpability. Those who give the orders can indulge in fantasies of destruction and all-potency. Many of the effects discussed by Mitscherlich (1970) are apparent in the Sambia material.

Where culpability is culturally repressed, the ability to see the injustice and the inadaptation of the whole cultural war fabric—ideology, symbols and institutions—is repressed with it. I consider war to be a cultural scotoma; we are no longer able to see that institutions such as obligatory military service, or symbols such as national pride, patriotism, courage or masculinity are not defenses against war, but the very instruments used to implement it. Freud (1963:240) remarked that as society does not tolerate the expression of aggresive needs in individuals, it monopolizes aggression and redirects it according to its interests.

Frustration during childhood socialization is inevitable. If the affects associated with this socialization become attached to aggressive and destructive tendencies in the adult, instead of being attached to their socializing origin, this will lead to an identification with these aggressive, destructive and sadomasochistic tendencies (see Mitscherlich, 1970:73).[3] A child interiorizes an event much more in terms of its affective load than in terms of its cultural significance. Moreover when justified aggressive expression by a child is invariably repressed and channeled through certain defense mechanisms (as in the Sambia case), these aggressive impulses will remain largely uncontrolled in the adult, who is then liable to destructive outbursts when provoked. Mitscherlich (1970:140) therefore pleads for psychoanalysis as a means of enlarging the field of consciousness gradually so that we come to understand our own destructive tendencies as well as those in socialization and society. Both psychoanalysis and anthropological training work toward such understanding.

Besides making aggressive impulses consciously more manageable, psychoanalysis may also assist in the development of education programs in which libidinal value would attach to conflict-avoidance mechanisms, instead of implementing destructive abreaction. It is no accident that some authoritarian and dictatorial regimes prohibit psychoanalysis, although some analysts tend to reinforce submission to society, under the pretext of adaptation.

Rather than encouraging mastery of aggressive impulses, contemporary Western society covertly encourages them if they promote its interests, even though they may be contrary to the overt value code (Mitscherlich 1970:81,90–91). Thus, "free" citizens are forcibly conscripted into armies, and authorities deliberately use propaganda and false information in conflict situations. It is clear that war goals are not initially those of the whole community, but are promulgated by a ruling caste (politicians, military-industrial complex) whose members can avoid public control, especially with regard to "security" matters, even in democratic countries. When opponents both operate in this way, neither is completely innocent of promoting conflict, even when threats to peace seem only to come from one side. Mitscherlich (1970:93) concludes that a cure implies not only a reconciliation with one's own being and history, but also an unyielding vigilance and suspicion of "public virtues."

Conclusion

Sambia male existence is relentlessly conditioned by a history of constant war (Herdt, 1981). The creation of an intense phallic masculinity, admitting of no alternatives, counters the constant threat from enemies who would feast on the slightest sign of weakness. But this is only half the truth; selection of aggressive attitudes in males, breeding of aggression through conditioning and affective attachment to it, with even war raids being launched for confirmatory initiation, clearly institutionalizes war and is its major cause. Herdt's (1981:303) argument that war creates a need for certain types of men and women has it backwards, for groups of men are culturally conditioned to choose to become and to breed warriors, and once war begins, a vicious circle with continued fighting and intensification of aggression is established. The question is how to interrupt this cycle.

The above discussion of Sambia masculinity shows clearly that modification must be carried out the in the sociocultural domain. According to Devereux (1982b:111), cultural change cannot be brought about only by changes in education. Adults must agree on a new set of values and cultural interactions that will create new identification models for the coming generations. The Sambia illustrate that a male gender identity that perverts the normal aggressive potentiality into destructive and autodestructive impulses is a crucial factor, leading to the conclusion that stable peace cannot be reached without corrections of that identity. Adult men must be made conscious that the values of aggression, with which they are conditioned to identify, entail destruction and self-destruction, and rest on models of infantile sadomasochistic relations that they have internalized. We know that not all men interiorize this model to the same extent, but those who have completely identified with it, for example the war leaders, have a stirring effect on their fellows and on the whole community. Not only the deviant and neurotic individual man, so consumed with demonstrating ruthless masculinity that he constantly and destructively broadcasts misogyny, creates such a climate, as Herdt (1981:162) would have it, but also a collective cultural neurosis.

Differentiation as a fundamental mechanism in identity formation is panhuman. Roheim (1967:417) rightly says that we are all alike affectively, precisely in that we think that all others are different from us. To identify with somebody or something means also to differentiate oneself, but when one identifies oneself as one of a kind, or as belonging to a "superior race," or a group or institution denies any value to others, this cannot but end in confrontation and (self-) destruction. Yet all military structures, armies and military education, operate on that principle (Mitscherlich, 1970:39ff.). Not surprisingly the army is often portrayed as a means of unifying a nation. But the nation-state represents a threat to international peace, for it is difficult to unify a people on behalf of nationality, religion or ideology without claiming superiority for your own nation, religion, or ideology (Patterson, 1977:93). Symbolic anthropology is of great value in developing methods to uncover implicit elements in a cultural symbolic system. An example is Devisch's structural logic of verticality/horizontality and hierarchy/equality which allows for cross-cultural comparison and analysis.

Psychoanalysis can help us to discover the origin of the hatred that so blinds people that they become self-destructive and to understand how such an alienating, oppressive and infantilizing situation can be maintained. But to understand the implicit logic of the cultural order, symbolic anthropological analysis is more useful. We need to understand war in industrialized countries, where economical and political structures are very complex. Despite this complexity, it is comparable to tribal warfare on the level of structural logic, and of the underlying psychodynamic mechanisms. Sambia culture seems unique in many ways, but its developmental pattern is not. A cross-cultural comparison shows that developmental patterns exist that entail less anxiety, less violence, and also a less paradoxical masculinity. Most Sambia men are not really happy with a warring situation and rarely mourn the passing of warfare violence (Herdt, 1981:50). Herdt (1981:305) holds that Sambia boys are reluctant men, who take far more pleasure in the stereotypical fantasy than in the hard-won reality of an aggressive warrior's life.

We must now recognize that cultural adaptation mechanisms based on the warrior ideal are evolutionarily condemned, and we with them. New political decisions are necessary, for war is a political activity. We must also submit cultural values, and especially those values entailing differentiation and hierarchization, to critical and liberating scrutiny. Finally, the individual must become critical of his or her own aggressive potentiality in order to master its destructiveness. These levels are linked as one single reality seen from different perspectives. Thus progress in one should also entail progress in the other. But social and moral revolutions have often failed because they tried to implement their goals with means employing a structural logic contrary to these goals. In other words, it is impossible to create a peaceful world by destructive and nonreciprocal authoritarian means, which make use of the infantile sadomasochistic aspects of human personality. If we want peace, more is needed than negotiation on nuclear or other weapons, or even more than reduction of economic inequalities. Reduction and suppression of military service, military institutions and military ideologies must be undertaken, for if war disappears as an institution, as a cultural convention, then the conditions will be created for its psychological correlates to disappear also.

We should take advantage of every possibility to break the vicious cycle we are in, lest we be caught again in it for the last time.[4]

Notes

1. Overpopulation (e.g. in urban space) as a cause of aggression, as sometimes suggested, seems to be extremely culturally dependent. Among other factors, the

cultural value put on close physical contacts with other society members plays a role.

2. From bottom to top, this hierarchy includes boys, preinitiates, initiates, first- and second-stage ritual novices, bachelors, third-stage ritual initiates, men, married, completed sixth-stage initiation, fatherhood, elders, grey-headed senior men (Herdt, 1981:25).
3. The terms sadism and masochism as used here do not refer to sexual perversions in adults, but to the reactualization of infantile, phantasmatical and deforming models of human relations, corresponding to an infantile, pregenital mode of libidinal organization: the sadistic-anal phase during which the parents are not yet perceived as total human persons, but as omnipotent beings with, among others, sadistic traits. In this relationship the child is always the weakest partner (see Freud, 1979a:140). As the genital phase unfolds, a more or less successful remolding of these early libidinal attachments, strongly influenced by the parents' own unconsciously determined attitudes, will take place. A person's later ability to engage in social relations on equal and satisfying terms will largely depend on this process.
4. Written from the psychiatrist's point of view, this paper may seem biased toward the psychoanalytic side, but it intends to open perspectives for further research.

References

Bastide, R. 1972. *Sociologie et Psychanalyse*. Paris: Presses Universitaires de France.

Clastres, P. 1977a. "Archéologie de la Violence." Libre 1, Payot: 137–73.

_____. 1977b. "Malheur du Guerrier Sauvage." Libre 2, Payot: 69–109

Devereux, G. 1972. *Ethnopsychanalyse Complémentariste*. Paris: Flammarion.

_____. 1977. *Essais d'ethnopsychiatrie Générale*. Paris: Gallimard.

_____. 1980. *De l'angoisse à la Méthode dans les Sciences du Comportement*. Paris: Flammarion.

_____. 1982a. *Femme et Mythe*. Paris: Flammarion.

_____. 1982b. *Psychothérapie d'un Indien des Plaines*. Paris: J.C.Godefroy.

Devisch, R. 1981. "Spatial Rationale of Good and Ill-health Among the Yaka." Paper prepared for the African Studies Association Meetings, Bloomington, Indiana.

_____. 1983. "Beyond a Structural Approach to Therapeutic Efficacy." In *The Future of Structuralism*, edited by A. De Ruijter and J. Oosten, pp. 403-21. Göttingen: Herodot.

Divale, W. and Harris, M. 1979. "Population, Warfare and the Male Supremacist Complex." In *Issues in Cultural Anthropology*, edited by D.McCurdy and J.Spradley, pp. 322-40. Boston: Little Brown.

Falconnet, G. and Lefaucheur, N. 1975. *La Fabrication des Mâles*. Collection Points. Paris:LeSeuil.

Foucault, M. 1966. *Les Mots et les Choses*. Paris: Gallimard.

Freud, S. 1962. *Trois Essais sur la Théorie de la Sexualité (1905)*. Paris: Gallimard.

_____. 1963. "Au-delà du Principe du Plaisir (1920)," "Psychologie Collective et Analyse du Moi (1921)," "Considérations Actuelles sur la Guerre et sur la Mort (1915)." In *Essais de Psychanalyse*. Paris: Payot.

_____. 1971. *Malaise dans la Civilisation (1929)*. Paris: Presses Universitaires de France.
_____. 1976. *Jokes and Their Relation to the Unconscious (1905)*. Translated by J. Strachey. The Pelican Freud Library vol.6. Harmondsworth, England: Penguin Books.
_____. 1979a. "Hysterical Phantasies and Their Relation to Bisexuality (1908)," "The Disposition to Obsessional Neurosis (A Contribution to the Problem of Choice of Neurosis) (1913)," "A Child Is Being Beaten, a Contribution to the Study of the Origin of Sexual Perversions (1919)," "Some Neurotic Mechanisms in Jealousy, Paranoia and Homosexuality (1922)." Translated by J.Strachey. In *On Psychopathology*. The Pelican Freud Library vol.10. Harmondsworth, England: Penguin Books.
_____. 1979b. "Psychonanalytic Notes on an Autobiographical Account of a Case of Paranoia (Dementia Paranoides) (1911)," "From the History of an Infantile Neurosis (1918)." Translated by J.Strachey. In *Case Histories II*. The Pelican Freud Library vol.9. Harmondsworth, England: Penguin Books.
Gell, A. 1975. *The Metamorphosis of the Cassowaries*. London: Athlone Press.
Herdt, G. 1981. *Guardians of the Flutes, Idioms of Masculinity*. New York: McGraw- Hill.
Huyghe, B. 1982. "La Violence: Une Réciprocité Manquée?" *Culture* 2(2):15–29.
_____. 1983a. "Spatial Metaphors and Psychosomatization: Some Perspectives in Transcultural Psychiatry." In *New Perspectives in Belgian Anthropology*, edited by R.Pinxten, pp. 217–35. Göttingen: Herodot.
_____. 1983b. "Structuration Metaphorique du Corps et Identite dans l'anorexie Mentale." *International Journal of Psychology*18(5), Special multidisciplinary issue on symbol and symptom. R.Devisch and A.Gailly, eds.
La Barre, W. 1980. *Culture in Context*. Durham, N.C.: Duke University Press.
Macchiocchi, M.A. 1975. "Sexualité Féminine dans l'idéologie Fasciste." In *Sexualite et Politique*. Documents of the International Congress on Psychoanalysis. Edited by A. Verdiglione. Milan: Giangiacomo Feltrinelli Editore.
Mauss, M. 1950. *Sociologie et Anthropologie*. Paris: Presses Universitaires de France.
Mitscherlich, A. 1970. *L'idèe de Paix et l'agressivitè Humaine*. Paris: Gallimard.
Ortigues, M.C. and Ortigues, E. 1966. *Oedipe Africain*. Paris: Plon.
Patterson, O. 1977. *Ethnic Chauvinism: The Reactionary Impulse*. New York: Stein and Day.
Radcliffe-Brown, A.R. 1940. "Preface" in *African Political Systems*, edited by E.E.Evans- Pritchard and M.Fortes. Oxford, England: Oxford University Press.
Reich, W. 1972. *La Psychologie de Masse du Fascisme*. Paris: Payot.
Roheim, G. 1967. *Psychanalyse et Anthropologie*. Paris: Gallimard.
_____. 1970. *Hèros Phalliques et Symboles Maternels dans la Mythologie Australienne*. Paris: Gallimard.
_____. 1972a. *La Panique des Dieux*. Paris: Payot.
_____. 1972b . *Origine et Fonction de la Culture*. Paris: Gallimard.
Rosolato, G. 1975. "Culpabilité et Sacrifice." In *Psychanalyse et Sèmiotique*, edited by A.Verdiglione. Paris: Union Generale d'Editions.
Weber, M. 1947. *The Theory of Social and Economic Organization*. New York: Free Press of Glencoe.

4

Fighting for Peace

Carol J. Greenhouse

Military discipline gives birth to all discipline
—Max Weber (1978:1155)

Implicit Premises in Social Science

Anthropological contributions to the study of war tend to share a fundamental premise that war is a form of social pathology (see especially, Nader, this volume), a sign that something is seriously amiss in the social, cultural, or ecological order. The topic is largely limited to what has been called "primitive warfare," that is, armed conflicts between groups whose recourse to nonviolent, verbal modes of conflict resolution has failed. Thus, anthropological investigations of warfare are studies of sociocultural failure.

Studies of "primitive warfare," therefore, stress the social and cultural deficits that increase the risk of warfare. Koch's (1974) study of the Jalé of Highland New Guinea, for example, proposes that peace fails there because of the absence of a shared and explicit normative order and the absence of stable interest groups. The ethnology of war also provides the imagery of a metaphor for the international arena: the analogy is that nations, like small groups without reliable judiciaries, inescapably incur risks of war. Barkun (1968), for example, develops this theme explicitly.

In our common premise that war is pathological, anthropologists betray an important bias—important because it reflects a professional value orientation that opposes armed aggression, and also because it has obscured some cultural questions from examination. The fact is that war is not always and not only an accident or a function of sociocultural breakdown in international relations. Warfare and the ability to mobilize for war can be signs that in the eyes of its members, society works, that its social order is viable. The argument of this paper is that war is not necessarily a form of structural disorder but, quite the contrary, the reflection of a successfully organized society. This paper offers a brief examination of an American cultural conception of war that suggests just this: that war is order. That these notions are perhaps repugnant raises additional issues that are beyond the scope of my discussion.

One of the peculiarities of the present moment in history is that it is fair to say that the next war will not require soldiers. But in the last war fought by the United States, the one that ended in Vietnam ten years ago, obedient soldiers were still the prerequisite of war. This fact was widely understood among the American people. For example, the draft resistance movement intended to deny the war its soldiers by bringing the Selective Service to a halt by means of petitions, appeals, and direct action. Indeed, in 1968, high-level administrators at Selective Service worried that even five thousand burned draft cards would burden the system to the point of collapse (Congressional Quarterly Service 1968:12). With the exception of legally recognized conscientious objectors who accepted noncombatant roles or civilian duty in lieu of combat, people who violated any point of the Selective Service Act of 1967 were subject to federal criminal prosecution. Convictions for failure to report for induction, for example, involved fines of up to ten thousand dollars or incarceration for up to five years (Butter, 1971:150). Thus it is perhaps understandable that public attention focused on the resisters, who were a very small proportion of draftees (e.g., in 1967, there were just under one thousand convictions and about two hundred thousand inductions (Congressional Quarterly Service 1968:17).

Social scientists, on the other hand, did not find resistance problematic, but, rather, *obedience*. It was obedience that raised spectral images of unquestioning compliance with authority (cf., Milgram, 1974; 180–89 for the applications to the Vietnam conflict). Obedience calls into question assumptions about the place of self-interest in cultural life: How is it that an individual would prefer to risk death in war than to risk a fine or imprisonment? But to approach the question of obedience in this way—as if all draftees thought about service as a question—is too narrow a view. Did those men who served *elect* to serve in the sense that they rejected resistance or conscientious objection?[1] Quite probably not. Obedience is not necessarily a decision made in terms of national interest versus self-interest, life versus death, but can be the consequence of a different sort of cultural process. That process involves the formation of propositions that positively connect the state, the law, and the individual, that is, a cultural conception of order that has specific consequences, including the acceptance of military service. For these reasons, the agenda of anthropology in questions of war and peace is not only in gaining an understanding of the *decision* to fight, but of the sociocultural logic that simultaneously requires and obviates that decision.[2]

Orientation toward Militarism

Weber's (1978:312--313) discussion of the nature of the legal order provides the framework for what follows:

> The fact that some persons act in a certain way because they regard it as prescribed by legal propositions...is, of course, an essential element in the actual emergence and continued operation of a "legal order." But... it is by no means necessary that all, or even a majority, of those who engage in such conduct, do so from this motivation. As a matter of fact, such a situation has never occurred. The broad mass of the participants act in a way corresponding to legal norms, not out of obedience regarded as a legal obligation, but either because the environment approves of the conduct and disapproves of its opposite, or merely as a result of unreflective habituation to a regularity of life that has engraved itself as a custom. If the latter attitude were universal, the law would no longer "subjectively" be regarded as such, but would be observed as custom. As long as there is a chance that a coercive apparatus will enforce, in a given situation, compliance with those norms, we nevertheless must consider them as "law." Neither is it necessary—according to what was said above—that all those who share a belief in certain norms of behavior actually live in accordance with that belief at all times. Such a situation, likewise, has never obtained, nor need it obtain, since, according to our general definition, it is the "orientation" of an action toward a norm, rather than the "success" of that norm that is decisive for its validity. "Law," as understood by us, is simply an "order" endowed with certain specific guarantees of the probability of its empirical validity.

Following Weber, I propose that, for many Americans, the prospect of military service does not raise questions of obedience. Rather it allows them to articulate a cultural orientation toward the nation that obviates questions of *deciding* to obey. Consequently, anthropologists can contribute to an understanding of war and peace not only by examining situations in which disorder has escalated beyond a society's control, but also by examining cultural conceptions that positively orient social groups toward armed aggression.[3] More specifically, the anthropological problem is not first and not only one of interpreting a pattern of choice making by obedient soldiers, but rather one of examining the cultural premises that culminate in their service.

Unfortunately, but intriguingly, direct ethnographic evidence of Americans' attitudes toward compliance in wartime is virtually absent. At first glance, the question of the "good soldier" is not an anthropological question at all, if current publication is any guide.[4] Indeed, the soldier who answers the call to duty is of less obvious relevance to the *fact* of war than, say, foreign policymakers whose activities are generally secure from anthropological investigation.[5] Good soldiers fall between the slats of inquiry: studies of warfare elsewhere focus on socialization to violence (e.g., Huyghe, this volume; Koch, 1974) and on affiliative behavior (e.g., van de Vliert, 1981), but these perspectives presuppose decisions to fight for a cause—not quite the situation of the American draftee. American soldiers are not driven to fight by extreme conditions such as starvation (see Dirks's 1980 discussion of the effects of starvation on interpersonal tension, for example), nor necessarily by the perception that they personally have something to gain (for a contrastive argument about imperialism and expansionism generally, see Barroll, 1980). Perhaps the absence of a clear cultural question to ask about soldiers' acceptance of duty has precluded anthropological contributions in this area.

But here, the ethnography of other societies at war is of some considerable help. How do individuals among the Jalé, or the Kapauku, or the prereservation Cheyenne enlist the aid of others in battle? In fact, we do not know *how* they mobilize recruits, but we know *who* their recruits are. They turn to their brothers, their affines, their friends, their debtors; they turn to people who do not question their own obligation to give aid. These soldiers are recruited so effectively, in fact, that anthropologists tend not to question the efficacy of their recruitment strategies, tend not to question the "primitive" soldier's enthusiasm for the fight. Examples of data about recruitment to war are extremely general. Koch (1974:35, 82) writes on Jálemó, where individuals mobilize support however they can, generally from within their own men's houses or villages. Of the Jibaro, Karsten (1967:309) writes that it is "the family's sense of justice as well as the duty to the deceased" that require revenge. Murder "naturally awakes the desire for blood" (Karsten 1967:309). Blackfoot raiders seek personal gain and prestige (Ewers, 1967:329). The Kapauku fight for their best friends or because the legal authority compels it (Pospisil, 1964:86–95), Maori warfare "was organized on the bases of kinship and loyalty" (Vayda, 1967:364). These studies implicitly suggest that to explain a soldier's acceptance of what someone else calls his duty is to explain society itself. That acceptance is the very stuff of the organization of society, seen from below as an undeniable discipline, seen from above as compliance.

Weber's (1978:1155) reference to discipline (cited above as the epigraph to this paper) entails more than the subordination of the individual (as the draft resisters put the issue), but the cancellation of the individual. This is at once a cultural and historical process that has long roots in the West. Foucault (1977:308) identifies the equation of discipline and domination as an explicit formulation in the West, and dates its genesis at the seventeenth and eighteenth centuries. The methods of discipline of the eighteenth-century soldier, played out in his very body,[6]

> became general formulas of domination.... The historical moment of the disciplines was the moment when an art of the human body was born, which was directed not only at the growth of its skills, nor at the intensification of its subjection, but at the formation of a relation that in the mechanism itself makes it more obedient as it becomes more useful, and conversely . . . The human body was entering a machinery of power that explores it, breaks it down and rearranges it. A "political autonomy" which was also a "mechanics of power," was being born. . . . In short, (discipline) dissociates power from the body; on the one hand, it turns it into an "aptitude," a "capacity" which it seeks to increase; on the other hand, it reverses the course of the energy, the power that might result from it, and turns it into a relation of strict subjection (Foucault, 1977:138–39).

The essence of Foucault's argument is that in eighteenth-century Europe the state completed its business of creating a sociology of domination by creating individuals. American individualism explicitly rejects domination by the state, in this precise sense, but nevertheless comprehends it, as Tocqueville's analysis so persuasively demonstrates (Tocqueville, 1945). His analysis is of a cultural logic in which authority and power are negatively valued except to the extent that they are conceded by individuals for their own good (Tocqueville I, 1945:67):

> Why, then, does (the individual) obey society, and what are the natural limits of this obedience? Every individual is always supposed to be as well informed, as virtuous, and as strong as any of his fellow citizens. He obeys society, not because he is inferior to those who conduct it or because he is less capable than any other of governing himself, but because he acknowledges the utility of an association with his fellow men and he knows that no such association can exist without a regulating force. He is a subject in all that concerns the duties of citizens to each other; he is free, and responsible to God alone, for all that concerns himself.

Individualism, which amounts to a claim that the individual pursuit of self-interest contributes to the public good, requires considerable symbolic support to provide clarity where the everyday ambiguity of personal gains and losses cannot. Fundamental American symbols revolve around the nature of the social order and around the nature of the social activity necessary for the maintenance of that order. The nature of the social order is held to be a continual process of homogenization, or normalization, and self-regulation. The "melting pot" is one expression of this symbolic complex, necessitated by the cultural paradox of accepting the need for regulation while rejecting regulating in principle. Significantly, in the absence of regulation, the activity requisite to normalization is self-control, or discipline. Schools figure prominently in the mythicized process by which aliens become Americans, but, as several writers have indicated, it is not education which makes an American, but rather an individual's attitude toward work and its significance as central to one's social life. (For the clearest statement of this position, see Warner, 1962.) It is through work, through participation in the market (where the relation between personal gain and public good can be most readily measured) that individuals can learn the fundamental importance of conceding private autonomy for the good of the group. For the affluent, the rewards of this discipline take the form of disposable income. For other Americans, the discipline must be held to be rewarding in and of itself. In this way, self-control and self-sacrifice become inextricably linked, since they lend each other meaning. Thus, the discipline demanded by war can be seen to differ by degree, not by kind, from the discipline exacted by ordinary life.

The discussion in this paper is intended to make the point that an American conception of order, that is, the individualist's conception, built of symbols of discipline and self-sacrifice, makes possible a cancellation of the potential opposition between war and everyday life. In his discussion of a semiotic theory of the self, Singer (1980:500) argues against an approach that would define the individual as being in conflict with the society around him: "The problem . . . is not a conflict between personal identity and a social-cultural identity, for they are both personal and sociocultural. The problem is, rather, the empirical one of discovering the bonds of feeling that hold people together or tear them apart, and what their interrelations and conditions are." This brings us to a point that can be illustrated by some ethnographic material from the United States.

The View from an American Town

My data come from a small suburb of a major American city; at the time—1973 to 1975—the town was smaller than it is now that the city has grown toward it.[7] I did not go there to study soldiers, obedient or otherwise, but to investigate how people in general thought about interpersonal conflict and conflict resolution. Working primarily but not exclusively with a group of devout southern Baptists, I found that people's antipathy to overt expressions of conflict was very strong. The Baptists' rationale was that since the world and its people are in God's hands, and since only God can judge, interpersonal disputing was merely a vanity, a temptation to be resisted by Christians. Other people, who were not Baptists, expressed similar thoughts in somewhat more secular terms, that people who care about their communities do not dispute in public. Most of my work was among the Baptists and the rest of my remarks have to do with that group, but it is important to understand that their negative attitude toward conflict is different in its stylization, but not in its substance, from that of other townspeople.

The ethic against disputing is profound. Needless to say, these people do not bring problems to court, nor to lawyers. The adversarial process—*any* adversarial process—is too tainted with self-interest to be acceptable to them. Even softer modes of dispute resolution such as mediation or arbitration, as have been reported in church communities elsewhere and at other times (see, for example, Konig, 1979; Nelson, 1981) are intolerable. Thus, local Baptists appear to confirm recent research on disputing in the United States, which suggests that most Americans have a strong preference for doing nothing about their interpersonal problems (Felstiner, 1974; Tomasic and Feeley, 1982). From the Baptists' perspective, however, they are actively committing their problems to Jesus, who resolves them in his own way in his own time. In essence, these people's tolerance of conflict is very high, not only because they feel powerless to change their personal situations, but also because they feel they have no right to attempt to do so, given Jesus' supreme authority. The active involvement of Jesus in believers' lives is an important dimension to this discussion, since it constitutes one axis of a cultural paradox.

In 1973, when I arrived in the field, there were two major conflicts beyond the borders of the town that preoccupied the nation: The revelation of President Nixon's involvement in the Watergate break-in, and, of course, the aftermath of war in Vietnam. These issues were notable in the community I studied primarily by the relatively total silence surrounding them. The Baptists' "position" on Watergate was the less problematic of the two, from my perspective: Baptists consider politics to be pure conceit. Corruption is no surprise. People were inclined to be loyal to the president until the transcripts of his secret tapes revealed that he used profane and obscene language. In general, Watergate and the fate of the Nixon administration comprised a very minor focus of public concern.

If Watergate was a minor issue, the war in Vietnam was not an issue at all, except perhaps for the handful of men in the church who had fought in it. In the core group whom I knew best, three men had served in Vietnam. Given their attitudes toward interpersonal conflict, their military service (and reenlistment in two cases) seemed paradoxical, although I never said so. But I did not need to. One night, as often happened, a group of ten or so young people, including one of the veterans, was gathered for an evening of television, cards and idle conversation. The television was almost always on at any social gathering, but the program was only rarely even a temporary focus of the event. On this occasion, the program was a war film, and a scene portraying killing in the trenches caught the attention of one young woman. She said to no one in particular, "I just don't understand how someone can kill and still call himself a Christian." Her remark was a cruel mistake, since she had evidently forgotten that one of her peers was just such a person, returned from Vietnam with memories of death and now rebuilding his life around the church and his own spiritual rebirth. He murmured something about "serving one's country" but otherwise let the moment pass.

I was inclined to see this young man and the others as victims; after all, they had served while my cohort and I had not. But I have no evidence to suggest that they considered themselves victims. Any sense of victimization that they spoke of came after they returned home; one, for example, declined to attend college even with the GI Bill paying his tuition, since he did not want to endure what he expected would be vilification from fellow students who had opposed both the war and its soldiers. For the most part, their peer group treated these men in the same way that they treated another one of their number who had too much knowledge of inappropriate things, the one among them who had been married and divorced. Sex, conflict, war, these were equivalent in the requirement of public etiquette that they be deemed inconsequential. Eventually, I listened at length on several occasions as one of the men talked about his years in the service both to me and to others. I never felt that he sought exoneration, nor that he shared his friend's feeling that killing in the service of one's country and a version of Christianity that forbids even raising one's voice in anger might be at odds.

I eventually learned what these men already knew and accepted: that the resolution to the paradox is in the meaning of war and in the meaning of citizenship. These soldiers did not go to war in anger, they did not kill Vietnamese because they hated them; they fought as the artists of war they had been trained to be. The veteran's accounts to me were of the discipline of war: the ability to hear danger, to shoot without being able to see one's target, to be able to repair any machine without adequate tools, to be able to master fear and grief and revulsion. War demands perfection, and war is a mighty judge, since mistakes cost lives. Submitting to this discipline is an act of faith, as life at home requires the discipline of faith. The need for this discipline is experienced as the continual effort to strip oneself of vanity, anger and mortal terror.

Christian discipline and military discipline are not incompatible if one gives priority to narrow questions of discipline and service, and allows questions of one's individual acts, and of the merits of the war itself, to recede (see Kehoe, this volume). How it is that these latter questions *fail* to be the urgent ones is the cultural question that follows.

Let us return to the town, and the prevailing ethic there that expressions of conflict are inappropriate. A central component of this idea for Baptists and non-Baptists alike is a strong sense of local identity. The *ideology* of conflict is a general one, but their *experience* with conflict and conflict resolution is personal and local. In other words, sustaining their moral commitment to harmony is a very strong sense of community, and of the essential homogeneity of their particular community. As the people's relative indifference to issues beyond their town indicates, they compartmentalize their locality from their state, region, and nation rather effectively. The quality of their attitudes toward these other, wider groups varies inversely with their familiarity: the townspeople express negative attitudes toward their neighbors in the nearby city, for example, but on the other hand feel that most communities (in the abstract) are very much like their own, filled with good people. Furthermore, their sense of the nation and national citizenship are structured by a sense of duty which is sanctioned by Scripture (Romans 13:1–3): "Everyone must obey the state authorities; for no authority exists without God's permission, and the existing authorities have been put there by God. Whoever opposes the existing authority opposes what God has ordered; and anyone who does so will bring judgment on himself. For rulers are not to be feared by those who do good but by those who do evil."[8]

Thus, the local view is that while politicians may be corrupt, the government is not. While laws may be conceits, law is not. While one's neighbor may be un-Christian, the nation as a whole is the work of God. The only war that puts these ideas to the test is the war of the soul against its own "bodily passion" (1 Peter 2:11). Wars between nations do not. Quite the contrary, war creates an opportunity for service that people consider not only right, but sacred (Romans 12:1): "Offer yourselves as a living sacrifice to God, dedicated to his service and pleasing to him. This is the true worship that you should offer." The image of sacrifice in war also has secular significance, as Warner's much earlier analysis of the American celebration of Memorial Day reveals (Warner 1962:5–34). Warner's conclusion is:

> The Memorial Day rite is a cult of the dead, but not just of the dead as such, since by symbolically elaborating sacrifice of human life for the country through, or identifying it with, the Christian church's sacred sacrifice of their god, the deaths of such men also become powerful sacred symbols which organize, direct, and constantly revive the collective ideas of the community and the nation.

The striking element of the American ethnography reported in this paper is that the ideals that create harmony at the local level—discipline and faith—are exactly the same ones that bring soldiers to war. In other words, there is something in the American conception of order that cancels the opposition between peace and war; peace and war are on the same side of a larger opposition between order and disorder. The men in the town did not make the war in Vietnam, yet they could not have failed to serve any more than they could have renounced their church, or their families, or their own selves. I make no claims that the town I studied was typical of American communities, nor would I claim that its individualism is unique. The war is over, but anthropology still has a role to play, not so much in explaining their decisions to serve, but in explaining why, for many soldiers, there was no decision to make.

Notes

1. One anonymous contemporary commentator noted with some surprise that soldiers in the field voiced opposition to the war in Vietnam, and inferred from this evidence that they must have rejected conscientious objection as being too troublesome to pursue (Congressional Quarterly Service, 1968:17).
2. Indeed, the lottery itself, implemented in 1969, deemphasized one decisional aspect of military service by eliminating the question of who should be called up first. The lottery attached priority numbers to birthdates by a randomization procedure. The apparatus of the lottery was literally a wheel of fortune in the form of a spherical wire basket containing numbered chips; the basket was rotated by a crank between each call of a birthdate. In this way, military service was presented as not being a decision. It was, in the Army's symbolic terms, a consequence of birth.
3. In a recent study, Kriesberg and Klein (1980) examined the rise in American public satisfaction with current levels of defense expenditures over the years 1973–1978. They conclude that the decline in the (negative) impact of the Vietnam war, the rise in "conservative" ideology, and increased anti-Soviet and anti-communist sentiment account for the rise in levels of public satisfaction. In general, they conclude that satisfaction with arms spending reflects "solidarity and integration with the community" (Kriesberg and Klein, 1980:103, 107).
4. For an earlier and parallel observation of American anthropology, see Fried, Harris and Murphy (1968:x). To their edited volume, Tax contributed an article opposing the draft (Fried, Harris and Murphy 1968:195–207). In his comment, Hoebel (208–10) rejected both Tax's argument and his anthropology.
5. But see Levi and Tetlock's (1980) psychological study of the cognitive maps of Japanese policymakers in their debate over the decision for war in 1941.
6. Foucault (1977:135–36) begins his discussion of "docile bodies" with the following evocative description:

   > Let us take the ideal figure of the soldier as it was still seen in the early seventeenth century. To begin with, the soldier was someone who could be recognized from afar; he bore certain signs: the natural signs of his strength

and his courage, the marks, too, of his pride; his body was the blazon of his strength and valour; and although it is true that he had to learn the profession of arms little by little—generally in actual fighting—movements like marching and attitudes like the bearing of the head belonged for the most part of a bodily rhetoric of honour. . . . By the late eighteenth century, the soldier has become something that can be made; out of a formless clay, an inapt body, the machine required can be constructed; posture is gradually corrected; a calculated constraint runs slowly through each part of the body, mastering it, making it pliable, ready at all times, turning silently into the automatism of habit; in short, one has "got rid of the peasant" and given him "the air of a soldier" (ordinance of 20 March 1764). Recruits become accustomed to "holding their heads high and erect; to standing upright, without bending the back, to sticking out the belly, throwing out the chest and throwing back the shoulders; and, to help them acquire the habit, they are given this position while standing against a wall in such a way that the heels, the thighs, the waist and the shoulders touch it, as also do the backs of the hands, as one turns the arms outwards, without moving them away from the body. . . . Likewise, they will be taught never to fix their eyes on the ground, but to look straight at those they pass . . . to remain motionless until the order is given, without moving the head, the hands or the feet . . . lastly to march with a bold step, with knee and ham taut, on the points of the feet, which should face outwards" (ordinance of 20 March 1764).

7. Fieldwork was funded by a training grant from the National Institute of Mental Health to the Department of Anthropology at Harvard University (1973–1975) and by a faculty grant for research in the humanities at Cornell University (1980).
8. Scriptural references are from the version of the New Testament most widely read among local Baptist young people, *Good News for the Modern Man* (American Bible Society). It is an ordinary-language, illustrated edition.

References

Barkun, Michael. 1968. *Law without Sanctions.* New Haven, Conn.: Yale University Press.

Barroll, Martin A. 1980. "Toward a General Theory of Imperialism." *Journal of Anthropological Research* 36(2): 174–95.

Butter, Stephen H. 1971. *Legal Rights to Draft Deferments.* Steubenville, Oh.: Centre House Publishers.

Congressional Quarterly Service. 1968. *U.S. Draft Policy and Its Impact.* Washington, D.C.

Dirks, Robert. 1980. "Social Responses during Severe Food Shortage and Famine." *Current Anthropology* 21(1): 21–44.

Ewers, John C. 1967. "Blackfoot Raiding for Horses and Scalps." In *Law and Warfare*, edited by Paul Bohannon, pp. 327–44. Garden City, N.Y.: Natural History Press.

Felstiner, William L.C. 1974. "Influence of Social Organization on Dispute Processing." *Law and Society Review* 9(1):63–94.

Foucault, Michel. 1977. *Discipline and Punish.* New York: Vintage.

Fried, Morton; Harris, Marvin; and Murphy, Robert, eds. 1968. *War: The Anthropology of Armed Conflict and Aggression*. Garden City, N.Y.: Natural History Press.

Hoebel, E. Adamson. 1968. "The Draft and the United States Congress." In *War: The Anthropology of Armed Conflict and Aggression*, edited by Fried, et al., pp. 208–10. Garden City, N.Y.: Natural History Press.

Karsten, Rafael. 1967. "Blood Revenge and War among the Jabaro Indians of Eastern Ecuador." In *Law and Warfare*, edited by Paul Bohannon, pp. 303–26. Garden City, N.Y.: Natural History Press.

Koch, Klaus-Friedrich. 1974. *War and Peace in Jálemó*. Cambridge, Mass.: Harvard University Press.

Konig, David Thomas. 1979. *Law and Society in Puritan Massachusetts*. Chapel Hill, N.C.: University of North Carolina Press.

Kriesberg, Louis, and Klein, Ross. 1980. "Changes in Public Support for U.S. Military Spending." *Journal of Conflict Resolution* 24(1): 79–111.

Levi, Ariel, and Tetlock, Phillip E. 1980. "A Cognitive Analysis of Japan's 1941 Decision for War." *Journal of Conflict Resolution* 24(2): 195–211.

Milgram, Stanley. 1974. *Obedience to Authority: An Experimental View*. London: Tavistock.

Nelson, William E. 1981. *Dispute and Conflict Resolution in Plymouth County, Massachusetts, 1725–1825*. Chapel Hill, N.C.: University of North Carolina Press.

Pospisil, Leopold. 1964. *Kapauku Papuans and Their Law*. Yale University Publications in Anthropology 54. Reprinted by Human Relations Area Files Press.

Singer, Milton. 1980. "Signs of the Self: An Exploration in Semiotic Anthropology." *American Anthropologist* 82(3): 485–507.

Tax, Sol. 1968. "War and the Draft." In *War: The Anthropology of Armed Conflict and Aggression*, edited by Fried, et al., pp. 195–207. Garden City, N.Y.: Natural History Press.

Tocqueville, Alexis de. 1945. *Democracy in America*. 2 vols. Edited by Phillips Bradley. New York: Vintage.

Tomasic, Roman and Feeley, Malcolm M. 1982. *Neighborhood Justice: Assessment of an Emerging Idea*. New York: Longman.

van de Vliert, Evert. 1981. "Siding and Other Reactions to Conflict: A Theory of Escalation toward Outsiders." *Journal of Conflict Resolution* 25(3): 495–520.

Vayda, Andrew P. 1967. "Maori Warfare." In *Law and Warfare*, edited by Paul Bohannon, pp. 359–80. Garden City, N.Y.: Natural History Press.

Warner, W. Lloyd. 1962. *American Life: Dream and Reality*. Rev. ed. Chicago, Ill.: University of Chicago Press.

Weber, Max. 1978. *Economy and Society*. Edited by Guenther Roth and Claus Wittich. Berkeley, Cal.: University of California Press.

5

The Culture of United States Military Enclaves

Alexander Randall 5th

This paper is based on three and a half years of working with a most unusual tribe. I have chosen to call them "Conians" from a place they call "The World." I call them this because the official term for their homeland is CONUS, an acronym for Continental United States. In fact, every official document carries the reference to CONUS, but the people who come from CONUS generally call it The World. The World refers to any place in CONUS that is home, and is used to invoke the memory one has of the life and lifestyle one led before becoming a Conian. It is heavily weighted with emotional and personal memories.

The Conians are members of the American armed forces who live on American military bases around the world. For three and a half years I was a traveling member of the faculty of the University of Maryland's Overseas Division, and taught college-level anthropology and psychology to military students. My work does not constitute traditional anthropological fieldwork since I lived on no base for more than two months. However, I was given an opportunity to live and work on more than forty military bases, and see a broad cross-section of the lifestyle of the Conians. I write from the perspective of one who has seen the common factors in Conian life.

The Conians live in an archipelago of enclaves. These enclaves, called "bases," are self-contained environments in which Americans work and live. Most of the bases are within the Continental United States and, when surrounded by their home culture, the Conians disappear into its mainstream. A substantial number of these military enclaves are located in Germany and Japan, and a few in Spain, Italy, Belgium, the Philippines, and elsewhere. When surrounded by foreign cultures, the Conian's home base becomes an island of American culture in the ocean of otherness.

The enclaves range in size from small stations with as few as a dozen Americans to massive complexes where as many as five thousand are living and working. While the climate of the military base varies from arctic to tropical, there are certain common environmental features.

Here I will be concerned with some of the social, recreational, and psychological aspects of living in an American enclave, providing some insights into the mind set of the military community, and of the Conian enclaves as a microcosm of American life.

Bases have common features. It is the stated policy of the U.S. Department of Defense that an American living on a military complex should not be deprived of the lifestyle or of the essential life-support systems commonly found in the United States. To this end, each base has uniform standards for housing, water supplies, schools, churches, shopping facilties, social services, and uniform standards for dress and appearance. These minimum standards are the common denominator that gives Conians a sense of security. As a by-product of this policy, there is a drab continuity to Conian life. No matter where you are in the Conian world, the base looks just like every other base. The locations of particular services may vary, but on the whole, you can be assured that all of the core elements are there. If the core elements are not present, then the people are entitled to hardship allowances.

Peripheral to the stated mission of each base is an array of social and family activities that maintain a social and interpersonal lifestyle that is a truncated version of American culture. In the effort to compress the core of American culture into the confines of government budgeting, some of the variety of American culture is inevitably lost. Every enclave has a bowling alley and a shopping complex. The large ones rival a major suburban shopping complex, while on some of the smaller bases there may be no more than a single-lane bowling alley with a group of vending machines. Every base has access to the unofficial newspaper of the American armed forces and to the Armed Forces radio network. The radio programming is packaged in the continental United States and shipped to the enclaves on long-playing records complete with public service reminders, banter from the disc jockey, and the latest songs. The programs are dateless and timeless.

All life-support systems, mission exercises, and recreation activities flow through a Department of Defense conduit, giving each component a bureaucratic overtone. If presented with Weber's (1978) description of bureaucracy, Conians inevitably agree that U.S. military life is an example of classic "total institutional bureaucracy." Social and recreational services, schools, and life-support systems are built, maintained, and supplied by the lowest bidder and channeled through a single supply system in which there are few economic rewards for exceptional service.

The Conian economy is centrally planned in structure and has been described by one economist as the largest socialist enterprise outside the Soviet Union. The consequence is that Conians are used to waiting in line for inefficient service and to a general bureaucratic tangle of paperwork and errand running.

The enclaves are usually surrounded by a semipermeable membrane of chain link fence and barbed wire. There are generally two openings and the flow from the outside to the inside is regulated by a security force. Each enclave has a small outside population which regularly comes and goes. These are host nationals who perform skilled labor for wages, and usually a group of Americans who choose to live outside the enclave "on the economy."

The size of these groups varies with the severity of conditions in the host nation and the desirability of the lifestyle off the base. At one extreme is Iceland where the local government keeps the Americans sealed on the base, and at the other is the Philippines where there is a lively black market in goods, operated through the base gates. In places like central Germany and the United Kingdom, where the host cultures resemble the dominant American culture, the membrane is quite porous.

In general, the citizens of the host nation know little more about the activities of the Americans on base than of the mission of the base itself. Details of American base life are largely unknown. Conians generally keep to themselves and work and live quietly in the enclave. The majority seldom ventures beyond the perimeter fence. Those who do go outside spend most of their time in the local bars and restaurants, where a few may get rowdy and cause problems with the local population. Host nation and base relations are, however, generally cordial.

The housing on base is uniform and is available on the basis of rank and seniority. The nicest houses on base are reserved for the officer class, with a lower grade of housing assigned to the lower ranks. Those with the least tenure in the tribe, or those without families, live in barracks. The barracks are less than ideal living quarters, and many of the young Conians choose to marry because married couples are entitled to better housing. These marriages are often short-lived since they are based on convenience and not on romance or love. Within the larger enclaves the class distinction between top rank and lowest is quite dramatic, yet all housing falls within middle American housing standards. While the top officer may enjoy a larger lawn and garden than the enlisted ranks, the housing conditions of the latter are generally better than a comparable income could buy in CONUS. It is not unusual for a family to have a washer and dryer or similar appliance supplied by the government when it lacked such a convenience before joining the military.

The population of the enclaves is drawn from a cross-section of the American population. Despite the range of people who join the military, and the breadth of ethnic backgrounds represented, all have adopted the uniform standards of Conian culture. They literally come from everywhere that could be called America: from the inner city to the suburbs to the rural country, and from all American territorial possessions. It is not uncommon to find Samoans, American Indians, Blacks, middle-class whites, and Hispanics.

The official doctrine of the military is egalitarian, and people of all origins have an equal opportunity to rise in the ranks both occupationally and in terms of the perquisites and benefits that accrue from service. However, in actuality, the Conian enclave is a strictly hierarchical society where rank is the major determinant of lifestyle.

The Male Conian

This hierarchy based on military rank has effects throughout the Conian system. One takes orders from above and passes orders below to the individuals under one's command. The resulting psychology is one in which resentment and anger are transmitted down the line and the lowest ranking members often contend with nagging and bullying. It is my belief that the rank hierarchy is a significant factor in the psychology of the Conian people. The task orientation of the base also influences this psychology. There is an official military mission for every base, and most of the time Conians are preparing themselves for the accomplishment of that mission. This involves regular exercises of the equipment and troops, although usually it is well known that an exercise is only an exercise. The fact that one is always preparing for a mission that may never come is demoralizing, and maintaining an alert status is a matter of constant work.

The news services are diligent in maintaining enthusiasm for the whole process of perpetual readiness. A content analysis of the major news organs shows that they report all matters that might have military significance in great detail. The illusion is thus created that warfare or local hostilities may spring up at any moment. The Soviets, always referred to as "Russ" in the headlines, are always on the move, and the need for security and safety are regular features of the news. The news media also present an image that life in The World is worthy of fond memories, although unemployment statistics also figure prominently. Since the news is filtered through the official and sanctioned unofficial channels it always has a certain editorial slant. The news media carry no advertising except for that which is sponsored by the military. There is a focus on safety, base services, and the benefits of remaining in the service.

Depending on the remoteness of the site, news may be late. In the most remote sites, like the Azore Island enclave, even television news can be a week behind. This tends to support the feeling that The World is where things really happen, while life in the enclave is substandard.

Another factor contributing to the psychology of the Conians is the fact that so many young males are assigned to overseas duty when they first join the military. These American males in a foreign culture, in seeking fulfillment of their American dream, are prone to act out the traumas of the late-adolescent identity crisis. Many marry available local women and begin the process of starting a family. The resulting mixes of Conian and local gene stocks produce a wide array of skin tones and body features in the Conian enclave. The young males are also known to act out their late-adolescent rowdiness, and to gain support of their peers through normative aggressive activities.

While Conians have essentially permanent job security, they are subject to regular changes of work location, and at a maximum are reassigned to a new enclave on a three-year rotation. Within any period they are also subject to remote assignments, temporary duty and other dislocations. The cost of moving to another base is borne by the military, but there are additional costs involved, which frequently require a bank loan backed by one's contract to continue working in the service. Some families report that most of the three-year rotation is needed for repayment. This sets up a repetitive cycle for some families, because reenlistment to pay off the old debt is necessary.

Despite a wide array of other social and recreational activities, the consumption of alcohol is a predominant social feature. It is sold in recreational clubs and in most dining facilities, and the result is a rate of alcoholism higher than in the home population. One single woman claimed that there were only three kinds of men in Conian society: drunk, married, or immature.

Role of Women

Women have recently been given greater opportunities to work in the American armed forces, and their role in the Conian enclave is still being defined. Women are not permitted in combat positions, and they form a distinct minority in their professional activities. Those who have children face special problems since military duty requires long hours and frequent separations. They must find caretakers during duty hours, and a single mother may be called upon to leave the enclave on a few hours notice for long periods of time. There is a substantial body of research on the effects of frequent separation as members of the service perform their duties away from their families. The general conclusion is that the frequent separations have negative consequences for military children.

Women in the service, like other minority groups, enjoy the egalitarian rights of military life, while wives of military members form a distinctly lower social group. Wives and families have no direct bearing on the mission of the base, and are seen only as a morale-boosting factor in Conian life. Their status is determined by the rank of the service member, and their rights are set by the base command structure.

The network of wives cuts across their husbands' job lines, and there are subgroups of wives who gather according to their husbands' rank, or according to ethnic and linguistic ties. Wives and children are considered to be the responsibility of the service member, and their behavior is a direct reflection on the service member. A disorderly wife or child could count against future advancement. The pattern of dominance in the rank structure carries over into family life. It is not uncommon for Conian children to complain that their parents are always giving orders and treating the children as though they were part of a command structure.

The general American pattern of male dominance is exaggerated in Conian life. One Conian wife reported that she told her husband that she did not want him to stay in the service when the end of an enlistment occurred, but her husband re-enlisted, and she only found out through the wives' network. There are no figures on how common this is, but the pattern of dominance would suggest that it is not uncommon.

Role of the Children

Children hold a special position in the Conian enclave. They share rank and status with their parent in the service, though they have no formal position in the hierarchy. Their rank entitles them to a position in the school social hierarchy. The sharp distinctions between the enlisted ranks and the officer ranks pervades the lives of children of Conians. While the school facilities are equally available to all, there are subtle ways that a child's "rank" is reinforced. There are separate swimming pools for the officer and enlisted ranks. Similarly, children report that their games and recreational activities show the influence of rank. In a school game it is frequently officer's children on one team against the enlisted rank children. Or if the game is homogeneous, an officer's child will be chosen as the team leader. Choices of activities reflect the rank distinctions. The officers' children are directed toward golf and tennis, while the enlisted children are more often involved with the bowling teams.

Child abuse and neglect are well documented in the Conian enclave. A search of the major social science databases on child abuse in the military reveals that a veritable army of research scientists have devoted themselves to this line of research. The abstracts on this topic alone fill a document nearly an inch thick. The results of two studies should be enough to give the flavor of the whole. The rate of child abuse in the army is 147.4 cases per hundred thousand people, while the same figure for the City of New York is only 34 cases per hundred thousand. A second piece of research shows that deaths from abuse or neglect are higher in the military than in the general American population.

Many Conian children are born on a Conian base and spend a major portion of their childhood in the Conian environment. They often have little contact with mainstream America or any role models outside Conian society. There is a strong tendency to follow in the footsteps of those who have gone before, and after high school graduation, Conian youths often begin their own military service.

Dominant Themes of Conian Culture

In terms of the reward structure of Conian society, high honors are placed on faithful, loyal, honorable service. Because the opportunities for heroism are rare in the modern military, the reality is that honor is paid to the Conians who come to terms with the grind of bureaucratic management.

Held high above simple service is the willingness to fight and die for onc's country. This premium on willingness to fight pervades the whole self-selection process that maintains the flow of young Americans into Conian society. The natural tendency of an institution permanently prepared for war is to collect those people for whom the idea is valued.

Every few years the Conian must decide whether to reenlist in the armed forces. The value of military activity is measured by the "bennies" and "perks" offered for reenlistment. At the high end of the scale, aviators can receive a bonus large enough to buy a new sports car, while at lower levels the bonus may be only a promotion and a modest raise.

When asked why they chose to remain in Conian society, a substantial majority answered that security was the most important reason. Others mentioned poor prospects for selling military skills in The World, and still others said that their payday to payday life could not support any major dislocations. The decision to stay for a second enlistment usually leads to a Conian career with a monthly retirement check after twenty years of continuous service.

In this context it is important to note that the ranks of the military swell and shrink with the ebb and flow of the economy in The World. The military system takes up the slack when a recession forces Americans out of work. Once a Conian has been in the service, he or she knows that there is always a job available working for Uncle Sam. It is also apparent that interruptions to this career mean a loss of benefits in the long run; thus it is advisable for the Conian to decide early whether Conian life will be permanent. This decision is influenced by advertisements in the daily paper which show a former military person struggling to pay a grocery-store bill while thinking of the benefits he enjoyed in the military.

Conian life is, in general, a truncated version of the middle American lifestyle, although some elements of the American lifestyle are highly exaggerated. As it is normal for Conians to move every three years, they tend to develop very shallow roots in any community while interacting in a friendly manner with other Conians. Children reported that they had no interest in making deep friendships, since it was clear that there was no chance of maintaining the friendship past the date of transfer.

There are other paradoxes to Conian life. Its moral foundation is work on a military base to preserve the famous freedoms on which the United States prides itself. Yet to be a Conian, one must sign a pledge that effectively signs away most of those Constitutional rights. While one is defending the world's largest free-enterprise system, the military itself is not a free-enterprise system. It is interesting in this context to note that when profitable businesses just outside the enclave provide services that compete with base services, the profitable businesses inevitably thrive.

My sense of Conian life is that it is a tightly regulated society with the major pathologies of our society standing out in bold relief. It is self-perpetuating, drawing to it those people who are most in need of security and giving them a guaranteed minimum level of personal safety and security. The military is ideally suited to manage the needs of the first levels of Maslow's (1971) hierarchy of needs. It is interesting to note that the safety and security needs are met by the socialized system, while the Conian society is not clear on its stance on individualism. On the one hand, the individual wears a uniform and must respond to most matters with stock answers. On the other hand, the military seems to be constantly creating new awards, medals, citations, and other markers of individuality.

I conclude on a note about the overall Conian psychology. Conians face one of the most intractable double-bind situations imaginable. In the recent past, it was easy to imagine a war fought in a distant location with no direct impact on the people at home. Warfare could be honorably conducted and most of the fighters could face a reasonable chance of survival.

They could rest well with the certainty that what they were doing would keep the homeland free and safe.

Since the beginning of the era of Mutual Assured Destruction, the Conians have had to face a wholesale transformation of their purpose. (See also Sarkesian, this volume, for a discussion of this transformation.) It has become painfully apparent to all Conians that any significant warfare utilizing the advanced weapon systems of the modern military would not serve to save the people at home, but to destroy them. I believe that this is a classic form of Gregory Bateson's (1972:206–7) "double bind." They are damned to repetitive preparation for their work with virtually no chance of putting it into action. The other side of the double bind is that if they are ever called upon to perform their work, it would bring their own destruction.

As Kenneth Boulding put it, "We have all become hostages of our own militaries." The Conians are aware of this, yet there are still no orders from above telling them how to deal with the psychological consequences of perpetual preparation for something that should never occur. One aviator said, "For me to fulfill my duty I have to be willing to commit genocide and suicide at the same moment."[1] I believe that it is demoralizing to most Conians that they are deeply involved with a power that is so vast that it could destroy all life.

I went into the Conian archipelago without a hypothesis to test or study. I observed the lifestyle, social conditions, and core social parameters of life in a Conian enclave, and while I have merely scratched the surface of this unusual group, the fact that they are from the core of America, but in the simplified setting of an overseas enclave, exaggerates some of our cultural pathologies. This microcosm appears to me to be an ideal setting for exploring many social issues in the larger society.

Note

1. Personal communication to the author

References

Bateson, Gregory. 1972. *Steps to an Ecology of Mind*. New York: Ballantine Books.

Maslow, A.H. 1971. *The Farther Reaches of Human Nature*. New York: Viking.

Weber, Max. 1978. *Economy and Society*. Edited by Guenther Roh and Claus Wittich. Berkeley: University of California Press.

6

Is War Necessary?

Mary LeCron Foster

We are so accustomed to warfare, to periodic outbursts of organized violence between and within nations, to a proliferation of armaments justified as war prevention, and to the influence of national military establishments on our political thinking, that we rarely ask if warfare is a necessary and inevitable fact of the human condition. We view war as belonging to the same class of inevitable disasters as earthquakes, volcanic eruptions, hurricanes and contagious diseases—all inevitably recurrent catastrophes to be coped with and surmounted as we get on with the business of living.

Even authors well aware of the extent to which metaphoric usage reveals our covert ideology, classifying war, along with love, time, labor, health and the like, as a natural rather than a cultural experience (Lakoff and Johnson, 1980:118). Books emphasizing our biological nature, such as *The Territorial Imperative* (Ardrey, 1966) or *The Naked Ape* (Morris, 1967) reinforce our assessment of war as natural by giving this view a semblance of scientific validity. Sociobiology, following the leadership of E.O.Wilson (e.g.,1975:573–74), has now reified the evolutionary "naturalness" of warfare as a function of the "selfish" as against the "altruistic" gene.

It is, of course, obvious to all of us that man, like other sentient creatures, can be motivated toward aggression. Woman, too, may become aggressive, especially when her children are threatened. Some of this aggression may be territorially motivated, as Ardrey, Morris, and others emphasize. Human beings, like other animals, are moved to action when emotionally motivated.

War is obviously an aggressive act, but it is not clear that it is necessarily emotionally motivated. War can be waged very effectively by individuals who are quite devoid of aggressive emotions. Military leaders may simply be applying a skill for which they have been professionally trained, within a career often selected among other alternatives (see Sarkesian, this volume). Some soldiers join the army because they need a secure job with regular pay; others because they have been drafted by their government to perform a patriotic duty. (For discussion of civilian response to military duty, see

Randall and Greenhouse, this volume.) Political leaders attempt to arouse aggressive emotions and incite soldiers toward retaliation for presumed threats to their security and to that of their families, but in general, their lives now are lived so far from the scene of potential threat that they respond to the call to arms not from aggressiveness but from fear of governmental sanctions if they refuse. It is clearly not the genetic response of the modern warrior that makes war "natural."

By the same token, it is highly unlikely that it is the genetic disposition of political leaders to incite to aggressive action. War, as a historical entity, is a highly calculated maneuver triggered by the ideology of a complex cultural organization rather than by a genetic predisposition. Swanton (1943) surveyed the anthropological literature for warlike attitudes and actions among the world's societies and found that there were as many that were peaceable as warlike.

Unfortunately, neither he nor the anthropologists responsible for his data seem to have explored in depth the ideological background that favored one disposition over the other. My conclusion, like Swanton's, is that genetics cannot explain war and it is not necessary for genetic reasons. It is ideology that must be investigated for roots of war or peace, rather than biology.

Like health, favorable weather, and adequate employment, peace is classified by most people as a desirable state. Even military leaders, trained for the professional pursuit of war, claim an ideal of peace for their own. The overtly expressed morality of most (if not all) of the world's societies seems to require that they remain at peace with one another. Yet, covertly, a great deal of human behavior reflects quite the opposite position. Modern Western governments seem almost routinely to place their citizens in a double-bind situation (Bateson, 1972:206–7), talking peace while supporting military institutions and glorifying war heroes and the military life. Religious institutions do the same: prohibiting killing in peacetime and sanctioning it in wartime. Discussion in the papers of Greenhouse, Sarkesian and Randall (all in this volume) reflect this anomalous behavior.

National symbols of patriotism are virtually entirely bound up with military successes. We revere bravery—especially bravery in battle. National heroes tend to be war heroes—either successful military leaders like George Washington, Dwight Eisenhower, or Simon Bolivar, or heads of states, like Winston Churchill, or Abraham Lincoln, who guided their nations and allies to victory in war. American presidents elevated to "greatness" in the popular mind are invariably those who shepherded the country successfully through a perilous war. The national anthems of most (perhaps all?) nations stir patriotic sentiments by reference to battle. Could there be patriotism without reference to past or future enemies?

Is it a cultural universal that common purpose requires common perception of threat? Anthropologists could usefully investigate this. Other areas of research also come to mind. Because of the danger of global destruction threatened by use of nuclear weapons it would be useful to determine cross-culturally what precedents for the reduction or elimination of other powerful, threatening technologies exist. Poison gas as a weapon in World War I comes to mind. And, as Kehoe (this volume) notes, the Japanese gave up gun-powder weapons in favor of the traditional sword. Are such technologies eliminated because of fear, superseded because more effective ones have been devised, or abandoned because a changed ideology makes their use obsolete?

One can imagine that nuclear energy would be superseded if it became technically feasible to procure less expensive energy from sun or sea. Its development has also been slowed in the United States because of fear. Neither alternative necessitates ideological restructuring that would affect lifestyle. Are shifts in lifestyle from more complex to less complex modes ever made, on the order of "Small is Beautiful," as is sometimes advocated? What factors might bring about such a change?

The course of history has been toward technological complexity, and complexity of lifestyle has inevitably followed. The first Paleolithic tools were undifferentiated in purpose. Over many millenia they became more specialized and complex, the speedup toward complexity being cumulative. Human beings grew to be compulsive tinkerers, finding more and more ways to improve on nature.

Not only do we tinker; we also speculate and devise moral systems based upon our speculations. For most of history these moral systems have been reinforced by the belief that there are powers beyond those of man to which man must adapt or perish. With the success of science, the individual became intoxicated with his or her own power to improve his world. Technology became ideology rather than a tool to serve it. The "good life" became inextricably bound with material improvement in living conditions, and technology became the primary motivation for human activity. Adhering to this standard of progress, mankind is now in a position to perish by means of creations of its own devising, far more powerful than the dread diseases, droughts, and natural disasters thought to have been sent by vengeful gods.

Change could not occur if the same ideological position were taken by every member of a given culture. Cultural viability depends on considerable ideological sharing; but, within a matrix of implicity shared goals, there can be strong differences of opinion over the means used in their pursuit. In the United States today there is such a conflict over the road to peace and the "good life." "The American Way of Life," long an effective political rallying cry, has come to mean different things to different people. In a certain sense, in recent years the Republican party has succeeded in "capturing" the flag, which used simply to be a symbol of citizenship. Adroit right-wing rhetoric identifying the flag with "defense" and the nuclear arms build-up has made Democrats and those farther to the left reluctant to be "flag-wavers." For example, the Berkeley, California, City Council has, for some time, refused to perform the traditional flag salute to open meetings. This has resulted in right-wing labeling of such people as "anti-American," "pro-communist," and the like. In a reverse effort to "recapture" the flag, one national, peace-promoting organization calls itself "People for the American Way."

In Western countries, if not elsewhere, we have moved into a period—probably the first in history—where many implicit values are being questioned. One of these is the necessity and inevitability of war. In this century an initial, widespread Western questioning followed the First World War; it virtually ceased during the Second World War, but was dramatically renewed and intensified during the war in Vietnam. More recently, questioning of the inevitability of war has once more mushroomed in the face of the confrontation of the two, heavily armed, superpowers and the growing threat of global nuclear disaster.

The argument is often made by politicians as well as military and political analysts that it is only the nuclear threat that is preserving peace between the most heavily armed nations, that only the possibility of total destruction is preventing them from "having at" each other militarily, and that with the nuclear genie well out of the bottle there is no turning back. According to this view, the only alternative, at least for the foreseeable future, is to continue the nuclear confrontation, with each side increasing its arsenal by investing enormous intellectual and financial resources in the attempt to equal or become superior to the other. According to one knowledgeable political scientist,

> the nuclear future will be like the past. There will continue to be nuclear weapons, but they will not be used, at least not by the two most heavily armed countries against each other. Their rivalry will continue, but will be confined to politics, to the arms race, and to proxy wars, as it has been since 1945.
>
> The reasons that all this was true in the past will hold for the future. They may be simply summarized: the alternatives, disarmament and war, are either too difficult to achieve or too terrible to risk.
>
> The message is that the bomb is a disease that is incurable but not fatal. As long as the world recognizes the illness and takes the proper precautions, it can continue to lead a normal life (Mandelbaum, 1983:121).

To assess the validity of this fatalistic view of a future guaranteed only through fear, we can draw upon anthropological theories about the nature of culture, and refer to history to discover potential alternatives. If no alternatives can be found, then there can be no rationale for trying to establish a different course, and we must yield to the logic of this argument.

A possible theory with which to begin is that of the universality of the effect on culture of the human propensity to create and extend classifications by means of binary opposition. I begin here because the opposition of two superpowers with strongly opposed political ideologies is largely responsible for the current threat of global annihilation. Ever since Lévi-Strauss first focused anthropological attention upon the fact of polarization in cultural systems, it has been the cornerstone of structural analysis. He also called attention to the structured mediation of opposition in myth and provided a formula for its resolution (Lévi-Strauss 1963, especially pp. 206–31). This formula may be applicable to resolution of the present impasse. One simple message that also can be derived from the formula is that while cultural oppositions inevitably exist, there are also cultural premises that allow for their resolution.

Human beings could not exist as cultural creatures unless they shared classificatory ground. Behavioral rules are derived from the assessment of likenesses among phenomena. These may be "real," as the shape of leaves or the number of petals in botanical classification, or they may be established through an implicit process of metaphorical extension. Whatever the grounds, there can be no class of phenomena which are "like," unless some other class exists which is "unlike" according to the terms of the classification. This fundamental principal of cultural organization has been explored by Hertz, Needham (e.g., Needham, 1973) and many others. All cultures seem to have implicit chains of metaphoric likeness, linking phenomena of human experience and exerting a strong influence on social behavior. In terms of this principle, if we did not perceive some things as "evil" it would be impossible to perceive others a "good." This creates both an opposition and the possibility of a hierarchy of values. It also gives rise to a "we" versus a "they" ideology in which "we" belong to the "good" class and "they" to the "evil." The universality of such a classification is attested in studies like that of White and Prachuabmoh (1983).

One solution that societies have devised to mediate we/they oppositions is war. Lévi-Strauss' mythological solution mediates opposition by redressing the balance through the adoption and adaptation by one of the adversaries of some feature possessed initially by the other. A third possibility that might have still more permanent effect is establishment of a common goal between adversaries with active participation of both in its pursuit.

During World War II, for example, the hatchet of political ideology separating communism and democracy was buried in the pursuit of victory over Nazi Germany. Although the effect was not, in this case, permanent, such a break in mutual suspicion builds toward a lasting peace.

War, as a means of mediation, has sometimes settled things once for all, as in the case of the American Revolution, after which the British and the Americans became allies. Again, following the American Civil War, although wounds have never entirely healed, although North and South resumed their former alliance without serious subsequent conflict. Counter-cases can also easily be found: after World War I the conditions of the Versailles Treaty festered in the German psyche and became ideological grounds for the outbreak of World War II.

Common ground between communist and democratic powers is presumably the desire for peace. If asked which alternative is preferable, war or disarmament, both sides would opt for disarmament. However, the desire of each side to secure worldwide acceptance of its own social philosophy interferes with this solution. The mediational trick then becomes the discovery of common philosophical grounds on the basis of which common goals can be predicated. Perhaps what is most needed is not disarmament talks, with each side jockeying for advantage, but talks on social philosophy intended to develop common social aims.

The example of the alliance of the Soviet Union and the allied Western powers in the defeat of Nazism suggests that the discovery of a common enemy can be a useful mediation technique. However, this technique promotes rather than discourages war. Quite possibly, enemies need not be other human beings. In Bali, Covarrubias (1937:281) described ritually prescribed, annual battles to expel from the community the evil "other"—in this case the class of supernatural demons responsible for all social ills. The demons become scapegoats for all forms of evil, eradicated through demon expulsion. The use of human scapegoats is probably more frequent than projection of evil onto supernatural ones, but common ills, redefined in other than human terms, might be designated as targets of a mutually agreed upon battle by erstwhile adversaries.

What I am attempting here is to open the field for examination of a variety of culturally attested means to subvert the necessity of war—an end to which anthropology, with its depth of understanding of the range of cultural patterning and its cross-cultural perspective seems to be particularly well adapted. Archaeological research shows that bureaucratically institutionalized war has not always been a cultural phenomenon. Fortified settlements did not occur until the late Neolithic and flowered only in the Bronze Age, when civil states or state cities replaced tribal or sedentary agricultural societies. It is impossible to discuss the history of war in a paper of this length, but it has many facets that need study if we are to understand the growth of the organization of war and its place in culture.

Struggle is both natural and cultural. Human beings have a special proclivity for pitting themselves against odds, even odds of their own devising, some constructive, many destructive (for a cogent discussion of this point, see Clark, this volume). The ultimate, most socially destructive, group struggle is war, and we regard successful strugglers as our greatest heroes. But many other cultural activities seem to satisfy the same emotional need, and with constructive results. Doctors and nurses struggle against disease, architects and builders against the structural problems presented by the intractability of materials. Even anthropologists struggle to gain a better understanding of human social behavior. These struggles classify as "good," while attitudes toward war are, at best, ambivalent.

In a study of definitions of war, Nettleship (1975:86) concluded that while "war is a civilized phenomenon different from primitive fighting" it is also "part of a continuum ranging from individual antagonistic actions to its present theoretically maximum development in nuclear holocaust." Traditionally, anthropologists have been more apt to study small scale antagonisms than full-scale warfare, but any study along this continuum can shed useful light on human belligerence and lead to understanding of the factors which lead to its escalation into wholesale slaughter. The interplay between technology and ideology involved in the generation of war is a natural target for anthropological inquiry, and it is just possible that knowledge gained from such studies may prove of use in making war unnecessary and, ultimately, obsolete.

References

Ardrey, Robert. 1966. *The Territorial Imperative: A Personal Inquiry into the Animal Origins of Property and Nations*. New York:Atheneum.

Bateson, Gregory. 1972. *Steps to an Ecology of Mind*. New York: Ballantine.

Covarrubias, Miguel. 1937. *Island of Bali*. New York:Knopf.

Lakoff, George and Johnson, Mark. 1980. *Metaphors We Live By*. Chicago, Ill.: University of Chicago Press.

Lévi-Strauss, Claude. 1963. *Structural Anthropology*. New York: Basic Books.

Mandelbaum, Michael. 1983. *The Nuclear Future*. Ithaca, N.Y.: Cornell University Press.

Morris, Desmond. 1967. *The Naked Ape: A Zoologist's Study of the Human Animal*. New York: McGraw Hill.

Needham, Rodney, ed. 1973. *Right and Left: Essays on Dual Symbolic Classification*. Chicago, Ill.: University of Chicago Press.

Nettleship, Martin A. 1975. "Definitions." In *War: Its Causes and Correlates*, edited by M.A.Nettleship, R. Dale Givens and A. Nettleship. The Hague: Mouton.

Swanton, John R. 1943. *Are Wars Inevitable*? Smithsonian Institution War Background Studies No.12. Washington, D.C.: Smithsonian Institution.

White, Geoffrey M. and Prachuabmoh, Chavivun. 1983. "The Cognitive Organization of Ethnic Images." *Ethos* 11(1/2): 2–32.

Wilson, E.O. 1975. *Sociobiology: The New Synthesis*. Cambridge, Mass.: Harvard University Press.

7

The Cultural Patterning of Risk-Seeking Behavior: Implications for Armed Conflict

M. Margaret Clark

In my position at the University of California School of Medicine, I have heard many discussions within the past twenty years about risk. Physicians have long known about risk: Hippocrates, in the oath he prescribed for his disciples in those barbarous days of septic surgery, was explicitly aware of the risks of "cutting for stone," and forbade his students to undertake it. Now the dangers of surgery have been minimized, and the consequences of neglecting a medical condition may far outweigh the dangers of surgery to correct it. The calculation of the relative dangers of action versus inaction are known to almost everyone who deals with the medical world as the "risk-benefit ratio"; assessment of such ratios is called "risk-benefit analysis." Today special committees are established in most health institutions to make such assessments in cases where human beings are to be the objects of research or the recipients of new drugs or experimental therapeutic procedures.

In the world of commerce, "risk" has been transliterated to "cost," a term believed more suited to investment of goods and services than "risk," with its connotations of possible loss of life, limb, or health. Cost-benefit analysis sounds relatively safe, sane, and orderly, even when it becomes a mode for calculating the aftermath of global holocaust.

The purpose of this paper is to draw a distinction between risk-taking behavior and risk-seeking behavior. In the former, as I have described above, there is a more or less conscious weighing of the value of that which can be gained against the harm that can be done by inaction. In the latter—risk-seeking—a different mode of thinking prevails. External evil is perceived (or even created) as omnipresent, threatening, and escapable only by the enlistment of extraordinary if not supernatural forces. These forces are rallied in various cultural institutions, whose rituals often demand sacrifice.

I suggest here that in the contemporary nuclear arms race there is a confusion between the conceptualization of these two kinds of behavior. Governmental respresentatives speak as though the consequences of nuclear war can be calculated by using the sort of cost-benefit or risk-benefit analysis appropriate to risk-taking behavior. This official view has been communicated so frequently to the society at large that it has come to characterize much of public sentiment, and has become expressed in social institutions. Examples of such institutions are the Civil Defense establishment, peacetime draft registration, and the organization of paramilitary sodalities.

My postulate is that this model is erroneous in the context of global thermonuclear warfare. An arms race with today's weapons is rather an example of risk-seeking behavior, with its singular world view of the pervasiveness of evil and the necessity for its confrontation. Further, I conclude that this confusion of conceptualization is a serious danger to rational efforts to maintain peace and to avoid the possibility of human extinction.

The Ethnography of Risk Taking and Risk Seeking

What have we learned as anthropologists about these two kinds of behavior? Let us first consider risk taking. Almost all human endeavor involves taking risks. Periods of absolute safety and security have sometimes been sought, or, at least, dreamed of, by human groups; but ordinarily periods of even relative safety have been brief interludes in flights from famine or danger, or fights over goods, land, or water. Migration, thought to be one of the earliest human activities, always involves danger. Existing resources are left behind, and much that is familiar and treasured is lost. The hazards of the journey and the danger of violent struggles over territory and resources in the new land are ever-threatening. Other risk-taking activities are raiding, territorial expansion, smuggling and other criminal activities, investment banking—a near endless list of endeavors in which much may be lost but perhaps even more may be gained.

Even the institution of Potlatching among the Indians of the Northwest Coast—although it is called "fighting with property" by some (Codere, 1950)—is actually a form of risk-taking behavior, in which wealth is exchanged for high status, with the probability of even greater power and wealth accruing to those who sacrifice their goods (Barnett, 1938).

Risk seeking has a quite different character. When we examine the ethnographic literature for behavior that involves the active seeking of danger with little regard for the probabilities of safe delivery, we find a strange assemblage of elaborate sociocultural institutions dedicated to these activities. The battle games of warriors throughout history and in many parts of the world seem to be of this sort. For example, the Plains Indians in their raiding parties were only partially involved in risk taking—stealing horses for gain; in part they were engaged in risk seeking, as this description of the Blackfoot indicates:

> Each raiding party . . . might never see action again as a military unit. Its members were motivated much less by tribal patriotism than by hope of personal gain—the economic security and social prestige that possession of a goodly number of horses would bring them. The killing of enemy tribesmen and the taking of scalps were not major objectives of these raids. Many of the most active Blackfoot horse raiders were members of poor families who were ambitious to better their lot. They were inclined to take the most desperate chances . . . but there were also rich young men who loved the excitement of these raids and coveted the prestige that could be gained through success in war. (Ewers, 1967:329)

Raiding, then, seems to have elements of both risk taking and risk seeking, as I am attempting to define them here. It is much less clear what material gain can be had from certain other cultural institutions. For example, when I was a child growing up in northern New Mexico near the Spanish-American villages of the upper Rio Grande valley, rites were carried out every Spring before they were abolished by government authorities. The cult of *Penitentes* practiced crucifixion: every Easter season a young man was selected as the *Cristo* and was immortalized symbolically (and sometimes, it was said, literally) by being crucified on a Good Friday at high noon on one of the rocky scrub-covered hills at the foot of the Sangre de Cristos—the "blood of Christ" mountains. The survivors of these rituals were forever after esteemed among the villagers.

Ethnographic accounts of similar instances of bodily harm or danger can be multiplied—ritually represented wolves among the Nootka of the Northwest Coast who stick spears into their bodies as a test of power (Sapir and Swadesh, 1939:139); the Hamadsa of the Kwakiutl who dance with knives and cut themselves with obsidian blades; the sun dancers among the Crow, the Cheyenne, the Shoshone and the Arapaho, who stare for days into the blinding light while they fast and dance for power, call it forth with incessant drumming and shrilling through eagle-bone whistles (Jorgensen, 1972). Pomo fire-eaters, another example, put live coals in their mouths and blow them into searing balls of fire (Aginsky and Aginsky, 1967: 195-96). Then there are the Toraja of Sulawesi in Indonesia, who dance into trance states then pierce their flesh with dozens of skewers (Belo, 1960). There are examples of this kind from all over the world—the firewalkers of Polynesia and Sri Lanka, the rope divers of Melanesia, and all those that drink poisons or handle live poisonous serpents (Parsons, 1937; LaBarre, 1962).

What are the psychocultural roots of this behavior? There seem to be multiple motivations. In some cases risk seeking is a part of initiation into a new and higher status. Circumcision, scarification, subincision, knocking out of teeth, piercing of earlobes, nostrils, and lips—all are widespread (Bettleheim, 1955). The Plains Indian vision quest was such an initiation rite. Lowie described it thus:

> The procedure was fairly fixed. A would-be visionary would go to a lonely spot, preferably to the summit of a mountain. Naked except for a breechclout and the buffalo robe to cover him at night, he abstained from food and drink for four days or more if necessary, wailing and invoking the spirits. Usually some form of bodily torture or disfigurement was practiced as an offering to the supernatural beings. Most commonly, perhaps, men would hack off a finger joint of the left hand, so that during the period of my visits to the Crow (1907-1916) I saw few old men with left hands intact. (Lowie, 1924:4)

In all similar descriptions of the vision quest, it is clear that the purpose of the behavior is to make an absolutely vital personal contact with the supernatural world—with one's own guardian spirit and source of personal power for the rest of one's life. I will return to a further discussion of initiation rites and their functions.

Snake-handling cults from the Appalachian area of the southern United States, as described by LaBarre (1962) and others, provide some insights into another aspect of risk-seeking behavior. These Christian Pentacostalists are not young initiates testing their courage and their right to call themselves adults or warriors; they are not the privileged of their society demonstrating their access to power. These people are different in that they are poor, chronically underpaid, and undernourished families of miners in the West Virginia coal fields. They are among the economically and socially powerless whose lives and welfare rest on the whims and machinations of the powerful. As we know from observations of such "cults of affliction" among the weak and downtrodden in many parts of the world (Lewis, 1971), danger is sought in order to ratify one's status as members of a spiritual elite. Seeking danger and encountering it successfully is a proof of faith and a sign of divine protection and privilege. Possession by the Holy Ghost confers immunity from harm, even from the toxicity of strychnine and the fangs of poisonous snakes. Signs of divine protection are manifested not only by immunity from poisons but also by the gift of power to heal the sick, and access to arcane knowledge such as the ability to speak in unknown tongues. Glossolalia is a sign to all the congregated people that the supernatural has indeed entered the worshipper—a further demonstration of spiritual exaltation.

Some anthropologists have suggested that such cult behavior has as its major genesis a drive for higher status, and it is clear, in the instance of the *Zar* cults of Ethiopia (Lewis, 1971), that such is often the case. The Christian Pentacostalists who handle snakes, however, seem to me to be moved by an additional potent force—a sincere belief in the presence of evil: in Satan and his unending struggle to destroy the human soul. A world view that is demonic is often a powerful stimulus to risk-taking behavior. (Parenthetically, the term "daredevil" seems to suggest such a connection in our English-speaking culture.) Certainly it occurs in the Indonesian possession religion described above, as well as in other shamanic systems of belief. I propose in the following pages that it is also a characteristic of those who pursue the current nuclear arms race.

Risk Seeking in Play

The universality of dangerous sports and games suggests that there is a strong element of play in risk-seeking behavior. The coup-counting of Plains Indian warriors, as I indicated above, can be thought of as a dangerous game. All over the world, for little or no material gain, people go into cages with wild animals, walk tightropes over fire pits or mountain gorges, leap off cliffs into rocky shoals, jump from airplanes, stand up on the backs of galloping horses, and skin-dive in shark-infested waters. A recent newspaper account reports that there are an "estimated 30,000 people who are hang gliders." . . . One of them said that hang gliding 'scares the living daylights out of me' and that 'everything else seems boring compared to it.'" (Klemesrud, 1983).

In a classical work on the function of play in the development of culture, the social historian Huizinga speaks of the extension of human play into the arena of warfare:

> Ever since words existed for fighting and playing, men have been wont to call war a game. . . . The medieval tournament was always regarded as a sham-fight, hence as play, but in its earliest forms it is reasonably certain that the joustings were held in deadly earnest and fought out to the death (1955:89).

As evidence of the play quality of war, Huizinga cites its "limiting rules," and the fact that a "declaration of war" must be made if subsequent hostilities are to be differentiated from peace on the one hand and criminal violence on the other.

He specifically denies the risk-taking functions of war—as I am using that term here:

> History and sociology tend to exaggerate the part played in the origin of wars, ancient or modern, by immediate material interests and the lust for power. . . . The great wars of aggression from antiquity down to our own times all find a far more essential explanation in the idea of glory, which everybody understands, than in any rational and intellectualist theory of economic forces and political dynamisms (Huizinga, 1959:90).

A 1983 American film called "Wargames" is a chilling reminder of the deadliness of the game of nuclear confrontation that world leaders are now playing. I will return to this point in a moment.

Motivations for Risk Seeking: A Summary of Factors

Now let me review the characteristics of risk-seeking behavior as it has been described in world ethnography. Following that, I will examine the current nuclear arms race in the light of those same characteristics.

Risk seeking contains many elements of play and is a challenging and engaging activity. In the face of danger, the autonomic nervous system is called into play and the subsequent outpouring of adrenaline and other endocrine substances sharpens the mind, quickens the pulse, stimulates the imagination, and heightens the senses. A few years ago I interviewed a hard-rock miner from Nevada who had incurred permanent disability as a consequence of being hit on the head with a 750-pound ore bucket. Yet he was mourning not so much that he was crippled by the accident, but that he found life outside the mines dreadfully dull. He explained that as soon as he set foot underground, he felt "really alive; the rock might break anytime, and you had to be ready every second to get out of there. It was wonderful!" Or, as I might paraphrase Mark Twain, nothing so focuses the mind as the knowledge that you are going to be hung at dawn. Danger can be a transcendent experience, provided one finally escapes it, and in play, one always expects to win.

Risk seeking involves aspects of social stratification. Most societies give special rewards to their warriors. In many instances the surest path to political power and wealth is through successful military adventures. Military heroes often become heads of state, as the most casual glance at the leaders of emerging nations around the world will demonstrate. Those who play games for high stakes and win are the stuff of song and legend. Our popular heroes in the Western world today are those who confront peril—the astronauts and cosmonauts, the surgeons who transplant living hearts, the divers who go down to imponderable depths of the sea in fragile metal shells, the climbers who conquer the airless and frozen peaks, the man who breaks the bank at Monte Carlo, the handsome actor who drives supercharged race cars. And then there are the most romantic and powerful of all—the new electronic wizards—the heroes who build and control the computers that control the buttons that control the missiles that control the future of the human species.

Risk seeking often incorporates supernatural elements. I will discuss three such elements that seem to me to have major significance for warfare. First, there is a *demonic world view* associated with much risk-seeking behavior, as I described above in connection with American snake-handling cults. Risks of the most extraordinary kind can be sanctioned as prerequisite to the destruction of evil, if evil is portrayed as sufficiently real and present. Second, a risk seeking frequently incorporates *rituals of divine protection.* Perhaps the most ordinary of these are prayers supplicating the deities to guard one or assure one's success and survival. Spanish bullfighters are usually portrayed as spending time in the chapel before entering the bull ring. There are special charms and amulets for risk takers. Special rituals convey personal or group immunity from destruction. A commonly cited example from American Indian ethnography is the Ghost Dance of 1890. By that date the Indians of the western United States had lost countless battles against the inexorable advance of White man's armies. Through the ritual of the Ghost Dance, dead comrades were to rise up against enemy forces, enemy bullets would be prevented from piercing the flesh, and all would be invincible through divine intervention. Mooney states that:

> The most noted thing connected with the Ghost Dance among the Sioux is the "ghost shirt" which was worn by all adherents of the doctrine. . . . In some cases the fringe or other portions were painted with the sacred red paint of the messiah. The shirt was firmly believed to be impenetrable to bullets or weapons of any sort. . . . The protective idea in connection with the ghost shirt does not seem to be aboriginal, . . . war paint had the same magic power of protection (1896:31,34).

In the Crow vision quest, supernatural benefits sought often included magical protection from harm:

> The character of a vision could determine the whole of a man's career. If he was promised invulnerability, as in the case of Scratches-face, his confidence in the supernatural patron's aid might lead him to snap his fingers at danger and to establish a reputation for reckless daring (Lowie, 1924:6–7).

The snake handlers, too, depend entirely on the protection of the Holy Ghost to render them impervious to harm. World literature is full of accounts of heroes with unpierceable armor, impenetrable shields, and unbreakable swords and spears.[1] The myth of invincibility, then, is a common characteristic of all risk seeking. As one daredevil reported, "I have a built-in denial of risk that's called surviving. I have an intellectual appreciation that it's risky. . . . But . . . it's always the guy on your right or your left; it's never you" (Klemesrud, 1983).

A third supernatural element in risk seeking is related in some ways to the other two, but for purposes of illustration I deal with it separately. This is the *sense of personal righteousness.* It is not enough to believe in the evil of the enemy and to seek protection; one must also believe oneself deserving of victory. A sense of moral superiority need not be couched in iconography or religious symbolism. Magical thinking can take remarkably secular forms. In the ethnographic and historical record, however, the doctrine of "manifest superiority" has been thought of as the will of the gods. In applying this notion to warfare, Huizinga has described it thus:

> One wages war in order to obtain a decision of holy validity. The test of the will of the gods is victory or defeat. So that instead of trying out your strength in a contest, or throwing dice, or consulting the oracle, or disputing by fierce words—all of which may equally well serve to elicit the divine decision—you can resort to war. . . . What we call "right" can equally well, archaically speaking, be "might"—in the sense of "the will of the gods" or "manifest superiority" (1955:91).

"God with us!" has been a battle cry throughout the long centuries of Western militarism; it remains implicit in the Cold War of today.

Assessing the Risks of Thermonuclear War

Thermonculear war is unthinkable. There is almost total agreement on that point among the nonmilitary and nongovernmental professionals in our society. For example, in 1981 the American Medical Association—not the world's most left-wing organization—issued the following statement:

> It is in a spirit of concern that the AMA Board of Trustees believes that it is incumbent upon the Association to inform the President and the Congress of the United States of the medical consequences of nuclear war and that no adequate medical response is possible (Kornfeld, 1983:211).

Another eminent group, the members of the National Academy of Sciences, in 1982 issued a near-unanimous statement that "science offers no prospect of effective defense against nuclear war and mutual destruction" and called upon the President and Congress "to avoid military doctrines that treat nuclear explosives as ordinary weapons of war" (Kornfeld, 1983:211). A recent interview with a former division chief of Los Alamos

Laboratory, the Nobel Prize winning physicist, Hans Bethe, contained these comments about all-out nuclear war:

> The United States as a functioning society would not survive. Such an attack, it has been estimated by the Defense Department, could mean 100 million immediate casualties, but that doesn't fully describe it. The worst part is the death of (many more) people by third degree burns, and that there is no possible medical help for them. . . . [Because of fire-storms] protection of the city population by shelters is totally futile. . . . Anyone who says we can recover from nuclear war in two to four years is crazy. . . . If there is an all-out attack on the Soviet Union and the United States, there will afterwards be no United States nor a Soviet Union (Scheer, 1982:276–77).

In view of this general appraisal of the nuclear path to Armageddon, how does it come about that the United States government, and to some extent that of the Soviet Union as well, continues to pursuade its citizens to support an arms race and listen seriously to projections of a "winnable nuclear war"? Such projections are reportedly contained in a 1982 5-year Defense Guidance Plan. One American journalist has written of this document:

> It would be difficult to exaggerate the implication of this strategy document, for it resolves a debate in the highest councils of government and places the United States for the first time squarely on the side of those extremists in this country and in the Soviet Union who believe in the possibilities of fighting and winning a protracted nuclear war (Scheer, 1982:8).

As Scheer says, the idea that nuclear war is survivable begins with the idea that it is possible to concoct an effective civil defense establishment. He cites Mr. T.K. Jones, then U.S. Deputy Undersecretary of Defense for Strategic and Theater Nuclear Forces, who said that American citizens could build primitive dugout shelters for protection from nuclear attack:

> Dig a hole, cover it with a couple of doors and then throw three feet of dirt on top. . . . It's the dirt that does it. . . . If there are enough shovels to go around, everybody's going to make it (Scheer, 1982:18).

Contrast this assertion with what has been published about the use of shelters in Hiroshima and even in Dresden during the fire storms following the bombings.

> A fire storm can increase the size of the lethal area five times. In such a case shelters would become death traps because the fires consume all available oxygen as the temperature in the shelters rises to levels of 1,500 degrees,

> roasting and asphyxiating the occupants. In Dresden . . . the only persons who survived were those who fled their shelters (Cassell, 1983:215–16).

Discrepancies of this kind can be multiplied when one compares public statements of government officials of the present administration with the observations, accounts, computations and judgments of physical scientists, engineers, physicians, and political scientists. How, then, can such an activity as a nuclear arms race be foisted upon citizens as reasonable behavior that should be supported both politically and economically? One possible answer lies in the analysis of the arms race as risk-seeking behavior.

The Nuclear Arms Race as Risk-Seeking Behavior

Going back to the analysis of ethnographic data in the preceding pages, we can understand the ways in which government officials are attempting to convince us to support an arms race.

First, convince the public of the presence of evil in the world, incarnated in those you wish to label as the enemy. Dr. Bethe has spoken to this point:

> The main increase of danger, in my opinion, is psychological. People are scared when the Reagan government says we are in mortal danger and need to increase our armaments. . . . Human beings who are very scared don't act rationally. My greatest fear is that it will make the American people less rational, and then anything can happen (Scheer, 1982:277–78).

Second, exploit panhuman urges for play, excitement, and new experience. Remind people of how much fun it was during World War II when we all got out of the drudgery of everyday life. Set up computer games for teaching young people war strategy; convince them that they can join the Navy and see the world, or join the Space Cadets and defeat Darth Vader. Make fighter planes faster, more beautiful, and more deadly.

Third, offer secular rewards to those who promote risk taking. Give them high positions in the government, and access to millions upon millions of dollars in defense appropriations. Provide them with opportunities to help their friends in the business end of the military-industrial complex. Let them fly all over the world in private planes with personal entourages. Let them eat in elegant private dining rooms and furnish their offices with European antiques. Drive them here and there in limousines. Give them access to secret knowledge and let them speak in unknown tongues as a sign of power. One official of a previous administration commented on this latter process.

> What's going on right now is that the crazier analysts have risen to higher positions than is normally the case. . . . Neither the current President nor his immediate backers in the White House nor the current Secretary of Defense have any experience with these things, so when the ideologues come in with their fancy stories and with their selected intelligence data, the President and the Secretary of Defense believe the last glib person who talked to them (Interview with Herbert York, in Scheer, 1982:13).

Fourth, convince people of their invulnerability. Speak to them of the righteousness of the American character and the nobility of democratic purpose. If they are Soviets, assure them of the secular morality of those whose only concern is for the people in their struggles against worldwide imperialism. Assure them that their leaders are sincere, selfless, and god-fearing. Remind them that they can be protected by vigilance and preparedness, and see that every household has—if not a ghost shirt—at least a shovel.

Conclusion

In the German pre-Nazi era, a political theorist named Carl Schmitt advanced the then popular notion that the essential function of the state is to prepare for war and then to wage it. All real relationships between nations had to be based on either affiliation or on enmity—there could be no neutral ground, no simple detente based on agreements to disagree and let live (Huizinga, 1955:209). We have since fought a global war, invented and used the atomic bomb, and are living in a qualitatively different age of potential destruction of our species. Yet we continue to live by the demonic and magical principles that have engulfed our minds since the dawn of time. Only when we recognize our irrationality for what it is—playing with snakes armed with multiple hydrogen warheads—will we be able to draw back from the abyss.

Almost a century ago, Kipling hoped for the day when "The tumult and the shouting dies;/ The captains and the kings depart." Perhaps, when that happy day comes, the nations of the world will have learned that it is possible to live without enemies.

Note

1. Space forbids a discussion of the clear sexual symbolism of these protective rituals, but the reader is referred to Campbell (1949) for such an exposition.

References

Aginsky, B. W. and Aginsky, E.G. 1967. *Deep Valley: The Pomo Indians of California.* New York: Stein and Day.

Barnett, H. G. 1938. "The Nature of the Potlatch." *American Anthropologist* 40:349–58.
Belo, Jane. 1960. *Trance in Bali*. New York: Columbia University Press.
Bettelheim, B. 1955. *Symbolic Wounds: Puberty Rites and the Envious Male*. Glencoe, Ill.: Free Press..
Campbell, Joseph. 1949. *The Hero with a Thousand Faces*. Princeton, N. J.: Princeton University Press.
Cassel, Christine. 1983. "An Epistemology of Nuclear Weapons Effects." *Western Journal of Medicine* 138:213–18.
Codere, H. 1950. *Fighting with Property: A Study of Kwatiutl Potlatching and Warfare, 1792–1930*. New York: J.J. Austin.
Ewers, John C. 1967. "Blackfoot Raiding for Horses and Scalps." In *Law and Warfare: Studies in the Anthropology of Conflict*, edited by P. Bohannon, pp. 327–44. Garden City, N.Y.: Natural History Press.
Huizinga, Johan. 1950. *Homo Ludens: A Study of the Play Element in Culture*. Boston, Mass.: Beacon Press.
Jorgensen, Joseph G. 1972. *The Sun Dance Religion: Power for the Powerless*. Chicago, Ill.: University of Chicago Press.
Klemesrud, Judy. 1983. "The Risk-takers: The Sport of Putting Your Life on the Line." *San Francisco Chronicle: This World*: 17 July.
Kornfeld, Howard. 1983. "Nuclear Weapons and Civil Defense—The Influence of the Medical Profession in 1955 and 1983." *Western Journal of Medicine* 138: 207–12.
LaBarre, Weston. 1962. *They Shall Take up Serpents: Psychology of the Southern Snake-Handling Cults*. Minneapolis, Minn.: University of Minnesota Press.
Lewis, Oscar. 1970. *Anthropological Essays*. New York: Random House.
Lowie, R. H. 1924. *Primitive Religon*. New York: Boni and Liveright.
Mooney, James. 1896. *The Ghost Dance Religion and the Sioux Outbreak of 1890*. Bureau of American Ethnology Fourteenth Annual Report, 1892–93.
Parsons, Elsie Clews. 1937. *Pueblo Indian Religion*. 2 vols. Chicago, Ill.: University of Chicago Press.
Sapir, Edward and Swadesh, Morris. 1939. *Nootka Texts: Tales and Ethnological Narratives*. New Haven, Conn.: Yale University Press.
Scheer, Robert. 1982. *With Enough Shovels: Reagan, Bush and Nuclear War*. New York: Random House.

PART II
THE DYNAMICS OF CONFLICT

8

Land Disputes and the Gods in the Prehispanic Mixteca

Jill Leslie Furst

Identification with the land, and ownership of it, often lie at the root of conflict. The origins of land disputes may eventually be forgotten, especially in the absence of written records, and symbolic and mythic assertions of rights to territory are often added to or blended with the practical reasons for a war, by both sides, to justify a land claim. When such claims are based upon such divine sanctions, war may become endemic, as seems to have been the case in this political conflict-in-microcosm, painstakingly reconstructed from ancient pictorial records.

War in the Mixteca Alta

Several hundred years before the Spanish conquest of Mexico, the Mixtec- speaking people of the Mixteca Alta, or highlands of Oaxaca, had a legend which told of their descent from two groups of magically born ancestors. The story was published in 1593 by Fray Antonio de los Reyes (1976), a Dominican who labored for the Faith at the town of Teposcolula, in the prologue to his grammar of the dialect spoken in that area, *Arte en Lengua Mixteca*. Reyes wrote that:

> It was a common belief among the native Mixtecs that the origins and beginnings of their false gods and lords was in Apoala, a village of this Mixteca, that in their language they call *yuta tnoho*, that is, River [yuta] where the lords came out because they were said to have been cut off [tnoho] some trees that came out of that river. . . . (1976:i).

These rulers, the myth continues, divided themselves into four groups which dispersed to the four directions. They took possession of the land, gave names to geographical features of the Mixteca and the surrounding territory, and brought the laws (for later versions of this myth, see Burgoa, 1934:i, 274; Furst, 1977, 1978a:132–39).

According to Reyes' native informants, the tree-born lords were the later rulers of the Mixteca because an earlier group

> inhabited this land before and possessed it and had it for their own . . . and those were said to have come out of the center of the earth that they call *anuhu*, without descent from the lords of Apoala, but that had appeared over the earth and took possession of it, and those were the real and true Mixtecs and lords of the language that is now spoken (Reyes, 1976:ii).

Exactly what this division meant is not known, but the later lords conquered the "real and true Mixtecs" when they took possession of the Mixteca Alta. This conflict is confirmed in the prehispanic native screenfold manuscripts that generally deal with the marriages, births, ceremonial activities, and occasionally, the deaths of the indigenous caciques. Both genesis from the ground and from a tree are represented in the codices, and when a dispute arises, an individual is often able to trace his or her lineage back to one of the two groups, while the opponent is descended from the other. One case in point is the long-term struggle at "Hill Split by Hands-Insect," a town that was ruled by descendants of the later, tree-born caciques. While its actual identity with a site on the modern map has not been established, its position is known relative to other towns which were under the patronage of the earth-born lords. Let us look first at "Hill Split by Hands-Insect" and the surrounding territory as it appears on the front, or obverse, of Codex Vindobonensis Mexicanus 1 (hereinafter called Vienna), in a section that presents a map of the Mixteca in primordial times.

On Vienna 42c (fig. 1, bottom of the third column from the right), "Hill Split by Hands-Insect" is shown in its most elegant and complete form. An insect is enclosed in a hill that is pried open by an unnamed, barefoot male who wears only black body paint and a white loincloth. His color and attire indicate that he is not supposed to be seen. Instead he functions rather like the black-clad figures in Japanese Noh drama or puppet plays, who offer aid but do not come to the attention of the audience. The place sign also includes a platform on the hill, a tripod vessel with the face of the rain deity on its side, two shells resting on their points, and a precinct containing two maize plants. Although some of these elements may be added when the site is pictured elsewhere, the insect and the split hill are usually sufficient to identify the town.

We get some idea of the position of "Hill Split by Hands- Insect" relative to two toponyms that have been deciphered. On Vienna 42d (far left center), a hill, with a cloud band around its middle and its top patterned with black dots, stands for Magdalena Jaltepec (Smith, 1983), a small town in the south arm of the Nochistlán Valley about five miles off the Pan-Amer-

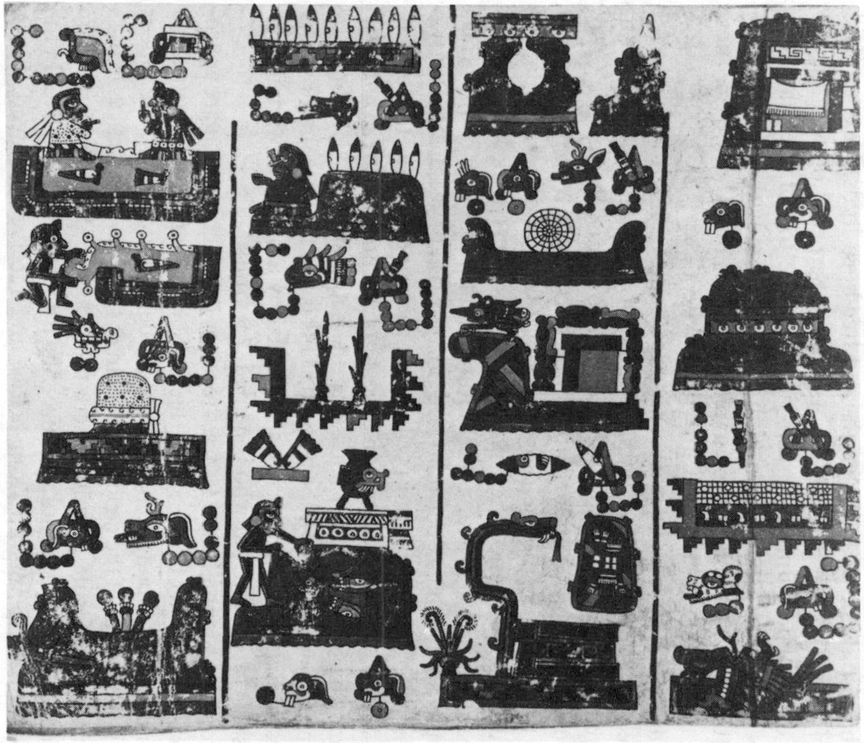

Figure 1. Codex Vindobonensis 42. In this map of the Mixteca, Magdalena Jaltepec appears in the center of the far left column, Tilantongo at the upper right side of the page, and "Hill Split by Hands-Insect" at the bottom of the third column from the right, next to "Place of the Ascending Serpent."

ican Highway. On Vienna 42a (far upper right), a hill with the skyband embedded in its top and a building with a piece of cloth hung over its entrance represent Tilantongo (Smith, 1973:55, 57). As Jaltepec is a good morning's walk to the north of Tilantongo, "Hill Split by Hands-Insect," or its ruins, probably lies somewhere between the two towns. The area of the Mixteca under dispute is clearly quite small.

Also represented on Vienna 42 are two place signs that become important in the dispute between the earth- and tree-born lords. Next to "Hill Split by Hands" is the "Place of the Ascending Serpent" on Vienna 42b (bottom of second column from the right). At the top of Vienna 42c is "Place of the Flints," shown as a multicolored frieze with red and white flints on top. With the relative geographic positions in mind, we may now examine the conflict at "Hill Split by Hands-Insect."

According to the geneaological manuscript Bodley 2858, the site comes to be ruled by ♂ 12 Lizard "Mountain Woman" (fig. 2). He inherits it from his paternal grandparents (for a commentary to Codex Bodley, see Caso, 1960), but his maternal grandmother was born from a tree at Apoala (Bodley, 1–V) and became the progenitrix of a large and powerful family that included at least nine other rulers of various sites (Bodley, 1, 2–III–I). ♂ 12 Lizard marries a woman, 12 Vulture "Feathered Sun," who brings "Hill of the Split Sun" as her marriage portion (Bodley, 4,3–II). The two towns are united politically, but perhaps not geographically, as the "Hill of the Split Sun" is not represented on page 42 of Vienna. In any event, ♂ 12 Lizard and his wife have four sons, and the succession to "Hill Split by Hands-Insect" would seem to be assured. This is not the case, however, for ♂ 12 Lizard, his wife, and four sons are killed by a powerful woman who wears a skull for a head and who is named ♀ 9 Grass.

According to Vienna 15b, ♀ 9 Grass receives the offerings that are appropriate to her and to her divine status (fig. 3). She is given human hearts and blood, and cups of blood are poured onto a field of growing maize. She is also given the bodies of the dead in the form of funerary bundles. ♀ 9 Grass is the personified fertile ground, where the hearts and blood of man are exchanged for the life- sustaining maize. She is the woman who lives in the earth, pushes the plants up from below, and receives the dead (Furst, 1978a:245–49, 1978c, 1982, 1983, forthcoming). Even the characteristically Mixtec flanged pectorals are appropriate gifts to the earth goddess, for the jewelry is used in ceremonies with chthonic associations.

In Bodley, then, the descendants of a tree-born dynasty are destroyed by the earth deity, who is by definition the "mother" of the earth-born lords in an ideological, if not physical, sense. Bodley says nothing about who inherits "Hill Split by Hands-Insect," and indeed, is more concerned about the sisters of the last ruler who marry into other lineages and escape their

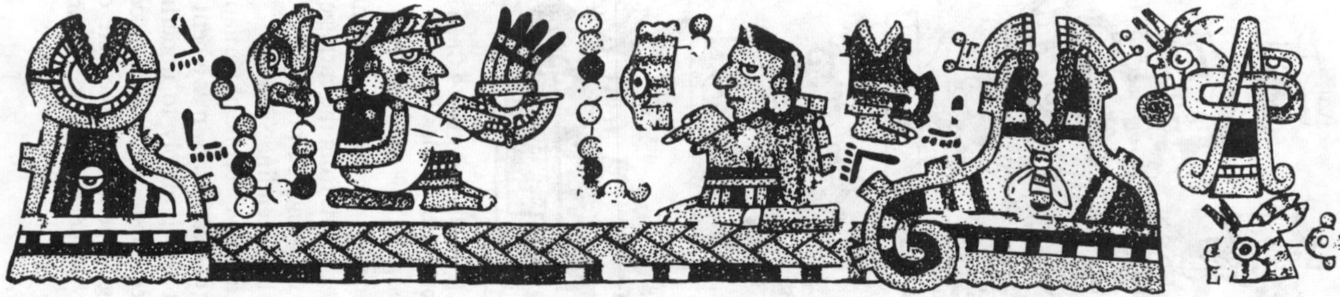

Figure 2. Codex Bodley 4, 3–II. ♂ 12 Lizard "Mountain Woman" from "Hill Split by Hands-Insect" faces his wife, ♀ 12 Vulture "Feathered Sun" from "Hill of the Split Sun."

Figure 3. Codex Vindobonensis 15b. The goddess ♀ 9 Grass receives the objects appropriately given to her as the personified fertile field.

brother's fate. In yet another genealogical manuscript, Codex Nuttall, however, one family that benefits from the carnage at "Hill Split by Hands-Insect" is depicted, and these, not surprisingly, are earth-born lords of the adjacent site, "Place of the Ascending Serpent."

On page 14 of the Nuttall obverse, one or perhaps two people, ♂ 5 Flower and ♀ 3 Flint, come out of a cave, shown as a bent stone band bordered on the inside by the night sky, probably to underline the darkness of the interior of the earth (see Furst, 1983, for a discussion of the lineage of "Place of the Ascending Serpent"). As the date of the event, the Year 7 Reed, day 5 Flower, also includes ♂ 5 Flower's name, he, at least, is generated from the ground.

After many ceremonies, ♂ 5 Flower and wife, ♀ 3 Flint "Shell Quechquemitl" succeed in making themselves rulers of "Place of the Ascending Serpent" (Nuttall, 15a-17b). Their daughter, also named ♀ 3 Flint, but with the different personal name or epithet of "Jeweled Quechquemitl," marries ♂ 12 Wind "Smoking Eye" and comes to rule at her parents' site (Nuttall, 18b–20) (fig. 4, upper right). After the younger ♀ 3 Flint is wedded, the war at "Hill Split by Hands-Insect" is depicted, complete with the funerary bundles of that town's defunct ruler, ♂ 12 Lizard, and his wife ♀ 12 Vulture (fig. 4, center). Further, the funerary rituals in honor of two of their sons, ♂ 3 Monkey and ♂ 4 House, are also represented (fig. 4, lower left).

The rulers of "Place of the Ascending Serpent" do not take "Hill Split by Hands-Insect" for their own. Instead, the earth-born caciques manage to move into the area at the expense of the tree-born lords. By comparing the generations, the younger ♀ 3 Flint is the contemporary of ♂ 12 Lizard, so that her earth-generated father, and perhaps her mother as well, are born one generation after the tree-born grandmother of ♂ 12 Lizard. Despite the belief that the rulers who came out of the ground were the original, "true" Mixtecs, they do not necessarily have a longer lineage nor an earlier ancestor. Primacy of claim seems to rest not on being at a site first, but on an ideological identity as a first inhabitant of the land.

As a descendant of an earth-born lord, the younger ♀ 3 Flint is secure at her site, even though the battle rages at the adjacent town. In fact, she and her husband do not even lift a spear to gain their advantage. They are the "children" of the earth, and the earth goddess herself settles the dispute with the rulers of "Hill Split by Hands-Insect." In Codex Nuttall, ♀ 9 Grass has as her allies men with diagonal multicolored stripes on their bodies that indicate "stone" in Mixtec pictorial convention (Smith, 1973:47, 50). The "stone men" were probably also believed to have come out of the ground in the primordial first times (Smith, 1974:68–71; Furst, 1983).

Later in the story on the Nuttall obverse, ♂ 12 Wind, the husband of the younger ♀ 3 Flint, offers to reconcile with several members of the tree-born family by marrying his daughter to a cousin of the defunct ♂ 12 Lizard—a wise move because ♂ 12 Lizard comes from an influential lineage. The wedding takes place (Nuttall, 22), but it does not prevent future antagonism between the rulers of the site and the descendants of the earth-born lords.

The war at "Hill Split by Hands-Insect" has yet another chapter, this one focusing on Magdalena Jaltepec and its ruler several generations later, the irrepressible ♀ 6 Monkey "Serpent (or Warband) Quechquemitl." This story is told in Codex Selden 3135 (A.2) for a commentary to Codex Selden, see Caso, 1964).

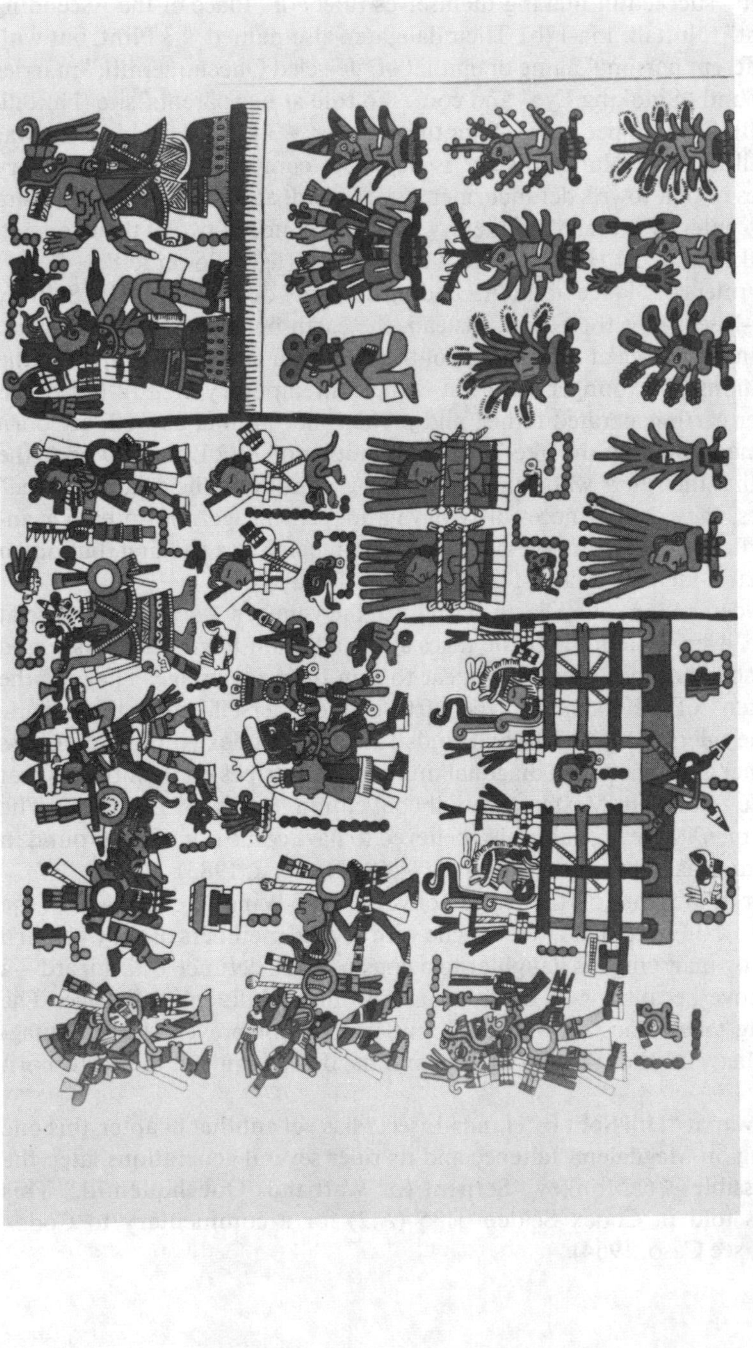

Figure 4. Codex Nuttall 20. ♂ 12 Wind "Smoking Eye" and ♀ Flint "Jeweled Quechquemitl" of "Place of the Ascending Serpent" are represented at the upper right, while the war of "Hill Split by Hands-Insect" occupies the left side of the page and includes the deaths of ♂ 12 Lizard and ♀ 12 Vulture (center) and two of their sons, ♂ 3 Monkey and ♂ 4 House (lower left). The goddess ♀ 9 Grass appears at the top of the page.

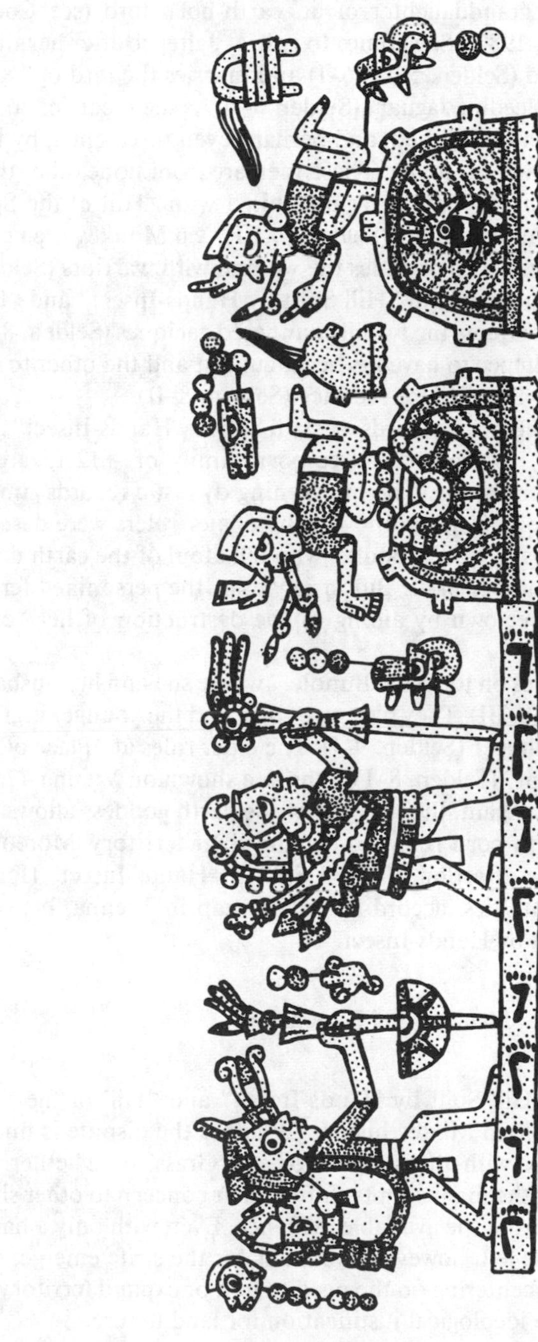

Figure 5. Codex Selden 7–III. ♀ 6 Monkey is carried (far left) past "Hill Split by Hands-Insect" and "Hill of the Split Sun" (far right), whose rulers insult her with "flinty words" (small flints attached to the speech scrolls that come from the lords' mouths).

♀6 Monkey is the granddaughter of an earth-born lord (see Codex Nuttall,1; Furst, 1978b, 1983). She comes to rule at Jaltepec after her three elder brothers are killed (Selden, 5–IV, 6–I) and marries the lord of "Xipe Bundle," ♂11 Wind "Bleeding Jaguar" (Selden 7–I). As she is carried to her husband's site (fig. 5), she is insulted, and perhaps even threatened, by two men who speak "flinty words" to her. These men are from none other than "Hill Split by Hands-Insect," still or again united with "Hill of the Split Sun," as it was in the earlier conflict (Selden, 7–III). ♀6 Monkey then goes to consult with ♀9 Grass, who provides the woman with warriors (Selden, 7–IV, 8–I). ♀6 Monkey returns to "Hill Split by Hands-Insect" and "Hill of the Split Sun" and conquers the two ill-mannered caciques (Selden, 8–I), taking one home to Jaltepec to have his heart cut out and the other to her husband's site of "Xipe Bundle" for sacrifice (Selden, 8–II).

The relationship of the two late lords of "Hill Split by Hands-Insect" and "Hill of the Split Sun" to the earlier tree-born family of ♂12 Lizard is unknown, if indeed there is one. The intervening dynastic records simply do not exist, so that we may never know if these later rulers were descendants of those first lords in Codex Bodley who fell afoul of the earth deity, or if the quarrel had another basis. But in any case, the personified fertile ground takes care of her own by aiding in the destruction of her "children's" enemies.

♀6 Monkey continues on to "Xipe Bundle," where she and her husband rule for a time (Selden, 8–III). They have two sons, and the younger is given his mother's town of Jaltepec (Selden, 9–I). The elder rules at "Place of the Flints," or simply, "Flint" (Selden, 8–IV), the site shown on Vienna 42c as being close to Jaltepec. Again, the support of the earth goddess allows the descendants of the earth-born rulers to expand their territory. Moreover, the expansion is in the direction of "Hill Split by Hands-Insect" (Furst, forthcoming) for "Flint" lies, according to the map in Vienna, between Jaltepec and "Hill Split by Hands-Insect."

Ideology and Expansion

After this episode, "Hill Split by Hands-Insect" and "Hill of the Split Sun" cease to play a role in Mixtec history. Whether the dispute is finally settled by ♀6 Monkey with the support of ♀9 Grass, or whether the conflicts continued but the manuscripts shifted their concern to other sites, cannot be determined from the available evidence. Even with only a handful of native documents left, however, two bases for the strife emerge, one intensely practical and centering on the need to find or expand territory, or both, and the other the ideological justification for land tenure.

Without the Vienna map, we would have no idea about the practical reasons for the war around "Hill Split by Hands-Insect." The area under dispute is small, and when a lineage occupies a site or gains territory, it does so at the expense of its neighbors. At the very least, an intrusive dynasty poses a threat to the territorial holdings and integrity of another. The necessity of defending borders seems justification enough for an already established family to fight, but the intruders assert their rights by an appeal to primacy of claim as members of the original inhabitants of the land, even when their lineage is not so ancient as that of later lords. ♀ 6 Monkey seems to inherit an old quarrel. Occupation of land is supported by the earth goddess, to whom the "original" inhabitants may have a special relationship, being under her care much as her other "children," the maize and the food plants. Further, the earth-born lords enlist the active aid of the deity or of her troops, saying in effect that "god (or, in this case, the goddess) fights on our side."

Without pushing the analogy too far—for any analogy becomes absurd when taken too literally—the situation in the area around "Hill Split by Hands-Insect" has a curiously modern ring to it, and especially echoes the Middle East today, where primacy of land claim rests not on actual possession of the land but on identification with a group that claims to be descended from its original inhabitants. Believing that a deity fights on one's side is too obvious to require any comment. The Mixtecs seem to have found no solution to this problem; perhaps an attempt was made at one point, after the first round in the war, to settle it by an intermarriage between the two groups. But this did not succeed, and several generations later the earth-born lords once again asserted themselves against their neighbors. Such a solution to a modern conflict is, of course, impossible where people are divided by differences in language, religion, and culture. Perhaps the lesson here is that before any solution can be found to a conflict, there is a need to separate quite firmly the practical reasons for a war from its rhetoric.

Note

I thank Dr. Hans Biedermann and the Akademische Druck-und Berlagsanstalt of Graz, Austria, for permission to publish page 42 of *Codex Vindobonensis Mexicanus1*.

References

Burgoa, Fray Francisco de. 1934 (1674). *Geografica Descripcion*. 2 vols. Mexico City: Publicaciones del Archivo General de la Nacion, vols. 25 and 26.

Caso, Alfonso. 1960. *Interpretation of the Codex Bodley 2858*. Mexico City: Sociedad Mexicana de Antropologia.

_____. 1964. *Interpretacion de Codice Selden 3135 (A.2)/Interpretation of the Codex Selden 3135 (A.2)*. Mexico City: Sociedad Mexicana de Antropologia.

Furst, Jill Leslie. 1977. "The Tree Birth Tradition in the Mixteca, Mexico." *Journal of Latin American Lore* 3(2):183–226.

_____. 1978a. *Codex Vindobonensis Mexicanus I: A Commentary*. Institute for Mesoamerican Studies, Publication 4. Albany, N.Y.: State University of New York.

_____. 1978b. "The Life and Times of ♀ 8 Wind 'Flinted Eagle.'" *Alcheringa* 4(1):2–37.

_____. 1978c. "The Year 1 Reed, Day 1 Alligator: A Mixtec Metaphor." *Journal of Latin American Lore* 4(1):93–128.

_____. 1982. "Skeletonization in Mixtec Art: A Re-evaluation." In *The Art and Iconography of Late Post-classic Central Mexico*, edited by Elizabeth Hill Boone, pp. 207–25. Washington, D.C.: Dumbarton Oaks Research Laboratory and Collections, Harvard University.

_____. 1983. "The Lords of 'Place of the Ascending Serpent': An Exploration of Pages 14 to 22 of the Nuttall Obverse." In *Symbol and Meaning Beyond the Closed Community: Essays in Mesoamerican Ideas*, edited by Gary Gossen. State University of New York, Institute for Mesoamerican Studies, Publication 9. Albany, N.Y.: State University of New York.

_____. Forthcoming. "Gifts to the Underworld: The Symbolism and Function of Gold Among the Mixtecs of Mexico." In *Images of Cibola: The Symbolism of Precolumbian Gold and Precious Stones in the Americas from Ancient Times to Conquest*, edited by Suzanne Engler and Luanne Hudson.

Reyes, Fray Antonio de los. 1976 (1593). *Arte en Lengua Mixteca*. Nashville, Tenn.: Vanderbilt University Publications in Anthropology, No. 14.

Smith, Mary Elizabeth. 1973. *Picture Writing from Ancient Southern Mexico*. Norman, Okla.: University of Oklahoma Press.

_____. 1974. "The Relationship between Mixtec Manuscript Painting and the Mixtec Language: A Study of Some Personal Names in Codices Muro and Sanchez Solis." In *Mesoamerican Writing Systems*, edited by Elizabeth P. Benson, pp. 47–98. Washington, D.C.: Dumbarton Oaks Research Library and Collections, Harvard University.

_____. 1983. "Codex Selden: A Manuscript from the Valley of Nochixtlan?" In *The Cloud People: Evolution of the Zapotec and Mixtec Civilizations of Southern Mexico*, edited by Kent V. Flannery and Joyce Marcus, pp. 248–55. New York: Academic Press.

Codices Cited

Codex Bodley 2858. 1960. Facsimile ed. Mexico City: Sociedad Mexicana de Antropologia.

Codex Nuttall. 1902. Facsimile ed. Cambridge, Mass.: Peabody Museum of American Archeology and Ethnology, Harvard University.

Codex Selden 3135 (A.2). 1964. Facsimile ed. Mexico City: Sociedad Mexicana de Antropologia.

Codex Vindobonensis Mexicanus 1. 1974. 2d facsimile ed. Graz, Austria: Akademische Druck-und Verlagsanstalt.

9

Directed Change and the Hope for Peace

Paul L. Doughty

Introduction

Acculturation has been a major concern of anthropologists since the 1936 "memorandum" on the subject (Redfield, Linton and Herskovits, 1936). Nevertheless, they have said relatively little about the consequences of peace and war, about the "shock of contact" in this context, or about how these might relate to planned change. Although the subject of war in the context of tribal societies and among "nonliterate" or "nonindustrial" peoples has occasionally been treated (Swanton, 1943; Turney-High, 1949; Fried, Harris and Murphy, 1968), this literature is not impressive when compared to other anthropological literature. The subject of peace has claimed even less anthropological attention, although the idea is a major conceptual product of some human cultures.

In contrast to the dearth in anthropology of studies of peace and war as cultural processes, such studies dominate historical and political descriptions of human life. During anthropology's emergence as a field of study, emphasis on "things as they are" and aversion to address the vital contemporary issues of society *as anthropological topics* reflect the national cultural visions of Euro-American scholars living in colonially dominant countries (see Lewis, 1973; Bonfil, 1966). The shortcomings in the social sciences in these respects are becoming clearer as major life issues take center stage and as we seek explanations from past experience (Wolf, 1982). The traditional lack of concern for the study of contemporary Euro-American culture and society by anthropologists was a product of the ethnocentric exclusion of ourselves as legitimate subjects of our own research. More importantly, this lack of attention kept us from dealing with some of the most vital aspects of cultural behavior which bridge industrial societies and the rest of the world. We must not perpetuate such "traditions." One significant change during the past decade has been the growing involvement as advocates for stateless societies and cultural minorities within nations of many academic anthropologists who previously had little to do with such action.

In other respects, during field research anthropologists increasingly face scenes of human conflict into which they can easily be drawn. We are asked to take sides on issues in local contexts or, at the very minimum, to provide direct feedback to the people we study and whose permission to be studied is now de rigueur for even the most simple of projects. The explosion of interest in the "ethics" of social research in the past decade deals with the practical issues of working as anthropologists and the obligations which might obtain between the scholar and the people. Just as the importance of such ethics to culture theory and behavior is undeniably relevant, our failure as a discipline to come to grips with the "large" issues such as war and peace is an ethical matter which can no longer be ignored.

Anthroplogy has long been interested in problems of planned change as well as acculturation processes. In this context the discipline has often dealt with the consequences of directed change programs at local or even regional levels. However this area of anthropological research has not been joined with the wider questions raised by war and peace. This paper is based on the premise that planned change efforts are closely linked in theory, policy, and practice with attempts to achieve peace and how well they do or do not succeed.

Planning for Change and Peace

Contemporary approaches to planned change stem in significant degree from the brave and idealistic statements which justified World War II. Franklin Roosevelt's declaration of the "Four Freedoms" embodied what was later to serve as the intellectual underpinning for foreign assistance. The "supremacy of human rights everywhere" rested upon freedom of speech and religion and freedom from want and fear. Achieving these conditions would result in a peaceful new world order without tyranny (Rollins, 1960:261).

Development and directed social change in the post-World War II era were born of the impact of war, the demise of colonialism, and emergence of new nations. During 1945 to 1952 the "revolution of rising expectations" around the world was manifested in such diverse movements as new cargo cults in Oceania and massive migrations of people seeking socioeconomic advantage. Ironically, just as the Cold War was beginning as a conflictive form of international relations, hopes for a "new tomorrow" were expressed with buoyant optimism in the introductory statements of United Nations agencies and foreign-aid programs.

In this context, it was commonly felt that one of the greatest sources of human unhappiness was war, and that this lamentable state was produced by grave socioeconomic stress and political injustice, often in combination. These sentiments are amply expressed in various United Nations statements, and particularly in the "Universal Declaration of Human Rights" (United Nations, 1967). The next world war is envisioned as apocalyptic. The reasoning of assorted analysts from Erich Fromm to the Club of Rome follows a consistent pattern that links the development of Third World areas and equitable wealth distributions to prospects for peace (cf., Fromm, 1961:248–52; Ward, 1962:111–59; Pearson, 1969:7–22; Mesarovic and Pestel, 1974:143–57). Thus the resolution of human suffering and deprivation through directed, planned change is regarded as the major pathway to peace: that is, a method of avoiding war.

Developmental Change

The developmental change approach to planned change, was to be accomplished by "friendly hands across the sea." The industrialized, former colonial nations would lend their know-how and resources to alter the conditions of the world's poor. Development obligations were to become the new "white man's burden." In this scenario, development was to occur by opening access to technology, and through democratic education by increasing general participation in the exercise of power. Know-how was the key notion, and unquestioned confidence was expressed in an industrial, technological "can-do" philosophy. With such aid and values, *any* country and people could engage in an operation bootstrap to pull themselves upward, as the Marshall Plan in ravaged Europe and in Puerto Rico were demonstrating. And there would be peace.

The enrichment of nations and societies would come fundamentally from the production of new wealth rather than the redistribution of existing wealth. Planned growth and utilization of untapped resources were the keys to development. However, the fact that the special constellations of resources, commitment, populations, cultural values and opportunity are rarely in place (or remain available) to permit long-term, consistent, planned growth and expansion, has led to disenchantment and modifications in the development approach to peace.

Redistributive Change

The quest for peace through the organized redistribution of resources is also a major strategy of planned change. By correcting imbalances and felt injustices as a basic means to address the ills which produce war and strife, such redistribution is intended to create peaceful conditions. Rather than resting the potential for planned change on the development of new wealth and untapped resources, this approach corrects problems of poverty and social value primarily through the reallocation of existing wealth. At one level, for example, there is the Food for Peace approach of the United States, which seeks to give surplus food to needy nations through various strategems embodied in the Titles of Public Law 480. The awarding of various types of "soft loans," whose interest or payback requirements are not stringently enforced, also redistributes substantial wealth from rich nations to poor ones.

In an energetics view it is accepted that the world resource base and ecology are to some degree renewable but nonexpanding. This version of the limited good concept implies that the potential for some conflict-producing process may be inherent to redistributive change: in redistribution, what I get is taken from someone else, somehow. At a personal level it means sharpened competition and/or theft (Richards, 1975:93–110). Within or between nations, it requires asymmetrical trade relations (dependency) or changes in balance and it may mean the adoption of coercive violent methods such as revolution and war.

A modern hope is that global redistributive change may be achieved without violence. The world has witnessed many examples of warfare generated by attempts to coerce change and has reacted ambivalently to them. Radical upheavals like that of Kampuchea under Pol Pot, or like the Mexican and Russian revolutions, leave such bitterness in their vindictive wake that the attractiveness of developmental change through tapping new and underused resources is more closely identified with peaceful change. This does not necessarily dislodge the wealthy and dominant classes. Rather, by obliging the poor to change (to become educated, skilled, ambitious and competitive within an existing system), it places the burden of development on the poor. Some see a model of this process in the development of the United States. However, with few frontiers left, most countries find the model at best difficult to emulate, even in small ways. Short of revolution, reformist, mildly coercive actions, such as the Peruvian "revolution" during the regime of Juan Velasco Alvarado (1968–1975) appeal to many as alternatives worth pursuing, because they combine the developmental and redistributive approaches.

The Rejection of Planned Change

Another reaction to the redistributive and developmental approaches to planned change is to reject all change that threatens the status quo. Despite the ubiquitous notion that change is inevitable, at a popular level the possibility is essentially rejected: the extreme of this view is the present survivalist movement, a nonaltruistic, highly ethnocentric (and egocentric) philosophy. This is not the first time that such a philosophy has appeared: in the late 1950s, during the public debate of and rising consciousness about the dangers of nuclear bombs, private fallout shelters were proposed by politicians and scientists alike. As one anthropologist demonstrated, by posing brandishing a Polynesian club next to a shelter for *Life* magazine in 1959, it was "anthropologically" sound to beat off any challenge to one's private resources.

On a societal level the survivalist alternative opposes significant development or redistribution supposing that conditions can be held as they are and the have-nots will be forced to accept the consequences (e.g. "Fortress America") in political- economic terms. The policies of numerous governments follow such philosophies on internal matters, as in Chile, South Africa, El Salvador and Guatemala. At the international level, the "let 'em eat cake" approach leads to restrictive policy, a kind of apartheid applied to other world citizens: others must be given only limited access to one's own country and be kept where they "belong." In this context, coercion and war are seen as essential means to maintain one's own way of life.

Millenarianism and Planned Change

By and large, the developmental strategy has been identified with the highly technologically oriented approaches of the Western industrial nations, while the redistributive theme has become associated with socialist and Marxist policy. Be that as it may, such pure approaches to planned change are rare. Most programs, regardless of ideological origin, involve a mix of developmental and redistributive techniques in an attempt to tease along the desired change.

However differently planned change might be visualized, it is widely assumed that once the goals have been reached, the developed and reordered society will be self-perpetuating. This seems to be the implication of many delineations of the development/redistribution challenge. According to Roosevelt the "Four Freedoms" goals were tangible and by implication, permanent: "That is no vision of a distant millennium. It is a definite basis for a kind of world attainable in our own time and generation" (Roosevelt, cited in Rollins, 1961:261). In other words, the two approaches share the same basic assumption about the outcome of effectively executed planned change: once resources and human potential are developed or effectively redistributed the peace-status goal will have been achieved.

The millenarian assumption in planned change does not allow for failure or backsliding. Where help has been given to little avail, there are complaints such as: What more do they need? We give them millions a year and get no gratitude; they still want more! Or the idea that Argentina could "lapse" after having received the best of Europe ("It's not Latin America; it's like Europe") is not understood. Nor indeed is the reality that formerly "nice" neighborhoods in New York City have become "Fort Apache."

The fact that after making investments planned to achieve progress, situations do not continue to fulfill expectations is disheartening. In any of these scenarios, however, the millenarian vision remains: the assumption that with the attainment of the status desired, it will last and that other less desirable conditions and variables of the past will not reappear. Unfortunately for the millenarian assumption, support, investment and maintenance of interest are not constant or consistent because planned change assistance programs, like the government process itself, follows political dictates—usually of short duration—almost exclusively.

I now turn to some Peruvian illustrations of these matters and ask: Is it reasonable to expect that peaceful conditions will result from almost forty years of developmental and redistributive efforts. Peace at the community level is not usually a question of killing, heavy weapons or armies. It might rather be considered the equivalent of domestic tranquility in a given culture, and to embrace notions such as the "Four Freedoms" or the United Nations "Universal Declaration of Human Rights."

Directing Change in a Repressive Society

Although Peru has not been a pacific society, its modern experience has been one of far less bloodshed than that of some of its neighbors. Bolivia, Paraguay, Chile, Argentina, and Colombia have all suffered violent nationwide strife in the past half century. On the other hand, Peruvians have endured a kind of social oppression for several centuries which has often produced localized rebellions temporarily lifting the blanket of endemic exploitation (Kapsoli, 1977). Its rigid social and economic structure, drawn along cultural lines and sharply discriminatory on the basis of race, language, dress and behavior, was widely recognized as unjust and archaic (Gonzalez Prada, 1960).

In particular the highland haciendas embodied the vital elements of this system of human relations and have been well described (Saenz, 1933; Vázquez, 1961; CIDA, 1966) as one of the principal factors in Peru's underdevelopment. Its spirit was a survivalist rejection of any change. In 1951, Cornell University's Allan R. Holmberg, in collaboration with Peruvian colleagues, initiated a bold program to work with the serfs of Vicos (Ancash), a traditional hacienda, for the purposes of abolishing serfdom and creating a viable community which could fend for itself and improve the levels of living of its members (Vázquez, 1952; Holmberg, 1960). Jointly operated by Cornell and the Peruvian government under a special agreement, the program lasted about fourteen years, achieving its goals despite a variety of problems, not the least of which was the covert opposition of the conservative Peruvian government itself (Dobyns, Doughty and Lasswell, 1971). Among the many dimensions of sociocultural change exemplified by the Cornell-Peru Project (CPP), the project illustrates a number of things at issue here.

Hailed by many as a sample of peaceful change under the most challenging of conditions, the CPP and the community's postproject experience demonstrate how planned change can be balanced precariously between peaceful process and violence. In concept, the CPP utilized aspects of both developmental and redistributive approaches. On the one hand, as an attempt to transfer power and control of the hacienda from its elitist owner-renters to the serfs, who were coerced into giving their labor in exchange for subsistence land, the plan was clearly redistributive in nature. On the other hand, improvements introduced into crop production were developmental by virtue of making new use of badly managed resources. Similarly, the appearance of educational opportunity, vocational training, and encouragement of initiative were key new resource elements.

The culture of the Vicos people, while rooted in ancient native Quechua traditions, also bore the scars of three centuries of serfdom. One of the special manifestations of this aspect of Vicos culture was a deep fear both of outsiders, "mishtis"—the mestizo landlord class—and of any changes in the brittle world of poverty in which people had long struggled to survive (Holmberg, 1967). At Vicos the landlord could whip the Vicosino, throw him in the hacienda jail, or take his animals at the slightest whim, with no fear of retribution. The Vicosino who might object to such behavior ran the risk of being abused, deprived of his belongings or expelled from the estate with nowhere to go. Vicos culture had evolved over the years in response to such conditions: peace was the hacienda undisturbed.

Change was not only unexpected but, as it presented uncertainty and insecurity, it was also feared. Overcoming this obstacle to planned change, even to alleviate the stresses identified by the community itself, was a major task of the CPP (Doughty, 1971). The deep resentments provoked by Vicosino recognition of their plight—"we are nothing but slaves"—was always a latent factor in interpersonal relations between Vicosinos and their mestizo neighbors, whom they feared and despised.

The system was held static by virtue of the land tenure arrangements, the isolation of Vicosinos from free intercourse with the rest of Peruvian society (through language, fear, and denial of economic enterprise), and coercion. The local upper class looked upon the "brute Indians" of Vicos as "animals" and considered them as undeserving of developmental attention or perhaps incapable of changing. The complementarity of landlord and serf attitudes solidified this static system.

Not unexpectedly, the CPP encountered opposition both inside and outside the hacienda. Those with modest advantages under the hacienda rule were reluctant to sacrifice their ascendency. Outside, the factor which most aroused the opposition of those with vested interests was the redistributive aspects of the project. While regional landlords could tolerate such products of developmental investments as increased potato production, they could not abide the implications of change in land tenure and attempted to frustrate the success of the program by blocking sale of the property to their former serfs (Dobyns; Doughty; and Lasswell, 1971:9–12).

Events also showed that they objected to allowing the serfs access to increased skills, respect and, certainly, power. While local authorities could not intervene directly in Vicos because of the project's sponsorship by the government, they could intimidate and suppress change at the perimeters. Landlord reaction was demonstrated in 1960, when the serfs on the adjacent hacienda of Huapra attempted to emulate Vicos by constructing their own school, financing it by planting and harvesting some unused hacienda land. Through his friend, the Prefect of Ancash Department, the landlord secured the services of a detachment of police, who rounded up the serfs while they were working in the wheat field and shot several of them, killing three outright.

In the tense days which followed the Huapra massacre, the Vicosinos were on the verge of marching on the nearby mestizo town of Marcara to take revenge. Several Huaprinos were jailed (accused of attacking the police), and an arrest warrant for the field director of the CPP was issued, accusing him of provoking the event by encouraging the serfs to be educated, and thus threatening the landlord's property. In subsequent years, the Huapra situation clarified. Fearing for his life if he returned, the landlord gave up his attempts to regain his property, and the serfs gradually assumed control of the estate. After the 1969 land reform declaration, the property became officially theirs.

In Vicos, despite the constant opposition of the landlord groups in the region and nationally, sale of the property to the people was obtained in 1962 after the opportune intervention of Edward Kennedy (see Mangin, 1979) and the persistence of CPP directors and community leaders. The years that followed the end of the CPP after 1964 saw numerous additional changes (Doughty, 1982), including the loss of community cohesion and several failed projects in which Ministry of Agriculture representatives played nefarious roles.

With the declaration of universal land reform in 1969, the Vicos community, whose pioneering experience had presaged the national event, entered a new phase. Anxious to place their own ideological stamp on progress, government representatives decreed a reorganization of Vicos to make it conform to the new national peasant community regulations. The Vicosinos resisted this when they were told that the CPP had deceived them. Manipulated by government interests and its leadership, misled by corrupt ministerial employees promoting a cattle feedlot project, the community dropped into a relatively disorganized state in the mid 1970s. Adding to its problems, a regional potato blight sharply lowered Vicos income. The community often presented an embittered image to outsiders.

Visitors to Vicos during this time, apparently expecting to see gleaming buildings and the operations of a slick community cooperative, were dismayed and found the situation inexplicable (Morse et al., 1976). Others perceived a negative situation, noting that Vicosinos had seemingly developed anxieties over change, conflicts were more visible, and social differentiation was increasing (Babb, 1976).

There was also a demographic problem at Vicos. In the early years, with development aid through which Vicosinos came to share more of the land's wealth, former residents had returned to the community from the coast (Vázquez, 1963:98), a virtually unique event in Peru. Today, however, with its population more than 2.3 times its 1952 level, there is a strong current of migration from Vicos *to* the coast. This follows the universal national demographic pattern. Did the project fail because the community could not hold its population or adopt birth control faster than the rest of the region?

The answers to this question can be found in the implications of the impact of planned change. Vicosinos, formerly imprisoned in the considerable homogeneity of serfdom, had now gained an opportunity for social differentiation. Changes in community class structure, age and peer relationships, educational opportunity, and sex roles are inevitable as the processes of development and redistribution continue. Project research had predicted the demographic increase and eventual Vicosino participation in patterns of national migratory change (Alers, 1971). The CPP stands guilty of having precipitated these things. The domestic tranquility of the status quo had been destroyed.

The migration of people, first back to Vicos and then to the coast, is also part of the redistribution process. In a larger sense it also is diagnostic of conditions in the country as a whole. The government's lack of coherent and consistent rural development or redistributive programs has had the effect of promoting vast migrations of highlanders to the primate city, where migrants have access to a larger share of wealth, power, health and whatever else they fail to gain through planned change in their Andean homeland.

And what of peace? The orderliness of past years—even during the CPP era—is gone. New conflicts and different anxieties have replaced those which occurred under hacienda conditions, where fear of repression was a dominant theme. Under the new conditions one cannot simply hunker down and be saved through ignorance. Skill and wider knowledge are needed.

If the CPP were successful, how could Vicos have lapsed into apparent disarray? The answer to this lies in viewing development and redistribution as *process* rather than *state*. The real question is whether or not community institutions are able to weather temporary adversity and whether or not in pursuing change they remain task oriented. By 1983 Vicos had rebounded from its mid-1970s malaise and was proceeding with its plans, which include finishing the new high school building, extending the 5-year-old residential electrical system, fixing its roads, and initiating ambitious plans for formalizing its new urban area. In the latter task the community has an agreement with the local university for technical guidance. Whether the community will continue to maintain its communal fields is being debated. A Vicosino was elected to the district government and now plays a key role in directing regional affairs. These self-initiated plans for change can be seen to conform to more general developmental and, particularly, redistributive patterns. As Vicos becomes urban in character, social stratification within the community will intensify as will the need for urban skills.

While the programs of planned change transformed Vicos, they also produced conflicts which had not existed before. There is no doubt that some of these are uncomfortable and even undesired, but how were they to be avoided? Do such changes lead away from peace? Resolving the visceral questions of outright oppression found in the old hacienda system was a step in that direction. On the other hand, once that had been accomplished, Vicos entered another stage of the process, one that is more demanding, problematic and less secure.

Peace and Change in Peru

For the past thirty years Peru has awakened its population to the possibilities of individual and family improvements in levels of living and greater participation in national life. But it has also failed to fulfill its promises of development and redistribution in any consistent manner. One of the distinguishing features of the Vicos project, in contrast, was the fact that it lasted fourteen years —through four presidential administrations— a rare event in a country where social and economic policies rarely endure two years. The Vicos success emerged in part because the CPP lasted long enough to accomplish something in the complex sphere of community organization, the development of new skills, knowledge, and opportunity for effective participation in the national society.

Unfortunately, during this same period, at a national level Peru did not develop a consistent, effective policy for constructive change. The country has "solved" its problem of planning rural change and defused increasing demands through a policy of uncontrolled urban growth, permitting provincial migrants to seek life improvements in Lima. Here government action is easily confined to providing newcomers with basic urban services. While the labor force in agriculture and industry has dropped, the service employment has grown in the past twenty years (World Bank, 1983:188). Presently this strategy is supported by Peruvian government investments in the urban coastal areas and, to a significant degree, by United States Agency for International Development. "Food for Peace" programs which provide cheap foods that are largely distributed through urban coastal markets (Johnson et al., 1983). The Public Law 480 program is the largest component of the USAID economic assistance package to Peru, amounting to about 70 percent of the total budget. P.L. 480 foods are also used to support rural and urban food-for-work and nutrition programs. Most participants in these programs are in Lima and other coastal cities where a largely female workforce is employed in the construction of sidewalks, new streets, school rooms, and street cleaning. Only a small percentage of the food-for-work projects could be called productive or income producing investments. Although the "Food for Peace" programs may well be assisting in keeping the peace in Peru's urban areas, it would be hard to argue that these resources were part of a strategy of directed change targeted at solving Peru's socioecnomic dilemmas.

Meanwhile, Peru's desperate agricultural situation shows a steadily declining rate of basic food production, caused in considerable part by the loss of farm workers through migration. Peru now ranks 112th out of 125 nations in per capita food production (World Bank, 1983:158). The lack of effective comprehensive rural development programs coupled with the constant *promise of redistribution and development* is particularly provoking. Indeed it is this aspect of the "R and D" scenario which most aggravates: the failure to fulfill pledges of planned change. Underlying the present "Sendero Luminoso" guerrilla movement centered in the impoverished highland departments of Huancavelica, Apurimac, and Ayacucho is a long history of provocations and bitter resentments over failed hopes. It is worth noting that both of these departments have had very high rates of migration to Lima since 1961. Can it be that the migration escape valve has finally clogged?

Conclusion

The CPP demonstrated that planned change requires a constant, consistent policy through several years to succeed even at the local level. It is a process, not simply the investment in infrastructure or the arrival at a state from which there will be no reversal or change. The peace-producing capabilities of planned change are tempered by this condition. In the process of redistribution particularly, conflict is often produced as anxieties and uncertainties interrupt the "peace" of stagnancy under oppression. Indeed, the survivalists or the old regime can be expected to resort to violent acts to thwart change. What can be done in such a context to avert this hostility as more humane and equitable institutions are built?

One lesson is clear: the road of planned change must follow consistent goals with the determination to see things through to the end and, indeed, beyond. The promise of change without fulfillment in the face of felt need is a provocation looking for expression. The deep alienation and violence provoked by deception is a bitter consequence of poor development and redistribution efforts. Palliative efforts such as current "Food for Peace" programs may only serve to exacerbate difficulties because rather than addressing true goals of development and redistribution they may in fact deepen dependency and undermine local capacity to deal with problems such as food production. In a Third World context such as that of Peru, planned change thus has a high possibility of resulting in violent reactions either by conservative survivalists or by disenchanted advocates of development and redistribution. Planning for change and achieving peace are thus tightly linked and call for integrated and coherent holistic strategies with the authority to execute them over spans of several years. Can this be done?

References

Alers, José Oscar. 1971. "Well-being." In *Peasants, Power, and Applied Social Change: Vicos as a Model*, edited by Henry F. Dobyns, Paul L. Doughty, and Harold Lasswell, pp. 115–36. Beverly Hills, Cal.: Sage.

Babb, Florence. 1976. *The Development of Sexual Inequality in Vicos, Peru*. Special Studies No. 85. Buffalo, N.Y.:Council on International Studies, State University of New York.

Bonfil Batalla, Guillermo. 1966. "Conservative Thought in Applied Anthroplogy: A Critique." *Human Organization* 25:89–92.

CIDA. 1966. *Tenencia de la Tierra y Desarrollo Socio-económico de Sector Agrícola: Perú.* Washington, D.C.: Unión Panamericana.
Dobyns, Henry F.; Doughty, Paul L.; and Lasswell, Harold, eds. 1971. *Peasants, Power, and Applied Social Change: Vicos as a Model.* Beverly Hills, Cal.: Sage.
Doughty, Paul L. 1971. "Human Relations: Affection, Rectitude and Respect." In *Peasants, Power, and Applied Social Change: Vicos as a Model*, edited by Henry F. Dobyns, Paul L. Doughty, and Harold Lasswell, pp. 89–114. Beverly Hills, Cal.: Sage.
_____. 1982. "What Has Become of Vicos? The Aftermath of a Classic Program." Paper presented at the Annual Meeting of the American Anthropological Association, Washington, D.C.
Doughty, Paul L.; Burleigh, Elizabeth; and Painter, Michael. 1983. *Peru: An Evaluation of P.L. 480 Title II Food Assistance.* Binghamton, N.Y.: Institute for Development Anthropology.
Fried, M.; Harris, M.; and Murphy, R., editors. 1968. *War: The Anthropology of Armed Conflict and Aggression.* New York: Natural History Press.
Fromm, Erich. 1961. *May Man Prevail?* New York: Doubleday Anchor.
Gonzalez Prada, Manuel. 1960 (1882). *Pájinas Libres.* Lima: Ediciones Pajinas Libres.
Holmberg, Allan R. 1960. "Changing Community Attitudes and Values in Peru." In *Social Change in Latin America Today.* New York: Vintage.
_____. 1967. "Algunas Relaciones entre la Privacion Psicobiologica y el Cambio Cultural en los Andes." *América Indígena.* 27:3–24.
Johnson, Twig, et al. 1983. *The Impact of PL 480 Title I in Peru: Food Aid as an Effective Development Resource.* Washington, D.C.: U.S. Agency for International Development.
Kapsoli, Wilfredo, ed. 1977. *Los Movimientos Campesinos en el Perú: 1879–1965.* Lima: Delva Editóres.
Lewis, Diane. 1973. "Anthropology and Colonialism." *Current Anthropology* 14(5):581–602.
Mangin, William P. 1979. "Thoughts on Twenty-four Years of Work in Peru: The Vicos Project and Me." In *Long-term Field Research in Social Anthropology*, edited by G. Foster, et al., pp. 65–84. New York: Academic Press.
Mesarovic, Mihajlo, and Pestel, Eduard. 1974. *Mankind at the Turning Point: The Second Report to the Club of Rome.* New York: E.P. Dutton.
Morse, E., et al. 1976. *Strategies for Small Farmer Development.* Boulder, Colo.: Westview Press.
Pearson, Lester B. 1969. *Partners in Development: Report of the Commission on International Development.* New York: Praeger.
Redfield, Robert; Linton, Ralph; and Herskovits, Melville J. 1936. "Memorandum for the Study of Acculturation." *American Anthropologist*, 38:149–52.
Richards, Cara. 1975. "The Concept and Forms of Competition." In *War: Its Causes and Correlates*, edited by M.A. Nettleship, et al. The Hague: Mouton.
Rollins, Alfred B. Jr. 1960. *Franklin D. Roosevelt and the Age of Action.* New York: Dell.
Saenz, Moisés. 1933. *Sobre el Indio Peruano y su Incorporación al Medio Nacional.* México, D.F.: Secretaria de Educación Pública.
Swanton, John R. 1943. *Are Wars Inevitable?* Baltimore, Md.: The Lord Baltimore Press.

Turney-High, H.H. 1949. *Primitive War: Its Practice and Concepts*. Columbia, S.C.: University of South Carolina Press.

United Nations. 1982. *Universal Declaration of Human Rights*. Adopted by the General Assembly of the United Nations, 1948. In *Encyclopedia Britannica*, 15th edition, 1982. s.v. "Addenda to Volume x."

United States 83rd Congress. 1954. *Agricultural Trade Development and Assistance Act, 1954 as Amended, Public Law 480*. Washington, D.C.: U.S. Government Printing Office.

Vázquez, Mario C. 1952. "La Antropologia Cultural y Nuestro Problema del Indio." *Perú Indígena* 2:7–157.

_____. 1961. *Hacienda, Peonaje y Servidumbre en los Andes Peruanos*. Lima, Peru: Editorial Estudio s Andinos.

_____. 1963. "Proceso de Migración en la Comunidad de Vicos." In *Migración e Integración en el Perú*, edited by H.F. Dobyns and M.C. Vazquez, pp. 93–102. Lima, Peru: Editorial Estudios Andinos.

Ward, Barbara. 1962. *The Rich Nations and the Poor Nations*. New York: W.W. Norton.

Wolf, Eric R. 1982. *Europe and the People without History*. Berkeley, Cal.: University of California Press.

World Bank. 1983. *World Development Report*. New York: Oxford University Press.

10

Ethnic Targeting as a Defense Strategy

Nancie L. Gonzalez

Appalling though it may seem, serious consideration has been given recently by both United States and Soviet strategists to the idea of selective targeting for annihilation of certain population segments in each other's country (See Albert, 1976; Burt, 1980; Foster, 1978). The technology for accomplishing this comes with the development of incredibly accurate new intercontinental ballistic missiles. At least one political scientist (Quester, 1980:232) suggested that ethnic targeting is a bad idea for two reasons: a) the cost in world image for the power which attempts anything like genocide, and b) the possibility of retaliation in kind by the other power. I would agree that ethnic targeting is a bad idea. The fact that it has been (and may still be) considered feasible by knowledgeable and influential people in both countries raises a number of questions which deserve serious consideration.

First, how has the concept of ethnicity become, in effect, both a household word and a tool for military strategists? What has been the role of social science, and particularly, anthropology, in fostering this situation?

Second, is it "natural" for human beings to discriminate on ethnic grounds? What are the roles of biology and of culture in the process, and what has been the history of such discrimination in different times and places? What have been the advantages and disadvantages of using ethnic criteria as bases for the classification of peoples?

Third, could the proposed ethnic targeting work? Is ethnicity an important and comparable variable in the United States and the Soviet Union, and are ethnic categories and ethnic conflict in the two countries strong enough to override national loyalties, thus contributing to the downfall of the state?

Fourth, has ethnic discrimination outlived its usefulness at the present stage of global development? What can anthropologists contribute to a better understanding of the reasons for its persistence, and to its potential for endangering world peace?

Ethnology and Ethnogenesis

Sumner introduced the concept of ethnocentrism into American social science in 1906. Since then, the concept of ethnicity has been widely adopted by many academic disciplines, as well as by politicians and the public at large. The literature contains a bewildering variety of definitions and opinions as to how ethnicity is manifested. Sociologists have contributed most of our information on and analysis of ethnicity in the United States (Glazer and Moynihan, 1975), and political scientists have used these ideas imaginatively, especially in relation to international affairs (Dreyer, 1976; Enloe, 1980; Suhrke and Noble, 1977; Wiarda, 1981).

Yancey, Ericksen and Juliani (1976) distinguish between ethnic salience—the selection of putative traits to characterize a social group—and ethnic identification—or the proclivity of group members to accept these attributions. Following Etzioni's 1959 discussion of "situational ethnicity," Yancey and his colleagues question the importance of heritage as an essential aspect of ethnicity. They believe, rather, that it has to do with the exigencies of survival and the structure of opportunity. Thus, the effect of ethnic or national heritage will vary depending upon the situation of the group (1976:399).

Anthropologists have covered much of the same ground. But, probably because we have examined the interaction between ethnic groups in a wide range of societies over time, we have taken a broader perspective than most on the kinds of things and events which have come to be associated with, or symbolic of, ethnic groups or characteristic of ethnic behavior. Furthermore, anthropologists have provided a cross-cultural dimension to the *theory* of ethnicity and have discussed how the concept has changed as social science itself has matured and become more adept at understanding the changing contemporary world (Bennett, 1975). We owe a great debt to those British social anthropologists who witnessed, recorded and analyzed the transformation from "tribe" to "ethnic group" in many African urban areas (Cohen, 1974; Gulliver, 1969; Mayer, 1961; Mitchell, 1956).

We also learned a good deal by paying increasing attention over the past two decades to macrolevel problems and global issues, both contemporary and historical. The model of the plural society, originally used by the economist, Furnivall, in reference to Southeast Asia (1948), was expanded by M.G. Smith (1965). It deals with societal institutions, rather than with ethnicity per se, but it has proven highly popular and useful in many quarters. In addition, anthropologists are better prepared than other social scientists to consider biological components of ethnicity, both in relation to the nature-nurture controversy, and in the way in which racial, or genetically transmitted, characters contribute to human behavioral variability and are themselves affected by it. Thus, we are aware, and can document that aggression toward other humans has frequently focused on ethnicity as a means of differentiating friend from enemy. The record for "ethnic targeting" contains entries ranging from various attempts over the past 2,000 years to annihilate Jews through more recent Brazilian and Guatemalan efforts to eliminate Indians.[1]

In a less well known case, I reviewed historical documentary evidence of a British plan to eliminate Black Caribs on the island of St. Vincent in 1797 while preserving the so-called "Yellow" Caribs, at the time thought to be a separate ethnic group. Ironically, the result was to further solidify a weakly defined ethnic division, and to preserve and strengthen the Blacks, while contributing to the cultural assimilation and social degradation of the Yellow Caribs (see Gonzalez, 1983). This caused me to ponder further the idea that ethnicity is better seen as the product or outcome of human classificatory efforts, rather than something biologically or culturally inherent in certain groups of people or in individuals (Barth, 1969; Cohen, 1978). In other words, ethnicity is a convenient means to identify both the in-group and the various out-groups with which any society and its members may have to deal. And by extension, it may be used to assign individuals to "appropriate" groups. Of course, the definition of ethnicity itself, as well as the specific criteria used to distinguish any one group or its members, is culturally relative, and may vary not only from people to people, but for the same people through time.

There are several other important dimensions to the issue. Cross (1978) has emphasized that the meaning of ethnicity and ethnic consciousness differs according to the level of national development. Bidney (1953) distinguished between what he called "benign" and "vicious" ethnicity, the former being more typical of advanced societies, in his view. However, most anthropologists today would not go along with such a value-laden dichotomy. On the other hand, Lanternari's (1980:55) statement that in tribal societies with communal economics, "organized mass ethnocentrism is hardly developed," cannot go unchallenged, for such societies are often among the most ethnocentric anywhere (Hohenthal and McCorkle, 1955). A key problem is how the societies in question discriminate between insiders and outsiders, and whether we choose to label the resulting behavior "ethnocentric."

In the Soviet Union there has been continuing interest in ethnic phenomena, and concern as to how to classify different kinds of ethnic allegiances and groups—by language, social class, territoriality, or culture—has preoccupied Soviet social scientists (see Armstrong, 1976; Bromley, 1983; Kozlov, 1980). The terms "nation," and "nationality" have been more commonly used in earlier Soviet scholarship, though Bromley (1983) has recently attempted to clarify, refine and improve on these and other terms, focusing more on the concept of ethnicity as it has been generally used in the West. Some American observers of the Soviet scene still do not use the term "ethnic," preferring "subcultural" or "national" to refer to the various population components in that country (Bertsch, 1982, cf. Zwick, 1979). Probably this reflects the fashion of the day, as well as differences in the writers' familiarity with the theory of ethnicity.

Marxists do not agree on the extent to which class overrides ethnicity in capitalist countries, but it is clear from Chinese, Cuban and Soviet evidence that ethnic distinctions do not disappear under socialism or communism, even though official policy in such countries has long been to centralize control, downplay ethnic differences, and create a melting pot. Khrushchev said in 1961, "Communists will not conserve and perpetuate national [read "ethnic"] distinctions. . . . Even the slightest vestiges of nationalism should be eradicated with uncompromising Bolshevik determination" (quoted in Burkey, 1978:128). Lately, however, the Soviets seem to tolerate some ethnic allegiance, so long as it does not become a political issue (see Kubbel, Sedlovskaya, and Tishkov, 1983).

An analysis of the significance of discussions concerning ethnic targeting by the United States and the USSR in the current tense situation is, therefore, not simple, and must take into account a number of factors. First, it will be useful to reexamine how ethnicity has been defined and brought into existence as a classificatory tool by social scientists.

The Bases of Ethnic Classification

Racial, linguistic and cultural variations are the raw material from which ethnic categories are built in all societies. Race, or the shared possession of a set of genetically determined, phenotypically visible characteristics, is perhaps the most convenient basis for ethnic classification, and may once have been more useful than it now is. With widespread migration, new rules governing endogamy and exogamy, and the rise of large, complex societies, gene pools are larger and more heterogeneous than ever before, leading to considerable racial variability, even within ethnic groups. In the United States, for example, "black" is likely to include many persons who are phenotypically white.[2]

The idea that aggression between "insiders" and others is a biologically determined primordial urge has been implicit in much of the literature since Sumner (1906:12–13), and most of it has assumed a link with racial or other ascriptive characteristics. Pierre van den Berghe (1974) suggests that ethnic and race relations are extensions of the idiom of kinship, and others conclude that primary kinship categories are themselves "natural" categories (Fox, 1979:132). There are two separate, though related, problems here. The first has to do with whether we are programmed to recognize and react more positively to individuals who share our own genetically determined traits. The second is whether aggression as a survival mechanism is built into human nature (Ardrey, 1966; Tiger and Fox, 1971).

Although critics of sociobiology are quick to point out that aggression between different social groupings is rare in the nonhuman animal world (Reynolds, 1980:304; Wiens, 1983), the strength of kinship ties, whether based on biological or cultural mandates to preserve and perpetuate one's own kind, has been demonstrated to be exceedingly strong among humans, and perhaps among some other animals. Most psychologists and anthropologists would probably agree that it is the symbolism of the in-group, ranging from the so-called mothering instinct to patriotism, which motivates individual humans to become aggressive on its behalf. If we accept the idea that ethnic or racial consciousness is an extension of kinship, it is not unreasonable to postulate the existence of some biological substratum. Certainly we cannot dismiss it out-of-hand, and it warrants further investigation. Probably those theories attempting to link biology and culture will be most fruitful for future analysis (see Alexander, 1979; Durham, 1979; and Irons, 1979).

It has been shown repeatedly, however, that ethnic salience and identification hardly ever depend upon genetic criteria alone, even though there is usually an underlying assumption of common descent among members of ethnic groups. Phenotypes, even within an interbreeding population, are simply too variable, and many characteristics are modified by the environment. But if biological traits are indeterminate, what else can be used? Language is also convenient, particularly when a group retains exclusive use of a tongue—sometimes consciously—as a boundary-maintaining mechanism. The only way to learn such a language, which is most often unwritten, is to do so as a member or quasi member of the group.

But political hegemony, whether achieved through military conquest or voluntary amalgamation, tends to spread certain languages across both racial and cultural groups, thus demonstrating, as Boas first noted, that race, language and culture vary independently. Some societies especially those whose members are likely to travel frequently outside their borders as adults, emphasize the learning of several languages from childhood. But even when one language becomes official and is taught in compulsory school systems, failure to use it frequently or widely causes some speakers to retain peculiar sounds or syntax, thus marking them as being "different" from the others. Again we have raw material for ethnic categorization.

Finally, even language may fail, as in civil wars, to distinguish the out-group, and at this point the richness and variability covered by the concept of culture may be brought to bear in creating ethnic groups. Religion has long been an important marker, but so also are food preferences, artistic tastes, and dress codes. Even economic activities may differentiate one ethnic group from another (Haaland 1969). To the extent that several traits or behavior patterns covary, an ethnic profile can be more easily established and people taught to recognize it.

Ethnic Targeting

The idea of ethnic targeting is based upon the recognition that in both the United States and the Soviet Union there are certain ethnic groups that do not share political power equally with the dominant group. These are then by definition ethnic "minorities" (Dreyer, 1976:1; Wagley and Harris, 1958:10). In the Soviet Union some groups have never become culturally assimilated. These include the formerly sovereign Caucasoid peoples in Ukrania, Latvia, Estonia and Lithuania. But race may also be a distinguishing characteristic (many northern and eastern Soviets being Asiatic, or Mongoloid.). Language, however, appears to be the most important barrier between the dominant Russians and all the others. In spite of efforts since the 1920s to stamp out national differences, many Soviet citizens still do not speak Russian well. Enloe (1980:67) claims that of the nearly 50 percent of Soviet citizens who are non-Russian, 62 percent cannot speak that language. Although Bromley has recently stated that "At least four fifths of the Soviet population have a free command of Russian" (1983:27), some Russian scholars will admit privately that the higher bureaucratic echelons, including the military, are still dominated by native Russian speakers and that a linguistic deficiency, with its associated educational disadvantages, is a major factor in this situation.

In the United States, Blacks, Hispanics, and Amerindians are identified as the major disadvantaged, or minority groups by observers both at home and abroad. As in the USSR, race, language, and religion are important markers, yet sociologists have shown our dominant White Anglo-Saxon Protestant ("WASP") category to be a melting pot of Catholic as well as Protestant Christians and Caucasians from all over Europe (Peach, 1980). Furthermore, by economic and political criteria, as well as by skin color, the American Jewish population now shares considerable power with the so-called Wasps, even though they remain ethnically distinguishable and still suffer prejudice in some quarters. Many white Hispanics, on the other hand, are denied majority status.

It might be argued that the United States has no configuration of ethnic groups comparable to that in the USSR since there were no native American states within what are now our borders at the time of the European settlement. The Amerindians, soon overwhelmed by massive and ongoing immigration, have still not been completely assimilated. Their situation seems not unlike that of some Soviet Asiatics in many respects. Furthermore, unlike Blacks and Hispanics, they have not yet been able to have much political impact, even in local areas—partly because of treaties assigning them to self-governing reservations.

The increasingly salient Asian ethnic component in our midst has commanded somewhat less recognition, though many social scientists have turned their attention to this situation recently. In Hawaii, of course, Asians have long formed a majority, though only recently has that been coupled with political power.

Some strategists think that it would provide an advantage to the attackers if missiles could be deployed so as to spare the minorities at the expense of the dominant group.[3] First, in the event of such an attack, it is thought that the minorities would seize the opportunity to rebel against their "oppressors," thus facilitating the latter's eventual defeat. Second, it is hoped that the fear of the loss of power, plus the unpleasant recognition that current leaders and their kind will be the first to die, will bring about changes in foreign policy such that the initial attack can be avoided altogether. But failing the above, the possibility of retaliation in kind is presumed a deterrent to either side ever using the technique offensively. Since both the United States and USSR continually characterize themselves as nonaggressors, this leads to the labeling of ethnic targeting as a "defense" strategy. Obviously, it can also be offensive.[4]

In both the United States and the Soviet Union, ethnic groups are not consistently located in identifiable areas. In the United States, depending on their economic fortunes, individuals can often move to a residential area not linked with their ethnicity. And the ethnic character of some urban areas has changed completely as one ethnic immigrant group has been replaced by another. In the Soviet Union there has been a deliberate attempt to settle White Russians in the interior, and to bring members of ethnic minorities into the mainstream of the Soviet system through military and other institutions.

The possibility of internal rebellion in either the United States or the USSR is unlikely, although for different reasons. The once-autonomous Soviet states might wish for greater self-determination than they now have, but there is no reason to believe that their citizens would be prepared to offer a united front in oppostion to the central system. Even though many Soviet ethnic groups are still territorially and linguistically distinctive, it is naive to believe that they have no loyalty to the Soviet Union. Two generations have now been raised under socialism. Besides, lacking any cross-ethnic links to each other, the chances of their uniting in opposition to *any* outside threat is miniscule.

Nearly two and a half centuries of institutionalized slavery in the United States have left marks unknown anywhere else in the modern world. Although bits and pieces of African culture survived and have been recast into something we now call "black culture," the basic world view of American Blacks is modern Euro-American, and they share more with Wasps than with Yoruba or Swazi. Although many of them hate "Whitey," they are not seeking violent overthrow of the government, nor are they any longer territorially or residentially segregated. Their political power at the local level is now apparent in many of our major cities.

The situation is still different for Hispanics in New Mexico, Arizona, Colorado and California, whose territory was seized from Mexico and annexed to the United States in 1846. Continuing in-migration from Mexico, in addition to a generally benign neglect on the part of the U.S. government, has made this area distinctively Hispanic in its cultural, linguistic, and even racial characteristics (Gonzalez, 1969). However, the Spanish-speaking population is now beginning to achieve the kind of political and economic clout associated with the more established and well-integrated ethnic groups in this country. Like the Blacks and the various Europeans who came here before 1924, they have won this through the institutions of the larger nation in which they are now inextricably embedded. Furthermore, they have found it expedient to join forces for some purposes with more recently arrived Spanish-speaking or Latin-derived groups such as Puerto Ricans and Cubans. The Hispanic Caucus in Washington, new in 1978, becomes more numerous and more visible each year.[5] Though their union may have been furthered by the prejudices they felt and by discrimination against them, the fact remains that many Hispanic leaders today express fairly conservative political views. It is difficult to conceive of any revolutionary movement deriving from this group, even were they to unite with the increasing numbers of undocumented Spanish- speakers who daily arrive in this country.

Members of many ethnic groups in the United States have arrived here voluntarily over the years as refugees from political and religious persecution. Rather than mount revolutions in their own countries, they sought to improve their condition through migration. Better economic opportunities in the United States were also important and continue to attract new migrants. Though often discriminated against, both as ethnic groups and as individuals, these migrants have often clung to their ethnicity as a source of comfort, mutual aid, and in some cases, political advancement. Again, they have done this by assimilating to the basic institutions of their adopted country (see Price, 1963 for a comparable interpretation of data from Australia).

Throughout the United States one finds thousands of voluntary associations built upon ethnicity. In the earliest period of immigration of an ethnic group, these function to preserve both the cultural patterns of the homeland and the ethnic identity of their members. They are not particularly political in nature, though they may take considerable interest in the politics of the country they left behind. As individuals become more successful in mainstream socioeconomic pursuits, they tend to drop out of these ethnic clubs, retain their membership in name only, or use the club for recreational rather than political purposes.

Ethnic residential communities function in the same way, whether they are small towns in North Dakota or neighborhoods in the Bronx. Many people move out when they "move up." Although they may retain a sense of nostalgia for the old ways, and affection for kin and old friends, they effectively remove themselves from the ethnic *group*. Whether they remain recognizable to others as members of the ethnic *category* depends upon the extent to which they have adopted mainstream habits of speech, dress, diet, and so on. Many are able to live in both worlds, and their ethnicity then becomes situationally determined. They can turn it on or off at will and in accordance with need.

I suggest that there is a kind of melting pot in the United States, even though it has not been fashionable, even among social scientists, to admit it. The common substratum is based upon consumerism; analyses of lifestyles, or consumption patterns, show that these crosscut racial, ethnic, and class lines (Sobel, 1981). Indeed, the promotion of ethnic salience and identification, which has become an ideological imperative since World War I (Willis, 1975:318), may owe its success to the existence of this countering force. Though Willis believes war has been the primary factor in the renewed American emphasis on nationalism and/or ethnicity, my sense is that an equally strong and sustaining impetus has been the Cold War need to counter Marxist assimilationist rhetoric. Furthermore, as ethnic minorities in the United States and elsewhere became more aware of and proficient in using their power, ethnic variability became more acceptable and increasingly apparent. Ethnic parades, fairs, and exhibits are now commonplace; a primary effect, of course, is to encourage further consumption of U.S. manufactured goods, many of which are produced especially for these occasions.

One might say we are trying to have our cake and eat it too, for though official and unofficial policy encourages ethnic identification, and stimulates competition in the market and in the political arena, at the same time we insist on identical treatment toward all in social, economic and political affairs and frown on aggressive behavior between groups or members of groups. Not surprisingly, examples of racial and ethnic conflict in the United States abound, though there is no way to document whether these have increased over the past fifty years. Even if they have, it is better than leaving the discrimination and prejudice underground and unchallenged. Indeed, some of the major changes in the status of minorities in this country might not have been possible without our having fostered greater respect for ethnic differences.

Various elements of minority cultures have even been adopted into the linguistic codes and lifestyles of our majority population—assisted, no doubt, by the advertising industry. The fact that the USSR has not been able to assimilate its minorities may, ironically, be related to its past inability to tolerate, much less respect, ethnic differences, as well as to the absence of a competitive market economy.

But the promotion of ethnicity may also be carried too far. During the past half century ethnic conflict has broken out in all, or nearly all, of the complex societies in the world. In addition to the United States, the following are well-known examples: Northern Ireland, Kenya, Ethiopia, Guyana, Brazil, The Netherlands, Australia—the list goes on and on. So far these conflicts have been fairly localized, and have reflected struggles for resources which have been distributed unfairly. The thought that ethnic conflict might escalate to larger-scale, even global, arenas should give all of us pause. Although, as I have indicated, I do not believe ethnic targeting would work in either the United States or the Soviet Union, the thought alone is, or should be, frightening. Nations, if we are to have them at all, must try to maintain the peace, both at home and vis-à-vis foreign powers, so that their citizens and residents may pursue lives in accordance with an overall (or underlying) set of philosophical tenets about "the good life". Situational ethnicity, as well as shared ethnicity, is compatible with the health of nations as so defined. So too may be a certain degree of ethnic salience and group identification for those individuals who find themselves either permanently or temporarily unable to pursue the kind of life they have come to appreciate and expect as a benefit of living in their particular nation.

But in the final analysis, too much emphasis on ethnicity may be a foolish and/or dangerous thing. The symbols of ethnic difference may become reified so that people react to others in continuing stereotypic ways. Social scientists have spilled much ink trying to educate the public about stereotypes, but the fact is that there are contradictory values in American life. One set tells us that anyone can achieve any kind of life here, but if people diverge too far from the patterns portrayed in the media, discrimination rears its ugly head and they are unable to sustain their alternate styles.

Thus, there is a number of forces in United States culture which make it difficult for ethnicity to survive after a certain level of affluence has been reached. Put another way, Williams (1981:137) has suggested, "The American way does violence to the poor masses." Some of the symbols used in scholarly and public rhetoric describing Black and Hispanic ethnicity are actually characteristic only of the poorer classes, while others are found only among the most affluent, and then merely as nostalgic reminders of their roots. Middle-class Blacks, for example, take little pride in being able to speak Black English, even though we have had programs designed to study, analyze, teach, and preserve it. It could be argued that it is the American "way" to obfuscate the issues by emphasizing ethnicity in order to divert attention from socioeconomic class distinctions. People are not so much "poor" as they are "ethnic."

Introducing ethnicity into the international arena as a means of dealing with nation-states we call our enemies, is a peculiarly twentieth-century American solution, which has derived from and reflects our own experience. As we know, domestic ethnic allegiances can be whipped up into frenzied protests, many of which become violent. Yet most of the members of these same ethnic minorities become docile cannon fodder against our external enemies. Perhaps it is due to the hope that eventually, as individuals, they may realize one of the accepted lifestyles which are tantalizingly held before them on television and elsewhere. The notion of "freedom" is powerful. Even the most poverty-stricken Blacks of whom Williams (1981) writes fiercely protected their right to behave as they wished—to work or not work. Such groups are not likely to defect to a communist and foreign government; it is the more educated and affluent who sometimes show such sympathies.

When will we reach the point where we can again, without embarrassment, treat ethnicity as the frosting on the cake, rather than the substance itself? First, we must face up to the fact that besides covering up poverty, ethnicity is often a euphemism for racism. People who look different have a harder time assimilating, regardless of how thoroughly they adopt the dominant culture. Second, we must recognize that our system has not succeeded yet in eradicating the enormous range of affluence which plagues most capitalist countries. As we move into an era of increased immigration, we must not let the myth of ethnicity, comforting though it may be for all concerned, divert us from the problems of poverty and inequality.

When ethnicity is elevated to the status of a causative factor in warfare, or as a means of dividing and conquering another nation, it should be examined very carefully, and steps should be taken to deemphasize the differences attributed to "heritage" and "custom". Anthropologists have appropriately called attention to these factors over the past 100 years, but now it may be time for us to put them back in their rightful place, and to help policymakers understand that since ethnicity is a creation of humankind, it can be used for both good and evil. World peace demands both a tolerance of different ways, as well as a recognition that the emerging global system contains imperatives, as well as rewards, for cooperation among peoples everywhere.

Notes

1. Examples are legion. These are intended only to introduce the subject. It might be argued that ethnicity is always somehow involved in warfare.
2. Many of these issues are illustrated by a recent incident in Louisiana, in which a middle-aged woman who had considered herself and her parents "White" all her life was declared to be "Black" following a genealogical analysis showing one of her great great grandparents was "Black". The example shows that phenotype alone is not enough, and that definitions of "Black" in the U.S. have meant different things at different times.
3. The question of whether such precision is possible with new missiles is a technical matter outside my competence. For purposes of this paper I must assume that it is, since the articles to which I am responding have all been based upon that conclusion.
4. What distinguishes the present case from many others is the targeting of the dominant ethnic group for annihilation. Haiti's rebellion in the late eighteenth century, triggered by the French Revolution and by the intolerable life of the slaves is one of the few success stories of this kind.
5. Barnett (1977), in reference to the Congressional Black Caucus, warns that much of what appears to be political strength and influence is only window-dressing, and hides a continuing second-class status. Much of what she says is also true for Hispanics. Still, no minority ethnic group has ever yet had real power at national levels in the United States.

References

Albert, Bernard S. 1976. "Constructive Counterpower." *Orbis* 19(2):362.

Alexander, Richard D. 1979. "Evolution and Culture." In *Evolutionary Biology and Human Social Behavior: An Anthropological Perspective*, edited by Napoleon A. Chagnon and Irons, William, pp. 59–78. North Scituate, Mass.: Duxbury Press.

Ardrey, R. 1966. *The Territorial Imperative*. New York: Atheneum.

Armstrong, John A. 1976. "Societal Manipulation in a Multiethnic Polity." *World Politics* 28(3):440–49.

Barth, Fredrik, ed. 1969. *Ethnic Groups and Boundaries*. Boston, Mass.: Little, Brown.

Barnett, Marguerite Ross. 1977. "The Congressional Black Caucus: Symbol, Myth and Reality." *The Black Scholar* 8(4):17–26.

Bennett, John W., ed. 1975. *The New Ethnicity*. St. Paul, Minn.: West.

Bertsch, Gary K. 1982. *Power and Policy in Communist Systems*. New York: J. Wiley & Sons.
Bidney, David. 1953. "The Concept of Value in Modern Anthropology." In *Anthropology Today*, edited by A.L. Kroeber. Chicago, Ill.: University of Chicago Press.
Boas, Franz. 1969. *Race and Democratic Society*. New York: Biblo and Tannen.
Bromley, Yulian V. 1983. "Ethnographic Studies of Contemporary Soviet Life." In *Studies in Ethnography and Anthropology*, edited by L. E. Kubbel, et al., pp. 22–28. Moscow: USSR Academy of Sciences.
Burkcy, Richard M. 1978. *Ethnic and Racial Groups: The Dynamics of Dominance*. Menlo Park, Colo.: Cummings.
Burt, Richard. 1980. "New Nuclear Strategy: An Inevitable Shift." *New York Times*, 7 August.
Chagnon, Napoleon A. and William Irons, eds. 1979. *Evolutionary Biology and Human Social Behavior: An Anthropological Perspective*. North Scituate, Mass.: Duxbury Pess.
Cohen, Abner. 1974. *Two-Dimensional Man*. Berkeley, Cal.: University of California Press.
Cohen, Ronald. 1978. "Ethnicity: Problem and Focus in Anthropology." *Annual Review of Anthropology* 7:379–404.
Cross, Malcolm. 1978. "Colonialism and Ethnicity: A Theory and Comparative Case Study." *Ethnic and Racial Studies* 1(1):37–59.
Durham, William H. 1979. "Toward a Coevolutionary Theory of Human Biology and Culture." In *Evolutionary Biology and Human Social Behavior: An Anthropological Approach*, edited by Napoleon A. Chagnon and William Irons, pp. 59–78. North Scituate, Mass.: Duxbury Press.
Dreyer, June Teufel. 1976. *China's Forty Millions*. Cambridge, Mass.: Harvard University Press.
Enloe, Cynthia H. 1980. *Ethnic Soldiers*. Athens, Ga.: University of Georgia Press.
Etzioni, Amitai. 1959. "The Ghetto: A Re-evaluation." *Social Forces* 39:255–62.
Foster, Richard B. 1978. *The Soviet Concept for National Entity Survival*. Arlington, Va: SRI International.
Fox, Robin. 1979. "Kinship Categories as Natural Categories." In *Evolutionary Biology and Human Social Behavior: An Anthropological Perspective*, edited by Napoleon A. Chagnon and William Irons, pp. 132–44. North Scituate, Mass.: Duxbury Press.
Furnivall, J. S. 1948. *Colonial Policy and Practice*. London: Cambridge University Press.
Glazer, Nathan, and Moynihan, Daniel P., eds. 1975. *Ethnicity: Theory and Experience*. Cambridge, Mass.: Harvard University Press.
Gonzalez, Nancie L. 1969. *A Heritage of Pride: The Spanish-Americans of New Mexico*. Albuquerque, N.M.: University of New Mexico Press.
———. 1983. "New Evidence on the Origin of the Garifuna." *New West Indian Guide*.
Gulliver, P. H., ed. 1969. *Tradition and Transition in East Africa*. London: Routledge & Kegan Paul.
Haaland, Gunnar. 1969. "Economic Determinants in Ethnic Processes." In *Ethnic Groups and Boundaries*, edited by Fredrik Barth, pp. 58–73. Boston: Little Brown.
Hohenthal, W. D., and McCorkle, Thomas. 1955. "The Problem of Aboriginal Persistence." *Southwestern Journal of Anthropology* 11(4):288–300.

Irons, William. 1979. "Natural Selection, Adaptation, and Human Social Behavior." In *Evolutionary Biology and Human Social Behavior: An Anthropological Perspective*, edited by Napoleon A. Chagnon and William Irons, pp. 4–38. North Scituate, Mass.: Duxbury Press.

Kozlov, Victor I. 1980. "The Classification of Ethnic Communities: The Present Position in the Soviet Debate." *Ethnic and Racial Studies* 3(2):123–39.

Kubbel, L.E., Sedlovskaya, A.N., and Tishkov, V.A., eds. 1983. *Studies in Ethnography and Anthropology. Papers Presented by Soviet Participants at the XI International Congress of Anthropological and Ethnological Sciences. Vancouver*. Moscow: USSR Academy of Sciences.

Lanternari, Vittorio. 1980. "Ethnocentrism and Ideology." *Ethnic and Racial Studies* 3(1):52–65.

Mayer, Philip. 1961. *Townsmen or Tribesmen*. Oxford: Oxford University Press.

Mitchell, J. C. 1956. *The Kaleia Dance*. Manchester, G.B.: Manchester University Press. Rhodes-Livingston Paper 27.

Peach, Ceri. 1980. "Which Triple Melting Pot? A Reexamination of Ethnic Intermarriage in New Hampshire, 1900-1950." *Ethnic and Racial Studies* 3(1):1–16.

Price, Charles A. 1963. *Southern Europeans in Australia*. Melbourne, Australia: Oxford University Press.

Quester, George H. 1982. "Ethnic Targeting: A Bad Idea Whose Time Has Come." *Journal of Strategic Studies* 5:228–35.

Reynolds, Vernon. 1980. "Sociobiology and the Ideas of Primordial Discrimination." *Ethnic and Racial Studies* 3(3):303–15.

Smith, M. G. 1965. *The Plural Society in the British West Indies*. Berkeley, Cal.: University of California Press.

Sobel, Michael E. 1981. *Lifestyle and Social Structure*. New York: Academic Press.

Suhrke Astri, and Noble, Lela Garner, eds. 1977. *Ethnic Conflict in International Relations*. New York: Praeger.

Sumner, W. G. 1906. *Folkways*. New York: Ginn.

Szymanski, Albert. 1976. "Racial Discrimination and White Gain." *American Sociological Review* 41(3):403–14.

Taylor, Douglas M. 1951. *The Black Caribs of British Honduras*. New York: Viking Press.

Tiger, Lionel and Fox, Robin. 1971. *The Imperial Animal*. New York: Holt, Rinehart and Winston.

van den Berghe, Pierre. 1974. "Bringing the Beasts Back In: Toward a Biosocial Theory of Aggression." *American Sociological Review*, 39:777–88.

Wagley, Charles and Harris, Marvin. 1958. *Minorities in the New World*. New York: Columbia University Press.

Wiarda, Howard. 1981. "The Ethnocentrism of the Social Science Implications for Research and Policy." *Review of Politics*, 43:163–97.

Wiens, John A. 1983. "Competition or Peaceful Coexistence?" *Natural History* 92(3):30–35.

Williams, Melvin D. 1981. *On the Street Where I Lived*. New York: Holt, Rinehart and Winston.

Willis, William S. 1975. "Franz Boas and the Study of Black Folklore." In *The New Ethnicity*, edited by John W. Bennett, pp. 307–34. St. Paul, Minn.: West.

Yancey, W.L.; Ericksen, E.P.; and Juliani, R.N. 1976. "Emergent Ethnicity: A Review and Reformulation." *American Sociological Review* 41:391–403.

Zwick, Peter. 1979. "Ethnoregional Socio-economic Fragmentation and Soviet Budgetary Policy." *Soviet Studies* 31:380–400.

11

Conflict in the Horn of Africa

Frederick C. Gamst

Ethiopia stands at the center of what is perhaps the most intractable and enduring political maelstrom in modern Africa.
—Edmond Keller

In this paper, I examine the historical roots of the elements that together lead to war in the Horn of Africa, focusing mainly on Ethiopia.[1] War[2] has long been ubiquitous in the Horn, owing largely to conflict over resources. Further, such war has complex roots often caught up in the strategies of global geopolitics. Three themes are discussed in this paper: the warlike nature of the state, how regional war in the Horn is often exacerbated by external intervention, and the warring response of local groups to attempts to suppress their autonomy. The focal point for this discussion is the areal political consequences of the introduction and use of firearms. This introduction critically upset the political equilibrium between centripetal and centrifugal forces in favor of state centralists and against in-group factionalists and ethnic-group separatists.

Historically, *conflict* has been endemic among and within states and near-states in the Horn, and *war* has been a customary way of regulating intra- and intersocietal relations. Imperialistic interventions from outside the Horn by technologically advanced states have usually exacerbated the intensity of war. This has been especially so since 1500 because those states introduced, then continued to supply firearms and other armaments. Since about 1850 this outside intervention has had two important effects. Through the use of these ever more efficient armaments, the centralist state of Abyssinia/Ethiopia has been able to control its internal factionalism and to expand effectively its traditional attempts to control other regional peoples. The present separatist wars raging in the Horn can be traced to the Ethiopian attempt during the past century to control the region. The human and economic costs of these wars are escalated by the importing of increasingly more deadly arms. These have provided separatists of conquered ethnic groups and factionalists from both conquering and subjugated ethnic groups with the means to wage effective war against the centralist Ethiopian government.

The State and War in the Horn

In his widely known introduction to Ethiopia, Edward Ullendorff (1973:200) says: "Military prowess in Ethiopia does not date from the days of Adwa but has been a characteristic feature since ancient times." And Richard Pankhurst (1961:178) similarly concludes: "Frequent warfare remained the curse of the country throughout the greater part of the period covered by this study" (200 B.C. to A.D. 1800). War has been continuous in the Horn since 1800 (Pankhurst, 1968a), and although not the only present conflagration in the Horn, the Eritrean war has been the longest and most intense in modern African history (Davidson et al., 1980).[3]

From around A.D. 900 to 1974, Abyssinia/Ethiopia was a form of feudal, hence military, state, structurally well adapted for internal war between factions.[4] Controlled by Abyssinians (Amhara, Tigrean, and Agew), Abyssinia/Ethiopia has been a classic imperialistic state, periodically expanding and contracting its territorial control. Imperialistic conquest reached a peak from 1855 to 1900. In this period, the ancient core state of Abyssinia doubled its size by force of imported firearms, thereby becoming the present state of Ethiopia. With a central dominating people (Amhara-Tigrean) controlling peripheral dominated peoples (various others) the Ethiopian empire was similar to those of Austria-Hungary, Russia, Persia, and Ottoman Turkey.

From 1900 to 1974, feudal Ethiopia developed a more bureaucratic government and a more modern economy, as it became part of the world capitalist market. Since the 1974-75 revolution against the old monarchical feudal order, a ruling *Derg* ("committee") emerged and it remains in control of Ethiopia's new military- revolutionary order, striving toward a Marxist-Leninist socialism. This quest occurs while the *Derg* holds under strong Amhara military restraint an ethnically fragmenting, polynational state.

Premodern Period of Outside Contact in the Horn, 1500–1855

Just before 1500 the Portuguese contacted the legendary Prester John of the Indies (that is, the Christian King of Kings, or Emperor, of Abyssinia; Beckingham and Huntingford, 1961). The few guns acquired immediately after 1500 were exotic new artifacts to the Abyssinians. In the 1520s and 1530s, Amed Gran, a strong leader of the Islamicized Somalis, invaded the Ethiopian highlands with a small army, at first unsuccessfully. In 1529, using firearms supplied by Muslim neighbors, he succeeded in defeating a far larger Abyssinian army (Basset, 1897–1909, Pankhurst, 1967). In 1541, Cristovao da Gama arrived in devastated Abyssinia with 450 Portuguese musketeers, 700 muskets, and eight cannon. With these weapons in 1543, the Portuguese and Abyssinians defeated Gran and restored the government of the core state of Abyssinia. In 1557, the Ottoman Turks occupied the island port of Massawa on the Eritrean coast to cut off the Abyssinian supply of guns. The Turks were turned back in their later attempts to expand into what is now Eritrea. This was the first of many foreign attempts to sever Eritrea from Abyssinia, all of which failed until the Italians succeeded in 1890.

The native pastoral Somali of the Horn and the alien Turks did not establish permanent presence in the Ethiopian highlands. However, the Oromo expansion from the south in the sixteenth century made use of their age-graded organization in establishing strong military formations and order in combat (Legesse, 1973). Fighting between Amhara and Oromo persisted in north and central Ethiopian highlands. Toward the end of this period of Oromo expansion, the Amhara-Tigreans used European firearms to stop these pastoralists, some of whom were then becoming assimilated into Amhara culture. In fighting Turks, Arabs, Somalis, Muslim Oromo, Beja, Afar, and other Islamic peoples, the Orthodox Christian Amhara-Tigrean-Agew had been waging crusades against the *jihads* of the Islamic peoples. To this day the Christians of the highlands feel and react militarily as if surrounded by a lowland "continent" of Islamic antagonists.

During the Era of the Princes of 1769 to 1855, Abyssinia barely existed as a unitary state, and the emperor was almost powerless. State authority had dissolved, and a number of autonomous principalities existed in constant warfare. Increasingly, those Oromo who were partially Amharized played a greater role in Abyssinian government (Abir, 1968). The many bellicose states and chiefdoms to the south of feudal Abyssinia continued their endemic wars.

Early Amhara-Tigrean Reactions to Outside Intervention, 1855–1889

The Era of the Princes was brought to an end when a brigand soldier fought his way against rival factions onto the Abyssinian throne (Rubenson, 1966). Crowned as Tewodros, the new emperor fought constant battles and inflicted harsh repressions to remain King of Kings. He also had the resources to reestablish firm Abyssinian control over the northernmost Oromo. He took the throne name of Tewodros because of an old millenarian legend about how an emperor with this name would someday successfully crusade against neighboring Muslim peoples.

The French development of the Suez Canal between 1856 and 1869 allowed European states more closely to exert economic and political control over the resources of the Indo-Pacific basin. Accordingly, the canal was the communications pivot in European domination of most of the eastern hemisphere (Farnie, 1969). European and Egyptian relations with the Horn took on new significance as the region was transformed from a global backwater to the strategic focal point of world trade and naval movement.

During the mid 1860s, Tewodros had taken hostage a few Britons and other Europeans because Britain had sided with Muslim Egypt and Turkey rather than with Christian Abyssinia. (Owing to a shortage of American cotton during the United States Civil War, English mills realized their critical dependence upon the great cotton crops of Egypt.) Then, in 1867-68, a British expeditionary force of 12,000 troops successfully invaded Abyssinia and easily defeated Tewodros, who was killed or killed himself (Rassam, 1869; Pankhurst, 1968a:11–16).

The ease of the British conquest emboldened the Egyptians. In 1868 Egypt expanded south along the Horn's Red Sea coast through Somali territory, then west into central Eritrea. Generally, the European powers gave Egypt free rein in the Horn. Egypt had earlier attempted to invade Abyssinia a number of times. They would soon be stopped by the weapons supplied to the Tigreans by the British.

In their campaign against Tewodros, the British had been given safe passage through the Tigray region by its ruler, *Ras* Kassa, in return both for their promise to leave the country after punishing the emperor and for 700 rifles and a number of cannon (Pankhurst, 1968a:16). With these weapons, Kassa defeated all rival claimants to the throne and consolidated his rule as Emperor Yohannes IV (1872–1889). In what was the first of his two popular crusades against Islam (1875–76), Yohannes also destroyed three of four invading Egyptian armies and captured many modern breech-loading rifles. Using these weapons, Yohannes further strengthened what was becoming the expanding Ethiopian state, including its hold over factious Amhara-Tigreans and over subject peoples. In 1882, Britain took direct military control of Egypt, and in 1885, at the Treaty of Berlin, the European powers divided the African continent but could not, at first, agree upon who would control Ethiopia. The core state of Ethiopia was made powerful and united because of European arms, but the European military noose was tightening around it. However, in 1887 Yohannes turned back an Italian incursion at Dogali.

In their Islamic revitalization movement of the 1880s, led by the Mahdi,[5] Muhammad Ahmad, Sudanese Mahdists defeated Egypto-British forces occupying Sudan, killed General Gordon, and then invaded Ethiopia. The Mahdists at times linked up with the Oromo, then being subjugated by the

Shewan Amhara King Menelik, a rival of Yohannes. Receiving no military support from Menelik, in his second crusade, at Metemma in 1889, Yohannes defeated the Mahdists and was killed in his victory. Menelik then ascended the Ethiopian throne and became King of Kings. To gain the throne, Menelik "had to increase his revenue for the purchase of expensive modern weapons" (Marcus, 1975:57).

Britain was maneuvering to diminish French control over the Suez Canal and greater northeastern Africa and to quell local uprisings against British colonial rule. Thus Yohannes was a temporary British ally against the Sudan's Mahdists. But Britain did not honor its treaty arrangements with the Ethiopians and instead allowed Italy to expand to control, by 1890, all of Eritrea. Eritrea's eastern peoples were extensions of those found in now landlocked Ethiopia. Its western peoples were Beja, stretching northward through Sudan into Egypt.

Later Amhara-Tigrean Reactions to Outside Intervention, 1889–1900

Menelik, emperor from 1889 to 1913, was greatly concerned with the modernization, consolidation and expansion of the Ethiopian state, *and* importation of firearms (Marcus, 1975). The firearms had the most profound of political consequences. "The last decades of the nineteenth century . . . constituted a veritable fire-arms revolution in Ethiopia . . ." (Pankhurst, 1971:69). While still King of Shewa before 1889, Menelik received arms from Italy for use in fighting Yohannes, who blocked the Italians in Eritrea. He also received arms from France to check rival Britain's influence in the Horn (Pankhurst, 1968a:21). With these arms, at first as king and then while emperor, Menelik was able to double the size of the core state of Abyssinia, and formed present-day Ethiopia by conquering the states and chiefdoms to the south. Some of this region earlier had periodically been under Amhara-Tigrean control. In Menelik's reign, control of the import of arms passed from the Tigreans to the Amhara (Pankhurst, 1968b:128). Thus the Amhara began to dominate their ethnic partners, to the enduring frustration of the Tigreans.

As with the Christian zealots Tewodros and Yohannes before him, Menelik conducted forced conversions of non-Christians in Ethiopia in order to control them more effectively and, in turn, to forestall outside intervention. What was firmly controlled by the Amhara could not be taken easily by outsiders. Even small, militarily weak peoples in the Amhara heartland such as the Felasha, Qemant, and Weyto were more directly controlled, and the first two were forced to convert. Under Tewodros and Yohannes, Islamic beliefs were outlawed and Muslims were ipso facto rebels against the state. Many Oromo and others either nominally conformed to enforced Christianity or emigrated to areas beyond Amhara-Tigrean control (Marcus, 1975).

In an attempt to stabilize their domination of the region, the British encouraged their Italian allies to expand in the Horn. Despite defeat in 1887, by 1890 Italy controlled what is now Eritrea. At Adwa, in 1896, Menelik defeated the Italians with weapons the latter had originally supplied to counter the military prowess of Yohannes. In an earlier version of Dien Bien Phu, at Adwa the Italians had very heavy casualties. With Italy unable to conquer Ethiopia and Ethiopia unable to retake Eritrea, a military stalemate ensued. For another forty years, Italy did not attempt further conquest of Ethiopia. This guaranteed that Eritrea would develop more rapidly and in a differentiated fashion from Ethiopia proper and set the stage for the present war between Eritrean secessionists and Ethiopian centralists.

Some scholars have labeled as "colonialism" the southward expansion of the Amhara-Tigrean core state to encompass all of what is present-day Ethiopia (except for Eritrea—reacquired in 1952). The Amhara-Tigrean parallel to the post-1885 European scramble for Africa is usually viewed, correctly I think, as not existing apart from European interests in the Horn. Europe's introduction of the rifle and its military intervention in the Horn also had nonpolitical concomitants too numerous to recount. These ranged from the destruction of Weyto habitat and lifeway (Gamst, 1979), to the creation of new "indigenous" art patterns for the Felasha (Gamst and Baldia, 1980:136–37).

Many present Amhara and Tigreans are now totally acculturated from peoples of formerly different cultures conquered by Abyssinia in past centuries. The distinctive aspects of the late-nineteenth-century imperial conquests are their swiftness, absoluteness, and vastness (of territorial expanse). At times indirect rule was used by the Amhara-Tigrean conquerors (Natsoulas, 1981:5), and often they became feudal landholders. As a result of the southward Amhara-Tigrean expansion of the Ethiopian state from 1855 to 1899, the military elite of these two peoples exercised a superior claim to part of the production of the masses of conquered commoners, largely peasants (Gamst, 1974:3–19). This repressive feudal control of the southern peoples is a root of many present separatist movements. Even more than the road and railroad, the newly introduced telephone and telegraph were used to tie together militarily the new Ethiopian empire (Garretson, 1980).

The Egyptian domination of the Somali coasts and Harer highlands, begun in 1875, was short-lived. In 1887, Menelik took for Ethiopia the trading city of Harer and its environs and in the late 1890s, invaded the Ogaden steppe inhabited by Somali and Oromo pastoralists. Coastal

Somali territory was partitioned from north to south without negotiation with Somalis, by France, Britain, and Italy. Somali military reaction in the form of a *jihad* against the partition was led by the Mahdi, Muhammed Abdulla Hassan (Cassanelli, 1982:183–253).

Four British expeditions in the early 1900s could not defeat the Somali Mahdi, but in 1920 using RAF warplanes the British finally prevailed. Introduction of aerial ordnance decisively shifted the distribution of power in the Horn against native Amhara, Tigreans, Somalis, and Sudanese, and in favor of the Europeans.

A century of conflict between the British and French for control of northeastern Africa was ended in 1898 in favor of the British. At the Shilluk village of Fashoda, in southern Sudan, General Kitchner, fresh from his machine-gun victory over the Sudanese Mahdists, forced away a French detachment marching from West Africa (Michel, 1900). In any event, the strategic global dominance of British naval power probably necessitated French withdrawal from Fashoda. The British south-north axis of Africa, Cape to Cairo, was secured, and the French west- east axis, Dakar to Djibouti, was forever thwarted (Lesage, 1906:238–40, Marder, 1940:320–40). The Amhara-Tigreans could no longer depend upon France in the Horn and increasingly feared what Britain might allow its ally Italy to do.

Amhara Consolidation of Power, 1900–1952

In the face of growing German threats, better Franco-British relations developed by 1904. Hence, in 1906, a Tripartite treaty among Britain, Italy, and France gave these countries spheres of influence in Ethiopia. In World War I, the Central Powers of Turkey and Germany found an ally in Menelik's successor, Lij Iyasu, who believed Ethiopia would gain from a defeat of the Tripartite powers and a return to Turkish control of Egypt and Sudan. Lij Iyasu became pro-Islamic and turned Ethiopia from an enemy to an ally of the Somali Mahdists, supplying them in their war against the Tripartite states. Rebelling Amhara nobility, including the future Emperor Haile Selassie I, feared government control by Muslim Oromo through Lij Iyasu. Troops of the Amhara nobility defeated Lij Iyasu's forces in 1917 during a battle with modern arms that claimed some 32,000 Ethiopian military lives. Thus Amhara-Tigrean subordination under a Muslim Oromo control of Ethiopia was averted, and an interesting attempt at Ethio-Somali ouster from the Horn of the Tripartite states was aborted (Marcus, 1975:249–281).

In 1925, the future Haile Selassie, then regent *Ras* Tafari, successfully used the League of Nations to block Britain and its ally Italy from strengthening their spheres of influence in Ethiopia. However, it appears that

Chamberlain and Mussolini may have reached an accord for future Italian Fascist conquest of Ethiopia (Iadarola, 1979). Haile Selassie's early success at resolution of conflict through negotiation in the League may have led him to believe that for successful negotiation with a powerful state it was not necessary to be prepared to go to war. Limited amounts of European arms and military training of his troops helped Haile Selassie crush several Oromo and Amhara revolts in the late 1920s and allowed him to become emperor in 1930. During his reign, Belgian, and later Swedish, military training missions helped him consolidate an Ethiopia disunited after the rule of Menelik. In 1932, a revolt in support of Lij Iyasu was easily suppressed by the well-armed forces of Haile Selassie.

In 1935–36 Italy successfully invaded Ethiopia and crushed the Ethiopian armies in an undeclared war. The Italian victory resulted from the use of vastly superior quantities and qualities of ordnance, especially aerial. Britain, among others, then recognized Ethiopia as Italian territory. Italy built the beginnings of an infrastructure for development in Ethiopia (CTI, 1938; Quaranta, 1940), but exacted a high price for it in atrocities by the armed forces used to stifle armed Ethiopian resistance (Ethiopia, 1944). During World War II, Italy conquered British Somaliland and thrust into the Anglo-Egyptian Sudan. British-African, and regular and guerilla Ethiopian forces defeated the Italians in Italian East Africa during 1941. Collaboration with the Italians by Ethiopian factions had been widespread, and Haile Selassie punished collaborators with imprisonment. Also, he fought rebellious Oromo and others through 1943, sometimes with RAF support. Britain occupied Eritrea into 1952 and part of the Ogaden through 1955. Britain at first treated Ethiopia as conquered enemy (Italian) territory. But Haile Selassie reestablished the authority of his government and received British military aid until 1952.

Great Britain thought Eritrea should be partitioned between the Anglo-Egyptian Sudan and Ethiopia along ethnic lines. Ethiopia wanted the entire former Italian colony and this antagonized some elements of Eritrean society. A loose federation of Eritrea and Ethiopia under the emperor was negotiated by the United Nations in 1952. This solution was doomed to fail because of armed violence and other conflicts between pro-Ethiopian irredentist and pro-Eritrean separatist factions. In 1962, Ethiopia seized control of Eritrea by nonmilitary means. The British exit from Eritrea in 1952 was part of its 1950s military withdrawal from east of Suez. Britain's decline as a world power and as an intervener in the Horn left a military vacuum in the region (Weeks, 1979:49).

The Horn as a Pivot of Global Politics, 1953–1983

The Horn of Africa, despite a temporary closing of the Suez Canal, remained strategically important to the Western bloc, the Soviet bloc, and the Arab world because of its closeness to Middle Eastern petroleum areas, Indian Ocean trade routes, and the Red Sea maritime corridor (Chaliand, 1978; Novik, 1978). From 1952 to 1977 the United States spent about $500 million to arm Ethiopia. Hence, the United States provided support for the suppressions of Haile Selassie. United States military aid to Ethiopia increased after pro-Western Somalia, with its Italo-British background, was forced to turn to the USSR for arms in its conflict with Ethiopia over the Ogaden Somali territory. Ethiopia also became allied with the United States client, Israel. While serving its own goals by furnishing military aid to Ethiopia, Israel helped soothe the ancient Amhara-Tigrean fear of Arab power. For example, Israel and Ethiopia cooperated in destabilizing Islamic Sudan by sending arms to the southern Sudanese rebels who were combating the northern Sudanese Arabs.

After breaking ties with the United States and Israel in 1978, Ethiopia began to receive Soviet military aid. Accordingly, the USSR is the latest supporter of the Ethiopian central government in its foreign and domestic wars. This support, in the amount of $1.5 to $2 billion in military aid, is legally correct in that the USSR now supports Ethiopia in its suppression of an internal war in Eritrea and its preservation of its international border against Somali attack. Soviet ordnance and military advisors, along with Cuban troops, helped Ethiopia win the Ogaden war against the Somalis in 1978, and turned near defeat in Eritrea in 1979 into partial victory (Halliday and Molyneux, 1981:211–67).

In 1974–75, the Ethiopian monarchical government—still partially feudal in its organization—was toppled by a creeping revolution. Among the elements contributing to the progressive spread of a revolutionary new order were: extreme poverty of a country with little in the way of a developmental infrastructure, conflict between feudal aristocracy and new bureaucrats (Hess, 1970), political and ethnic fragmentation of the state (which helped maintain the feudal prerogative of exploitation in the southland), tensions from the developing capitalism found in a small part of the overall economy, shocks of a devastating famine, and rise in world oil prices.

Especially important in the revolution was the dissatisfaction of officers and enlisted men of the Ethiopian armed forces, which contained most men in the country with a high school education. There was discontent over inadequate personal salaries and living conditions, and over lack of general societal reform. In June 1974 a committee of radical junior military officers was formed. This *Derg* became the nucleus of growing political power in the creeping coup. Haile Selassie was eventually arrested by the *Derg* and a Provisional Military Administrative Council (PMAC) now controlled the government. The central government of Ethiopia had changed from a monarchical-feudal *military* form to one without monarchist-feudal aspects. By the end of 1974, key leaders of the old regime had been executed without trial and the *Derg*/PMAC was voicing and developing a socialistic and nationalistic policy. A national, socialist, military order was in place, but not yet definitely in control. Other revolutionary factions of social upheaval such as students, teachers, blue-collar workers, and government employees were over the next few years firmly suppressed.

With the declining importance of the United States communications base at Kagnew, Eritrea, and with Ethiopia becoming more of a liability than a military asset, the United States could afford to support Somalia politically. In 1977 the United States sought improved relations with Somalia in conjunction with United States construction of its new chain of Indian Ocean bases. These bases in Somalia, Kenya, Oman, and Diego Garcia are strategically important and secure—a luxury not available in Ethiopia.

Recent Wars of Ethnic Self-Determination in the Horn

Without a stake in a vigorous national economy and without a pluralistic participation in government, many of the subjugated peoples in Ethiopia were ready for a destruction of the old order. Most of these peoples have traditions of war for autonomy, or for sovereignty from Amhara-Tigreans. The 1974 fall of the Ethiopian monarchy was perceived by most Ethiopian peoples as a signal of the end of Amhara-Tigrean military domination and as a time to fight for traditional separatist goals. Various interpretations of this signal ranged from a demand for greater ethnic participation in government, to ethnic autonomy, to ethnic sovereignty. For Eritreans and Somalis, this last option was already being sought by war, and other ethnic groups would again seek their goals of self- determination by armed force. After all, arms were plentiful in the Horn and more could be acquired from outside powers. As Halliday and Molyneux (1981:159) explain, Ethiopia's "post-revolutionary history has been marked by extremes of bloodshed that have cost many lives, destroyed areas of the country, stored up new resentments. . . ."

The colonial boundaries fixed by Europeans for all African states, including those allowed for Ethiopia, are held sacrosanct by nearly all of Africa, the United Nations, the Organization of African Unity, the United States, and the USSR. Therefore, Eritrea's efforts at independence and Somalia's demands for the Somali-inhabited territories of the Ethiopian Ogaden, Kenyan Northern Frontier District, and eastern Jubuti are not received with the anticolonial fervor and military support given by Africans to former independence movements and uprisings (cf., Matties, 1977:413–15).

Somali fighting with the Amhara-Tigreans is actually older than the Eritrean war and goes back at least to Amed Gran's combat with Ethiopian forces. The difference today is that the balance is tipped against the Somalis in favor of the Amhara-Tigreans by the Soviets' supply of modern armaments. The Somali movement differs from all others in Ethiopia in that it advocates a Greater Somalia which would result from the expropriation of parts of Ethiopia and Kenya (Hoskyns, 1969). The idea of Greater Somalia was once endorsed by some British leaders, but now has little support outside of hardline Arab states.

With the revolution in Ethiopia, the Somalis perceived the new *Derg* as militarily weaker than the old monarchy. So plans underway for negotiating the Ogaden dispute were abandoned by the Somali state, and war was begun. The Western Somali Liberation Front (WSLF) fighting in Ogaden, but supplied from Somalia, was joined by Somalia in what became an invasion of Ethiopia by another state. Thus, highland Christian Ethiopians were compelled to unite in a crusade against the latest in a long history of onslaughts from the Muslim lowlands. After considerable initial success, both the WSLF and the Somali army were decisively defeated in their attacks in and beyond the Ogaden during 1977–78. The WSLF wants separation of Ogaden Somalis from Ethiopia, but it is now cool on union with Somalia and its increasingly despotic regime, maintained in power with the help of American arms.

The military government in Somalia uses the costly Ogaden liberation issue to help quell internal conflict between traditional Somali groupings (Halliday and Molyneux, 1981:203). By choosing war over negotiation, "the Somali regime brought catastrophe upon its fellow Somalis in Ethiopia and laid enormous additional burdens upon its own impoverished people as a result of the manner in which it purported to champion the . . . legitimate rights of the Ogaden Somalis" (Halliday and Molyneux, 1981:204).

Although not as long standing as the Somali dispute, the Eritrean conflict erupted into a major war in the mid 1960s. The Eritrean Liberation Front (ELF) began open combat with Ethiopia in 1961, around the time of Haile Selassie's annexation of the federated former colony of Eritrea. By 1965 the ELF had weakened Ethiopian control of the province. The ELF was nationalistically Eritrean and Muslim in its initial orientation, but became increasingly Marxist in its leadership. Its separatist movement originated in the western Muslim lowlands among Beja pastoralists (a people never firmly in the Ethiopian state), but eventually spread to the eastern Christian highlands. In 1970 the Marxist, Eritrean Peoples' Liberation Front (EPLF) broke away from the ELF to become the largest and militarily most powerful Eritrean faction. In turn, the Eritrean Liberation

Front-Popular Liberation Forces (ELF-PLF) broke away from the EPLF as a small, nationalistic anti-Marxist force. Saudi Arabia and other conservative Arab states have supported both the ELF and the ELF-PLF. Between 1972 and 1974 and in later years, the various Eritrean factions have fought bloody civil wars among themselves.

Because the new *Derg* appeared militarily weaker than the old monarchy, Eritrean separatists became very active combatants after 1974. The *Derg* responded with a massive invasion of Eritrea by a peasant militia including many Oromos. This invasion was a debacle, and the crusading peasant militia was devastated in a battle by Muslim and Christian Eritreans. However, no Eritrean faction was militarily strong enough to negotiate with the *Derg*, which talked of a negotiated Eritrean solution while reorganizing the regular army. Hence, the ELF and EPLF, two similar Ethiopic socialist-military forces, faced a third such force in the *Derg*. After the massive Soviet arms aid and the support from Soviet advisors and from Cuban troops, the *Derg* achieved military victory in the Ogaden, in the southeast, and also, during 1979–80, broke the military supremacy of the Eritreans in the north. With its formidable destructive power, the Ethiopian army easily defeated the factionalized Eritreans. Clearly, the imported military might of Ethiopia has come a long way along the path of destructiveness since the use of breech-loading rifles by Yohannes and Menelik in their expansion and defense of the empire.

The *Derg* saw Eritrean separatism as a part of a Western and conservative Arab imperialism and as a reaction against an Ethiopian socialism, which was bent on liberating the oppressed Ethiopic masses of Eritrea. Any concession given to the Eritrean fronts would be a model and inspiration for other long-smoldering separatist movements in Ethiopia. Therefore, the *Derg* used its modern ordnance juggernaut to crush the Eritreans in a very traditional Amhara-Tigrean fashion.

Although no Eritrean cultural groups exist apart from those found in neighboring Ethiopia and Sudan, an Eritrean nationalism has been slowly developing. This development is in part created by the Ethiopian political and military reaction to the growing sense of Eritrean self-identity. Accordingly, among Beja-speaking pastoralists, urbanites with Italian acculturation, and conservative Tigrean peasants, modes of ethnicity are gradually evolving. These increasingly set Eritreans apart from non-Eritreans and make for genuine ethnic groups of this former Italian colony. In Ronald Cohen's terms, ethnic boundaries are not necessarily stable and continuing but, instead, situational (Cohen, 1978:385–86). Therefore, Tigreans in Eritrea can, with changing circumstances, gradually become different Tigreans from their brethren with whom they were once territorially continuous. As the ethnicity of Eritrea and Ethiopia becomes more polarized, both increasingly believe they have the just cause. The polarizing ethnicity of the Eritrean conflict becomes catastrophic with the use of modern imported armaments. "In its dimensions, both human and political, Eritrea has been a tragedy of great proportions, in which no simple attribution of responsibility or of socialist credentials is possible" (Halliday and Molyneux, 1981:172). Just as the Tigreans in Eritrea province feel increasingly differentiated from the majority of the Tigreans, who live immediately to the south in Tigray province, so too the latter feel increasingly alienated from the Amhara.

Although the Tigreans have long been the venerable, albeit smaller, half of the Amhara-Tigrean dominance in the Horn, some of them are in armed revolt against the *Derg*. Located in Tigray, the Tigrean Peoples' Liberation Front (TPLF) began in 1974, largely as a reaction to the military government of Ethiopia and in resentment over Amhara dominance in the partnership since 1889. This came about when the Amhara began to control the trade in modern firearms once channeled by the Tigreans. The TPLF is nationalistic, with a Maoist variety of Marxism. Its goals are unification of all Tigreans (including, interestingly, those in Eritrea), and autonomy in, or independence from, the Ethiopian state. The TPLF has used its armed forces to help the EPLF fight the ELF as well as to interdict the Amhara-Oromo lines of military communication to Eritrea, located directly to the north of Tigray province. Part of the Tigrean's dissatisfaction with what they see as Amhara-Omoro dominance is the old Ethiopian military tradition of having field armies live off the land. The huge peasant militia invading Eritrea used Tigray as a staging area. By force of arms, Tigrean peasants were forced to feed and house the militiamen. This created a need for an additional Ethiopian military force to quell unrest among Tigrean peasants in Tigray and Eritrea, which, in turn, created more conflict—to the point of armed revolt.

Within the core of Ethiopia two joint Amhara-Tigrean fronts also combat the *Derg*. (Factionalism is endemic in both Amhara and Tigrean history.) One of the fronts is the Marxist-Leninist, Ethiopian Peoples' Revolutionary Party (EPRP) fighting for a civil Marxist government. The other is the moderate, monarchist Ethiopian Democratic Union (EDU), fighting for a more democratic government. Both the EPRP and EDU have been diminished in military effectiveness since victories freed the heavily armed Ethiopian forces in Ogaden and Eritrea.

The Muslim Afar people situated to the east of the Tigreans, in the Red Sea lowlands, are led by conservative, traditional leaders in a movement, also traditional, for autonomy. The Afar Liberation Front (ALF) has helped the Eritreans and is aided by conservative Arab states and Somalia. As the military might of the *Derg* has waxed in Eritrea, the power of the

ALF has waned. This inverse relationship of core-Ethiopian and Afar power is recurrent in Horn history.

Still militarily significant is the nationalistic and socialistic Oromo Liberation Front (OLF), representing what is probably the largest ethnic group in sub-Saharan Africa, the not too homogeneous 7 to 18 million Oromo (Baxter, 1978). Receiving military aid from Somalia and Syria, the OLF wants either autonomy or independence. The proposed state of Ormoia could include one-half of Ethiopia and would include many non-Oromo within its borders. That would trigger conflict and war between the Oromo and the non-Oromo enclaves. The Oromo range from those with strong Islamic backgrounds to Amharized Christians. Once strong in the *Derg*, Oromo influence has diminished. After 1976, the OLF launched armed attacks on the new Ethiopian government. This government could not exist if, through armed revolt, it lost one-half of its central territory to an Oromia state.

Conclusion

Whatever the effectiveness of the counterbalance of military terror of atomic, biological, and chemical warfare among technologically advanced industrial states, the counterbalance does not apply to third- and fourth-line states. These use conventional weapons supplied by first- and second-line industrial powers. Since the Renaissance, Western man has increasingly come to believe that unsanctioned violence and war can be diminished or prevented by a reasonable discussion of grievances (Kiefer, 1972:52–111). But Quincy Wright (1942) in his monumental study of war found that state legal systems cannot resolve interstate conflict and that interstate mechanisms for adjudication or repression of conflict are weak. Further, even within polynational states such as Ethiopia, interethnic enmity is so deeply rooted in a culture history of war over control of resources, that any political settlements by the state are usually fleeting. Healthier, expanding economies for poor states and their factions would remove some of the pressures and provide disincentives for conflict resolution by war as would discontinuance of the outside armament supply. Because underlying material inequities are not resolved or resolvable, invective and war rather than reason and peace are the legacy of interethnic relations, both within and between states.

In the Horn, complex, ancient, materially based hatreds are expressed ethnically by means of modern weapons. For centuries the Horn has been caught in global conflicts, and it is unlikely in the near future that powerful outside states can declare the Horn a sort of neutral Antarctica. Thus peace in the Horn may be more an ideational post-Renaissance chimera than a materially based solution endurable in the real world.

Notes

1. The *Horn of Africa* includes the states of Ethiopia, Somalia, and Jibuti and adjacent parts of Kenya and Sudan. The term *Ethiopia* is often used to refer to the modern state enlarged to its current boundaries from 1855 to 1900 by force of Amhara-Tigrean firearms. *Abyssinia*, or the core state of Ethiopia, usually refers to the Amhara-Tigrean-Agew state and culture area existing from around A.D. 900 to the late 1800s within the northern and central part of present-day Ethiopia (Gamst, 1977).
2. Western social scientists, in attempting to consider social behavior objectively are often fettered by common ideas and conventions. Therefore, I provide as the conceptual basis of my discussion the widely held anthropological view that warfare among humans is not innate, but is a social institution ordinarily resulting from economic and political causes, often for the control of resources. War is more reinforced than caused by ethnic antagonisms. It is one result of intra and intergroup relations in and among human societies, be they organized as state, stratified, rank, or egalitarian groupings. As a society's energy base and organizational complexity increase, so does the frequency of its warring (Fried, et al., 1968:181, 214; Otterbein, 1970:75, 78).

   The basis of human life is social interaction. Social conflict is one major variety of this interaction. Conflict often has the potential for violence even when it does not erupt. War is the use of armed force between groups as a means of resolving social conflict. Some theorists, in the vein of Georg Simmel, find it useful to distinguish between external armed conflict as *war*, and internal armed conflict as *feud* or factional strife, and not as *civil war*. In the present paper, I discuss *all* intergroup armed conflict as war. Conflict may also be resolved by negotiation (see Wright, 1942:853). *War* then is *negotiation* (or litigation) by other means; or, the two are polar types on a continuum of interaction. Thus, *war* and *peace* are also polarities on a continuum. An irregular cycle exists in war and peace with transition phases, for example, peaceful wartime (Sitzkrieg) and hostile peace (Cold War). Actual determination of the occurrence of war must necessarily be done by arbitrary definition. At times war occurs with the assiduous avoidance of its formal labeling as such. War, then, is not the textbook or legalistic formal declaration of hostilities by one state upon another. Besides negotiation and war, other forms of conflict exist, such as *competition, economic pressure, invoking of supernatural or political ideology* (Simmel's conflict of impersonal ideals), and, perhaps, *sport* and *ritualized attack* (see Spies, 1975).

   War is not necessarily now viewed by social scientists as pathological or socially aberrant, but often as having social-evolutionary selective attributes (Simmel, 1955; Coser, 1956, 1967; Murphy, 1957; Dahrendorf, 1962; Vayda, 1968). Such a view may seem anathema in the present age of potential thermonuclear holocaust, but is objectively valid.

   Whatever the resolution of arguments for the existence or nonexistence of war in certain egalitarian societies (cf., Gardner, 1966; Dentan, 1968:2, 55–59), it is ever present with states. Few state societies are at peace for very long, and war could well be a function of state structure. Not just writing, advanced agriculture, and monumental architecture, but also periodic open warfare is a hallmark of civilization, agrarian or industrial. War is an enduring reciprocal relationship between states. The state exists by and for its monopoly on violent force, wielded by central authority, for a territory's internal order and external defense. Especially in the case of the state, we can agree with Gerhard Lenski that "military power has been the basic determinant of societal survival" (1970:93). Given the full-time political leaders having martial orientations and military specialists honing combative prowess, it may be well that, generally, a state is a war waiting to happen.

3. Although the present paper necessarily focuses, through time, upon the warlike nature of the Amhara-Tigrean state, it must be emphasized that all states and chiefdoms in the Horn of Africa have been lethally combative throughout their histories (Levine, 1974; Bartnicki and Mantel-Niecko, 1978). In fact, the states in the Horn could be considered synonymous with war. Reviewing the overall military preparedness and the military engineering fortifications of Kefa and neighboring southwest Ethiopian states, George P. Murdock (1959:191) says in his encyclopedic *Africa*: "The country is thoroughly organized for war. . . . With the exception of the Great Wall of China, and possibly a few sections of Imperial Rome's frontier defenses, no other known people has lavished such effort on military protection."

   Horn ethnic/language groups discussed in this paper include the peoples below, listed with their ethnic/language name, linguistic affiliation, and (in parentheses) roughly estimated 1970 population:

   Ormo: Afro-Asiatic –East Cushitic (7 to 18 million)
   Amhara: Afro-Asiatic -- Ethio-Semitic (8 million)
   Tigrean/Tigrinya: Afro-Asiatic -- Ethio-Semitic (3.5 million)
   Various groups/Tigre: Afro-Asiatic (117,000 +)
   Somali: Afro-Asiatic –East Cushitic (4.35 million)
   Beja: Afro-Asiatic –North Cushitic? (700,000 + in 1956)
   Afar: Afro-Asiatic –East Cushitic (363,000?)
   Agew (various groups): Afro-Asiatic –Central Cushitic (125,000)
   Hareri: Afro-Asiatic –Ethio-Semitic (50,000?)

(Sources: Nelson and Kaplan, 1980; Nelson et al., 1973; Cassanelli, 1982).

4. The appropriateness of the political model of feudalism (as correctly applied to Europe and Japan) in application to Ethiopia has been controversial. The use of the term *feudal* for Ethiopia in the present paper is in accord with a critical use of the concept as defined by Jack Goody in his reflection upon feudalism in Africa and as outlined by Marc Bloch in his study of the nature of feudal society (Gamst, 1969:15–16; 1970:384–87).
5. The Mahdi (Expected One) is the awaited messianic leader, predicted in certain *hadiths* (sacred writings) to achieve the final triumph of Islam, create social equity, end oppression, and herald the last judgment of God.

References

Abir, Mordechai. 1968. *Ethiopia: The Era of the Princes: The Challenge of Islam and Reunification of the Christian Empire, 1769–1855*. New York: Praeger.

Bartnicki, Andrzej, and Mantel-Niecko, J. 1978. *Geschichte Athiopiens (von den Anfangen bis zur Gegenwart)*. 2 vols. Edited by R. Richter. Berlin: Akademie Verlag.

Basset, René M.J. 1897. *Historie de la Conquête de l'Abyssinie (XVIe Siecle) par Chihab El-Din Ahmed Abd el-Quader Surnomé Arab-Faqih*. Paris: Ernest Leroux.

Baxter, P.T.W. 1978. "Ethiopia's Unacknowledged Problem: The Oromo." *African Affairs* 77(308):283–96.

Beckingham, Charles F., and Huntingford, G.W.B. 1961. *Prester John of the Indies*. 2 vols. Cambridge, England: Hakluyt Society at the University Press.

Cassanelli, Lee V. 1982. *The Shaping of Somali Society: Reconstructing the History of a Pastoral People, 1600–1900*. Philadelphia, Pa.: University of Pennsylvania Press.

Chaliand, Gérard. 1978. "The Horn of Africa's Dilemma." *Foreign Policy* 30:116–31.

Cohen, Ronald. 1978. "Ethnicity: Problem and Focus in Anthropology." *Annual Review of Anthropology* 7:379–403.

Coser, Lewis A. 1956. *The Functions of Social Conflict*. Glencoe, Ill.: Free Press.

_____. 1967. *Continuities in the Study of Social Conflict*. New York: Free Press.

CTI (Conscoiazione Turistica Italiana). 1938. *Africa Orientale Intaliana*. Milan, Italy: Conscoiazione Turistica Italiana.

Dahrendorf, Ralf. 1962. *Gesellschaft und Freiheit*. Munich, Germany: R. Piper.

Davidson, Basil; Cliffe, Lionel; and Selassie, Bereket Habte. 1980. *Behind the War in Eritrea*. Nottingham, England: Spokesman.

Dentan, Robert Knox. 1968. *The Semai: A Nonviolent People of Malaya*. New York: Holt, Rinehart and Winston.

Ethiopia. 1944. *La Civilisation de l'Italie Fasciste en Ethiopie*. Addis Ababa: Gouvernement Imperial D'Ethiopie.

Farnie, D.A. 1969. *East and West of Suez: The Suez Canal in History, 1954–1956*. Oxford, England: Clarendon Press.

Fried, Morton; Harris, M.; and Murphy, R., eds. 1968. *War: The Anthropology of Armed Conflict and Aggression*. Garden City, N.Y.: Natural History Press.

Gamst, Frederick C. 1969. *The Qemant: A Pagan-Hebraic Peasantry of Ethiopia*. New York: Holt, Rinehart and Winston.

_____. 1970. "Peasantry and Elites without Urbanism: The Civilization of Ethiopia." *Comparative Studies in Society and History* 12:373–92.

_____. 1977. "On 'Abyssinia,' a Response to Bender." *American Anthropologist* 79:902.

_____. 1979. "Wayto Ways: Change from Hunting to Peasant Life." *Proceedings of the Fifth International Conference on Ethiopian Studies, Session B*, edited by Robert L. Hess, pp. 233–38. Chicago, Ill.: University of Illinois at Chicago Circle.

Gamst, Frederick C.; and Baldia, M.O. 1980. "Ueber die Sogenannten 'Fruchtbarkeitsidole' der Falascha von Abessinien." *Zeitschrift für Ethnologie* 105:134–44.

Gardner, Peter M. 1966. "Symmetric Respect and Memorate Knowledge: The Structure and Ecology of Individual Culture." *Southwestern Journal of Anthropology* 22:389–415.

Garretson, Peter P. 1980. "Ethiopia's Telephone and Telegraph System, 1897–1935." *Northeast African Studies* 2(1):59–63.

Halliday, Fred, and Molyneux, M. 1981. *The Ethiopian Revolution*. London: NLB.
Hess, Robert L. 1970. *Ethiopia: The Modernization of Autocracy*. Ithaca, N.Y.: Cornell University Press.
Hoskyns, Catherine. 1969. *The Ethiopian-Somali-Kenya Dispute, 1960–67*. Oxford, England: Oxford University Press.
Iadarola, Antoinette. 1979. "The Anglo Italian Agreement of 1925: Mussolini's 'Carte Blanche' for War against Ethiopia." *Northeast African Studies* 1 (1):45–56.
Keller, Edmond. 1980. "Review of: Tom J. Farer, *War Clouds on the Horn of Africa*; and Colin Legum and Bill Lee, *The Horn of Africa in Continuing Crisis*." *Northeast African Studies* 2:91–93.
Kiefer, Thomas M. 1972. *The Tausug: Violence and Law in a Philippine Moslem Society*. New York: Holt, Rinehart and Winston.
Legesse, Asmarom. 1973. *Gada: Three Approaches to the Study of African Society*. New York: Free Press.
Lenski, Gerhard. 1970. *Human Societies*. New York: McGraw-Hill.
Lesage, C. 1906. *L'Invasion Anglaise en Égypte: L'achat des Actions de Suez*. Paris: Plon.
Levine, Donald N. 1974. *Greater Ethiopia: The Evolution of a Multiethnic Society*. Chicago, Ill.: University of Chicago Press.
Marcus, Harold G. 1975. *The Life and Times of Menelik II: Ethiopia 1844–1913*. Oxford, England: Clarendon Press.
Marder, A.J. 1940. *British Naval Policy 1880–1905: The Anatomy of British Sea Power*. London: Putnam.
Matties, Volker. 1977. *Der Grenzkonflikt Somalias mit Äthiopien und Kenya*. Hamburg, W. Germany: Institut fur Afrika-Kunde.
Michel, Charles. 1900. *Vers Fashoda*. Paris: Plon.
Murdock, George P. 1959. *Africa: Its Peoples and Their Culture History*. New York: McGraw-Hill.
Murphy, Robert F. 1957. "Intergroup Hostility and Social Cohesion." *American Anthropologist* 59:1018–35.
Natsoulas, Theodore. 1981. "Ethiopia: The Anatomy of an Indigenous African Colonial Empire." *Horn of Africa* 4(3):3–6.
Nelson, Harold D., et al. 1973. *Area Handbook for the Democratic Republic of the Sudan*. Washington, D.C.: U.S. Government Printing Office.
Nelson, Harold D. and Kaplan, I. 1980. *Ethiopia: A Country Study*. Washington, D.C.: U.S. Government Printing Office.
Novik, Nimrod. 1978. *On the Shores of Bab al-Mandab: Soviet Diplomacy and Regional Dynamics*. Philadelphia, Pa.: Foreign Policy Research Institute.
Otterbein, Keith F. 1970. *The Evolution of War: A Cross-cultural Study*. New Haven, Conn.: HRAF Press.
Pankhurst, Richard. 1961. *An Introduction to the Economic History of Ethiopia, from Early Times to 1800*. London: Lalibela House.
______. 1967. "The History of Firearms in Ethiopia Prior to the Nineteenth Century." *Ethiopia Observer* 11:202–25.
______. 1968a. *Economic History of Ethiopia, 1800–1935*. Addis Ababa: Haile Selassie I University Press.
______. 1968b. "An Inquiry into the Penetration of Firearms into Southern Ethiopia in the 19th Century Prior to the Reign of Menelik." *Ethiopia Observer* 12(2):128–36.

______. 1971. "Linguistic and Cultural Data on the Penetration of Firearms into Ethiopia." *Journal of Ethiopian Studies* 9:47–82.

Quaranta, Ferdinando de San Severino. 1940. *Development of Italian East Africa.* New York: Italian Library of Information. Outline Studies, Series IV, No. 7.

Rassam, Hormuzd. 1869. *Narrative of the British Military Mission to Theodore, King of Abyssinia.* 2 vols. London: J. Murray.

Rubenson, Sven. 1966. *King of Kings: Tewodros of Ethiopia.* Addis Ababa: Oxford University Press.

Simmel, Georg. 1955. *Conflict.* Translated by Kurt H. Wolff. Glencoe, Ill.: Free Press.

Spies, Richard G. 1973. "War, Sports, and Aggression: An Empirical Test of Two Rival Theories." *American Anthropologist* 75:64–86.

Ullendorff, Edward. 1973. *The Ethiopians: An Introduction to Country and People*, 3d ed. London: Oxford University Press.

Vayda, Andrew P. 1968. "Hypotheses about the Function of War." In *War: The Anthropology of Armed Conflict and Aggression*, edited by M. Fried; M. Harris; and R. Murphy, pp. 85–91. Garden City, N.Y.: Natural History Press.

Weeks, Albert L. 1979. "Soviet Geopolitical Momentum." *Horn of Africa* 2(1):42–53.

Wright, Quincy. 1942. *A Study of War.* Chicago, Ill.: University of Chicago Press.

12

Christianity and War

Alice B. Kehoe

Perhaps the greatest paradox of the last seventeen hundred years is the pursuit of war by professed followers of Jesus of Nazareth. Jesus said, "Resist not evil: but whosoever shall smite thee on they right cheek, turn to him the other also. . . . Love your enemies, bless them that curse you, do good to them that hate you" (Matt. 6:39,44).[1] During the first two centuries of the Christian era, Jesus' followers endeavored to imitate the example set in his acceptance of crucifixion, of pacifism and nonresistance. These early Christians refused to use weapons. By A.D. 173, the opposition between Christians and the power of the state began to wane, and some professed Christians were soldiers of the Roman Empire.

The great reversal occurred in A.D. 312: on 28 October of that year, Constantine, Augustus (senior emperor) of the west of the Roman Empire, fought a rival at the Milvian Bridge at Rome. Constantine won although he had fewer men than his rival, and he attributed this victory to his use upon his banners and his soldiers' shields of a magic symbol, the *labarum*. On the way to Rome, the emperor and his army had seen in the sky a cross superimposed upon the sun, and the words "Hoc signo victor eris." That sign, in its earthly rendering, was a monogram of the Greek letters chi and rho, the first two letters of the word Christos.

In gratitude to the god who had favored him in battle, Constantine ordered that the persecution of Christians end, and he was generous to Christian churches and charities (Jones, 1948). The god of the Christians continued to support Constantine, enabling him in 324 to conquer the eastern half of the Roman Empire. As supreme Emperor, Constantine promulgated edicts that established Christianity as the preferred religion of the Empire. The Dutch pacifist Heering (1972:35) terms this establishment "the fall of Christianity."

In this paper I shall examine early Christianity and the tradition of pacifism; the tradition of the just war, developed by Augustine in the century after Constantine; the appearance of holy wars or crusades; and two factors that may explain, if not resolve, the paradox of Christians pursuing war: the assimilation into the ideology of Christian Europe of the Germanic ideal of battle glory and the function of the myth of the millennium in European Christian societies. Throughout the paper, the term "Christian" refers to professed followers of Jesus of Nazareth, the Christ, regardless of their doctrinal or sectarian allegiances or of their actions.

The three principal positions of Christians in respect to war, pacifism, just war, or crusade, have been set out by Bainton (1960). As in any typology, particularly any so ambitious as to condense two thousand years of discussion into three categories, Bainton's set of positions represents normative generalizations that distort any actual argument (Johnson, 1981:xxv–xxvi). Still, the typology does present a useful framework for discussion, and it has the virtue also of representing three distinct historical sources: the revolutionary ethos of Jesus and the early Christian communities, the classical philosophy accepted by the established Catholic Church, and the Germanic ideology.

Early Christianity and Pacifism

From a Mennonite perspective, Yoder (1971: chap. 1) insists that the New Testament is a gospel of revolution. The Greek texts, he argues, choose words—*euangelion, metanoia*—that connote societal and personal change. Jesus consistently repudiated the world as it was and urged upon those listening a life the opposite of their accustomed ways. "Seek ye first the kingdom of God . . . for great is your reward in heaven" (Matt. 6:33, 5:12), he instructed, specifying in detail the manner in which those who would obtain eternal life in heaven must reject conventional practices (codified as the Sermon on the Mount, Matt. 5–7). Yoder analyzes Jesus' possible actions, as a Jew in first-century Judea. Jesus saw as his mission the creation of a new community living by new precepts and renounced the accommodation to Roman custom exemplified by the Sadducees, the tabu-surrounded cleaving to Judaic law of the Pharisees, the withdrawal of the Essenes, and the rebellion of the Zealots. As a rule Jesus' precepts were opposites of convention—e.g., "Lay not up for yourselves treasures upon earth, . . . but lay up for yourselves treasures in heaven" (Matt. 6:19–20).

The central tenet of early Christianity was identification with the kingdom of God rather than with earthly kingdoms. For some, seeking the kingdom of God meant retreat into monastic communities in the desert; for others, nonparticipation in the rites, festivals, and official businesses of the state while remaining resident in ordinary communities. Jesus' words (Matt. 22:21), "Render therefore unto Caesar the things which are Caesar's;

and unto God the things that are God's," prescribed a limited engagement in mundane affairs. Paul (Epistle to the Romans: chap.13) later clarified the message. He explained that the ministers of the state are ordained by God "to execute wrath upon him that doeth evil," (13:4) and "Wherefore ye must needs be subject, not only for wrath, but also for conscience sake. . . . Render therefore to all their dues: tribute to whom tribute is due; custom to whom custom; fear to whom fear; honour to whom honour" (13:7). But Paul concludes, two verses further, "If there be any other commandment, it is briefly comprehended in this saying, namely, Thou shalt love thy neighbor as thyself. . . . Love is the fulfilling of the law" (13:9–10). Bainton (1960:77) asserts, "the early Church saw an incompatibility between love and killing." Thus, by the late second century there could be Christians in the Roman armies so long as the Christians carried out only police duties and refused to kill.[2] The simple notion that the Christian should ignore the demands of the state or of the body in order to attend to the soul, can be drawn from many of Jesus' teachings. Yet, hundreds of passages are ambiguous on the degree of abstention recommended (e.g., did Jesus mean that one should give all one's *denarii* to the Caesar's officers, or only that it is lawful to pay taxes?). Paul's expositions interpret Jesus' teachings in a relative not absolute way. Thus he leans toward accommodation to the state.

Bainton (1960:81–82) describes several bases for pacifism in the early Christian communities: Tertullian (A.D.150–230) emphasized the legalistic injunction, "Shall the son of peace be engaged in battle when for him it is *unlawful* to go to war?" and Marcion (fl.144) developed a Gnostic position thoroughly repudiating the physical, from marriage to killing; Origen argued that Christians should pray rather than fight: "The more any one excels in piety, the more effective help does he render to kings, even more than is given by soldiers. . . . We by our prayers vanquish all demons who stir up war" (Origen quoted in Marrin, 1971:33–34). These several reasons for pacifism build upon the straightforward consensus of the first two centuries of the Christian era, that a Christian must not kill another human.

During the third century A.D., Christianity became respectable. In A.D. 251 there were probably 30,000 Christians in the city of Rome alone and they were served by 154 recognized officers of an organized Church community (Barnes, 1981:53). Christianity was becoming more a sect than a cult. Constantine surely perceived it as one among many competing sects in the Roman Empire. Christianity became preferred when he achieved victory under the auspices of its god. Christians were no longer taken to be opposed to the state, but were rather seen as its guarantors. For their part, Christian citizens of Constantine's Empire do not seem to have been disturbed by their new earthly status. Yet, as Heering (1972:36) says, "That the association between Church and State in the fourth century began *in the army* and *in war* was of ill omen for its future" (his italics). One of the bishops recognized by Constantine, Athanasius of Alexandria (A.D. 295–373), declared, "Murder is not permitted, but to kill one's adversary in war is both lawful and praiseworthy" (*Epistle to Ammonius*, quoted in Heering, 1972:36).

The Doctrine of the Just War

Although Constantine after the Battle of the Milvian Bridge favored Christianity, he was not baptized until he lay on his deathbed, May 337.[3] Despite his forbidding of various pagan practices and desecration of shrines and temples, Constantine's personal conduct hardly befitted a follower of Jesus. As Voltaire said, Constantine "had a father-in-law and made him hang himself; he had a brother-in-law and caused him to be strangled; he had a nephew of twelve or thirteen years and had him throttled; he had a first-born son and he had his head cut off; he had a wife and he caused her to be suffocated in the bath" (*Dictionnaire Philosophique II*, quoted in Doerries, 1972:226–27). Yet, Christians revered Constantine as the Emperor who had (literally) seen the light, God's agent on earth. How could reverence for such a man be coupled with adherence to Jesus?

Augustine, Bishop of Hippo (354–430), developed for Christianity the doctrine of the just war. Bainton (1960:89) identifies Ambrose, former praetorian prefect and then bishop of Milan (339–397), as the first to formulate a "Christian ethic of war." He drew upon the Stoics, particularly Cicero (106–43 B.C.), and legitimized the view by refering to holy wars spoken of in the Old Testament from Abraham and Moses to Maccabeus. Ambrose further justified the view by arguing that Christianity was, and must be, protected against the barbarians by the armed force of the Roman Empire. Both Augustine and Ambrose saw the Christian Empire as empowered to resist paganism and heresy. It is generally assumed that Augustine's position was influenced by the fact that he lived during the period when the Goths sacked Rome (A.D. 410) and of other invasions including the Vandals' attack on Hippo in Africa. Augustine and Ambrose were defending a status quo in which they enjoyed power and prestige. Should the barbarians (who from 382 included many Christians following the Arian "heresy" [Thompson, 1963:68–76]), or the Roman Arians, not be fought off they would lose this status.

Augustine based his doctrine of the just war on Cicero's writings:[4]

> There are two ways of settling a dispute: first, by discussion, second, by physical force; and since the former is characteristic of man, the latter of the

> brute, we must resort to force only in case we may not avail ourselves of discussion. The only excuse, therefore, for going to war is that we may live in peace unharmed; and when the victory is won, we should spare those who have not been blood-thirsty and barbarous in their warfare. . . . As for war, humane laws touching it are drawn up in the fetial code of the Roman People under all the guarantees of religion; and from this it may be gathered that no war is just, unless it is entered upon after an official demand for satisfaction has been submitted or warning has been given and a formal declaration made [*De Officiis*, 1:xi–xii, quoted in Marrin, 1971:50–51].

Both the above and the following from Augustine are grounded in the Stoic concept of natural law.

> Whoever gives any moderate attention to human affairs and to our common nature, will recognize that if there is no man who does not wish to be joyful, neither is there any one who does not wish to have peace. For even they who make war desire nothing but victory—desire, that is to say, to attain peace with glory. For what else is victory than the conquest of those who resist us? And when this is done there is peace. It is therefore with the desire for peace that wars are waged, even by those who take pleasure in exercising their warlike nature in command and battle. And hence it is obvious that peace is the end sought for by war. For every man seeks peace by waging war [*City of God*, 19:10–13, quoted in Marrin, 1971:57].

Or,

> The natural order which seeks the peace of mankind, ordains that the monarch should have the power of undertaking war if he thinks it advisable, and that the soldiers should perform their military duties in behalf of the peace and safety of the community. . . . For there is no power but of God . . . the man (must) be blameless who carries on war on the authority of God . . . by the authority of his sovereign . . . everyone who serves Him knows that He can never require what is wrong [*Reply to Faustus the Manichaean*, 22:73–76, quoted in Marrin, 1971:61].

Augustine's presentation of the concept of the just war[5] was codified by Thomas Aquinas (1225–1274) in *Summa Theologica* (pt.II, Q.40), which forms part of the officially recognized doctrines of the Catholic Church (Marrin, 1971:69):

> In order for a war to be just, three things are necessary. First, the authority of the sovereign by whose command the war is to be waged. For it is not the business of the private individual to declare war, because he can seek for redress of his rights from the tribunal of his superior. Moreover, it is not the business of a private individual to summon together the people, which has to be done in wartime. And as the care of the common weal is committed to those who are in authority, it is their business to watch over the common weal

> of the city, kingdom or province subject to them. And just as it is lawful for them to have recourse to the sword in defending the common weal against internal disturbances, when they punish evil-doers, according to the words of the Apostle (Rom.13:4): *He beareth not the sword in vain: for he is God's minister, an avenger to execute wrath upon him that doth evil*; so too, it is their business to have recourse to the sword of war in defending the common weal against external enemies. Hence it is said of those who are in authority (Ps.81:4): *Rescue the poor: and deliver the needy out of the hand of the sinner*; and for this reason Augustine says (*Contra Faust.* xxii.75): *The natural order conducive to peace among mortals demands that the power to declare and counsel war should be in the hands of those who hold the supreme authority.*
>
> Secondly, a just cause is required, namely that those who are attacked, should be attacked because they deserve it on account of some fault. Wherefore Augustine says (*QQ. in Hept.*, qu.x): *A just war is wont to be described as one that avenges wrongs, when a nation or state has to be punished, for refusing to make amends for the wrongs inflicted by its subjects, or to restore what it has seized unjustly.*
>
> Thirdly, it is necessary that the belligerents should have a rightful intention, so that they intend the advancement of good, or the avoidance of evil. . . . For it may happen that the war is declared by the legitimate authority, and for a just cause, and yet rendered unlawful through a wicked intention. Hence Augustine says (*Contra Faust.* xxii:74): *The passion for inflicting harm, the cruel thirst for vengenance, an unpacific and relentless spirit, the fever of revolt, the lust of power, and suchlike things, all these are rightly condemned in war* [quoted in Marrin, 1971:69–70].

Francisco de Vitoria (1485–1546), a Thomistic theologian, and Francisco Suarez (1548–1617), a Jesuit Thomist, expanded the principle of just cause by expounding the principle of proportionality which says that to justify either war itself or means pursued in war, the good to be gained must be expected to outweigh the evil caused.

A contemporary statement of the theory of the just war sums up:

1. Just cause. All aggression is condemned; only defensive war is legitimate.
2. Just intention. The only legitimate intention is to secure a just peace for all involved. Neither revenge nor conquest nor economic gain nor ideological supremacy are justified.
3. Last resort. War may only be entered upon when all negotiations and compromise have been tried and failed.
4. Formal declaration. Since the use of military force is the prerogative of governments, not of private individuals, a state of war must be officially declared by the highest authorities.
5. Limited objectives. If the purpose is peace, then unconditional surrender or the destruction of a nation's economic or political institutions is an unwarranted objective.
6. Proportionate means. The weaponry and the force used should be limited to what is needed to repel the aggression and deter future attacks, that is to say to secure a just peace. Total or unlimited war is ruled out.

7. Noncombatant immunity. Since war is an official act of government, only those who are officially agents of government may fight, and individuals not actively contributing to the conflict (including POW's and casualties as well as civilian nonparticipants) should be immune from attack (Holmes, 1981:120–21).

The upshot of this position is that in this century the doctrine of the just war is seen as in principle *limiting* war and therefore coinciding with the many statutes of international law (O'Brien, 1981). This is no coincidence. Modern international law has largely been written by European Christians. The rationale for limited—that is, just—war is that the depravity of human nature makes power the basis of human affairs and therefore that Christians must deal with and in terms of power (e.g., Ramsey, 1961, 1968). Christian love is then to be expressed in efforts to bring justice tempered with mercy to one's fellows. Such efforts must involve the threat or use of power. As Augustine said, "Every man seeks peace by waging war." Subject and agent of the state which itself must posit its actions on the likelihood of war, the Christian must seek moral conduct in a world where physical force reigns.

The Crusade

The concept of a crusade or holy war to be waged by Christians to spread or protect their faith can be said to begin with Constantine, particularly with his conquest of the Eastern Empire in 324. Constantine's apologists justified the Christian Empire's wars by reference to the wars conducted by the Jews as the Chosen People in the Old Testament. Conventionally, however, the appearance of the Christian crusade is taken to be the speech of Pope Urban II in 1095 at the Council of Clermont:

> The Holy Sepulchre of our Lord is polluted by the filthiness of an unclean nation. Recall the greatness of Charlemagne, O most valiant soldiers, descendants of invincible ancestors, be not degenerate. Let all hatred depart from among you, all quarrels end, all wars cease [in Europe]. Start upon the road to the Holy Sepulchre to wrest that land from the wicked race and subject it to yourselves [quoted in Bainton, 1960:112].

The crusade was assumed to be a just war even if no arbitration were attempted, for the enemy was by definition faithless.

The sixteenth-century Protestant rebellions against the Church had the flavor of holy wars. Like the early Roman Catholic who did not distinguish between Arian Christian and pagan barbarian, the Protestant rebel was classed with infidels; persons who rejected the true faith earned ruthless extermination. The Reformation spawned a wide spectrum of attitudes toward war, ranging from the adamantly pacifist Anabaptists who emulated the earliest Christians, through Luther's separation of church and secular affairs which allowed war but noted the possibility of conscientious objection, to Calvin's theocracy which held that "no consideration could be paid to humanity when the honor of God was at stake" (Bainton, 1960:145). For those who wage one, a crusade is only a just war, the enormity of the enemies' denial of the faith justifying any means of war.

The distinction between a crusade and a just war is not comparable to the distinction between Christian pacifism and just war. The pacifist and the proponent of just wars fundamentally disagree about whether Jesus' teachings are to be followed in the historic Christian era or are meant only for the Millennium; whether Jesus' redemption of humanity began with his crucifixion or is limited to the heavenly sphere until his Second Coming. The crusader takes his justification in the tenets of the doctrine of the just war, the principle of proportionality allowing extreme actions. Thus, there are really only two Christian attitudes toward war: pacifism following Jesus' teachings, or just war following classical, especially Stoic, recognition of natural law.

Germanic Ideology

The doctrine of the just war can be seen as an apologetic developed from classical sources once it became generally accepted that the Millennium was not imminent. Theological and political arguments alone are not sufficient for an analysis of Christians and war. The New Testament gives much evidence of Jewish and Hellenistic influences, and Constantine's establishment of Christianity as the imperial religion moved it towards parallels with Roman government and traditional sects. Lastly, the Germanic barbarians influenced European Christianity, even though little scholarly literature deals with this.

After Constantine established Christianity as the imperial religion, and particularly in the fifth century with the final breakdown of imperial power in the West, Germanic peoples settling in the Roman provinces took on Christianity as part of their assimilation of civilization (Thompson, 1963:78). In the sixth century, Clovis, King of the Franks, converted to Christianity after he successfully called upon the Christian god to aid him in his battle against the Alamanni. This resulted in a shift of power, by 800, in Western Europe from Rome to Aachen (Hillgarth, 1969:83). The concept of God also shifted:

> Christ . . . was being approximated to this representation of God . . . terrible and strong. . . . A gravestone of the Frankish period near Bonn shows Christ as King of Heaven, with a lance in his right hand, towering over the conquered Serpent. . . . In the monastic *Rule* of St.Benedict [died 547], which was gaining ground throughout these centuries and was to conquer the Christian West with the Carolingians, Christ is above all a King and God a Judge. . . . The Church acquired a military and legal stamp in these centuries—when its hierarchy was modeled after the militarized hierarchy of the Late Roman Empire and its God after that Empire's despotic ruler and his lesser imitators, the barbarian kings—that is not yet effaced [Hillgarth, 1969:84–85].

The background to this militant Christ whose glory is in battles is probably the Germanic ideal (Aho, 1981:80) of honor. Lindow (1976: chap. 5) shows that the Germanic terms for "honor" connote also "glory," "rank," "respect," "fear," "hold in awe or reverence," "admire," "bright," "shining." In many dialects they also connoted "clemency" or "mercy." In the first millennium A.D. honor gained through the generous fulfillment of social obligations came to be commonly referred to in Germanic societies (Lindow, 1976:135–43). Although honor achieved in battle and honor achieved through social obligations had distinct developments, they were conflated, and the terms for each were used more or less synonymously. As Lindow explains (1976:141):

> Medieval Christendom, which entered Scandinavia at about the time the term *hird* did (early eleventh century) had its own notions of honor, none of which coincided even remotely with the pagan Scandinavian situation. To a Christian, honor was primarily what was due to God; man's duty was to be humble. Thus, in writing about Christian honor, men were faced with a wide variety of words from which to choose in order to express this new concept. As far as we can determine, words expressive of both the honor of martial glory and the honor of social utility were chosen indiscriminately.

It is important to note that in first millennium A.D. Germania, honor connoted both "proper actions in given social situations" (Lindow, 1976:137) and martial glory. Moreover, the advent there of Christianity did not alter this. Christ, to whom all honor is due, embodied martial glory as well as the other qualities of a society's leader.

Both Constantine, who established Christianity in the Roman Empire, and Clovis, who established Christianity within the greatest of the Germanic empires, were models of the Germanic ideal leader, brave warrior and generous patron. Established in both cases through identification with military victory, Christianity in northern Europe, as elsewhere, accommodated to the local ideology more than it altered it. (For example, the shrine to Wotan at Monte Gargano became a place of worship for Norman soldiers who saw the deity as Michael the Archangel [Aho, 1981:81]). Hillgarth

(1969:86) notes that the bishops and priests of the converted Germanic peoples created lengthy and elaborate rituals for blessing the kings embarking upon war, for their arms and for their soldiers, for example, in seventh-century Spain.[6]

Germanic ideology reasserted itself during the Protestant Reformation. By the latter eighth century the Frankish Carolingians had allied with the Roman papacy. However, other Germanic peoples and leaders chafed under Papal power. Thus, the Synod of Worms, 1076, deposed Pope Gregory VII, and the Concordat of Worms, 1122, gave the emperor the right to veto election of prelates. The Protestant break with the Church in the sixteenth century was the culmination of centuries of uneasy relations. Martin Luther (1485–1546) said of the Peasant Rebellion:

> The peasants would not listen; they would not let anyone tell them anything, so their ears must now be unbuttoned with musket balls till their heads jump off their shoulders. . . . He who will not hear God's word when it is spoken with kindness, must listen to the headsman, when he comes with his axe. . . . It is God's will that the king be honored and the rebels destroyed. . . . The Scriptures . . . see the temporal sword aright. . . . It is God's servant for vengeance, wrath, and punishment upon the wicked, but for the protection, praise, and honor of the righteous. . . . I am called a clergyman and am a minister of the word, but even if I served a Turk and saw my lord in danger, I would forget my spiritual office and stab and hew as long as my heart beat. If I were slain in so doing, I should go straight to heaven [quoted in Marrin, 1971:102–7, from *An Open Letter on the Harsh Book against the Peasants*].

Indo-European Mythology and the Warrior

Georges Dumézil (1970), in studying Indo-European mythical warriors, has discovered that these figures are peculiarly placed between heaven and earth. If the gods of Dumézil's first function, sovereignty, are primarily eternal and remote, and those of his third function, abundance/fecundity, are busy with minor happenings, the warriors who embody the second function, force, articulate the two others.

Since the New Testament gospels are cast in the structure of Semitic oppositional dualism (see Dumézil, 1973: Appendix) with the young, meek and mild Jesus against the old, proud, aggressive and conventional Jews and Romans, there is no direct correspondence between the Jesus of the gospels and pagan Indo-European heroes. But wherever Indo-European ideology was dominant in the first millennium A.D., God the Father must be a first-function deity: the Sovereign Judge. Christ the Son must be second function: the young, powerful warrior who guards the eternal order, who suffers grievous tribulations, and who can bring clemency to mitigate justice. (Mary, as the Mother, epitomizes the third function [Warner,

1976:196].) Thus the Christ, King of Heaven, towering over the conquered Serpent described by Hillgarth is, from Dumézil's perspective, really Indra, who in the Indian mythology kills the monstrous serpent son of Tvastr, and Heracles who killed serpents from his cradle and then the Hydra. Of course, the Jesus of the gospels remained known to the learned clerics of Europe, while the illiterate populace conceptualized Christ the Warrior, and there was a fruitful tension between the two. But the Indo-European Warrior is perenially engaged in "just" battles against demons and is the savior of the right order. This mythic figure thus is the model of holy war. Although the crusade is only a subclass of the just war, Bainton (1960) may be justified in giving it coordinate rank because of its reflection of the Indo-European personification of Force. (Or, Bainton may be so Indo-European himself that he feels compelled to distinguish three classes!) The doctrine of the just war is a classical thesis, founded on the classical principle of moderation, while the crusade comes from the tradition that glorified the *berserkir*.

The Millennium

The gospels of Matthew, Mark, and Luke agree that after his resurrection Jesus instructed his disciples to go forth and teach all nations his message. Building upon this, Paul and other writers of the developing Church sought to amplify and detail Jesus' teachings into codes of conduct appropriate for Christians in the various regions of Empire.[7] It became clear that Christ's Second Coming was not imminent, and that the establishment of his kingdom on earth would be a slow process, presumably dependent upon the conversion of all nations. The last book of the New Testament, Revelation, attributed to Jesus' "beloved disciple" John (the Divine) countered the disappointment and resignation that these realizations brought. Radically different from John's gospel, Revelation is a compendium of mystical portents of the avenging God of the Old Testament, who identifies himself as "alpha and omega, the first and the last," and who is attended not only by Jesus Christ but also by seven spirits (Rev. 1:8, 11, 4–5). The book decribes a massing of the creatures of Satan to battle the Lord at Armageddon, followed by a thousand-year reign of God and Christ over those who had not deviated from their worship, the release of Satan from his millennium of bondage and his subsequent destruction, and the resurrection of all the dead for the last judgment. The entire book is presented as a vision vouchsafed by God for the instruction of humanity.

It is common to link the gospels with Revelation by citing the nearly identical passages in Matthew 24:6–7, Mark 7–8, and Luke 21:9–10 that state: "Ye shall hear of wars and rumours of wars: see that ye be not troubled: for all these things must come to pass, but the end is not yet. For nation shall rise against nation, and kingdom against kingdom" (Matt. 24:6–7). "The end" that Jesus speaks of is to be Armageddon, and it is therefore said to have been prophesied that wars will continue until the beginning of the Millennium of the Second Coming. A contrast is created between this corrupt age (which began with Adam and Eve's Fall) and the Millennium. The fundamental premise is that the depravity of humanity makes wars inevitable until that corruption is cleansed by Armageddon (Nelson and Olin, 1979:17). The premise says nothing about the conduct of individual Christians. A corollary to the premise is that in the gospels Jesus' frequent references to the kingdom of heaven are references to his kingdom during the Millennium. The oppositional dualism that Jesus uses to elucidate the differences between his precepts and convention becomes a temporal opposition between the present age and the Millenium. Thus the Sermon on the Mount is the charter for the Millennial kingdom rather than for contemporary Christians. The Millennium functions as a mythic condition in which the realities of the world are inverted: the poor gain the kingdom, mourners are comforted, the meek inherit, those hungry for righteousness are filled, those persecuted for righteousness' sake gain the kingdom, and the peacemakers become the children of God. From Augustine through Paul Ramsey, the words of Jesus are set in the framework of the mythic Millennium (Johnson, 1981:364); those who would follow Jesus' teachings here and now are considered fools who cannot recognize eschatology. The Christian is the person who finds eternal life by accepting Christ as the savior—whose mortal corrupted body will be shed in order that its inversion, the immortal, pure soul, may be eternal. On this earth, we all sin; those who accept cleansing through Christ's sacrificed blood will be freed to live with the Lamb in holiness in the world that is to come.

Christians and War Today

The attitudes of contemporary Christians run the gamut from belligerency to absolute pacifist nonresistence. The majority, Catholic and Protestant, accept the doctrine of the just war (Ramsey, 1968:xi–xii). In our time this doctrine requires discussion of the morality of the use of nuclear weapons. It is now axiomatic that any just war will be a limited war (O'Brien, 1981). Can the effects of nuclear weapons be limited to combatants (a condition of just war)? If not, can the *threat* of the use of nuclear weapons—deterrence—be morally or pragmatically justified?

For those who hold the concept of the just war, nuclear deterrence poses exceedingly difficult questions. There are first the factual questions: can the effects of nuclear weapons be limited to targeted combatants, or would radiation and fallout affect populations indiscriminately? Scientists cannot give simple answers, for not only do effects of blasts depend upon complex factors of wind, topography, height of explosion, and so on, there are in each instance the more profound calculations of degree of risks such as delayed cancers or birth defects. Then there are the strategic questions: how many and what kinds of nuclear weapons are necessary to deter opponents? And the political questions: what overt attitudes (conciliatory? belligerent? shrewdly pragmatic?) might best elicit opponents' restraint? allies' cooperation? voter support? and of course what might win one bloc may antagonize another. Finally, there are the moral questions: given the probability of certain physical effects, given the probabilities of responses in kind from the opponent, from allies, from voters, what then are the preferred choices for Christian statesmen?

Debate among those who accept the concept of just war focuses on the principle of proportionality: will the good obtained outweigh the evil caused, and do the means proposed to achieve that good fit the situation? Ramsey and his predecessor, Reinhold Niebuhr, develop a Protestant position that emphasizes *jus ad bellum*, the importance of maintaining the political strength of Christian nations. Their rationale is the obligation of Christians to express love and charity toward humanity, which in the view of these theologians is first of all an obligation to extend the revelation of salvation. Evangelism is a pragmatic activity, and practical means must be taken to support and protect the evangelist, the converted, and potential converts. As Ramsey asserts (1968:7), "The use of power, and possibly the use of armed force, is of the *esse* of politics and inseparably connected with those higher human goods which are the *bene esse* of politics," and again (Ramsey, 1968:150–51):

> Intrinsic within the new foundation laid by Christ for the entire conduct of his disciples was the conviction that love and mercy are the fulfilling of the law, of natural justice. . . . The combatant stood at the point of intersection of many primary claims upon the Christian's life with and for his fellow man. . . . For love's sake . . . forces should be repelled and the bearers and close cooperators in military force should be directly repressed, by violent means if necessary, lest many more of God's little ones should be irresponsibly forsaken.

No citations of Scripture are given for any of these assertions. For Ramsey (1968:xi), Christian ethicists should be concerned with a "theory of statecraft . . . the nature of a proper *political act*—of 'government'—. . . from the perspectives upon the political life of mankind which Christians should share. The *military* doctrine—the just-war theory—is an outgrowth," a subfield of the problem of the Christian's political responsibilities (his italics). As Johnson (1981:332) points out, for Niebuhr "morality and realism were depicted dialectically," and the same holds true for Ramsey, Niebuhr's successor in tradition.

The deep pessimism of Protestant theologians such as Ramsey and Niebuhr, the dichotomy they see between the real world and the Millennial vision, is not common among Catholic thinkers (Ramsey, 1968:260; see also his remarks on John XXIII's *Pacem in terris*). The Second Vatican Council agreed that:

> Insofar as men are sinful, the threat of war hangs over them, and hang over them it will until the return of Christ. But insofar as men vanquish sin by a union of love, they will vanquish violence as well and make these words come true: 'They shall turn their swords into plow-shares . . . Nation shall not lift up sword against nation, neither shall they learn war any more' (Isa.2:4) (Vatican Council 1965, quoted in Marrin, 1971:279).

Catholic theologians are thus not convinced that war is absolutely inevitable, and this premise makes them less inclined to assume that the use of nuclear weapons is unavoidable. Their discussions on the principle of proportionality focus on,

> the kind of instruments which can now be found in the armories of the great nations . . . (which) compel us to undertake an evaluation of war with an entirely new attitude. . . . The unique hazard of modern warfare consists in this: it provides those who possess modern scientific weapons . . . occasion for perpetuating . . . abominations (Vatican Council 1965, quoted in Marrin, 1971:281).

Whereas Ramsey can flatly prohibit the indiscriminate harming of noncombatants and yet advocate, from his "Christian realist" position, a "deterrence posture" implicitly backed by nuclear weapons (Ramsey, 1968:ix), Catholics conclude that "the arms race is an utterly treacherous trap for humanity" (Vatican Council 1965, quoted in Marrin, 1971:282) and in May 1983, American bishops published a pastoral letter condemning the strategy of nuclear deterrence.

That notion of a "unique hazard" of warfare today which requires profound rethinking of the position of the Christians in regard to war is not a recent condition. In classical Greece, the introduction of fire arrows was considered an abomination; in medieval Europe, the use of the longbow destroyed the foundation of the code of war, leading the Lateran Council, 1139, to declare "The deadly art, hated of God, of crossbow-men and archers against Christians and Catholics is prohibited on pain of anthema" (quoted in Aho, 1981:95). More tellingly, the introduction of guns into sixteenth-century Japan led to "the discovery that efficient weapons tend to overshadow the men who use them" (Perrin, 1979:23–24). Men were mowed down before they had the opportunity to display their valor, stupid peasants slaughtered great nobles, war became work, and honor and glory were lost (Aho, 1981:156–57). After a century of high-fatality wars, dependent upon gunpowder, the Japanese reverted to their older traditions of war, concentrating their armaments technology upon the production of incredibly sharp swords of great beauty and, often, fame (Perrin, 1979:11). This is a precedent for abandoning more efficient weapons, though not from Christian love. Perhaps it can be taken as support for the Catholic theologians' relatively optimistic evaluation of the possible course of natural law. Indeed, the Japanese abandonment of gunpower took placc during the reign of the politically astute Tokugawa shoguns, who managed a state with real concern for the general welfarc and prosperity (Perrin, 1979:90–91). Pope John XXIII said:

> There is reason to hope . . . that by meeting and negotiating men may come to discover better bonds—deriving from the human nature which they have in common. . . . May He enlighten the rulers of peoples so that in addition to their solicitude for the proper welfare of their citizens, they may guarantee and defend the great gift of peace (*Pacem in Terris*, quoted in Marrin, 1971:276).

Pacifism persists in many varieties. The conservative Catholic theologian Murray (1960:70) faults what he calls "relative Christian pacifism," which would "affirm that war has now become an evil that may no longer be justified, given . . . the ruinous effects of today's weapons," for failing to conform in developing an argument within the Church's just-war doctrine, yet by 1968, the agonies of the Vietnam conflict had forced him to reconsider the issue, informed now by the Second Vatican Council's 1965 recognition of the validity of conscientious objection. He finds in 1968 that "selective conscientious objection" can be countenanced, and that the just war principle of discrimination is one of grave importance. Thus, where Ramsey sees the just war focused on the selection of military targets so as to avoid harm to noncombatants, Murray understands it to open the door to a carefully researched decision to refuse to participate in a war (Murray in Marrin, 1971:326–33).

Quite different from the casuistry of a Father Murray were the popular expositions of liberal humanist Christian pacifism by Canon Raven, then Regius Professor of Divinity at Cambridge University. Raven (1938:13–16) ingenuously begins by admitting that his Church has been seeking some issue that would attract general interest to theological discussion. Doctrinal questions no longer excited the public; education as an issue ran afoul of taxpayers' revolts; "leisure, housing, unemployment, . . . the Labour Party

. . . the Communists . . . 'Foreign Missions' . . . the changed status of womanhood," all failed to engage truly widespread popular concern; the issue of war succeeded. Having disarmed his reader, Raven then describes 1930s conferences that linked ecumenical movements to the achievment of peace, and concludes that, "War destroys the essential fellowship which exists and should be fostered between human beings as children of God . . . the blessed society which is the body of Christ. The primary tenet of our faith is outraged and blasphemed by war" (Raven, 1938:48–49). This conclusion had also been reached a decade earlier by the Catholic religious Franziskus Stratmann, O.P.: "Love is the . . . binding element in the Mystical Body, its fruit is that *unitas et pax* . . . want of Love and breach of unity reach their extreme point in War. Christ Himself suffers in each of His suffering Members (Col.1:24)" (Stratmann, 1928:29). Zahn (1960:119) repeated the imperative to pacifism given by the concept of Christians as the Body of Christ.

That a Christian at war attacks Christ himself and blasphemes God is developed at greater length by Lasserre (1962), a minister in the Reformed Church of France and one time officer of the International Fellowship of Reconciliation, which had been founded in England in December, 1914, by a Presbyterian minister and a Quaker (Bainton, 1960:207–8). Lasserre (1962:167–68, his italics) claims that "In killing *above all*, man takes the place of his Creator. . . . It cannot be done by chance that man's rebellion against God reached its climax in a murder, that of Golgotha. . . . 'For this is the message which ye heard from the beginning, that we should love one another. Not as Cain . . . who slew his brother' (I John 3:11)." Lasserre (1962:218) is convinced that:

> The Christian life is wholly a ministry of reconciliation. . . . The 'Christian soldier' can bear witness to nothing but this: that love, and therefore the Gospel, are inadequate and Utopian. . . . We have the choice between folly and crime; but all hesitation disappears as soon as we sense, behind that folly, the shadow of the folly of God [Because the foolishness of God is wiser than men; and the weakness of God is stronger than men] [I Cor. 1:25].

The best known Christian pacifist of our generation is undoubtedly Martin Luther King, Jr. (1929–1968), who stood for nonviolent resistance but not for nonresistance. He was strongly influenced by Gandhi, who was, in turn, influenced by Jesus, Tolstoy, Thoreau, and Ruskin (Marrin, 1971:216). King remarked that, "Gandhi was probably the first person in history to lift the love ethic of Jesus above mere interaction between individuals to a powerful and effective social force on a large scale" (quoted in Marrin, 1971:216), and said in 1967, "Our only hope today lies in our ability to recapture the revolutionary spirit and go out into a sometimes hostile world declaring eternal hostility to poverty, racism, and militarism" (quoted in Marrin, 1971:305). King's leadership of the American Black rebellion might not ordinarily be considered directly relevant to a discussion of Christianity and war, but it does point up one of the principal features of the just-war doctrine: a war, to be just, must be officially declared by a legitimate state. Since the United States government never openly declared that it was warring against its Black rebels, any action taken against them by United States soldiers was *ipso facto* unjust. The blacks, however, could claim to be fighting in *bellum justum* (O'Brien, 1981:162). King's principles, strategies, and tactics thus may be said to exemplify Christian nonviolent resistance as one position of Christians in regard to war.

True nonresistance continues to be manifested by the separatist churches, primarily the various Anabaptists and the Quakers. Their position is summed up:

> Whatever the nature of the millennium, this does not permit us to postpone, as though they are only applicable in a future millennium, the implications of the Sermon on the Mount and Jesus' ethical teachings. . . . [Their] stance is to be clearly interpreted as an evangelical and biblical stance, not as the stance of humanistic or moralistic pacifism [Augsburger, 1981:83,86].

From the perspective of these churches,

> properly read, Romans 13 is telling us that God ordains political institutions for ordering the society: But since God ordains the powers he remains above them. In that light our response on many occasions will be that as Christians, "we must obey God rather than men" [Acts 5:29]. . . . We are not to be lawbreakers . . . but we also cannot disobey a divine law to obey a contrary law by the government [Acts: 87].

(Hence the distinction between nonviolent resistance, which would allow lawbreaking, and nonresistance.) According to Augsburger (1981:87), "loyalty to Christ and his kingdom transcends every other loyalty," so that "Nonresistance is the claim of Christ upon his disciples as an expression of the reality of his kingdom" (Augsburger, 1981:90).

In that great bifurcation of Protestantism in the sixteenth century, what would become the antithesis of separatist pacifism began its career. Today, that antithesis is most dramatically seen when the separatists are compared with the fundamentalists. The latter should not be indiscriminately lumped with evangelicals, who may subscribe to more liberal interpretations on Biblical inerrancy and the importance of social reform (Wells and Woodbridge, 1977). Nor should all who insist upon a narrow view of Biblical inerrancy—i.e., fundamentalists—be assumed to agree on all other points of controversy. There is nevertheless a constituency in North America composed of professed Christians who hold Scripture to be inerrant and who believe it is the mission of Christians to evangelize both directly as preachers of the Gospel and indirectly as participants in all legitimate activites of citizenship: "The spiritual is to pervade and transform the political and other earthly tasks. [Christians] therefore have a mandate for full participation in all morally legitimate governmental functions, including military action" (Holmes, 1981:124). Some fundamentalist groups take this mandate as a spur:

> The forces of evil [are] being met in these last days with an aggressive, explosive reaction of men who are led and filled by the Spirit of God . . . not simply to withstand their attack, but to attack them. . . . As C.S. Lewis has put it, we who believe in Jesus Christ are little Christs. Just as Jesus "directly interfered in the affairs of men" by His coming to earth, so we believers today must continue to interfere with Satan's well-laid plans [V.L. Grose, a lay advocate of teaching Creationism in the public schools, quoted in Bredesen, 1971:148–49].

These are the militants who see the United States as the Redeemer Nation (Tuveson, 1968) and themselves as Captain America (Jewett, 1973), a remarkably pure example of the second function warrior of Indo-European myth, complete to his predilection to sin (Dumézil, 1970). Jewett notes this all-American crusader for God is:

> curiously immune to criticism if he happens to break one of the ideals or laws in the battle. . . . His initial desire is to be passive, but when he receives the clear call to battle he must faithfully but regretfully obey. . . . [He is] a perfectly clean and basically passive hero, committed to lawful obedience, carrying out his highest form of faithfulness by violating cleanliness, law, and passivity" [1973:153].

Francis Shaeffer, a theologian popular with fundamentalists, asserts that "Historic Christianity stands on a basis of antithesis . . . that there really are such things as absolutes . . . right and wrong . . . true and false" [Shaeffer, 1968:14–15]. From such a foundation it is possible to conclude with Phyllis Schlafly that the atomic bomb is a "marvelous gift that was given to our country by a wise God" (quoted in Felsenthal, 1981:51).

Peace for these crusaders lies in the hearts of born-again Christians and after the Second Coming, but not on this earth:

> *Peace, perfect peace, in this dark world of sin?*
> *The blood of Jesus whispers peace within.*

Peace, perfect peace, by thronging duties pressed?
To do the will of Jesus, this is rest.
Peace, perfect peace, with sorrows surging round?
On Jesus' bosom naught but calm is found.
Peace, perfect peace, our future all unknown?
Jesus we know, and He is on the throne.
Peace, perfect peace, death shadowing us and ours?
Jesus has vanquished death and all its powers.
It is enough: earth's struggles soon shall cease.
And Jesus, call us to heav'n's perfect peace. Amen.[8]

Notes

1. All Biblical quotations and references are from the *Authorized (King James) Version of the New Testament* (1977, The Gideons International, Nashville, Tenn.: National Publishing Company).
2. The Council of Arles, A.D. 314, gave as its Canon III, *De his qui arma proiciunt in pace placiut abstineri eos a communione*, which Bainton (1960:81) interprets to prohibit Christians from refusing to carry out police duty—laying down arms in peacetime—although in time of war the Christian would be expected to refuse to kill.
3. No doubt an example of the "deferred repentance" Ramsey (1961:12) allows statesmen!
4. Plato had even earlier expostulated the concept that wars should be conducted with a view toward reconciliation (Bainton, 1960:37).
5. Strictly speaking, *jus ad bellum*, justification for recourse to war; *jus in bello*, restrictions upon what may be lawfully done in war, was formally developed much later.
6. "May the king have, by Thy Grace, O Lord, strong armies, faithful generals, minds in concord, by which he may overcome the adversary and defend his own. Give him, O Lord, of Thy Spirit, to think of what are needful and to perform them, so that, fortified by Thy Protection, marching with his subject people and going out from this present church of Thy Apostles Peter and Paul with angel guardians, he may valiantly carry out the acts of war" (quoted in Hillgarth, 1969:90).
7. This period corresponds to the adaptation and transformation phases of the revitalization process postulated by Wallace (1956:274–75); routinization began in the fifth century under Theodosius II.
8. Hymn by Edward Bickersteth, 1875.

References

Aho, James A. 1981. *Religious Mythology and the Art of War*. Westport Conn.: Greenwood Press.

Augsburger, Myron A. 1981. "Christian Pacifism." In *War: Four Christian Views*, edited by R.G. Clouse, pp. 79–97. Downers Grove Ill.: InterVarsity Press.

Bainton, Roland H. 1960. *Christian Attitudes Toward War and Peace*. Nashville, Tenn.: Abingdon Press.

Barnes, Timothy D. 1981. *Constantine and Eusebius*. Cambridge, Mass.: Harvard University Press.

Bredesen, Harald. 1971. "Anatomy of a Confrontation." *Journal of the American Scientific Affiliation* 23:146–49.

Doerries, Hermann. 1972. *Constantine the Great*. Translated by R.H. Bainton. New York: Harper & Row.

Dumézil, Georges. 1970. *The Destiny of the Warrior*. Translated by A. Hiltebeitel. Chicago, Ill.: University of Chicago Press.

_____. 1973. *Mythe et Epopée*, III. Paris: Editiones Gallimard.

Felsenthal, Carol. 1981. *The Sweetheart of the Silent Majority*. Garden City, N.Y.: Doubleday.

Heering, Gerrit Jan. 1972. *The Fall of Christianity*. Translated by J.W. Thompson. New York: Garland.

Hillgarth, J.N. 1969. *The Conversion of Western Europe, 350–750*. Englewood Cliffs N.J.: Prentice-Hall.

Holmes, Arthur F. 1981. "The Just War." In *War: Four Christian Views*, edited by R.G. Clouse, pp. 115–35. Downers Grove Ill.: InterVarsity Press.

Jewett, Robert. 1973. *The Captain America Complex*. Philadelphia, Pa.: Westminster Press.

Johnson, James Turner. 1981. *Just War Tradition and the Restraint of War*. Princeton, N.J.: Princeton University Press.

Jones, A.H.M. 1948. *Constantine and the Conversion of Europe*. London: Hodder & Stoughton.

Lasserre, Jean. 1962. *War and the Gospel*. Translated by O. Coburn. London: James Clarke.

Lindow, John. 1976. *Comitatus, Individual and Honor*. Berkeley, Cal.: University of California Press.

Marrin, Albert, ed. 1971. *War and the Christian Conscience*. Chicago, Ill.: Henry Regnery.

Murray, John Courtney, S.J. 1960. "Theology and Modern War." In *Morality and Modern Warfare*, edited by W.J. Nagle, pp. 69–91. Baltimore, Md.: Helicon Press.

Nelson, Keith L. and Olin, Jr., Spencer C. 1979. *Why War*? Berkeley, Cal.: University of California Press.

O'Brien, William V. 1981. *The Conduct of Just and Limited War*. New York: Praeger.

Perrin, Noel. 1979. *Giving up the Gun*. Boston, Mass.: David R. Godine.

Ramsey, Paul. 1961. *War and the Christian Conscience*. Durham, N.C.: Duke University Press.

_____. 1968. *The Just War*. New York: Charles Scribner's Sons.

Raven, Charles E. 1938. *War and the Christian*. Reprinted 1972. New York: Garland.

Shaeffer, Francis A. 1968. *The God Who Is There*. Downers Grove, Ill.: InterVarsity Press.

Stratmann, Franziskus, O.P. 1928. *The Church and War*. London: Sheed and Ward.

Thompson, E.A. 1963. "Christianity and the Northern Barbarians." In *The Conflict between Paganism and Christianity in the Fourth Century*, edited by A. Momigliano, pp. 56–78. Oxford, England: Clarendon Press.

Tuveson, Ernest Lee. 1968. *Redeemer Nation*. Chicago, Ill.: University of Chicago Press.

Wallace, Anthony F.C. 1956. "Revitalization Movements." *American Anthropologist* 58:264–81.
Warner, Marina. 1976. *Alone of All Her Sex*. New York: Random House.
Wells, David F. and Woodbridge, John D. 1977. *The Evangelicals*. Grand Rapids, Mich.: Baker Book House.
Yoder, John H. 1971. *The Original Revolution*. Scottdale, Pa.: Herald Press.
Zahn, Gordon C. 1960. "Social Science and the Theology of War." In *Morality and Modern Warfare*, edited by W.J. Nagle, pp. 104–25. Baltimore, Md.: Helicon Press.

PART III
SOCIAL SCIENTISTS REACT

13

Sociopsychological Aspects of the Prevention of Nuclear War

Jerome D. Frank

As students of the structure and functioning of human societies, anthropologists and ethnologists can make major contributions to the prevention of nuclear war—certainly more significant contributions than psychiatrists, whose field of expertise is the more remote one of the psychopathology of individuals.

The topic is much too vast to be covered in thirty minutes, or even in the four days of this conference; so I have singled out for brief comment a few psychological aspects of the nuclear dilemma that are closest to anthropology and seem modifiable. Many have been or will be considered by other participants at this meeting.

As a psychiatrist, my point of entry was the recognition that leaders of the nuclear powers, although generally among the most emotionally stable members of their societies, behave like mental patients in one crucial respect: they perceive a danger and the means they use to cope with it make it worse. All national leaders regard a nuclear war as a terrible catastrophe. As President Reagan has said, "Nuclear war cannot be won and must never be fought" (Reagan, 1982). At the same time, according to the Army Field Manual (1980:1–2): "U.S. Army must be prepared to fight and win when nuclear weapons are used." To this end, the United States plans to spend 1.6 trillion dollars (a literally unimaginable sum) on armaments in the next five years and add 17,000 warheads to our already swollen arsenal of 30,000.

It reminds me of the story of the man who was afraid to fly because he was afraid someone would put a bomb on the plane. He went around and talked with various people and found out that the chances of one bomb being on the plane might be one in 10,000. And that wasn't enough for him, he still was scared. Then one day he heard that the chance of two bombs being on the plane would be around a hundred million. And that was something. So he drew the obvious conclusion and every time he flew he carried one bomb with him.

The basic dilemma facing the leaders of the nuclear powers arises from the need to cope simultaneously with two dangers: one as old as mankind yet in any given manifestation only temporary; the other brand new—thirty-eight years old to be exact—yet permanent. The familiar danger is the existence of another group perceived as an enemy—enemies have always existed, yet the perception of members of any particular group as enemies is transitory. Witness the vicissitudes of the relationship between the United States and Germany, for example. The new danger is, of course, nuclear weapons and, since humans will never forget how to make them, this danger will hang over humanity indefinitely, or at least until that far-off time when armed conflict has been abolished.

National leaders concentrate on dealing with the familiar, temporary danger —another nation perceived as an enemy—by the familiar means of seeking to confront the enemy with the threat of superior violence. In so doing, they exacerbate the new permanent danger of a nuclear catastrophe and, at the same time, intensify mutual hatred and mistrust.

The effort to accumulate more and more accurate nuclear weapons than any adversary possesses is based, I believe, simply on force of habit. When faced with a brand new problem for which no solution has yet been devised, humans inevitably try to make it look like an old familiar one and to solve it by methods which worked with the familiar problem. Almost all of today's national leaders started their climb to power in a world of conventional weapons and have reached their present positions in part because they are masters of the prenuclear international game in which war was the final resort and the nation possessing more and better arms won. So national leaders try to deal with nuclear weapons as if they were simply much larger conventional ones, instead of realizing that they are revolutionary. With conventional weapons, the appropriate national behavior is to try to outarm one's rivals, in the hopes of deterring them from resorting to force and defeating them if deterrence fails. Since, except for Hiroshima and Nagasaki, all wars are still being fought with conventional weapons, this behavior is still being reinforced.

The revolutionary feature of nuclear weapons is that, because of their enormous destructive power, there can in principle be no effective defense against them. For in contrast to nonnuclear weapons, against which even a highly imperfect defense was sufficient (the RAF won the battle of Britain by destroying only 10 percent of the Luftwaffe), to be of any use, a defense against nuclear weapons would have to be essentially perfect, and a perfect defense against any weapon has yet to be devised. Even if a theoretically perfect defense were miraculously created, the inevitability of error would defeat it. When an attacker can launch thousands of nuclear warheads, any one of which can destroy a city, even one mistake would be disastrous.

Actually, beyond a level long since passed by the United States and the Soviet Union, accumulating more powerful and sophisticated strategic weapons decreases the security of all nations, including the possessor. The more people who have hands on these weapons within and among nations, the greater the likelihood that one will be fired by misjudgment, malice or accident, thereby possibly triggering the computers poised to launch a strategic nuclear exchange.

The difficulty in grasping the revolutionary nature of nuclear weapons is compounded by their psychological unreality. Nuclear explosions lie outside any previous human experience. Moreover, nuclear weapons in their silos, planes and submarines do not impinge on any of the senses—they cannot be seen, heard, tasted, smelled or touched. As students of cultures will recognize, in the absence of direct sensory experience, our perception of reality is shaped by the words we use to describe it (Rapoport, 1980). Reality is what we tell ourselves it is.

Nuclear weapons emerged quite recently, and nuclear explosions lie outside human terrestrial experience. They are bits of cosmic fire that have no counterpart on earth. As a result, we have not yet devised a vocabulary appropriate to them, so we fall back on words used for prenuclear weapons.

Such terms, for example, as "equivalent," "superior," or "inferior" accurately described relationships between military forces when the destructive power of weapons was limited. However, they lose all meaning when the "inferior" country can destroy the "superior" country many times over no matter what the latter can do. Yet such is the power of words that President Reagan has described a larger United States arsenal of nuclear weapons than that of the Soviet Union as a "margin of safety." As this example suggests, since we think in words, if words don't correspond to reality, we're off on the wrong foot before we even are aware that we've started to think.

Since the management of technologically advanced societies requires much specialized knowledge, both the leaders and the public of the nuclear powers rely heavily on nuclear weapons experts for guidance. This guidance takes the form of scenarios of various types of nuclear exchanges. The rigorous logic and sophisticated computerized calculations of these scenarios conceal the fact that they are based on pure speculation. Since experts are as prone as everyone else to fall back on old solutions to new problems, behind the thousands of sophisticated computerized programs for fighting and "prevailing" through waging controlled, limited nuclear wars lies the persistent belief in the age-old, but now forever unattainable, goal of achieving victory through superior weaponry. This delusion is abetted by the fact that the great majority of nuclear experts have never witnessed a nuclear explosion or experienced a battle. As a result, to quote Admiral Noel Gayler (personal communication, 16 November 1982), who for years was in charge of targeting nuclear weapons, they literally don't know what they are talking about.

The relationship of nuclear weapons experts to nuclear weapons bears striking similarities to the relationship of priests to their gods. Like priests of old, nuclear experts are a breed apart, held in awe because of their claimed ability to communicate with and thereby control their gods. Being based on secret knowledge, this claim cannot be challenged. The experts communicate with each other and with their deities in an impressive arcane language, unintelligible to the layman. The computer language of the nuclear experts is particularly awe-inspiring because its quantitative precision invokes the image of Science, our contemporary god.

Leaders of the nuclear powers invoke these unprecedented, monstrous weapons to deal with an old, familar threat: other nations perceived as enemies. As a manifestation of ethnocentrism, the so-called image of the enemy scarcely requires elaboration before this audience.

Regardless of the actual characteristics of enemies, each typically attributes the same virtues to itself and vices to its opponents. "We" are honorable, good and peace loving; "they" are treacherous, evil and warlike. Although the enemy's behavior may be motivated initially by fear more than aggressiveness, the image becomes a self-fulfilling prophecy. That is, in combating what they perceive to be the other's cruelty and treachery, each side becomes more cruel and treacherous itself. Hence the USSR and the United States today have genuine reasons to fear and distrust each other.

A striking example of the virtuous self-image is provided by the statement of General John Vesey, Chairman of the United States Joint Chiefs of Staff: "The Russians know we're not going to attack them anyway" (cited in Smith, 1983:135). This is in the face of American vilification of Soviet leaders and an Advanced Strategic Missile System Program whose avowed purpose is to devise military equipment that "will insure the success of a nuclear attack on the Soviet Union."

General Vesey's assumption that, in spite of such official programs, the Soviets know that our nuclear build-up, is purely defensive is a prime example of failure of realistic empathy with the enemy (White, 1984). It has the further ominous implication that the Soviet claim that their nuclear build-up is purely defensive is simply a cloak to conceal its true aggressive purpose, thereby confirming our image of them as deceitful.

The ubiquitous perception of the enemy as demonic is one of the most dangerous aspects of the enemy image (see Foster, this volume, for a reversal in which the enemy is a "real" demon). For example, President Reagan has called the USSR "an evil empire" and its leaders "godless monsters." President Nixon (1980:314) has written: "It may seem melodramatic to treat the twin poles of human experience represented by the United States and the Soviet Union as the equivalent of . . . God and the Devil; yet if we allow ourselves to think of them that way . . . it can help clarify our perspective on the world struggle." To help maintain perspective, it is worth recalling that Khomeini calls the United States "the great Satan."

If the enemy is viewed as the incarnation of Evil, then whatever it perceives to be in its interest must by definition be disadvantageous to us. For example, the mere fact that the USSR supports a nuclear freeze is sufficient grounds for many Americans to reject the freeze out of hand. As an opponent of the nuclear freeze movement put it in the *Nuclear Times* (1983:7): "If the American people learn that the goals of the KGB and the Soviet Union are the same as those of the freeze movement, then we'll be doing all right."

To keep the record straight, according to Chairman Edward Boland of the House Intelligence Committee (*Nuclear Times*, 1983:20): ". . . the hearings provide no evidence that the Soviets direct, manage, or manipulate the nuclear freeze movement."

In short, the mutual image of the enemy leads to the perception of every conflict as a zero-sum game. Students of human societies can combat this perception by supplying evidence that outcomes of conflicts with enemies include not only those in which one side wins what the other loses, but also outcomes that are gains or losses for both sides. In the example, a nuclear freeze, to the extent that it would impede the nuclear arms race, would be a win for both the United States and the USSR.

So much for some of the psychosocial forces pushing the world to nuclear disaster. Fortunately, one can discern a few grounds for hope to place on the other scale of the balance. In the United States we have seen a progressive broadening of active efforts to check the nuclear arms race. It is encouraging that mass movements and demonstrations, such as the nuclear freeze campaign, have reached a size that influences policymakers, although, unfortunately, not yet to the point of affecting national policy. Highly encouraging has been the growing number of large, prestigious institutions and organizations, such as the American Catholic hierarchy and numerous national professional associations, that have adopted official antinuclear positions. In short, the message, succinctly stated by Admiral Noel Gayler (1982:1B), is being heard and acted upon by an ever-increasing number of individuals and groups: "There is no sensible military use for any of the three categories of nuclear weapons—strategic, theater, or tactical . . . there is no conceivable military objective worth the risk of nuclear war."

Campaigning against nuclear weapons, however, is not enough; for even if by some miracle they were entirely abolished, the sources of international strife that led to their creation would remain, as would the knowledge of how to make them. Humanity will be able to breathe easy only when international institutions exist that are powerful enough to eliminate war as a means of settling international disputes. The creation of such institutions lies in the hands of other disciplines than ours, but anthropologists especially can counter the widely held fatalistic view that because humans are biologically prone to violence, war cannot be eliminated. Anthropologists can document the fact that expression of all biological needs is channeled and shaped by cultural values and institutions. Therefore, one cannot draw any conclusions about social institutions such as war from biologically determined propensities. Other widespread, deeply ingrained social institutions, such as absolute monarchies, cannibalism, human religious sacrifices, and slavery, for which related biological propensities could be identified, have withered away when better ways of performing their functions emerged. Nuclear weapons have already undermined the ability of war to resolve international disputes. Since Hiroshima, no war that could have involved the nuclear powers has been fought to victory, except one—Vietnam—in which the nuclear power chose to lose rather than to resort to nuclear weapons. This raises hopes that eventually substitutes for war will be devised.

On the positive side, technologies as revolutionary as nuclear weapons are creating new ways of progressing toward the worldwide consensus that would provide the psychological preconditions for world government. These technologies provide powerful means of heightening awareness of worldwide threats posed by nuclear weapons, reducing national antagonisms, and, above all, fostering the realization that all the globe's inhabitants are passengers on the same fragile spaceship, the survival of which is threatened by nuclear war.

At least three new technologies can serve these ends: (1) international electronic communication by satellite; (2) international rapid mass travel; and (3) exploration of outer space. With respect to the first, national leaders already use the hotline and surveillance satellites to communicate rapidly and directly without the distorting effects of intermediaries. This reduces mutual fears by imposing restraints on secret preparation for hostilities.

Television and radio are by far the most effective means of communication ever invented. In contrast to the printed word, they jump the illiteracy barrier and, as all advertisers know, have immediate and powerful emotional impact. As an example, an article in a magazine with fifteen million readers elicited 75 letters. The same message sent over a national television network attracted 1,000 letters a week. Today, through television receivers in public places and transistor radios in the hands of individuals, communication satellites can reach almost everyone on earth simultaneously. Satellites are already capable of carrying some 30,000 voice channels simultaneously, and transmission capacities of 100 million bits per second are anticipated (Ahmad and Hashmi, 1982). The possibilities of international satellite communications are limitless for driving home on a worldwide scale the menace of nuclear weapons and promoting mutual appreciation among the world's peoples.

New methods of rapid mass travel permit face-to-face contact among millions. Of course, as cultural anthropologists well know, mere increase of contacts may exacerbate rather than reduce mutual antagonisms, but properly planned programs of personal contact have been shown to mitigate national stereotypes and promote mutual understanding. Two examples among many are the Experiment in International Living and the American Field Service exchange program. These provide the background of experience for programs that have been worked out but not yet activated such as massive interchanges of high school and college students.

Although space exploration has military implications, it has greater potential for promoting international peace than satellite communication or mass international travel because space exploration is a superordinate goal—that is, for full efficiency it *requires* international cooperation, as evidenced by the rudimentary but hopeful joint USSR-U.S. space program. Work toward superordinate goals has been shown experimentally to significantly reduce intergroup antagonisms (Sherif, 1966). Other examples of international superordinate goals technologically attainable for the first time are long-term weather forecasting, which requires inputs simultaneously from all over the world, combating pollution of the atmosphere and the oceans, and eradicating worldwide diseases such as smallpox.

The long-term considerations that I have touched on suggest specific ways that we professionals in the field of human behavior, as individuals and through our professional organizations, can contribute to survival in the nuclear world right now. The first, and perhaps the most difficult, task is to reorder our own priorities. The prevention of a nuclear catastrophe must receive at least as great a commitment as our customary professional concerns. We must ask ourselves what more we and our organizations can do than we are doing now to prevent a nuclear holocaust. In concluding this talk, let me offer a few suggestions.

As possessors of specialized knowledge, our primary efforts must be educational. We should expound the topics I've touched on, as well as many others, to as many audiences as possible. For example, we can repeatedly expose the fallacious ways of thinking of national leaders that are driving the world toward a nuclear catastrophe.

Those of us in a position to do so should intensify efforts to introduce into school curricula accurate information about the consequences of a nuclear holocaust and other topics relevant to survival in a nuclear world. We can also offer expert consultation based on our areas of expertise to the antinuclear mass movements in our various countries.

Finally, international organizations such as this, by virtue of their memberships and structures, have special opportunities to foster sustained, continuing international activities among their members. Successful models are the Pugwash Movement and the International Physicians for the Prevention of Nuclear War.

As I and many others can testify, to become active in antinuclear work is a good antidote to the despair that otherwise threatens to be overwhelming. Activity provides at least the illusion that one is accomplishing something. Combined with the emotional support of like-minded others, this provides a great boost to one's morale.

The road to survival in a nuclear age will be long, arduous and dangerous, but we must embark upon it. In doing so, I personally have found moral support in a line from an ancient Jewish religious tract, and you may too: "It is not incumbent upon you to finish the work. Neither are you free to exempt yourself from it."

References

Ahmad, I. and Hashmi, J.. 1982. "World Peace through Improved Perception and Understanding." Paper presented at the 32nd Pugwash Conference on Science and World Affairs, Warsaw, Poland.

Gayler, N. 1982. "A Plan to Cut the Risk of Nuclear War." *Detroit Free Press* 25 April 1982.

Nixon, R. M. 1980. *The Real War*. New York: Warner.

Rapoport, A. 1980. "Verbal Maps and Global Politics." *Etc.: A Review of General Semantics* 37:297–313.

Reagan, R. 1982. Camp David Address, April 14.

Sherif, M. 1966. *In Common Predicament: Social Psychology of Intergroup Conflict and Cooperation*. Boston, Mass.: Houghton Mifflin Co.

Smith, R.J. 1983. "The Search for Nuclear Sanctuary (II)." *Science* 221 (8 July):133–38.

United States Army. 1980. *U.S. Army Field Manual FM-3-87*.

White, R.K. 1984. *Fearful Warriors: A Psychological Profile of U.S.-Soviet Relations*. New York: Free Press.

14

The Drift to War

Laura Nader

Although our history books are filled with examples of incidents that touch off a declaration of war, the concept of drift (rather than incident) is central to an understanding of the processes that lead to war in the modern age. I refer here to the cumulative unplanned actions of people that have had the unintended consequence of moving their societies in a direction toward war. In this paper, I will elaborate on an argument that suggests that the way in which nation states have become structured on the basis of modern militarized science prefigures a "slope" toward war. In this view, what, independently considered, may appear to be relatively unimportant tendencies developing in systems, will be seen as a set of continuous changes increasing the likelihood of war (Nader, 1983).

A recognition of this drift or slope should encourage us to change or broaden our present strategies for avoiding war. If unconscious or unplanned tendencies in social behavior result in deep structures which prefigure a drift to war, solutions cannot be found through rational analysis of single incidents. We cannot see contemporary social systems as fixed systems that can be pushed to move away from or towards war with slight changes in current policies. Analogies to war as a game, whether ping-pong or chess, are equally unhelpful, except as data on how warriors think. In other words, theories relying only on one independent variable such as conflict or confrontation, "limited good," or gamesmanship, for example, will no longer be adequate (if they ever were) for the job of understanding why modern wars happen, or knowing what to do to prevent them from happening.

I distinguish nuclear from conventional warfare because I believe the two are the result of basically different sorts of drift processes, as different from one another as defense is from suicide. While no one can win a nuclear war, conventional war can be won in terms of territorial gain or increased control of other goods.

The historian E.P. Thompson deals with the idea of drift by introducing the concept of inertia in his analysis of the current crisis:

> But to structure an analysis in a consecutive rational manner may be, at the same time, to impose a consequential rationality upon the object of analysis. What if the object is irrational? What if events are being willed by no single causative historical logic . . . but are simply the product of a messy inertia? This inertia may have drifted down to us as a collocation of fragmented forces (political and military formations, ideological imperatives, weapons technologies): or, rather, as two antagonistic collocations of such fragments, interlocked by their oppositions (Thompson, 1980:3–4).

The most important aspects of drift are its unplanned nature and the fact that it is the cumulation of a series of decisions and actions (related and unrelated), that have led in the direction of war the most powerful world nation-states. It is the structural context of this drift and the ideologies that legitimize it that should be probed.

Structure and Ideologies

We have a number of studies of the power structures of twentieth-century nation-states. The power structure of these societies—the disparities of power and social distance between those with or without control of decision and the means of production—is relational. This structure has generated close social relations between the leading military, political and economic groups of the nations producing nuclear weapons. Such relations provide the context in which the following behavioral phenomena have emerged: "institutionalized insanity," organizational survival and momentum, and short-term self-interest.

I use the term "institutionalized insanity" to refer to groups with institutional power whose members are immune from the heavy social sanctions imposed on insane individuals without such power. Institutionalized insanity has not been widely recognized as a social problem, although exhibiting many of the same features as insanity among individuals. Those who suffer from it are members of power groups and as such are not counted among the socially insane. We hear individuals like physicist Herb York say about the Reagan administration: "What's going on right now is that the crazier analysts have risen to higher positions than is normally the case." U.S. Senator Alan Cranston refers to T.K. Jones, a high-ranking member of the Reagan administration as "far beyond the bounds of reasonable, rational, responsible thinking," when Jones suggested in relation to nuclear war that, "If there are enough shovels to go around, everybody's going to make it." Psychiatrist Jerome Frank (this volume), says that leaders of nuclear powers behave like mental patients because they increase danger in instituting coping strategies. President Reagan's reference to Russians as "godless monsters" is additional evidence of the kind of thinking that leads to messianic planning to defend presumed U.S. vulnerabilities. I say, "presumed," because both inside and outside the administration, deficiencies in arguments by the proponents of nuclear build-up have been challenged or qualified by many astute, responsible observers and participants, including Hans Bethe and Admiral Hyman Rickover (1982), and more recently by Frank von Hippel (1983).

The architects of the present U.S. nuclear policies are said to be intellectuals who, in the words of Robert Scheer (1982) can separate their rhetoric from the consequences of what they advocate. Another view was revealed to me by a man who had worked in the Pentagon for more than twenty-five years. When I asked him if the Pentagon was studying the problem of depressed white middle-aged men in positions of power and responsibility; he added, "and who are being advised by depressed men." It must be difficult to manage the inherent contradictions between what is considered "sane" within the organization and outside of it as well.

A recent letter in the *New York Review of Books* (Draper, 1983:33) refers to an article in the June 1983 issue of *Commentary* in which Albert Wohlstetter conceives of a nuclear war in which "nuclear warheads would drop 'precisely and discriminately' on each side's military installations 'without mass destruction'" —a school of thought that Draper refers to as indoctrination "in the feasibility of a nuclear war without mass destruction and civilian devastation." A nuclear war, we are being told, can be limited, controlled, and clean. Contradictions between what is sane or insane can only be resolved by blurring the distinctions between nuclear and conventional warfare. The term "institutionalized insanity" thus refers to the inability of certain groups to distinguish delusions derived from ideology from reality based on empirical fact.

Some scholars studying organizational behavior have found the concepts of organizational survival and momentum to be useful analytical tools for explaining organizational resistance to change and innovation. No matter what the explicit goals of an organization are, its most central, albeit implicit goal, is its own survival. An organization takes on a life of its own.

Institutionalized insanity and organizational survival are important factors in the nuclear arms race. When insanity is institutionalized in military and defense bureaucracies, behavior among them that outsiders might think crazy (like asserting that somebody can win a nuclear war) goes unnoticed and undebated within the organization. This situation can persist for so long that the very survival of such organizations depends on the continuance of policies arising from this insanity (Fallows, 1981). When this happens, the survival of the organization itself begins to take precedence over national or even personal survival. Ideologies and rationales are developed within these groups to defend their plan of action. These defenses are reinforced by actual or imagined outside criticism, and often become so strong that the organizations' insanity becomes even more firmly entrenched. This happened in the Cuban missile crisis (Janis, 1973).

The drift to war has been accelerated by the building of a permanent war economy, which Melman discusses in this volume. As Admiral Rickover made abundantly clear in his last testimony before Congress, the United States defense industry is self-interested and profit motivated. After World War II, Charles E. Wilson of General Electric (Barnet, 1972) who recognized the profitability of the emerging defense industry, talked of "building a permanent war economy." During the Eisenhower years, the theory was developed in the United States among liberal politicians, economists, and businessmen that large military spending would stimulate the economy. This theory was put into practice during the Kennedy administration through an enormous increase in military spending and investment in military science.

Due to government sponsorship, defense industries profit from long-term contracts, interest-free loans, payment by government of most plant and capital equipment, and government willingness to pay prices subjected to continuous upward renegotiation. These industries are among the biggest, most powerful, technologically advanced units of economic power in the country, and U.S. national security policy is directed by elite groups largely recruited from such businesses.

People have argued that high-level military spending is having an adverse effect on the civilian economy, and that increased military spending has weakened the U.S. position in the international marketplace and increased inflation at home. But surely the idea of a permanent war economy is hardly rational if one method of coping with the economy actually worsens it. The insanity of it lies not so much in the idea as in its institutionalization.

To understand the drift to war we need to examine both the nonrational and rational aspects of the arms race. There may be something about the way U.S. society has changed since the 1930s that has prompted this apparent drift. Some have said that Americans never found a civilian economic solution to the Great Depression. We simply postponed solutions by going to war. In fact, preparing for war has become endemic to the superpowers, which suggests that there may be internal structural reasons behind this pattern in both the United States and the USSR.

E.P. Thompson (1980) focuses his analysis on structures and explores the political implications of the types of defense communities found in the USSR and the United States. He argues that the division of the world, particularly Europe where it is most visible, into two mutually hostile blocs—keeping a nuclear balance between these blocs and freezing Europe and the world into a political scenario of Cold War—legitimates the military build-up of the two superpowers. He sees more similarity than difference between these countries. Both have produced an organization of production in which the division of labor, allocation of resources, and scientific innovation have assumed a militaristic character. Both are characterized by what Thompson calls exterminism—a situation in which the competition for nuclear dominance inevitably means fighting a nuclear war. He argues: "What may have originated in reaction becomes direction. What is justified as rational self-interest by one power or the other becomes, in the collision of the two, irrational" (1980:7), and Thompson concludes that both sides need this cold war for their economic and status survival.

In all this, ideology operates as an important driving force. Thompson argues in another work, *Beyond the Cold War* (1982), that the function of the Cold War is primarily ideological, serving to promote internal bonding among two rival states and to maintain cohesion and discipline within each bloc. While the ideologies of each state may be seen to be different in their purpose, they may be mirror opposites, that lead to similar consequences. Thompson speaks of the profit motive as a driving force behind the growth of a massive arms industry in the West, of competition between the branches of the armed services as a way of increasing the complexity of weaponry, and of the role of the weapons labs and the accommodation of politicans as a way of enlarging their power. In the Soviet Union, bureaucracy and ideology are the driving forces and, as in the West, the arms industry has become a major factor in the economy. In both countries nationalism, patriotism, and fear of the other are part of the ideological basis for national existence.

Ideology in this context is political and manifest. As Sutton, et al. defined it: "Ideology is any system of beliefs publicly expressed with the manifest purpose of influencing the sentiments and actions of others (1962:2)." Sentiments are aroused in support of nuclear build-up by the normative elements of the ideology (democracy, freedom, egalitarianism, individual liberty, free enterprise, individual property ownership, free marketplace, and so on for the United States; and, for the USSR, communal property ownership, the state representing the interests of all citizens, equality between all citizens, and so on). Nuclear buildup means a war economy and permanent preparedness which legitimizes huge spending for military programs at the expense of socioeconomic programs (see Melman, this volume). The need for public support for such programs has encouraged the use of binary opposites in ideologies supporting each superpower: for instance, freedom vs. nonfreedom, censorship vs. noncensorship. Democracy with all its principles is pitted against communism and vice versa, as the only desirable political system. Anthropology has demonstrated that binary opposites in human thought exist in all societies. (For a discussion of the tendency to symbolize in terms of binary opposites see Foster, this volume.) Those opposites, which form the basis of their ideological structures, reflect the actual power structures of particular social systems. The American and Soviet power structures have become wedded to the ideologies linked to an insider/outsider dichotomy that mobilizes the people of each state to work for defense, pay taxes for it, and be prepared for war. Ideology not only influences sentiments, but also action. Communism prompts the seizure of territory and its control in order to prevent the incursion of the free market of capitalism. Capitalism thrives on creating world markets and attempts to control those parts of the world that provide raw materials and labor for its enterprises.

Religion is also called upon for ideological justification. American leaders talk about the godless nature of the USSR and see the Pope's visit to Poland as the symbol of good versus the evil of that nation's communist government. Words like "nuclear gospel" are used to describe the notion of a controlled nuclear attack, capable of striking military targets "precisely and discriminately" (Draper, 1983:33, quoting Wohlstetter). Rhetoric becomes important in ideological warfare. Supporters of the nuclear build-up use a style of rhetoric that F.G.Bailey (1981) terms pseudocerebral; they appear to use logic and scientific evidence to support their position, while in fact, distorting or excluding important information. This appeals to the will rather than the intellect of the hearers.

Discussion

What are the implications of the foregoing? Is there any sign of a counterdrift away from war? The antinuclear movement is wise to plan its actions in steps beginning with the nuclear freeze and no-first-use declarations. At the samc time, we need to develop positive economies and plan futures for nation-state societies that are not dependent on war for continued existence. To achieve these goals, those concerned with the arms race might well link up with the environmental movements and with healthy alternatives being worked on by the women's movements. Specific recommendations that follow patterns of logical reasoning for stopping this drift toward nuclear war have begun to appear: for instance the slogan, "Nuclear war is not good for your health, and here is a series of paths that lead to the exit."

We also need plans for drawing people away from nuclear drift toward positive goals. We need to visualize peaceful worlds, a world bent on creation not destruction, on communication rather than distrust among nations (see Calder, 1981). The role of citizens will be crucial in this process; our voices will not be hindered by bureaucracies. In *Our Depleted Society* (1965), Seymour Melman has suggested alternate ways of using the $222 billion earmarked for "defense" if the emphasis on the arms race were reduced. There has been talk about the economic successes of Japan and West Germany, nonparticipants in the arms race. Why can't we imagine what the economies of the United States and the USSR might be without it? Can we find solutions for the Great Depression that do not include warfare and use these solutions as a positive enticement away from nuclear war? Can we address as part of the picture the very serious problem of personal powerlessness among top-level officials in military bureaucracies in countries like the United States or the USSR?

I am arguing that we must recognize the limits on what our military and civilian leaders can do to change our present direction. The public I believe is less limited. People need to realize the roles ordinary people might play in order to generate sufficient optimism to carry them into active participation in decisions affecting their lives. Such optimism might lead us to think about developing economies appropriate to the conditions of peace. National security is surely best guaranteed by a healthy society. Contests between nations, rather than focusing on war technology, might alternatively focus on developing peacetime high technology. Such effort will be carried out by people-to-people movements unconstrained by bureaucracies and alert to the potentials provided by development of nonmilitary goals. It may be that nation-states make war but people make peace (Willens, 1984).

References

Bailey, F.G. 1981. "Dimensions of Rhetoric in Conditions of Uncertainty." In *Politically Speaking*. Philadelphia, Pa.: ISHI.

Barnet, Richard J. 1972. *Roots of War*. Harmondsworth, England: Penguin Books.

Calder, Nigel. 1981. *Nuclear Nightmares*. Harmondsworth, England: Penguin Books

Draper, Theodore. 1983. "On Nuclear War: An Exchange with the Secretary of Defense." *The New York Review of Books* 30(13):27–33.

Fallows, J. 1981. *National Defense*. New York: Vintage Books.

Janis, I.L. 1973. *Victims of Groupthink*. Boston, Mass.: Houghton Mifflin.

McLaughlan, Greg, n.d. "E.P. Thompson on the Nuclear Arms Race." Unpublished manuscript.

Melman, Seymour. 1965. *Our Depleted Society*. New York: Delta.

Nader, Laura. 1983. "Two Plus Two Equals Zero: War and Peace Reconsidered." *Radcliff Quarterly*.

Rickover, Hyman. 1982. *No Holds Barred*. Washington, D.C.: Center for the Study of Responsive Law.

Scheer, Robert. 1982. *With Enough Shovels*. New York: Random House.
Sutton, Francis X., et al. 1962. *The American Business Creed*. New York: Schocken Books.
Thompson, E. P. 1980. "Notes on Exterminism, the Last Stage of Civilization." *New Left Review* 121 (May-June).
_____ . 1982. *Beyond the Cold War*. New York: Pantheon Books.
Von Hippel, Frank. 1983. "The Myths of Edward Teller." *Bulletin of the Atomic Scientists*. (March).
Willens, Harold. 1984. *The Trimtab Factor—How Business Executives Can Help Solve the Nuclear Weapons Crisis*. New York: William Morrow and Co.

15

The War-Making Institutions

Seymour Melman

Highly specialized and lavishly funded institutions dedicated to war making have become characteristic features of both industrialized and developing nations. Independently of variation in politics, ideology, history and culture, war-making institutions have been installed as state managements over the largest aggregations of industrial and allied enterprises, to serve the military functions of the state. Apart from their military effects, owing to weaponry of unprecedented lethality, the economic and social effects of the war-making institutions include economic retardation and authoritarian features of a garrison society. These effects are inherent in the concentrated use of production resources (capital) for the military, and are inseparable from the normal authoritarian structure of military organizations.

The idea that military spending spurs the economic development of communities by energizing economic activity is one of the most dangerous and destructive beliefs of our time. In industrialized and developing countries this idea is used as a spearhead and shield for the power and privilege of the occupations engaged in creating and wielding armed force.

Within the United States the cornerstone of this ideology is the claim that it took the onset of World War II to end the Great Depression and that the nation then enjoyed an abundance of guns and butter. In fact the draft and war production ended unemployment. But the guns plus butter combination was made possible by two special conditions: first, the U.S. mainland was untouched by war damage; second, U.S. participation in the war lasted only four years, during which the main industrial and other physical plant of the nation stood up well enough.

The World War II experience was not a competent baseline for predicting the effects of thirty-eight years of a permanent war economy. The long period of concentration of technology and other capital resources on the military enterprise has produced industrial deterioration without precedent in the U.S. economy and has had a primary role in destroying the historic advantage in high productivity that the United States enjoyed for more than a century. The mechanism of that development is the subject of this paper.

The main economic consequences of military economy are determined by: the nature of the military product; limits on industrial and other resources; military budgets as capital funds; the social costs of military economy in depleting industry and infrastructure; the cost and subsidy-maximizing character of the military microeconomy; and finally, its effects on productivity and employment.

Capital Resources Used for Military Budgets

In ordinary industrial management usage, capital is conventionally understood as composed of "fixed" and "working" capital. The fixed component includes land, buildings, and machinery. The working capital component comprises the tools, fuel, raw material, purchased components, and working hours of the very sort required to conduct production on a sustained basis. *Military budgets are important in relation to fixed and working capital because a modern military budget sets in motion precisely the sets of resources ordinarily understood as the capital of modern industry. A modern military budget is a capital fund.*

From 1946 to 1980 the Department of Defense budgets totalled $2,001 billion. The planned DOD budgets from 1981 to 1986 are $1,600 billion. One way of appreciating the magnitude of resources involved here is to compare the sum of military budgets, $3,601 billion from 1946 to 1986, with the money value of the reproducible national weath of the United States (as of 1975), $4,302 billion. This latter sum refers to the money value of everything manmade on the surface of the United States, all structures, machinery, public and private facilities, business and personal inventories. The money value of the land is not included here. The sum of military budgets 1946 to 1986 is a quantity of resources amounting to about 83 percent of the estimated money value of everything manmade on the surface of the United States. Stated differently, the military budgets have preempted resources approximately equivalent to those required for renewing the largest part of what people have wrought in the United States in terms of physical facilities and tangible goods of all sorts (Melman, 1983).

Another way of appreciating the size and effects of the U.S. military budget is by comparing the military budgets of the United States and other countries with some indicator of major new capital resources in an economy. For this purpose we can contrast the military budgets of a single year with the gross fixed capital formation achieved by economies during the same period. The latter category is a measure of all new civilian (private and public) structures, machinery and equipment added to an economy during a given year.

For 1979 (the last year of available data compiled by the United Nations) we observe that for every $100 of gross fixed capital formation in the United States, $33 was separately expended for military purposes. The ratios of military spending for each $100 of new fixed capital formation were:

Ratios of Military Spending to New Capital Formation

Country	**Percent for Military Spending** (per $100)	**Country**	**Percent for Military Spending** (per $100)	
U.K.	32	West Germany	20	
France	26	Japan	3.7	
Sweden	23	USSR	66	(my estimate, no U.N. data)

Within the American economy access to capital resources is limited for industrial managements by their ability to wield finance capital. We are indebted to President Eisenhower for calling attention, in his farewell address of January 17, 1961, to the fact that "We annually spend on military security more than the net income of all U.S. corporations." From 1951 to that date, the annual budget of the Department of Defense had, each year, exceeded the net profits of all corporations. That pattern has continued from 1961. Hence, the federal managers of the U.S. military economy have wielded, for thirty years, the largest single block of finance capital resources in the American economy.

This concentration of capital resources in behalf of military economy necessarily limits their availability for civilian economic purposes of every sort. Two conditions control this effect. The first is a limitation conferred by nature itself: materials or energy used in one place cannot at the same time be available at another place. A second limitation derives from the character of the products of military economy: *whatever other usefulness may be assigned to them, military products do not add to the ordinary goods and services of consumption or to capability for further production.* The extensive use of capital resources for military projects precludes the possibility of constructing needed industrial and allied plants and equipment (Melman, 1981).

The Effect of a Permanent War Economy on Productivity

For a century prior to the mid 1960s, industrial output per person employed in the U.S. manufacturing industry tended to increase at about 3 percent a year. This was a direct consequence of the sustained use of industrial capital to increasingly mechanize industrial work. So long enduring was this pattern that a 3 percent rate of industrial productivity growth came to be identified as virtually inherent in American economy. By 1965 this condition was transformed. Here are the average annual rates of productivity growth thereafter:

Productivity Rates, 1965–1980

Period	Average Annual Productivity Rate
1965–70	2.1 percent
1970–75	1.8 percent
1975–80	1.7 percent

These were not only the lowest annual rates of productivity growth recorded for American manufacturing but also the lowest rates of productivity growth in any major industrialized country for which data are available. Here is the comparison of average annual rates of growth in manufacturing industry productivity from 1965 to 1975 in the following countries:

Manufacturing Growth Rates, 1970–1975 and 1965–1970

Country	Average Annual Rate of Growth	
	1970–75	1965–70
Belgium	8.2	6.8
Canada	3.0	3.5
France	3.4	6.6
Germany	5.4	5.3
Italy	6.0	5.1
Japan	5.4	14.2
Netherlands	5.8	8.5
Sweden	4.4	7.9
Switzerland	3.5	6.2
United Kingdom	3.0	3.0
United States	1.8	2.1

We have already accounted for the fact that in Japan and Germany, as contrasted with the United States, capital resources have been used with priority to civilian economic use. The low and declining rates of U.S. productivity are a direct reflection of the lessened use of capital for the mechanization and other types of modernization of industrial work.

The declining rate of annual productivity growth in U.S. industry has also been vitally affected by the changed character of the decision rules governing the mechanization of work. While many factors surely affect output per person employed in industry, considerable evidence supports the understanding that average output per person is most directly controlled by the degree of mechanization of work and the accompanying organization of production. The mechanization of work in U.S. industry had long been governed by the continuing effort of U.S. industrial managers to minimize their costs of production the better to maximize profit. In the effort to minimize production costs, U.S. industrial managers typically had the opportunity to replace direct manual effort by machine production. *This replacement was spurred by the fact that prices of machinery had long tended to rise at a lesser rate than the wages of labor.* This important effect was obtained as the managers of U.S. machinery-producing industries in turn strove to minimize their costs. Thus as these managers responded to increasing costs, like wages of labor, with efforts to offset them by improving their own efficiency, they were able to offset all or part of the cost increase. *Therefore they did not have to increase prices of their machinery products to the same degree as the wages of their workers. For the users of machinery, this meant a sustained pattern of advantages in shifting from manual to machine performance of work. The consequence was automatic increase in productivity per person in manufacturing* (Melman, 1956).[1]

This classic pattern that had induced productivity growth in U.S. manufacturing was abridged during the 1960s as the cost-minimizing mechanism was altered by the institutionalization of a new decision-maker, the federal government and its Department of Defense, functioning as the effective central administrative office managers of 37,000 industrial firms or parts of firms (i.e., prime contractors).

The military establishment developed a sustained pattern of purchasing on a cost-plus basis. Also, the Department of Defense under Robert McNamara institutionalized a series of practices, like historical costing and concurrency in production scheduling, which had the automatic effect of inducing rapid cost and price increases for the industrial products produced to their specifications.

As these and related methods were made preferred and characteristic practices in military-serving industry, the tradition of cost-minimizing was displaced by an effective pattern of cost-maximizing. Insofar as this penetrated the machinery-producing industries, the results have included severe abridgment or termination of the traditional cost-minimizing process.

By the 1970s the results were plain enough. Here are the percent changes in the hourly earnings of industrial workers compared to changes in machine-tool prices from 1971 to 1978:

Wages and Tool Prices Compared

	Worker Earning per Hour	Machine Tool Prices
United States	+72	+85
Germany	+72	+59
Japan	+177	+51

These crucial data show that in Germany and in Japan machine tool prices advanced far less than the wages to industrial workers. In those countries the classic cost incentive favoring the further mechanization of work continued, with special strength in the case of Japan. *The Japanese pattern during the 1970s closely resembled the development in the United States during the first half of this century that had spurred productivity growth* (Melman, 1983).

In the United States, however, the 85 percent increase in average machine-tool prices, exceeding the 72 percent rise in worker earnings, marked the close of the classic process, which had induced industrial productivity growth. In response to this new pattern which reflected a cost-maximizing rather than a cost-minimizing style of managerial decision making, the users of American machine tools responded as one might expect. They proceeded to purchase fewer new machine tools, and of those that they did buy, an increasing proportion were purchased outside of the United States. During the 1970s the metalworking industries of the United States operated the oldest stock of metalworking machinery of any industrialized country. By 1980, 25 percent of the machine tools purchased in the United States were imported.

There has been a further effect of the military economy with far-reaching consequences for the viability of civilian production in the United States. During the 1960s and 1970s there has been a shift in the position of the United States, notably in relation to Germany and Japan, with respect to thc number of scientists and engineers serving civilian industry per 10,000 in the labor force. By 1977 the data were as follows:

Number of Scientists and Engineers Serving Civilian Industry

United States	38
Germany	40
Japan	50

This means that as compared with the United States, a larger proportion of the available population of scientists and engineers in Germany and

Japan, notably the latter, were functioning in the service of civilian product design and civilian production.

Effects on the Technical-Economic Competence of U.S. Industries

The normal functioning of the American military economy has withdrawn technical brains and hands, capital for production, and incentive for productivity growth from American civilian industry. Under these conditions, it should be no surprise that many American firms became progressively less able to hold market position in the face of competition from outside the United States (notably those firms endowed with less imaginative, less venturesome, and less production-oriented managements). By 1978–79, U.S. production of many classes of goods had been displaced by production performed abroad, especially in Western Europe and the Far East. The following is a sample of commodities with the indicated proportion of imports as a percent of U.S. consumption during 1978–79.

Sample of Imported Commodities

	Percentage of U.S. Consumption Produced Abroad 1978–1979)
Automobiles	26.7
Machine Tools (1980)	24.6
Steel mill products	15.4
TV sets, black and white	87
Calculating machines, handheld	47
Calculating machines, desktop and printing	39
Microwave ranges and ovens	22
Communications systems and equipment	16.3
Integrated microcircuits	33.8
X-ray and other irradiation equipment	24.3
Motion picture cameras (1977)	74
Sewing machines	51
Tape recorders and dictation machines, office type	100
Bicycles	22
Apparel	19.7
Leather gloves	37
Footwear (nonrubber)	45
Flatware	50.1

The percentage of production once performed in the United States translates directly into permanent loss of productive livelihood for the people of these industries (Melman, 1983).

Since the elemental task of an economy, any economy, is to organize people to work, it is evident that the military economy of the United States is an antieconomy. Independently of intention, the military economy of the United States disables the competences ordinarily required for the conduct of economic life.

I have estimated that $3,800 billion of fresh capital outlays will be required to repair the damaged U.S. industrial system and infrastructure. (See Melman, 1983:chap.14.)

The eroding effects of a permanent war economy on the largest and richest industrial economy lead one to expect that less industrialized countries are bound to be even more vulnerable to depletion by military economy.

Of $600 billion world military expenditures in 1980, 23 percent was accounted for by developing countries. Furthermore, during the 1970s these nations increased military spending at a more rapid rate than the industrialized states.

Until the late 1970s a much quoted but flawed book by E. Benoit (1973) was the basis for confident affirmations that military spending spurred economic development. Thereafter, a series of statistical studies (Kaldor and Kidron, 1976; Marcha, 1975; Nabe, 1982; Smith and Smith, 1980) established that there has been a systematic negative relationship between military spending and development.

In a report to the United Nations, *Barriers to Conversion from Military to Civilian Economy*, I estimated the 1979 military-industrial workforces of several key countries:

Estimated Military-Industrial Workforce

Country	Military-Industrial Workforce
USSR	4,800,000
United States (1974)	2,000,000
Great Britain	600,000
Federal Republic of Germany	325,000
India	270,000
Israel	70,000
Egypt	40,000

Military economy has become the sole livelihood for millions of men and women in industrialized and unindustrialized countries, notably for the many engineers, scientists, and managers who are employed in disproportionately great numbers by the military economy. That job experience is highly specialized and differs everywhere from what is required by civilian industry. In the absence of alternatives, this specialization, locking large numbers of educated and well-paid people into the military economy, translates into a political commitment to the arms race and to its supporting technical and production activity. That is the case in Western capitalism, the Soviet Union, and developing countries.

In each country the military organization controls the largest single block of industrial resources of the economy. Consider the crucial factor of supply of capital. In the United States the largest of Western military economies, the fresh resources made available to the Department of Defense have each year since 1951 exceeded the net profits (after taxes) left to the managers of all private corporations.

In each of these Western capitalist countries the military-industrial economy is organized and operated on a state managerial basis. A large central administrative office staff in the federal government of each society oversees the major operations of the military-serving enterprises. Thus, while buying and selling operate in each economy, the fact is that company (seller) behavior is monitored by an elaborate network of government (buyer) administrators who, functionally, manage the seller firm. The military-serving firms must comply with exacting regulations (Armed Services Procurement Regulations in the United States) that are written and administered by the central office staff of each ministry of defense.

In the USSR, a command of economy is operated in a context of shortages of goods so numerous and pervasive that some Soviet authorities characterize their economy as a deficit economy. Under such conditions, there is no "marketing problem," no issue of finding purchasers for all manner of goods. Supply is a central problem, quite possibly *the* central problem, for both the managers of the national economy and the managers of single enterprises in the Soviet system. Problems of supply in the USSR are addressed within the limits of a centralized priority system.

The military economy of the USSR commands a large but officially undesignated proportion of manufacturing resources and manufacturing products. The proportion taken by the military, however, is large enough so that priorities, as between military and civilian uses, are discussed at the highest levels of government.

Available (fragmentary) evidence suggests that cost-maximizing is operative within the Soviet military industry.

Military Economy in Developing Countries: Egypt, India, Israel

Wherever a developing country operates a military economy, its factories are islands of efficiency, modernity, and sophisticated production equipment, with management methods that closely resemble those in fully industrialized economies and, typically, the highest wages and salaries in the country. All these features of military industrial enterprise appear in surroundings of human and material underdevelopment that include unreliable communications, unclean water supplies, and impoverished conditions of production and consumption.

Military industry in a developing country is treated as a top priority area by government and suffers few or none of the supply problems that afflict the managers of civilian industry, which is chronically short of capital.

The managers and engineers of military industry in developing countries are not constrained by market pressures to minimize cost in design and production. The military product is sold before it is produced.

The military economies of developing countries display a unique set of characteristics—they combine the cost-maximizing and subsidy-maximizing pattern of the Western "market" economies with the power and privilege pattern of supply priority that characterizes the military economy of the USSR.

In each country a production ministry, which is part of the ministry of defense, wields top managerial control over a network of enterprises that produce weaponry of many sorts, and in each case these are government financed and owned. Privately owned firms participate in the military enterprise as subordinate suppliers of common use articles such as housekeeping equipment, textiles, and parts of raw materials that are the inputs for weapons fabrication.

In each country there is a central administrative office, and senior civil servants comprise the core of a team of state managers who operate the military economies on a continuing basis, giving the systems a policy continuity, independent of elections and party politics.

In Egypt, the military-industrial network draws 40,000 people from the total industrial labor force of about one million. In Israel the military-industrial enterprise employs 60,000 to 75,000 out of 300,000 in manufacturing. In India, military industry includes 270,000 out of the seven million employed in all the factories of the country.

But the economic and other importance of the military-economy networks in each society derives not only from the numbers involved, but also from the quality of the people and of the facilities they operate. For example, computer-controlled machine tools are part of the advanced "state of the art" in metalworking production around the world. Wherever civilian industrial managers must reckon with the cost of production and the price of the product as it affects salability, computer-controlled machine tools have characteristically been introduced as an offset to the cost of industrial workers and others earning high wages. Wherever there is a concentration of computer-controlled machine tools in civilian economy, it is clearly accompanied by the highest wages to production workers.

In the case of military production everywhere, cost-minimizing criteria are replaced by emphasis on the timing and quantity of production targets and the ease of maintaining militarily desirable quality standards. In underdeveloped countries the state managers, who have priority access to capital funds mobilized for them by the government, can and do requisition computer controlled machine tools for military industry. This produces the extraordinary sight of military factories laden with the most expensive and sophisticated metalworking equipment, even in areas where the ordinary civilian telephone system is unreliable and the supply of electric power is problematic.

Military production is shielded from the full impact of the surrounding conditions of economic underdevelopment. Where civilian telephone networks are unreliable, military-industry management has installed separate and private microwave communications systems. Where ordinary public transportation is obviously deficient—requiring long waits for overcrowded buses—military-industry managements deploy fleets of private buses to move their employees to and from the workplace. Where housing has been in short supply and so expensive as to be well beyond the reach of ordinary industrial workers, military-industry managements have used their priority access to capital funds to invest in housing for their employees.

In all three countries senior officials of the ministries of defense indicated that they had access to capital and other resources—effectively outside the limitations within which all other parts of the government must operate. In Egypt, a planning official said that if the Ministry of Defense asks for, say, one hundred million £E over and above planning ministry preliminary estimates, then the Ministry of Defense gets it. In India, a senior official of the Ministry of Defense Production told me that single capital investments in the magnitude of $100 million were completely plausible when priority military production is involved. In Israel, senior authorities stated that fresh allotments of capital in magnitudes of hundreds of millions of dollars were manageable when priority military items are involved.

Thus Israel and India are active producers of jet aircraft and military helicopters, and the Ministry of Defense factories of Egypt are fully equipped to produce small and heavy weapons, ammunition in quantity, and precision-built short-range rockets of several varieties. India now produces its own heavy tank—an immense and costly industrial undertaking in any country, and Israel has been in the midst of development and industrial investment for a heavy-tank program.

In these three countries the priority pattern is clear. Even where there are planning ministries, the ministry of planning doesn't interfere with the ministry of defense proposals. Whatever they ask for, they get. In India, during a lengthy discussion, a senior planning official repeatedly emphasized that neither his department nor any other division of the Planning Commission has any information on, or jurisdiction over, the Ministry of Defense or military industry. As reported by an Egyptian planner: under widespread conditions of shortage and the need to wait in line, the military-industry manager is usually first in the line.

The military-industry top managers of Egypt, Israel, and India report that cost plus is a dominant pattern for the internal operations of their military-industry enterprises. The idea that a cost-plus system of paying for military-industry products might induce a sustained escalation of cost (cost maximizing) has evidently not been considered by the senior administrators of military-industry networks. In Israel, an economist in the Ministry of Defense had only recently discovered that, while the military-industry firms were paying employees on the basis of a national job-wage schedule, the largest military-industry firm had been increasing its actual wage and salary costs 10 percent more rapidly than the rest of the country. This was the result of generous incentive payments, premiums, and fringe benefits. In India, informal reports from several major military industry enterprises indicate that employees, plants and equipment are being used seriously below capacity. In all three countries weaknesses of infrastructure, like power shortages and failures, reduce operations below capacity and thereby automatically prevent a sustaining cost-minimizing policy from emerging anywhere in the industrial economy. Furthermore, data from Egypt, Israel, and India reflect a pattern of imaginative enlargement of fringe benefits, even alongside "fixed" wage and salary systems; and these too have the effect of escalating costs.

To be sure, cost maximizing does not proceed indefinitely. It is limited by the readiness of the state to maximize subsidy. Therefore cost maximizing moves at a pace that is acceptable to the top administrators in each country. A further restraint on cost maximizing is the comparison often made between the prices of military products in Egypt, Israel, and India as against those for comparable products in Western Europe and the United States. Since the wage and salary schedules of these developing countries are well below West European and U.S. levels, the use of industrialized-country prices as a benchmark provides a wide margin within which the cost-escalating process can proceed.

Costs rise also in Egypt, Israel, and India because rules governing employment security are observed, while opportunities for economic conversion are neglected. Egypt, Israel, and India all have regulations, with the effect of law, that guarantee employment in the military-industry enterprises once a new worker has undergone an introductory or trial period. These arrangements are strongly reinforced by government policy and popular consensus: the government maintains employment and pay—with or without work. In Egypt and India, where the ranks of the unemployed and underemployed are very large, the pressure for employment/payroll maintenance is particularly intense. This is notably the case for the whole range of educated occupations, where the supply of applicants far exceeds the ability to organize such people for productive work. In all three countries, military-industry enterprises "stockpile" people in the guise of "providing employment." One inescapable consequence is escalation of the wage and salary overhead of military-industry firms.

The military budgets of these three and other developing countries represent the largest equivalent capital funds of those nations. The lack of contingency planning to use them for productive economic development is a definite limitation on their development prospects. Until such planning is begun, one may be confident that economic underdevelopment will continue.

In 1979, the world's developing nations spent over $90 billion on their own armed forces. In January 1980, a world conference of the United Nations Industrial Development Organization, held in New Delhi, India, marshalled the talents of representatives of all the developing nations and produced a consensus report whose keystone was a request that, from 1980 until the end of the century, the industrialized nations of the world should make available to the developing nations an additional $30 to $40 billion a year for the purpose of speeding industrialization. Assuming that to be a reasonable estimate of the sums needed, it is evident that the developing nations are themselves using up in their military enterprises a capital fund that far exceeds the requirement for accelerating their own economic development.

Compare the following 1979 ratios of military spending to civilian capital formation:

Selected Ratios of Military Spending to Civilian Capital Formation

Country	Ratio of Military Spending to Civilian Capital Formation
United States	33
U.S.S.R.	66 (Est.)
Japan	3.7
Israel	117
Egypt	100 (1977), 36 (1979)
Zimbabwe	99
Syria	96
Ethiopia	67
Kenya	20
Korea (South)	20

These ratios of military to civilian use of capital resources define a primary limit on economic development in the Third World.

The Arms Race and Economic Conversion

The main implications of my 1980 United Nations report apply in 1983. With respect to military economy and economic conversion, the similarities among the countries examined far outweigh the differences. Whatever the national differences of size, wealth, culture, geography, history, power, social and economic structure, the governing establishments of the United States, United Kingdom, West Germany, USSR, Egypt, India, and Israel share the common ground of having no contingency plans for economic conversion of their military economies. Diverse ideological rationalizations are advanced to justify a common decision: neither aggregate nor enterprise-level contingency planning should be done for economic conversion. The decision not to do alternative-use planning is paralleled, in each government, by the absence of assigned professional responsibility for developing workable blueprints for reversing the arms race.

Within each of these nations the military-industrial economy controls the largest block of industrial production resources under one management. These industrial systems enjoy subsidies that are generous beyond the hopes of the rest of society. Their internal operations are typically free from pressure for minimizing cost or for greater productivity.

For the state managerial establishment of each nation, the military-industrial network is the basis for dominion over scientists, engineers, managers and production workers. The capital intensity typical of military industry marks its rulers as the top economic decisionmakers of each society. The military/economic position leads rapidly to political power through the particular institutional channels of each nation.

None of this is to say that there are no policy differences to be found, not so much among, as within, the nation-states. Governments are the formal spokesmen of each state. However, manifest differences on conversion policy are emerging within states as a growing array of problems, domestic and international, are seen to be solvable only on the condition that the capital and technology resources preempted by the military economies are converted to civilian use.

From this growing recognition one may expect ever greater pressure within each nation to confront and cope with the problems of conversion. That action cannot be negotiated among states; it must be internally formulated and implemented. However, an international result can be predicted from that development. For just as the absence of conversion capability is a barrier even to formulating negotiating strategies to call off the arms race, the converse can also be true.

During the great armaments build-up that has followed World War II, the disposition of military economy, hence the conversion problem, has been the item omitted from the agenda of every meeting among states to consider the arms race in any respect. Therefore even a beginning of conversion capability within the nation-states will be a start toward reversing the arms race among the states.

That is why it is important to identify the barriers to economic conversion and to find ways to surmount them, everywhere.[2]

Notes

1. None of this is to say that other factors do not affect production competence or productivity. These include the training, morale, work competence and work traditions of the labor force, the presence of a long-term as against a short-term planning tradition among managers, the readiness of managers to invest in domestic industry rather than to seek investments abroad. And other factors are surely involved. However, studies in many industries and work operations have shown that major productivity changes are the direct effect of the degree of mechanization of work. This in turn is controlled—in cost-minimizing firms—by the relative cost of labor to machinery. This factor (and immediately associated variables) has been shown to account for about 78 percent of the observed variability in industrial productivity among major countries during the first half of this century (see Melman, 1956).
2. For further data and analysis, see the series of videotaped Briefings on Peace and the Economy: 1. The Military-Industrial Firm; 2. The Permanent War Economy; 3. Conversion from Military to Civilian Economy; and 4. On Reversing the Arms Race; and accompanying bibliography, available from the National SANE Education Fund, 711 G Street S.E., Washington DC 20003, (202) 546-7100.

References

Benoit, E. (1973). *Defense and Economic Growth in Developing Countries.* New York: Lexington Books.

Kaldor, M. and Kidron, M. 1976. "The Military in Development." *World Development* June.

Marcha, V.F. 1975. *The Impact of Military Expenditures on the Process of Industrialization in Latin America: Evaluation of Statistical Analysis.* D. Sc. Dissertation, Columbia University (University Microfilms, Ann Arbor Michigan).

Melman, Seymour 1983. *Profits without Production.* New York: Alfred A. Knopf.

_____. 1981. "Looting the Means of Production." *New York Times* July 26.

———. 1956. *Dynamic Factors in Industrial Productivity*. New York: John Wiley.

Nabe, O. 1982. *Military Expenditures and Socioeconomic Development in Africa*. Ph.D. Dissertation, Columbia University (University Microfilms, Ann Arbor, Michigan).

Smith, D., and Smith, R. 1980. *Military Expenditures, Resources and Development*. Mimeographed. London, England: Birkbeck College, University of London.

16

The Nature of War and the American Military Profession

Sam C. Sarkesian

Although war in this century had become progressively more complex and deadly, the development of nuclear and biological weapons following World War II signalled a dramatic broadening of the possible destructive dimensions of warfare. At the same time, modern revolution introduced another dimension of conflict that is less dependent on sophisticated and highly destructive weapons, but more protracted and potentially as destructive to a political system as nuclear war.

The different dimensions represented by nuclear war on the one hand and revolution on the other reflect not only the complexity of modern conflicts, but also unprecedented challenges to nation-states and international security. As a major world power with interests and alliances in virtually every corner of the world, the United States is placed in a position requiring an ability to respond across the entire conflict spectrum. This does not necessarily mean that the United States *must* respond; it does mean, however, that it must be prepared to do so.

The fundamental problem facing the United States is the translation of these issues of international security and challenges to it into reasonably clear national objectives and effective policy and strategy. One difficulty is created by moral and ethical dimensions that have emerged regarding war and American policy. Another involves disagreements over the qualitative nature of threats and the differing concepts and definitions of modern wars.

As a result, except in clear cases of threats to its national security, the United States is plagued by ambiguous national objectives, inconsistent policy, and confusing and often contradictory strategy. Nonetheless, the military instrument, as a major and often the primary instrument of American political-military power, is expected to respond to conflicts across the conflict spectrum, regardless of policy problems at the national level.

The purpose of this paper is to analyze the relationships between modern conflicts and the American political system as reflected in the state of the American military profession. The following specific points will be addressed: the character of modern conflicts as seen across a conflict spectrum, the capability and credibility of the American political system to respond to these conflicts, the relationship between America's response and its democratic value system, and the demands placed on the American military profession in carrying out political-military policy.

Two premises are necessary to the purpose of this paper. First, regardless of the variety of roles that the military institution must play in the modern era, and the complexity of domestic political and social forces that interact with the military, the primary purpose of the military remains as it has throughout history: to win wars. What has changed are the methods used to win, the concept of victory, the dimensions of military professionalism, and the relationship of the military to society.

Second, military professionalism cannot be realistically examined in the abstract. It must be studied in the context of the political system from which it evolves. While there are some universal principles of military professionalism, for the most part, the nature of the state determines the nature of the military system.

The Conflict Spectrum

For purposes of policy analysis and development wars can be characterized according to their scope and relative intensity. Such an approach complements rather than replaces other ways of characterizing war. Hence, in addition to the focus on intensity used here, wars may be viewed, for example, historically, geopolitically, or technologically.

Fig. 1 shows how various kinds of conflict can be organized on the "conflict spectrum" (see Sarkesian, 1981a:6). On the low intensity end of this spectrum are shows of military force and the giving of military assistance. At the high extreme, gallactic thermonuclear war. Other conflicts fall between these two extremes. What I call midrange conflicts are in general revolutionary or counterrevolutionary in nature. It is these midrange wars—conflicts like those in Nicaragua, El Salvador, Afghanistan, Cambodia, and Angola—that are most likely to occur in the foreseeable future (see, for example, Cohen's analysis of war-proneness in this volume.)[1]

Although this classification system distinguishes five levels of intensity between the lowest category and the highest two categories, the classification of the level of intensity of actual wars is not straightforward. This is because there is sometimes a relatively fluid shifting among these levels of

FIGURE 1
Conflict Spectrum

*Noncombat Force Employment	Surgical Operations	Revolution/ Counterrevolution	Conventional War	Nuclear War
		**I II III Vietnam	Limited General	
		INTENSITY		
LOW		MID-RANGE		HIGH

*Includes shows of force and military assistance.
**These indicate types from lower to higher levels of revolution and counterrevolution.
I-Weapons Assistance Teams: police training, advisory teams
II-Special Forces teams: care for indigenous forces (continuation with Type I)
III-Integration of U.S. combat units with indigenous forces (continuation with Types I and II)
Classification of all types includes requisite economic assistance.
Adopted from Sarkesian 1981a.

intensity in response to situational demands which indicate the possible need for escalation.

Further, low and midrange intensity conflicts tend to develop ambiguous sociopolitical and psychological dimensions that do not lend themselves to clear policy choices. Moreover, if a country has based its political-military posture on high-intensity conflict it is difficult to adapt it to the demands of low and midrange conflicts.

Nuclear Strategy and Military Posture

Since deterrence is a basic factor in the relationships between major powers, it is a logical starting point in studying high-intensity conflicts. In brief, deterrence is the ability of a state to appear ready, able, and willing to use superior military force to insure that another state will not take actions that are contrary to its self-interest.[2]

How deterrence is perceived differs, as do the capabilities of the major powers. In no small way, these differences can be attributed to the character of nonnuclear conflict. A nuclear power incapable of deploying credible forces in nonnuclear confrontations makes itself vulnerable to nuclear blackmail; either it must choose nuclear war or withdraw from the conflict. Thus, for example, Israel (a nonnuclear power, at least as of this writing) has a more credible nonnuclear capacity than England (a nuclear power). America's New Look strategy of the 1950s is also a case in point. Threatening nuclear devastation against any adversary challenging its "national interests," the United States placed itself in a zero-sum game situation. Either nuclear weapons had to be used or credibility would be lost. That such a policy did not work quickly became apparent. As one scholar has written,

> The shift to an overriding strategy of nuclear deterrence has placed the military in an anomalous, not to say philosophically absurd, position. Armed forces are now maintained in order that armed forces shall not be used; their major commitment is to psychological warfare waged by politicians; and the object is of course to prevent military action. Soldiers are asked to develop a professional ethos in line with the new technology of violence and at the same time to accept the almost total illegitimacy of the most advanced technology relevant to the goal for which the profession ostensibly exists [Abrams, 1965:246].

This "bigger bang for the buck" strategy was quickly discredited because of its inflexibility, and it was superseded by Flexible Response as the Kennedy administration attempted to demonstrate America's commitment to protect freedom anywhere. In so doing, the Flexible Response strategy broadened the concept of deterrence. Its purpose was to provide a controlled use of force that could respond to low-level aggression as well as other forms of threat. The Vietnam experience, however, showed that the strategy was not completely effective. It could operate only if the adversary was willing to accept the strategic rules of engagement. An adversary who was willing to raise the "ante" made Flexible Response militarily questionable.

Since the Vietnam War, American policy seems to have become based on a deterrence strategy that incorporates nuclear and conventional capabilities that are almost exclusively focused on Europe or on European-type conflict environments.

Low- and Midrange Intensity Conflicts

Current perceptions of American military capability and credibility vary relative to geographic area and level of conflict intensity. Fig. 2 shows the relationship between United States military capability and United States military credibility.

FIGURE 2
Conflict Spectrum
American Credibility and Capability

	*INTENSITY	
LOW	MID-RANGE	HIGH
	U.S. Credibility	
Adequate	Poor	Poor-Adequate
	U.S. Capability	
Adequate	Poor	High-Adequate

*See Figure 1.

Adopted from Sarkesian, in Sarkesian and Scully, p. 6.

As indicated, American capability and credibility in low- and midrange conflicts are suspect. This is due primarily to the difficulty that American policymakers have had in translating nuclear power into political power outside of the European and U.S.-USSR strategic framework. This makes it difficult to develop a convincing policy and capability for responding to low- and midrange intensity conflicts. The problem is made more difficult because of the inability (and impossibility?) of blending American democratic norms with the use of force.[3]

From the perspective of American strategy, low- and midrange intensity conflicts (particularly revolution and counterrevolution) have important characteristics that distinguish them from high-intensity conflicts. In the main, the political and social factors are more pronounced and constraining. In major wars and nuclear conflicts there is usually little question as to the purpose of the war in terms of national security, political, social, and economic factors. These factors are secondary to questions about the state's survival. In nonnuclear conflicts, the main purpose of military actions is a function of political considerations and limited social and economic goals, since the survival of the state may not be at issue.

Additionally, involvement in nonnuclear conflicts requires distinctive military training and education—quite apart from a conventional competence. In this respect, policymaking processes and the military institutional focus and structure cannot easily transfer from a major war posture, either nuclear or nonnuclear, to the highly constrained and politically demanding nature of nonnuclear conflicts of a lesser order.

Yet political and military planners face a fundamental conceptual problem. There is no consensus about the meaning and concept of "low intensity." Paralleling this, a further problem occurs when they deal with revolutionary and counterrevolutionary wars (and these are the most difficult and most likely conflicts in the 1980s). Despite terminological confusion in the literature, three concepts emerge as primary reference points: guerrilla war, insurgency, and revolution.

In developing the political-social dimension of revolution and distinguishing it from guerrilla war, Fall (1963:357) states,

> It is . . . important to understand that guerrilla warfare is nothing but a tactical appendage of a far vaster political contest and that, no matter how expertly it is fought by competent and dedicated professionals, it cannot possibly make up for the absence of a political rationale. A dead Special Forces sergeant is not spontaneously replaced by his own social environment. A dead revolutionary usually is.

Several observations are in order here. First, *revolutions* are a fundamental challenge to the existing political order and to those who hold power in the system (Dunn, 1972:1–23). Second, armed conflict may be necessary for revolution, but is not sufficient for revolutionary success. The focus of revolution is the political system. In this respect, armed conflict is usually tangential to revolutionary purpose. Third, insurgency may denote an attempt to correct an immediate policy issue or problem, while revolution focuses on long-term political-social change. Yet all of these concepts are closely linked and are often used to describe the same phenomena. Nonetheless, each concept suggests a different strategy and doctrine. And civilian-military response requires that agreement be reached on the meaning of the particular conflict.

Revolution encompasses both political and armed conflict dimensions; guerrilla warfare is an appendage of a political structure. The purpose of guerrilla warfare is to maintain constant pressure on the armed forces and political effectiveness of the existing system, in order to erode its credibility and its legitimacy, as well as to provide needed protection for the revolutionary political organization. Thus, counterrevolutionary response to guerrilla warfare is inadequate without an aggressive political dimension.

There are five other important considerations about low- and midrange intensity conflicts. First, it is likely that American involvement in low- and midrange intensity conflicts will be as an external intervening force.

Second, these conflicts are likely to be asymmetrical. For the revolutionaries, for example, the conflict is a total one. There is therefore a psychological commitment that is enduring and directly linked to the political-social goals of the revolution. In contrast, United States' commitment to these conflicts is limited, both as to resources and as to political goals.

Third, low- and midrange intensity conflicts are ambiguous. The highly political-social complexity of the conflict shifts attention from the actual battlefield to the political-social system. In simple terms, it is difficult to distinguish between friend and foe.

Fourth, such conflicts are primarily unconventional. Often combatants and noncombatants are not clearly distinguishable. The United States Army is trained and organized mainly for conventional battlefield-based conflicts, and the conventional criteria for measuring military success (e.g., number of casualities, amount of real estate taken, significance of weapons captured) may not be meaningful indicators of success for low-intensity conflicts that are not battlefield based.

Fifth, low- and midrange intensity conflicts usually develop into wars of attrition and are protracted. This makes it difficult to maintain a consensus within the body politic to continue a war which has no clear political goals, in which conventional responses are inadequate, and which promise to be long and drawn out. In addition, the lack of political consensus can be transformed into active resistance against the conflict, and this may have a negative effect on the morale and effectiveness of American forces engaged in third-country operations.

As General Weyand (cited in Summers, 1982:7) stated,

> Vietnam was a reaffirmation of the peculiar relationship between the American Army and the American people. The Army really is a people's Army in the sense that it belongs to the American people who take a jealous and proprietary interest in its involvement. When the Army is committed the American people are committed, when the American people lose their commitment it is futile to try to keep the Army committed. In the final analysis, the American Army is not so much an arm of the Executive Branch as it is an arm of the American people. The Army, therefore, cannot be committed lightly.

In sum, modern wars are likely to be a mix of political, social, economic, psychological, and military factors. Moreover, such wars rarely have unambiguous beginning or endings. Thus, it is a grave mistake to assume that warfare can be clearly delineated into civilian and military spheres or that policy choices can presume that since World War II nothing has changed in the international security environment. Equally unrealistic is the view that the military profession is merely a military instrument that carries out "pure" military actions without reference to political-social complexities.

The American Military Profession

Speaking to the graduating class of the U.S. Military Academy in 1962, President Kennedy (1963:454) said:

> The nonmilitary problems which you will face will also be most demanding, diplomatic, political, and economic. . . . Whatever your position, the scope of your decisions will not be confined to the traditional tenets of military competence and training. You will need to know and understand not only the foreign policy of the United States but the foreign policy of all countries scattered around the world who 20 years ago were the most distant names to use. You will need to give orders in different tongues and read maps in different systems. You will be involved in economic judgements which most economists would hesitate to make. . . . Above all, you will have a responsibility to deter war as well as to fight it. For the basic problems facing the world today are not susceptible of a final military solution.

This call for a broader concept of military professionalism has generally gone unheeded. Indeed, when seeking a clear definition of their roles, military professionals frequently focus on military skills and competencies that are narrowly construed. This approach is supported by opinion and scholarly assessments which tend to view the military as clearly distinct and separate from the general society, politics, and the policy process. Accordingly, this narrow view argues, the less political the military, the more likely it be highly professional.

As I showed earlier, however, the nature of contemporary conflicts means that if the military profession is to be an effective instrument in American national policy, traditional battlefield-based definitions of military professionalism *must* be greatly altered. The necessary changes require an understanding of the political and social consequences of military operations and of the close links between military and civilian systems. Thus, discussion about the development of war making and sustaining capabilities cannot be left either to the military or to civilians alone. Rather it requires that decisions be made by civilians who have knowledge of the nature of military service and about the capabilities of military systems, together with military professionals who understand the character of political systems and of politics.

> The catastrophic prospects of nuclear warfare, the multinational defense alliances, and the fusion of military and civilian defense functions have brought an increasing political role-expansion of military officers. Even minor military decisions may have repercussions for the escalation of international conflicts to the stage of nuclear exchange. The role-expansion has arisen as a natural counterpart to the growing overlap between strategic and political issues [Abrahamson, 1972:38].

The military profession is thus placed in a triangular relationship with the demands of modern war and the need to conform to the expectations and demands of democratic society. What makes this relationship particularly difficult is that the demands of one may be contradictory to the demands of the other.

The Military Profession and American Society

Scholars have long addressed the issues of civil-military relations and the role of the military in American society (Kohn, 1975; Huntington, 1957; Janowitz, 1971; Sarkesian, 1981b). I do not intend here to review these perspectives. Nevertheless, I do identify major views about the character of the military profession and give special attention to the relationship of society and modern war. Throughout United States history, even on the battlefield, American society expects attention to certain levels of morality and ethical behavior: regardless of how good the ends, military behavior must conform to basic values and norms of democratic society.

A fundamental democratic tenet makes the military subordinate to civilian leaders. As Huntington (1957:80–85) points out, there are both objective and subjective means of control. Accordingly, the American political system places the military under the constitutional control of a civilian leader—indeed, of several civilian leaders, while budgetary considerations and overall size and career structures of the military, for example, are under control of a civilian Congress.

Beyond such formal controls, there are also various informal controls. Military personnel come from a democratic culture and are educated and socialized into a democratic system. Equally important, in the modern period, the relative openness of the military lifestyle exposes military men and women to the civilian values and to the civilian quality of life. These reinforce the democratic norms.

Moreover, it is generally recognized that there is an interaction between the general society and the military. Part of this is a result of the nature of international conflicts, and part is due to the nature of democratic society. As Ambler (1966:372) notes with respect to France, "... the old solution of dividing defense neatly into political and military realms was always partly fiction; in revolutionary-guerrilla war it is altogether unfeasible." This applies equally to the United States.

Democratic cultural values disfavor military professionals who become involved in politics. Thus democratic culture usually places the military in a clearly subordinate position in the political system and demands a clear delineation between military and civilian sectors.

Today, this narrow traditional concept of military professionalism places the military system in a situation that limits its ability to conduct modern war by denying a political role to a highly competent military elite. Additionally, this creates an intellectual vacuum which constrains the development of strategic military policies relevant to the modern period. Continued emphasis on equating professionalism with battlefield competency severely limits military professionals.

The conclusion to which my analysis leads is that the military is not and cannot be apolitical. Moreover, describing civil-military relations in the United States in terms of civilian control and supremacy is much too facile. Military men and women influence political events and policymakers through a variety of formal and informal channels. Also, the variety of formal and informal linkages between society and the military obscures the traditionally presumed boundaries between them. A broadening of the horizons of military professionalism and the "civilianization" of parts of the military system would also mitigate against the kind of military subservience to which civilian leaders have been accustomed.

Additionally, an understanding of the political and social consequences of wars is an important professional requirement. The military cannot wait until after the first shot is fired before it becomes concerned about force structure, contingencies, and characteristics of target areas. Future major wars will probably engulf the entire political-social system. Even limited wars are likely to draw heavily upon the psychological sustenance of domestic society. In sum, the triangular relationship between the military, modern wars, and society necessitates the development of a military professionalism that accepts a political as well as a miltary role.

A New Military Professionalism

A military profession limited to competency in accordance with traditional battlefield concepts would not be prepared to undertake the variety of tasks facing it in the future, and the profession would find itself increasingly isolated from the system it is designed to serve. It would thus be unable to get the credibility and support it requires to succeed in modern conflicts, except perhaps in cases where national survival is clearly threatened.

The alternative is to develop a model of military professionalism that balances political, social, and military goals. Such a model presumes that the various subsystems share the same values and can agree upon the norms of behavior. Under a revised code the military and society would each maintain its own integrity and identity, while political-psychological support to all individuals would be drawn for both from the political-social order, because the military would exist to support the democratic political-social order.

There are a number of other considerations in applying such a model to the military. First, as a political institution, the military can now pursue its goals through the legitimate informal channels and processes, but its latitude in the official sphere is legitimately restricted. It interacts politically with others with greater political legitimacy and latitude. In sum, the military institution has a distinctly secondary and subordinate role in the official sphere, but much leverage in the unofficial sphere.

Second, the relationship between the military and society is symbiotic. This symbiotic relationship most closely reflects a civilian-military partnership based on common educational and socialization processes. Additionally, the partnership between the military system and other political actors, although at times adversarial, is mutually advantageous in the pursuit of the goal of perpetuation of the political system. Conflict, tension, and a give-and-take in such a relationship are not, as some presume, antithetical to democracy. On the contrary, many social scientists argue that this is a sign of a healthy democratic system as long as all share a common democratic ideology.

Third, equilibrium rests on a dynamic, interacting, and self-adjusting relationship. If variation goes beyond acceptable standards for democracy, political pressures are exerted to restore a reasonable democratic congruence. The acceptable relationship between the two sectors is determined by a variety of political linkages and influences. The critical mass of these relationships must be within the acceptable boundaries of democracy and must support the democratic system.

Thus there is a pressing need to review the prevailing concepts of civil-military relations and of military professionalism to determine how appropriate they now are. The evidence suggests that there is ample cause to question what has become an intellectual and military tradition—an ideal view of civil-military relations and a narrow definition of military professionalism.

Once these realities are accepted we can then ask what kind of military professionalism is needed if we are to be able to respond to modern conflicts and operate in a democratic system. To develop such a view requires "enlightened advocacy" (Sarkesian, 1981a, 1981b).

Enlightened Advocacy

Enlightened advocacy is a concept of military professionalism that is not bound only by military considerations. Also considered are social and political implications of military decisions and the need to set priorities that mix civilian and military considerations. In this context, enlightened means the ability to go beyond the bounds of military skills and to understand the nature of democratic society. Advocacy means the articulation of a particular point of view or policy while attempting to influence the political system to accept such a point of view or policy.

The military profession must study and understand its own society and political system if it is to be effective. To be sure, there are those who argue that such an approach would lead to a politicized military whose activity and function would eventually erode the basis of democracy. There is compelling evidence that suggests the opposite: those who understand the prerequisites, the history, and the evolution of democracy and democratic political thought are more likely to be committed to such a system. Those who are not fully cognizant of the process demanded by democratic systems are likely to distort the meaning of democracy and engage in activities inimical to the system. This is an argument for the kind of understanding and civic education that will provide the intellectual wherewithal for military professionals to be sensitive to the complexities and consequences of military-civilian struggles in democratic systems.

It is clear that no military system in a liberal democracy can legitimately engage in political action in support of one or another political party. Political knowledge, political interests, and awareness, however, are not the same as political action and bipartisan politics. Indeed, the more they have of the former, the less likely that the military will develop the latter.

Developing a new military professionalism is a task in which civilian policy makers and the public at large must participate. They must review their concepts and understanding of the meaning of military professionalism. Too often, these reflect simplistic notions about the military, and are too frequently clouded by demeaning and prejudicial attitudes.

Conclusion

The nature of modern wars and the complexities of democratic society make it particularly difficult for the American political system to develop and maintain a credible and capable military force. The use of military force in international politics has not diminished. But the use of military force by the United States in its role as superpower has taken on serious moral and ethical implications that are increasingly affected by domestic politics.

Complicating the problem is the fact that many effective responses to low- and midrange conflicts can threaten democratic norms. Additionally, United States involvement as an intervening power into revolution and counterrevolution evokes fears of Vietnam.

Regardless of the complexities facing the American system with respect to modern wars, the military profession is placed in the position of being required to be able to respond across the conflict spectrum. At the same time, the profession must operate within the norms of democratic society. Traditional concepts of military professionalism, particularly with respect to the nature of modern wars, may be inadequate to serve either the military or society.

A new professionalism can be based on the recognition that the military is a political as well as a military instrument. This demands that military professionals develop political understanding and an educational level that allows the synthesis of political with military requirments.

Besides the nature of political leadership with respect to national will and political resolve, one of the greatest responsibilities for developing and maintaining American credibility and capability in modern war rests with the military profession. What is needed for the future is well expressed by General Weyand (cited by Summers, 1982:25),

> As military professionals we must speak out, we must counsel our political leaders and alert the American public that there is no such thing as a "splen-

did little war." There is no such thing as a war fought on the cheap. War is death and destruction. The American way of war is particularly violent, deadly, and dreadful. We believe in using "things"—artillery, bombs, and massive firepower—in order to conserve our soldiers' lives. The enemy, on the other hand, made up for his lack of "things" by expending men instead of machines, and he suffered enormous casualties. The Army saw this happen in Korea, and we should have made the realities of war obvious to the America people before they witnessed it on their television screens. The Army must make the price of involvement clear *before* we get involved, so that America can weigh the probable costs of involvement against the dangers of noninvolvement . . . for there are worse things than war.

Notes

1. This kind of classification of conflict intensity applies at the group, not the individual level.
2. This is in reference to objections to nuclear war fighting or the planning of the use of nuclear weapons, on the basis of moral considerations. Such objections are reflected in the "freeze" movement and the stand of the Catholic bishops.
3. As former Secretary of State Dean Acheson expressed this:

> No American purpose, it could be pointed out, depends upon our using force against anyone. But we must be prepared to deter or meet the use of or the threat of force against our interests. When we speak of deterring the use of force against us, what do we mean? A deterrent is a threat under certain circumstances to do harm to another, which the other believes we will do and does not want to provoke. A threat is not believed, and therefore cannot deter, unless there is a general conviction that the threatener has both the capacity and the intention to carry out the threat. . . . Therefore, to deter or meet force used or threatened on a local basis, capacity in what are called conventional forces is required, that is, forces which can conduct limited warfare and keep it limited. Even these will not act as a deterrent or moderating factor unless others believe that they will be used [Acheson, 1957:464–65].

References

Abrahamson, Bengt. 1972. *Military Professionalism and Political Power*. Beverly Hills, Cal.: Sage.

Abrams, Philip. 1965. "The Late Profession of Arms: Ambiguous Goals and Deteriorating Means in Britain" *European Journal of Sociology* 6(2).

Acheson, Dean. 1957. *A Citizen Looks at Congress*. New York: Harper & Brothers.

Ambler, John S. 1966. *The French Army in Politics, 1945–1962*. Columbus, Oh.: Ohio State University Press.

Dunn, John. 1972. *Modern Revolution: An Introduction to the Analysis of Political Phenomenon*. London: Cambridge University Press.

Fall, Bernard B. 1963. *Street without Joy: Insurgency in Indochina, 1946–63*. 3d rev. ed. Harrisburg, Pa.: Stackpole.

Huntington, Samuel. 1957. *The Soldier and the State: The Theory and Politics of Civil-Military Relations.* New York: Vintage.

Janowitz, Morris. 1971. *The Professional Soldier: A Social and Political Portrait.* New York: Free Press.

Kennedy, John F. 1963. *Public Papers of the Presidents of the United States; Containing the Public Messages, Speeches and Statements of the President: John F. Kennedy, 1962.* Washington, D.C.: U.S. Government Printing Office.

Kohn, Richard H. 1975. *Eagle and Sword: The Federalists and Creation of the Military Establishment in America 1783–1802.* New York: Free Press.

Sarkesian, Sam C. 1981a. "American Policy and Low Intensity Conflict: An Overview." In *Potentials for Military Struggles in the 1980s: U.S. Policy and Low Intensity Conflict*, edited by S.C. Sarkesian and W.L. Scully. New Brunswick, N.J.: Transaction.

_____. 1981b. *Beyond the Battlefield: The New Military Professionalism.* New York: Pergamon.

Summers, Jr., Harry G. 1982. *On Strategy: The Vietnam War in Context.* Carlisle Barracks, Pa.: U.S. Army War College.

17

War and Peace: The View of a Soviet Scholar

Valery A. Tishkov

In the mid-1850s a Russian officer who took part in the Crimean campaign[1] wrote down the following while his experiences and thoughts under enemy fire on the bastions of Sebastopol, besieged by the English and French, were still fresh in his mind:

> A strange thought often occurred to me: what if one of the warring sides suggested to the other than each army remove one soldier apiece? The wish might seem strange, but why not carry it out? Then a second would be removed from each side, then a third, a fourth, etc., until only one soldier would remain in each army (assuming that the armies are of equal strength and that quantity would be replaced by quality). And then, if complex political issues among rational representatives of rational beings really can be settled by a fight let these two soldiers fight—one would besiege the city, the other would defend it [Tolstoy, 1979:103].

The Crimean War, already so remote from us, was no "ordinary," "local" war: according to some estimates, a million lives were lost (Urlanis, 1960).

These losses and devastations shook the Russian officer—the great Russian writer Leo Tolstoy—and today his words sound strikingly topical. But this is so not only because the proposed disarmament plan according to the principle of equal security—as his thoughts might, apparently, be translated into modern political language—is by no means easier to carry out today than it was over a hundred years ago. Leo Tolstoy's thought is close to us today mainly because he was shaken by men's very habit of settling their quarrels by means of massive, armed fights, that is, by war.

On the Nature, Origins, and Historical Types of War

Many of those who attempted to master the laws of human development came to a disconsolate conclusion that war as a social phenomenon was unavoidable and that it was a natural aspect of relations between countries and peoples. Some theorists and politicians maintained that war, with all its cruelty and destructiveness, was a virtue, not an evil. This outlook found its most crystallized expression in the ideology and policy of Hitler's fascism.

It might have seemed that the lessons of World War II should have done away forever with attempts to treat war as a means of solving problems faced by mankind. But even today, however, some of those in power are guided in their policy by the acceptability of a world nuclear war as if it were nothing to be afraid of. For instance, Zbigniew Brzezinski (1978) expressed an opinion that in the event of a nuclear conflict about 10 percent of the world population, i.e., over 400 million, would die, and, "it is inaccurate thinking to say that the use of nuclear weapons would be the end of the human race. . . . I don't know if it's a good thing or a bad thing to say that this notion is wrong, but I know it is wrong factually."

As to the students of origins and causes of wars, very few have dared to maintain openly that wars were useful and necessary for the functioning of human society. Most authors never failed to realize that for the vast majority of the population wars were far from attractive; on the contrary, they caused repugnance and fear. But quite often we come across an opinion that the popular masses have no choice other than accepting the inevitability of wars and that those masses, or man per se, cause the emergence and persistence of this evil.

This includes first the so-called psychological theory of the origins of war. The premise here is that violence and a desire to kill one's own kind are inherent and inevitable features of human psychology (Jaspers, 1951). According to this view, the causes of wars are rooted in the domain of the irrational, subconscious instincts of people, which are uncontrollable by the mind, inaccessible for scientific analysis, and unmanageable. Therefore, any attempt to comprehend the nature of war and to eliminate it is doomed to failure. Thus, it is alleged, there is no reason to blame a given social system or a social class or warmongering, since wars are caused by individuals, by nations consisting of bellicose people.

In accordance with the theory of social Darwinism, nations and states are either strong or weak, either fit to exist in today's complicated world or not, war being the only test for categorizing a given nation or state. Social Darwinism directly leads to racism, which professes a natural inequality of races, a superiority of certain races over others, and even a right of "superior" races to eradicate or enslave the "inferior" ones.

In another theory of the origins of war, the Malthusian theory, Malthus (1815, 1820) and his modern followers conclude that epidemics, hunger and wars are natural "safety valves" eliminating from time to time the "surplus" population.

The geopolitical theory of the origins of war is also closely linked to racism and Malthusianism. It is based on the premise that states, especially densely populated ones, like biological organisms, either grow and spread to the territories of other countries or die. It follows that it is neither the specific aspects of the state's social system nor its policy that leads to the pursuance of territorial aggrandisement, but its geographical location, the ratio of the size of its territory to the population. From a geopolitical viewpoint, war is but a necessary means to obtain *lebensraum* for the "surplus" population.

The twentieth century saw the emergence of yet another theory of origins of war which maintains that wars are an inevitable corollary of the existence of sovereign nations and states. Sovereignty, independence of one state from another, and the absence of a supreme supranational authority are alleged to lead to an inevitable anarchy in the world, to a conflict of interests among different nations, to contradictions between them which can be eliminated by war. According to these authors, the variety of causes of armed conflicts between states is indeed endless. For instance, it is maintained that the raison d'être of wars is incompetence, narrow-mindedness, and a lack of foresight in statesmen. It is stressed that wars are caused by personal ambitions of those holding the reins of state power, or by a lack of mutual understanding between leaders in various countries, by their inability or unwillingness to make a sober assessment of the states' legitimate rights and interests, and to reach reasonable agreements on this basis, thus eliminating the need to use armed force. The advocates of these views consider war easily avoidable. From their viewpoint, it would be sufficient to entrust state power to honest, enlightened and well-intentioned leaders who would always be able to find an honorable solution to the most complex problems, thus preserving peace and good relations with the like-minded leaders of other states.

There is no doubt that both the personalities of statesmen and the institutional forms of international relations do have a certain, and in some cases a decisive, role to play in the success or failure of measures to prevent an armed conflict. And in this sense, improving the means of peaceful settlement of international disputes is important and necessary. In the same vein, the conduct of the leading statesmen has a far from insignificant role in international affairs, especially in crisis situations. The role of these factors becomes extremely important in the age of atomic weapons when a very limited number of persons can make a decision to push the button which would unavoidably bring global war.

Therefore, those who stress the importance of all these aspects in the prevention of wars are justified. Their fallacy, however, is in that they regard them as the basic, if not the sole, cause of armed conflicts between nations.

Marx and Engels worked out a truly scientific view of war as a distinct social phenomenon. According to their theory, it was the division of society into classes with antagonistic interests that generated wars. Class and state politics can be implemented both by peaceful and by violent means. One of the latter is war. Strictly speaking, the formula: war is the continuation of policy by other means, belongs to General von Clausewitz (1918). "This famous dictum," V.I. Lenin observed, "was uttered by Clausewitz, one of the profoundest writers on the problems of war. Marxists have always rightly regarded this thesis as the theoretical basis of views on the significance of any war. It was from this viewpoint that Marx and Engels always regarded the various wars" (Lenin, 1977, 21:304).

War is by no means a mere continuation of the foreign policy of a state; it is also a continuation of its internal policy and of relations between classes within a state (Lenin, 1977, 24:400). Moreover, internal policy, being a direct reflection of the class nature of a state, in the final analysis determines the basic orientation of its foreign policy.

In determining the attitude toward a war it is important to keep in mind the class character of the war: what classes are pursuing their interests by waging it, and what historical and historico-economic conditions gave rise to it (Lenin, 1977, 24:398–99). From this, one very important conclusion on the legitimacy and progressive character of civil wars emerges, that is, "wars waged by an oppressed class against the oppressor class, by slaves against slave-holders, by serfs against landowners, and by wage-workers against the bourgeoisie, are fully legitimate, progressive, and necessary" (Lenin, 1977, 21:299). Thus, Marxism-Leninism regards colonial liberation wars against foreign oppression as just and legitimate.

In making a distinction between just and unjust wars, we think that both are caused by the system of class rule and by the exploitative nature of presocialist systems. It is not by the striving of the exploited to effect transformations that civil wars are caused, but by the exploiters' attempts to prevent the inevitable. National liberation wars are caused not by the peoples' desire for freedom, but by the wish of imperialists to suppress this desire by any means, including armed force, and to preserve the colonial system. The cause of wars between the capitalist states and the countries where socialist revolution has taken place is not the wish of the latter to spread revolution over to the former, but the striving of imperialism to eliminate socialism as such.

It is necessary to take into account not only the social orientation (progressive or regressive) and character (just or unjust) of the course followed by each of the belligerent powers, but also the quantitative aspect of the social consequence of war (the number of victims and the scale of devastation). More often in Soviet writings on peace and war we find an opinion, that since the consequences of even a just war may be disastrous for social development, war is now considered also from the point of view of its expediency. Irrespective of its moral and political characteristics, a world nuclear war spells irreplaceable losses and impedes social progress, and therefore it cannot be regarded as a rational way of overcoming political differences between states (Dodin and Zhdanov, 1983:51).

The historical typology of wars is linked with the social contradictions of its particular historical epoch. Thus, classification of wars is complicated by the fact that each war has its specific characteristics, and a particular category very rarely finds expression in a particular war.[2]

The main types of wars in slave-owning societies were: wars of slave-owning states against less developed tribes, wars between these states to gain the territory and goods of conquered countries, wars between different groups of slave owners, slave rebellions, peasants' and craftsmen's uprisings.

The main types of wars in feudal society were: wars between feudal states, wars between feudals for enlarging their possessions, wars to establish centralized feudal states, wars against invaders, peasant wars against feudals, urban uprisings against feudal exploitation.

Wars of the premonopolistic capitalism period may be classified into the following main types: colonial wars of capitalist countries against peoples of Asia, Africa, and Latin America; aggressive wars between states and coalitions of states for domination in certain regions; revolutionary, antifeudal, and national-liberation wars; wars for national consolidation; civil wars; and proletariat uprisings against the bourgeoisie.

The main types of wars in the contemporary period are: wars between states with different socioeconomic and political systems, civil wars, national-liberation wars, and wars between capitalist states. The Second World War, because of its complicated character, had a special place among contemporary wars.

Recent events suggest some additions to this classification. First, in this final quarter of the twentieth century, the most widespread type of armed conflict is war between developing countries. These military clashes are generated by religious and territorial disputes, by tribal strife, and by scrimmages for sources of raw materials, compounded by general social and economic backwardness and neocolonialist policy. Second, there is the new question of armed conflicts between states belonging to the world socialist system. Soviet observer A. Bovin (1982:109) explains this phenomenon as follows:

> It is clear in theory that such wars are contrary to the nature of socialism. But as we have already had occasion to see, the "nature of socialism" in historical reality does not exist by itself, in abstract theoretical purity. Socialism's development may be accompanied with deformations, some of them fairly considerable. The common reason for them is the social, economic, and political backwardness of many of the countries that take the socialist road, coupled with the lasting influence of petty-bourgeois views and notions. Fertile soil appears for nationalism and chauvinism, and that can easily affect the foreign policy of the country concerned. And a foreign policy shot through with chauvinism may be (and does become) a source of armed clashes between countries belonging to the world socialist system.

The Doctrine of Peaceful Coexistence

In its first decree, the Decree on Peace, the Soviet Republic proclaimed its central objective in foreign policy to be the struggle for a just and durable peace, for ridding humanity of the nightmare of senseless predatory wars. Peace was desperately needed by the young Russian Republic in order to strengthen the Revolution and to build a new society. But in the sixty-year history of the USSR, for every year and a half of a peaceful construction there has been a year of war or of recovery from the destruction of war. And it is an obvious fact that enemies of socialism have tried to destroy the socialist order by force many times in the past. Even today the greatest diehards in the ruling circles of bourgeois society are harboring similar plans for crusades against communism. In fact, capitalism created nuclear weapons with the view of "solving" the contradiction between the two social systems by destroying socialism in a nuclear war. There is enough evidence that the United States were preparing for a nuclear war against the USSR in 1945, even before World War II was completely over (Brown, 1978). Obviously socialism had to take this into account and create an appropriate counterpoise.

Ideally, socialism needs neither an army nor immense arms expenditures, for by its very nature it is a system which rejects war and aggression. Neither classes nor social or professional groups in the socialist countries have vested interests in war or expect to gain economically as a result of the arms race. Quite a number of problems confront the socialist countries, and they may be solved only under the conditions of durable peace. But as long as a real threat of attack from without exists, socialism is compelled to bear the burden of unproductive expenses so as not to be caught unawares, so as to defend what has already been won by the people.

An extremely important feature of the Soviet foreign policy, one of its fundamental principles, is the principle of peaceful coexistence of states with different social systems (see e.g., Gromyko and Ponomarev, 1980; Lebedev, 1980; Chubaryan, 1976). The vitality and effectiveness of the policy of peaceful coexistence have been tested by the practical experience of the USSR and other socialist countries. At present this course is meeting growing understanding and support in many nonsocialist countries, and the principle is reflected in the United Nations Charter. This policy responds to the needs of our time: promoting the opportunities which the scientific and technological revolution opens to humanity, the tendency toward internationalization of the world economy, the closer economic interdependence of different countries, cooperative efforts in solving important problems in the fields of energy, transportation, and raw materials, the improvement of various forms of communication and transmission of information, and so on.

The very concept of peaceful coexistence implies that the goal of such a policy cannot be achieved through the efforts of only one state. It is a two-sided process, assuming the mutual readiness of countries with different social systems not simply to refrain from fighting one another, but also to recognize negotiations as the only way to solve controversial issues, to reject a policy of aggression, to establish and develop equitable, mutually advantageous cooperation in the economy, science and technology, culture and politics.

Here we approach a very crucial question of the dialectics of social progress (or revolution) and peaceful coexistence. Arguments of Western writers concerning Moscow's so-called striving to "world domination" as a threat to peace are based upon the following postulate: since the core of the political system in the USSR was and remains the Communist party and Communists are for the revolution and allow for the violent overthrow of capitalism, there can be no talking about their peace-loving aspirations. Many writings by Western authors portray Communists as publicly expressing their devotion to peace but carefully concealing the fact that they allegedly want to use peaceful coexistence and disarmament to facilitate the armed overthrow of capitalism. The dialectic view of revolution and peaceful coexistence frequently seems inconsistent, contradictory, even insincere to people who are far from Marxism.

The Marxist approach to this question is that the forms of transition from capitalism to socialism depend on the concrete situation in a given country and on the general situation in the world as a whole. It is precisely the nature of these objective conditions which determines the way socialist revolution might be accomplished, and what forms it might take—peaceful or nonpeaceful. Communists are convinced opponents of the "export of revolution," that is, attempts to "make" a revolution for the working class of another country by force, by interference from without. That is why Communists have always and everywhere stressed so insistently that the policy of exporting revolution is fruitless and mistaken. Lenin wrote in 1918 that Marxism "has always been opposed to 'pushing' revolutions, which develop with the growing acuteness of the class antagonism that engenders revolutions" (Lenin, 1977, 27:71–72). Exactly the same position was expressed recently by the late General Secretary of the USSR Communist Party, Y.V. Andropov (1983), in his speech at the Plenary Session of the party's Central Committee:

> Communists are sure that the future belongs to socialism. That is one path of history. But it does not mean at all that we are going to "export revolution," to interfere in the internal affairs of other countries. To "export revolution" is absolutely impossible. Socialism grows only on the soil of objective demands for societal development in each country. We strongly believe that Socialism will prove its merits in peaceful competition with capitalism. And we are not interested in the military competition enforced upon us by imperialism.

Unexpected evidence against the theory of the export of revolution came from Z. Brzezinski (1979). Speaking at the annual meeting of the American Association of Newspaper Editors, he referred to the changes ("revolutionary," as the Communists would say) which are taking place in an "arc of crisis that stretches across Southern Asia to Southern Africa. . . . We [i.e., Americans] must not make the mistake of assuming that change and turbulence, by themselves, are evidence of external mischief . . . [on the contrary] they were usually the result of the internal dynamics of a particular country."

The Communists, while opposing the concept of the "export of revolution," which has nothing in common with their philosophy, ideology, or politics, also resolutely condemn the opposite concept, namely "export of counterrevolution." International reaction and imperialism go to the extreme in their attempts to establish their "right" to crush the revolutionary, democratic liberation movement in the world. In the nuclear age such an antipopular, antihumane, reactionary policy is fraught, apart from everything else, with the danger of critically aggravating international tensions and, conceivably, causing a nuclear catastrophe.

Peace and War in the Light of Nuclear Parity

The contemporary situation brings us back to Clausewitz's postulates, which need very serious corrections in the nuclear age. Clausewitz's formula has a double meaning. On the one hand, he states as a fact: "Politics is the womb which conceives war" (Clausewitz, 1918:94). This is certainly true when war is started. Then it is an instrument of politics, the continuation of politics, irrespective of what kind of war it is and what kind of weapons are used—conventional or nuclear. In this case Clausewitz's formula is quite up-to-date. On the other hand, this postulate offers the politician a choice—whether he should pursue his purposes by peaceful means or resort to armed force. But can anyone nowadays imagine a total nuclear war as "another" political means, as an example of rational political behavior? It is impossible to find arguments justifying nuclear war and yet remain within the limits of reason. No political purpose can justify jeopardizing the survival of civilization itself.

This new situation revealed itself clearly when the equalization of Soviet and American military potential brought about what Henry Kissinger (1979:6) described as "a revolution in the strategic balance."

Nuclear parity is a rather vague concept allowing for various interpretations. What is absolutely definite, however, is that neither side possesses such a mighty nuclear potential as to disarm the enemy. Therefore, he who strikes the first will die the second.

Under these conditions of "assured mutual destruction," nuclear balance and parity become essentially a means of preventing war. That is why Andropov (1983) made the following statement:

> Peaceful coexistence is objectively promoted by strategic parity between socialism and capitalism. The establishment of this parity is one of the most important achievements of recent decades. It has taken our people and the peoples of other countries of the socialist system enormous efforts and resources, and we shall not allow it to be disrupted. We are going to take all the necessary measures to maintain our security and that of our friends and allies, we are going to strengthen the defense capabilities of the Soviet Armed Forces, a powerful factor in restraining the aggressive aspirations of the imperialists.

Shifting from the realm of strategy to that of psychology, some specialists describe the resulting situation as an "equilibrium of fear." It is anything but cozy to live in the shadow of a global cataclysm. But we have no other choice. While the strategic equilibrium has worked for peace, not war, a peace resting on an "equilibrium of fear" cannot be stable and constant. Strategic parity tends to reproduce itself at an increasingly higher level. Armaments always play a dual role: they are the basis of security for one side and a source of danger for the other.

There may be two ways out of this nuclear stalemate. The first is resolute action against the threat of a head-on collision of the two systems, a gradual lowering of the level of strategic parity, and security obtained not through build-up but through limitation of armaments. The second is "rationalization" of nuclear war through perfection of technological means and techniques, and the premise that such a war can be won. The first leads to international detente, the second to intensified confrontation.

In the context of the imperative of detente we want to attract attention to such a notion as the historical limit to war, more and more used in recent literature. The military-technological revolution has filled the peace and war dilemma with new historical meaning and substance: on the global scale, it is not merely war or peace but a world nuclear war or peaceful coexistence, and from the point of view of the dynamics of social development, the situation is such that war cannot be regarded as a rational means of attaining political goals, or as a rational policy. Since there is actually no alternative to peaceful coexistence, it is possible to say that the world has reached the historical limit to war (Dodin and Zhdanov, 1983:55). The factors of reaching the historical limit to war are different: social (i.e., at present the threat of world thermonuclear war impels the masses to actions also in peacetime, not only with the opening of hostilities, as it was in the past), geographical (means of destruction has made peace necessary for humans and nature because the explosions will affect a territory exceeding the area of the globe), demographic (the threat of extinction of humanity), economic (unprecedented scale of annihilation of productive forces and products of labor), and so on.

Whence the Threat to Peace

All talk about contemporary problems of peace and war is fruitless without an attempt to discover who threatens world peace today. Practically speaking, we have three different points of view on this question. The first postulates that Soviet military build-up and external policy have caused the international tensions and are a threat to Western strategic interests. The second treats the rivalry between the two superpowers, with their ambition for world domination, as the major threat to world peace. The final view attributes the main reasons for international tensions and the growing danger of world catastrophe to the imperialist U.S. policy of world domination through nuclear superiority to prevent the development of socialism and national liberation throughout the world.

I share this last point of view, and analyze here major facts from postwar history which may give an impartial answer to the question of who really challenges whom, and who is building up military power without restraint, creating a menace to peace and the security of nations.

In August 1945, the world learned of the appearance of the most destructive weapon in history—the atomic bomb—developed by the United

States and used, with no military need, against the civilian population. The subsequent Soviet proposals for banning the use of nuclear energy for military purposes were turned down by the United States. So, in face of the threatening danger, the Soviet Union took countermeasures and developed its own atomic bomb.

In the 1950s the United States became the initiator of a race for strategic armaments. On the excuse of having "fallen behind in bombers," the Pentagon obtained large allocations from Congress and set in motion a large program for the construction of strategic bombers. After an armada of these planes had been built, however, it was discovered that the United States had deliberately exaggerated the number of Soviet bombers three to four times over.

In the early 1960s a howl was raised about a "U.S. missile gap," and the United States initiated a massive deployment of ground-based intercontinental ballistic missiles (ICBMs). Then, after more than a thousand of these had been deployed, it turned out that the Soviet "missile threat" had been exaggerated fifteen to twenty times over. Simultaneously, an American program was launched to build forty-one nuclear-powered ballistic missile submarines (SSBNs). At that time no one in the world had them. And, in the mid 1960s, the Pentagon began fitting submarine-launched ballistic missiles (SLBMs) with multiple reentry vehicle (MRV) warheads.

At the end of the 1960s and the beginning of the 1970s, the United States was the first to begin arming strategic ballistic missiles with multiple, independently targetable reentry vehicle (MRV) warheads, starting a new spiral of the nuclear arms race. Thereupon it began developing a new type of strategic weapon—air-, ground-, and sea-based long-range cruise missiles with nuclear warheads.

In 1981, the United States President ordered the full-scale manufacture of neutron munitions, and in 1982, the special command for space war activities was established and the United States started the militarization of space.

As for the Soviet Union, it has initiated no new types of weapons throughout postwar history. In building its armed forces, it has only reacted to dangers created by the West. The USSR has never aspired to positions of military superiority, and has always confined itself to measures ensuring security for itself and its allies. It is the United States that is trying to upset the military parity and the military-strategic equilibrium. That is the goal pursued by the United States President in his program of comprehensive strategic arms build-up announced in October 1981. Reagan's program extends to all the components of the strategic offensive forces, and includes deployment of MX intercontinental ballistic missiles and new strategic bombers, construction of Trident nuclear-powered missile submarines, escalated production of various types of cruise missiles, and other projects.

In its Soviet Military Power pamphlet, the U.S. Defense Department says the Soviet Union has 1,398 ICBM launchers, 950 SLBM launchers, and 156 heavy bombers with a total payload of nearly 7,000 nuclear weapons. These figures, taken in isolation, sound impressive. But the pamphlet makes no mention of the 10,000 nuclear weapons of the U.S. strategic offensive forces, which have 1,053 ICBM launchers, 648 SLBM launchers, and more than 570 heavy bombers, plus 65 medium bombers. In addition, the United States has thousands of nuclear-capable aircraft in its forward-based forces in the proximity of Soviety territory in Europe, the Far East, and the Indian Ocean (USSR Ministry of Defense, 1982:6).

It should also be borne in mind that the Soviet Union is confronted not only by the United States, but also by two other Western nuclear powers.

Some Western officials and propagandists allege that the Soviet Union seeks a "global projection of Soviet military power." In reality, the Soviet Union has military contingents in the territory of only some of its East European allies and in neighboring Mongolia and Afghanistan, while U.S. military units are deployed in dozens of countries up and down the world, and there are more than 1,500 U.S. military installations and bases overseas, chiefly in the proximity of Soviet borders.

Questions about the arms trade, especially involving arms shipments to developing countries are very controversial and complicated. In a Pentagon pamphlet the USSR is portrayed as the biggest exporter of military hardware, though the United States accounts for nearly 45 percent of world arms trade and other NATO countries for more than 20 percent of the arms trade. According to the report prepared by the democratic fraction in the U.S. Senate, the United States shipped abroad in 1982 alone, war munitions for $21.5 billion (see Pravda, 1983). And it is common knowledge that U.S. arms go to shore up reactionary and dictatorial regimes, to suppress revolutionary and national liberation movements, and to consolidate the U.S. military presence in the recipient countries.

It is of interest to compare some other aspects in the development of atomic and thermonuclear technology. In 1954, the USSR launched an atomic power plant, the first one to be built in the world. This signalled the beginning of the development of atomic power engineering designed to serve peaceful purposes. In 1958, the first nuclear-powered vessel also intended for purely peaceful purposes, the icebreaker *Lenin*, was launched. According to the president of the USSR Academy of Sciences, academician A. Alexandropov (1982:18): "The USSR has always considered the knowledge related to the development of the civilian aspects of its nuclear technology common property of mankind." For this reason, detailed information on the working principles of the first atomic power plant, the Siberian APP and the icebreaker *Lenin*, was communicated to the First and Second Geneva conferences. During his 1956 visit to Great Britain, academician I. Kurchatov read the first communication on the use of controlled thermonuclear fusion for peaceful purposes. In the years to follow, Soviet scientists continued to inform the world's scientific community on the results achieved in those areas of nuclear power engineering where they took the lead.

In most recent years two very different attitudes are present in world politics in reaction to the danger of nuclear war and struggle for peace and disarmament. The Soviet Union, the other socialist countries, and the majority of states stand unequivocally for peace. Soviet initiatives in the 1960s and 1970s led to several important agreements and treaties:

- on nuclear nonproliferation
- on the prohibition of nuclear weapons tests in three media
- on the prohibition of the placement of weapons of mass annihilation on the sea and ocean bed
- on the prohibition of bacteriological weapons, and so on.

On the initiative of the USSR, Soviet-American agreements in the field of strategic arms were reached. While SALT 1 still holds today, SALT 2 was rejected by the present administration in the United States.

Committing itself unilaterally not to be the first to use nuclear weapons, the USSR confirmed once again that concern for removing the threat of war remains the chief element of its policy. The USSR and its allies in the Political Declaration, adopted by the Warsaw Treaty member countries in Prague in January 1983 proposed that an agreement be concluded between the Warsaw Treaty and NATO countries that would contain a reciprocal commitment not to resort to the use of any weapons—either nuclear or conventional. In other words, not to use force *at all* in relations between them. The proposal to prohibit force thus was proposed for the first time in history.

Today, Soviet initiatives and proposals comprise an all-embracing program of measures, from individual steps in the field of arms limitations to general and complete disarmament, including a total ban on nuclear weapons and favoring their destruction. The USSR has made proposals on overall and complete measures of control.

Opposed to this resolute course of peace, of ensuring international security is the policy of the aggressive imperialist forces. That policy is the source of the serious aggravation of the international situation in recent years. This is happening because representatives of circles with clearly expressed imperial ambitions, preaching the cult of force in international relations and bent on remaking the world according to their own standards, are now at the helm of Washington's foreign policy.

The United States has derailed the SALT 2 Treaty, broken off a whole series of negotiations, and refuses to resume the talks on the complete and universal prohibition of nuclear tests, on limiting the deliveries and sales of conventional weapons to other countries, on limiting military activity in the Indian Ocean and on a number of other questions. The U.S. administration is now pursuing an obstructionist line at the Soviet-American talks in Geneva on the problems of limiting and reducing strategic arms and also on limiting nuclear arms in Europe. Besides large programs for modernization of its weapons of mass destruction, the United States has in effect violated SALT 1 by its decision to commence the deployment of a large-scale ABM system.

The Reaction of Humans to the Danger of Nuclear War

The predominant form of human or public reaction to the danger of war has been, and still is, a denunciation of war as a negative, immoral, and frightening phenomenon. Metropolan Yuvenaly (1982:147), quoting a verse from the New Testament, "Glory to God in highest heaven, and on earth his peace for men on whom his favor rest" (Luke 2:14), pointed out that "this hymn of praise marked the beginning of the Christian era on earth." This reaction found its most characteristic reflection in antiwar, peace, or pacifist movements which have a long historical tradition and experience. I do not attempt to cover this question here in historical perspective, and only analyze the current antiwar movement as a prevailing form of contemporary man's reaction to the danger of nuclear war.

More and more people in various regions and countries of the world realize that the international situation has reached a crucial stage and that the maintenance of peace and prevention of global war depend on their own efforts. The scale and character of antiwar public activities allow us to describe the whole movement as acquiring a qualitatively new stage in its development. This was especially true in 1983, when millions of people took part in antiwar activities, especially in Western Europe.

The most important feature of the contemporary antiwar movement is the steady expansion of its social and political base. New professional and political groups begin to participate in it. In addition to Communists, it has been joined by influential sections of social-democratic, liberal, and other bourgeois political parties, as by the trade unions and various women's and youth organizations, by environmentalist groups, by businessmen's organizations, by various pacifist bodies, by writers and artists, and by members of parliaments.

Among the most active participants in the antiwar movement are scholars from various countries who are specialists in a wide range of fields, representative of major scientific centers. This is probably due to both the level of information which scientists have acquired about the destructive force of the H-bomb and to the level of the sense of responsibility of the most educated strata of society.

This can also explain the very strong movement of physicians for the prevention of nuclear war: medical workers know better than any other professionals the real results of using nuclear weapons. In this case the knowledge of catastrophic consequences of nuclear war acts not as a damper but as a catalyst of public action.

The well-known authorities in the medical world participating in this movement see its mission as convincing the world public and the governments of the nuclear powers of the danger inherent in the continuing arms race and accumulation of nuclear weapons. For example, according to the estimations of Soviet physicians (Chazov, 1982:53–54, Chazov, et al., 1982), a ground explosion of a one-megaton nuclear device in a city with a population of one million will destroy one-third of its inhabitants. The shock wave and the fires will demolish buildings almost throughout the city. There will be no housing, no electricity, and no water. Food deliveries will be disrupted. Thermal (luminous) radiation will cause third-degree burns even at a distance of 12.5 kilometers from ground zero. The huge casualties will cause a host of sociohygienic problems, with the emergency treatment of injuries among the most acute. The experience of Hiroshima and Nagasaki shows that a nuclear attack will annihilate 50 to 90 percent of medical personnel. Those who survive will hardly be able to care adequately for the people injured by the nuclear blast. There will be a shortage of blood plasma, oxygen, and medical supplies. Mass outbreaks of contagious diseases are quite possible among the population weakened by radioactivity, injuries, hunger, the lack of fresh water, and excessive psychological stress.

During the past two years antiwar sentiments have grown among religious leaders, who now play a quite considerable role in this movement. No doubt this position of Church leaders reflects the antiwar inspiration among its rank-and-file believers, who look at the nuclear war as immoral. In this context, from an interview with Filaret, Metropolitan of Minsk (1983:10), we find that

> Most religious leaders rise against the threat of nuclear catastrophe, compelled by the awareness of their human nature and dignity, by the conviction

> that people must not let themselves be overcome by fear, but believe in the ultimate victory of the good, of reason, and of good conscience. I admit, however, that fear may come in here. For when one comes to know of the consequences of even the very first nuclear explosion in Hiroshima, one is stricken with fear, despite oneself. However, it is not only fear, of course, that inspires the anti-war struggle. The doctrine of threatening people with nuclear war, with ecumenical catastrophe, is repugnant to man's common sense, irrespective of his being a believer or atheist . . . For we cannot help but call this mad arms race launched by the Western powers a sin. This is the main theological foundation of all of our peacemaking activities.

Religious forces in the antiwar movement use more and more active forms of struggle: refusing to pay taxes, gathering signatures in support of proclamations, participating in peace marches. The National Council of Churches in India announced its support to make Asia a nuclear-free zone. Important antiwar actions were also taken by the Asian Buddhist Conference for Peace and the All-African Conference of Churches.

These new features in the character and struggle of the antiwar movement have not cancelled out the fundamental ideological and political distinctions between its separate segments. It is naive to ascribe the activity of such a broad movement to any guidance from some single international or national center, and to portray the antiwar actions, as is sometimes done, as "Communist-inspired."

The main reason for the growth of the peace movement is the deterioration of the international situation and the appreciation of the fact that the plans of the Pentagon and NATO are pregnant with the threat of nuclear war for Western Europe and other regions of the world. Ever broader sections of the public see that the recklessly tough line of the U.S. administration could turn Europe, and not Europe alone, into a war theater involving the use of nuclear weapons. People also remember the beneficial effects of detente, which had not only scaled down the war threat and inspired hopes for a peaceful future, but had also yielded immediate benefits through the broader economic, scientific, and cultural cooperation between states.

The mood of the masses is also influenced by the fact that in the present state of economic and structural crisis in major capitalist countries, the expenditures on social and cultural needs are being cut back while military budgets are skyrocketing. The success of the struggle for continued detente, for peaceful international relations, and for gratification of the immediate social and economic demands of the working people depend in many ways on the consistency and resolution of the actions against war preparation. Under present conditions these two aspects are closely linked.

For a better understanding of the origin and nature of the peace movement it is important to analyze priorities and slogans advanced by the different groups as well as the various forms and methods of actions in different regions and in capitalist, socialist, or developing countries. For example, in the European peace movement, the first task is to make this continent a nuclear-free zone. The thrust of all antiwar slogans here is directed to forbidding the manufacture of the barbarous neutron bomb (scheduled for use in the European war theater), and to preventing the deployment in Western Europe of new medium-range U.S. missiles. In Arab countries the struggle is against aggression, for liberation of occupied territories, and for peaceful and just regulation of the Near-East conflict. In countries of the Indian Ocean basin, it is a struggle for liquidation of foreign military bases and to make this region a zone of peace.

The strength and effectiveness of the antiwar movement also varies. It is strongest in Europe, where in the 1980s it achieved certain concrete results. In the early stage of the antimissile movement (1979), its participants did not succeed in preventing the adoption by NATO of its nuclear-missile decisions, but they did achieve some results. Under public pressure, the governments of Belgium and the Netherlands—two of the five countries in which the new weapons were to have been sited—had postponed their decisions on the matter. The mass actions and discussions at various forums displayed a considerable degree of agreement among representatives of various political trends and their awareness of the special danger that the NATO decisions contained for densely populated Western Europe. In the early 1980s the movement grew so much as to become an increasingly effective barrier to the implementation of the NATO decision.

The grass roots movement against NATO's missile decisions is gaining an ever-broader support. Besides the FRG, it encompasses Britain, Netherlands, Belgium, Portugal, Norway, Denmark, and a number of other countries. The demand not to deploy new U.S. weapons in Western Europe merges with specific local slogans.

Actions for nuclear-free zones have proliferated. A consultative meeting of peace organizations, gathered in Helsinki in August 1981, called on their governments to work out practical measures for establishing a nuclear-free zone in Northern Europe. At a 1981 Gröningen conference on nuclear war in Europe, prominent scholars and public leaders from Western Europe and the United States said that a nuclear-free zone stretching across Europe from Portugal to Poland would greatly help to eliminate the war threat. The slogan "A Europe Free of Nuclear Weapons from Poland to Portugal and from Italy to Ireland" is seen frequently nowadays at mass antiwar demonstrations in Western countries, especially Belgium, Portugal, the FRG, and Greece. At the moment of preparing this paper (June 1983) about three million signatures were collected in Sweden, Norway, Denmark, and Finland under the proclamation "For the Nuclear-Free North."

An important factor in the contemporary antiwar movement is the position of the developing countries of Asia, Africa, and Latin America that are being directly militarized. The United States has military bases and military advisers in eight Arab countries. Since the autumn of 1982, American soldiers have been stationed in Lebanon. The United States has been allowed to set up bases in Kenya and Somali. The United States is creating new military units and strong points in Central America and the Caribbean. Military expenditures in the developing countries themselves have grown almost two-and-one-half times, and the total military expenditures in the world are quoted as having risen from 10 to 19 percent. Therefore, the present deterioration of the international situation as a result of the imperialist policy of aggravating international tension and continuing the arms race, does the peoples of the developing countries much harm, both as to the general human interest in preserving peace and in specific subsequent problems in international relations.

Not very long ago the populations of developing countries underestimated the urgency of the problems of war and peace, believing that they only applied to the developed states or even exclusively to the greatest powers. These attitudes have now changed. The peoples and governments of the developing countries are beginning to oppose imperialism in questions of war, peace, and disarmament, and now place these in the foreground of their foreign policies.

These shifts in attitudes revealed themselves clearly in 1983 at the Seventh Conference of the Nonaligned Countries in Delhi. Attention was focused on the fundamental problems of the international situation, especially those of defense of peace, detente, and restraint of the the arms race. The conference named these objectives as the key tasks of the foreign policy of the nonaligned countries. In its final declaration, blame was laid on the United States and other imperialist states for the creation of hotbeds of tension and crisis situations in the Near East, Central America, South Africa, and the Indian Ocean basin. Peoples of these areas set themselves a twofold task: to help save humanity from the nuclear threat and to clear the path for socioeconomic development. They are coming to understand that imperialism, forcing conflicts and the arms race upon the peoples of the world, aims at keeping them in submission.

For a number of reasons, I want to give special attention to the peace movement in the Soviet Union. First, because it is characterized by certain specific features, determined by the sociopolitical structure and foreign policy of a socialist country. Second, because information spread by the Western mass media about this movement is either distorted or ignored. President Reagan's announcement at the second special session on disarmament of the United Nations that the struggle for peace is banned in the USSR can only be explained by ignorance or by ill will.

In actual fact, it is not the struggle for peace, but propaganda for war that is banned in the Soviet Union. It is forbidden by the basic law of the country—the Constitution of 1977. The Soviet government, which is itself a body of elected representatives of the people, works in the interest of the entire population of the country. The whole of the sociopolitical structure allows the people to control effectively the activities of the government bodies in the sphere of both home and foreign affairs, and to realize, through the channels of the political system, their aspirations and demands—in particular, those concerning the question of war and peace. In the Soviet Union it is unimaginable to be elected to any state, political, or social office on the platform of propaganda for war or calls to use force or even the threat of its use. Professing these views would mean the instant political death of the person involved, and his or her persistence in these would entail criminal prosecution up to imprisonment. This testifies to the complete unanimity of views on war and peace of the masses, on the one hand, and of the state and political mechanisms of power, on the other.

One important trait distinguishes the Soviet peace movement from that in the Western countries. It contains no antistate trend like that in many social and public movements in capitalist countries. This does not mean, however, that the movement is wholly "controlled" or "directed from above" and does not express the true sentiments and interests of the people.

In the USSR, various committees, unions, associations, and other public organizations are engaged in large-scale activities to popularize and translate into reality the ideas of peace, international cooperation, and disarmament. Millions of people representing all strata of the multinational Soviet society take part in the activities of these organizations on a voluntary basis. This includes workers and farmers, young people, Communists and nonpartisans, scientists, trade unionists, war veterans, the intelligentsia and clergy.

The forms and methods used are varied: mass meetings and demonstrations; collection of signatures on peace appeals; news bulletins and magazines; books and booklets on peace and disarmament; seminars, talks, and scientific conferences; sponsoring of international assemblies and public forums; and participation in press conferences on radio and television broadcasts.

The Soviet Peace Committee (SPC), founded in 1949, is a public coordinating body of the peace movement in the USSR. Members of the Committee (450 persons) represent all major public organizations, industrial and agricultural enterprises, research institutes, educational establishments, the mass media, and so forth. There are republican peace committees in the fourteen Union and sixteen autonomous republics of the country. If territorial and regional committees are included, the number of local committees totals 120. The supreme body of the peace movement in the USSR is the National Conference which convenes regularly and elects the SPC. Like the Soviet peace movement as a whole, the Committee is financed entirely by the donations of millions of citizens to the Soviet Peace Fund.

The Soviet Peace Fund (see Kharkhardin, 1982:211–19; Polevoi, 1982:229–34) was established in 1961 and at the present time over 80 million people contribute to it. In all republics and regions of the country, in cities and villages, at factories and on state and collective farms, committees have been set up to promote the Fund. They have over 4.5 million activists. Forms of contributing to the Fund are very different: donating a day's salary, benefit concerts and performances, art auctions, honoraria of scholars. School children collect waste paper, scrap materials for recycling, and medical herbs, and send the money obtained to the Fund. The Church makes voluntary contributions to the Fund as well, and the Fund also receives money and gifts from people of other countries.

Here are some data on the activities of the Soviet participants of the peace movement in the year 1982 alone:

In May-June, in support of effective measures of disarmament by the special session of the General Assembly of the United Nations, 60 million people participated in over 20,000 demonstrations and meetings.

In July-August, 700,000 Soviet people took part in the meetings with the participants of the international marches for peace, Stockholm-Minsk, and Moscow-Kiev-Budapest-Bratislava-Vienna.

In October, during the week of the mass action for disarmament about 50 million people took part in over 80,000 meetings, marches, and manifestations.

More than 12 million participants of these actions signed a letter to the United Nations demanding a stop to the arms race. This was circulated as an official document at the thirty-seventh session of the General Assembly.

Over 15 million Soviet youths sent protests against the preparation of nuclear war to the headquarters of NATO in Brussels (Zukov, 1983:90–91).

The contemporary antiwar movement as whole would seem to be the greatest in history. The postwar period witnessed at least four points of increase. The first occurred in the early 1950s, when 500,000 people signed the Stockholm appeal for banning nuclear weapons, which helped to frustrate General MacArthur in his plans to use the atom bomb in Korea. The second wave of the antiwar movement came in the 1960s, when demonstrations, meetings, petitions and protests hastened the victory of the Vietnamese people over the American aggressors. The third occurred in the 1970s when supporters of peace collected about 700 million signatures in support of the second Stockholm Appeal, rejecting plans by the United States to station neutron bombs in Europe. The future will show what fruits today's movement bears.

Notes

1. The Crimean War (1853–1856) was fought between Turkey, England, and France on the one side and Russia on the other.
2. The following classifications are based on the Grand Soviet Encyclopedia , vol. 5, 1971. (In Russian)

References

Alexandrov, A. 1982. "Science, Peace, Cooperation." In *Peace and Disarmament, Academic Studies*, edited by N.N. Inozemtsev, pp. 15–23. Moscow: Progress Publishers.

Andropov, Y.V. 1983. *Selected Speeches and Articles*. 2d ed. Moscow: Politizdat. (In Russian)

Bovin, Alexander. 1982. "Politics and War." In *Peace and Disarmament, Academic Studies*, edited by N.N. Inozemtsev, pp. 95–111. Moscow: Progress Publishers.

Brown, A.C., ed. 1978. *Dropshot: The United States Plan for War with the Soviet Union in 1957*. New York: Dial.

Brzezinski, Z. 1979. *The New York Times* 2 May.

Chazov, Y. 1982. "International Physicians for the Prevention of Nuclear War." In *Peace and Disarmament. Academic Studies*, edited by N.N. Inozemtsev, pp. 51–58. Moscow: Progress Publishers.

Chazov, Y.; Ilyin, Y.; and Guskora, A. 1982. *The Danger of Nuclear War: A Point of View of Soviet Physicians*. Moscow: APN Publishers. (In Russian)

Chubaryan, A.O. 1976. *Peaceful Coexistence: Theory and Practice*. Moscow: Politizdat. (In Russian)

von Clausewitz, Carl. 1918. *Vom Kriege*. Berlin and Leipzig: Behr.

Dodin, E.J., and Zhdanov, E.A. 1983. "Socio-philosophical Problems of War and Peace in Recent Soviet Literature." In *Peace Research in Finnish and Soviet Scientific Literature*, edited by Jakob Berger and Unto Vesa, pp. 48–64. Tampere Peace Research Institute, Research Report N. 26.

Filaret, Metropolitan of Minsk. 1983. "World Needs a Hope." *Literary Gazette* 18 May.

Gromyko, A.A., and Ponomarev, B.N., eds. 1980. *History of USSR Foreign Policy, 1917–1980*. 2 vols. Moscow: Nauka.

Jaspers, Karl. 1951. *Rechenschaft und Ausblick*. Munchen: Piper.

Kharkhardin, O. 1982. "The Soviet Peace Committee." In *Peace and Disarmament. Academic Studies*, edited by N.N. Inozemtsev, pp. 211–18. Moscow: Progress Publishers.
Kissinger, H.A. 1979. "The Future of NATO." *Washington Quarterly* (Autumn 1979):3–17.
Lebedev, N.I. 1980. *USSR in the World Politics: 1917–1980*. Moscow: Progress Publishers.
Lenin, V.I. 1977. *Socialism and War: Collected Works*. Moscow: Politizdat.
Malthus, T.R. 1815. *An Inquiry into the Nature and Progress of Rent, and the Principles by Which it is Regulated*. London: Murray.
———. 1820. *Principles of Political Economy Considered with a View to Their Practical Application*. London: Murray.
Polevoi, B. 1982. "The Soviet Peace Fund." In *Peace and Disarmament, Academic Studies*, edited by N.N. Inozemtsev, pp. 229–33. Moscow: Progress Publishers.
Pravda. 1983. 8 April.
Tolstoy, L.N. 1979. *Collected Works*, Vol.2. Moscow: Nauka. (In Russian.)
Urlanis, B.I. 1960. *Wars and Population of Europe*. Moscow: Sozegiz Publishers. (In Russian.)
USSR Ministry of Defense. 1982. *Whence the Threat to Peace*. Moscow: Voenizdat.
Yuvenaly. 1982. "The Russian Orthodox Church in the Struggle for Peace and Disarmament." In *Peace and Disarmament, Academic Studies*, edited by N.N. Inozemtsev, pp. 247–57. Moscow: Progress Publishers.
Zukov, Y. 1983. "A Mighty Force." *Communist* 3 (May):83–98. (In Russian)

PART IV

CONFLICT AND THE NATION-STATE

18

Ideology and Institutions in Peace and War

Silviu Brucan

Ideology and institutions are inextricably linked in human society. Old ideologies purport to perpetuate existing institutions; new ideologies serve to change them. Institutions need a legitimating ideology to lead people to accept their authority. Once an institution emerges, it often molds ideology to consolidate itself. In fact, the potency and viability of each depend on those of the other.

Since ideology is a highly controversial concept, I will define it as the particular view of the world that a class or social group acquires as a result of its conditions of existence and environment. As such, ideology is indispensable to any social group having a common interest and striving to promote it. However great the falsc clement it contains, ideology keeps a class together by common consciousness. It is ideology that drives men and women to act together, fight together, resist together, hold onto power together. Without ideology there can be no large-scale social action.

The struggle between peace and war revolves around institutions of power; only the possession of power makes it possible for the supporters of an ideology to realize its goals. I submit that the institution most directly involved in peace and war is the *nation-state* with its military machinery. While police forces generally belong to municipalities or other subnational entities, military forces belong to nations. This reflects the fact that the very existence of nation-states subjects us to the threat of war, thus requiring preparation against it. Such a vital aspect could not but exert a strong influence on ideologies; all nation-states acquire national coloration, causing citizens and their leaders to view the world through a common national periscope. Bourgeois ideology in the United States is somewhat distinct from that in France or Japan, as is Marxist ideology in the USSR from that in China or Romania. It is in this context that I will deal with institutions involved in peace and war from their origins to the way they appear in the world today.

Origins of War and Its Abolition

From time immemorial people have been fighting in groups for land and hunting grounds, for water and food, for dominance, sex, and revenge. We may ask: When did regular warfare with its institutional arrangements emerge as an organized and purposeful social exercise? We need to know in order to determine whether war is a historical rather than a natural category and, if it is, to infer when and how war will disappear or be abolished.

Although I consider Engels' thesis on the origin of the state to be of great theoretical importance, I am also aware of the limited information about ancient societies that was available in his time. Therefore, I shall risk some generalizations from anthropological research that acquired major dimensions only in the 1920s and 1930s when political anthropology came of age.

War as an organized social exercise developed only when politics took over as the regulating factor of human society and corresponding institutions were set up.

As a transition from primeval acephalous societies of the Paleolithic to the tribal organizations of the Neolithic Revolution took place, several constituent units (towns, villages, ethnic groups) coalesced, and some sort of centralized power was required to control this larger territory and to defend it against predatory neighbors and invaders. Multiethnic communities could not function without central authority and political organization. To the degree that a social group lost its autonomy and was assimilated into a larger unit—from band to tribe and to tribal unions or confederations—force became the inevitable companion of politics and required some sort of military organization.

So long as tools were relatively simple, food scarce, and no surplus of goods was available for trade, armed conflicts were fought along genealogical lines and territorial cleavages. With the development of more efficient tools, the emerging division of labor and subsequent accumulation for surpluses and wealth, economic gains and political territorial conquest played an increasing role in the outbreak of military hostilities.

Briefly, politics took over when (a) kinship ceased to be the social regulating factor; (b) large unions and confederations were constituted; and (c) surplus goods became available, providing a new motivation for territorial conquest. As a consequence, an armed force in embryo was set up.

With the division of primitive society into classes, politics turned into class domination, and the state became its main instrument.

A repressive public force, including a regular army, was created to serve the state in its dual capacity as the instrument of social domination inside society, and the armor of the city (or nation) against the external competition raging in the world arena.

Even so brief a consideration of primitive society demonstrates that the origin of war must be sought in both basic types of human aggregation—ethnicity and class—and in the dynamics generated by both ethnic and class inequalities. Although the two intertwine and interact, each has a different root, different cohesive ties, and an evolution of its own. Historically, the elimination of class antagonisms has not been enough to eliminate war. War will be eliminated when not only class contradictions but also discrepancies in power, wealth, and development among nation-states have been overcome.

Ideology and Relations between Nation-States

In international studies, "the state" is too abstract and lifeless a concept unless one fills it up with a national component. Experience shows it is not enough to mention the form of the state—whether authoritarian or democratic, capitalist or socialist. To understand its external behavior one must add that it is French or American, Russian or Chinese, Argentinian or Vietnamese, which brings the ethnocultural elements into the picture with all that comes from the strategic circumstances which mark the state's place in world politics. I can hardly think of a concept more meaningful and fruitful in explaining orientations and options, strategies and policies in the world arena than the nation-state.

Since the modern international system originated with the expansion of capitalism and the formation of nation-states in Europe, the patterns of behavior in interstate relations have been shaped by that historical symbiosis. Although the October Revolution of 1917 in Russia and subsequent revolutions in other countries have brought profound changes in the international system, they did not alter the basic structure of nation-states nor the patterns of disparities in interstate relations.

Unlike previous class societies that were split communities, the nation embraces all classes of the population in a given territory with the bourgeoisie striving to strengthen its political and ideological control by promoting the common ties and interests of the respective nations. We thus find in modern nations a replica of the two conflicting tendencies so characteristic of a tribal society: between the centrifugal effect of autonomy and territorial dispersion driving villages and tribes, and the centripetal urge for their aggregation into larger units to meet external competition. On the one hand, nations are torn by social conflicts and class struggles; on the other hand, whenever nations are waging a war, struggling against foreign domination, or perceiving a threat from outside, an impulse toward unity permeates all the component classes. As one or the other facet expands on a large international scale, it may well become predominant in the whole international system. Hence, modern history beginning with the French Revolution has been marked by class conflict alternating with sharp national rivalries. I have called this the seesaw of class and national motive forces, for, as one comes to prevail, the other goes down.

World War II is a classic example of the priority gained by national motivation and the strategic interests it entails. The United States, Britain, and the USSR passed over their class-ideological differences to unite against the common enemy, Germany. In occupied countries also, class conflicts were minimized in the name of national liberation.

After the war, as the revolutionary process extended into Eastern Europe, the United States and other Western powers countered with the containment policy, the Marshall Plan, the Truman doctrine, and so on. Class conflict with its ideological commitments divided the world into two large camps, capitalism and socialism, each one tightly lined up behind its leading power, the United States or the USSR. The Cold War became the virulent expression of that division.

With the halting of the revolutionary wave in Europe and the powerful national resurgence of the newly independent states pervading world politics, a new stage arose in the early 1960s. The two nuclear treaties jointly drafted by the superpowers to consolidate their strategic supremacy, the de Gaulle rebellion against U.S. domination in the West, and the Sino-Soviet rift in the East, are all signs of national-strategic considerations overriding ideological ones. Whereas in the 1950s ideological conflict was viewed as the most likely to produce wars, now the big power game and national rivalries are threatening peace. The 1980s started with a strong outburst of superpower confrontation over spheres of influence and strategic positions. Soviet military forces are fighting in Afghanistan, while the United States is striving to establish a *pax Americana* in the Middle East and in Central America.

After the American rejection of the SALT 2 agreement, the nuclear race is out of control; an all-out race for military superiority, whatever that means today, is running wild. President Reagan has revived the Cold War view that all international troubles, whether political turmoil in Central America or turbulence in the Middle East, tribal wars in Africa, and terrorism all over the world, originate in a sinister Communist masterplan unceasingly directed by Moscow against the United States and the West. To counter that conspiracy, America must build more and bigger weapons while arming any regime, no matter how despotic, corrupt, or repressive, that shouts anti-Communist slogans, including the regime of apartheid. Thus the arms race is exported to Africa, Asia, and Latin America, distorting there the development process (see Pinxten, this volume) and infecting some countries with militarism, an appetite for domination, and an aspiration to play regional policeman.

At the same time, when strategic interests are at stake, Washington will not hesitate to make deals with China and sell it modern weapons. This shows once more that ideology in international relations never appears in a pure form —it always mingles with power. Great powers are very good at that; they mold ideology according to their strategies and use power either "to make the world safe for democracy" or "to save socialism." Moreover, ideology is the best instrument to strengthen control over NATO or the Warsaw Treaty and compel allies to fall in line.

The United Nations

While the United Nations has the historical merit of helping the extension of the state system to all continents, it has proved inadequate as an institution designed to achieve peace and international security. Owing to the veto power provided in the Charter for the United States, the USSR, China, Britain, and France, the Security Council is unable to take effective action whenever one of the five is directly or indirectly involved in a conflict. Even in a local conflict, like the current Iraq-Iran war, the United Nations has been ineffective.

One can hardly avoid the conclusion that present international institutions do not have a significant impact on either the outbreak of conflicts or the settlement of disputes already going on. For one thing, the use of force, as provided in the U.N. Charter, has a rather limited effect, since in the sphere of international relations there are no tribunals and no police to enforce the law. Moreover, the principle of sovereignty which lies at the very basis of the United Nations allows every member state to decide whether or not to obey U.N. decisions. To be able to make decisions and enforce them, a world institution must be empowered by its members so to act. In other words, a transfer of power (gradual to be sure) must take place from the nation-state to the world institution.

Conclusions

Present arsenals of nuclear missile weapons may blow up the whole world and kill its population many times over. Yet, by using them no political aims can be achieved; no national interests of any country can be served; no ideology can benefit; no nation can overcome poverty and underdevelopment. What is more, global problems that have come to the fore in recent decades—development, population, food, ecological balance, energy and resources, weather control—are of such a nature that it is difficult to see how military violence can hope to cope with them.

And yet, the mightiest states continue to make preparations for war, their leaders keep invoking "national security" reasons, and their generals, by virtue of the very institution they command, formulate doctrines for "winning a nuclear war." External competition, the traditional law of the interstate system, has been compounded by the ideological antagonism between capitalism and socialism. But what could one or the other gain from a nuclear war?

Let me here state that whenever ideological reasons are given to justify the use of force against a nation's right to self-determination, the net outcome is a loss of ground by the respective ideology both within that nation and in the world at large. Ideology, however noble its aims, cannot be imposed by tanks and bombs.

The fact is that nuclear weapons have developed so rapidly in international life—in less than a generation—that political institutions and their ideologies have remained well behind. In no other domain of social life is there so great a contrast between the speed of change stimulated by the technological revolution and the capacity of institutions, both national and international, to adapt in so comparatively short a time.

In the nuclear age, traditional parochial views regarding national and international security must be redefined in a way that recognizes world peace as the overriding interest of each and all. Institutions must be restructured accordingly, and since the arms race is the specific form of movement that keeps the war system going, we must start with a halt to the arms race, a nuclear freeze. Just as a cease-fire is a must in order to start fruitful negotiations between two belligerent parties, so is a nuclear freeze for successful arms control talks.

Whether this historical challenge will be met is the central question of our time.

19

War and War Proneness in Pre- and Postindustrial States

Ronald Cohen

In a recent paper (Cohen, 1983) I pointed to important continuities and similarities among pre- and postindustrial states. Looking at the conditions leading to the end of the "early" state I reasoned that states as centralized political systems have become steadily more powerful and capable of greater center-periphery control. Industrialization simply increases this quality by integrating the society more tightly economically, culturally, and politically. The end of such a system is therefore to be seen in the diminution of centralized, and the growth of localized or peripheral, control. This process has, I believe, now begun to occur because technology allows for social and political integration outside the exercise of centralized authority.

This does not mean, however, that it is possible to fully equate and lump pre- and postindustrial states and regions. Significant differences in social formations and culture between the two modes of production are associated with other significant distinctions, not the least of which, I shall argue, is warfare and the degree to which it is an acceptable and desirable foreign policy option for the leadership and the masses in each kind of society.

In what is to follow I shall look at theoretical ideas on war proneness in pre- and postindustrial society, examine some of the relevant data and discuss the results. The data lead to an interpretation of war proneness that claims it is significantly less likely once a society becomes fully industrialized not only in its economy but also in its social and political culture.

The Problem

Some societies are more warlike than others. That is, the number of times per year or per decade that political leaders decide to unleash organized, deadly violence against those of another polity vary from one society to another. No matter how one views the Moutain Arapesh or the Hopi on the one hand, and the Apache or Sparta on the other, proneness to warfare differs; Arapesh and Hopi being at the lower end of a scale, Apache and Sparta at a much higher level of frequency. Accounts of these societies tend to explain the tendencies in terms of local cultural development, intersocietal relations, socialization, religion, or other institutions that increase or decrease proneness to warfare. Comparative research has shown that ecological factors such as protein deficiency (Harris, 1980), or social factors such as lack of peace-making capabilities (Koch, 1974) can help to explain these differences. This contrasts with sociobiologists' attempts to explain aggressiveness on the basis of genetic factors (Alexander, 1980). This last view infers genetic variation from behavioral differences, then takes the inference as the cause, but does not demonstrate the relationship empirically.

Sociobiological theories tend to look at the development of warlike reactions among the total gamut of social formations available for study in the evolutionary record of our species. However the question for our times is: how, why, and under what circumstances, states resort to interstate warfare. Specific details and empirical correlates for actual wars are the concern of military history and the more general study of international relations. The anthropological problem is more comparative, more closely related to explaining the differences between the Hopi and the Apache, or between Switzerland and Germany. Such an approach asks questions about factors in societal adaptation which predict warfare proneness.

Theoretical Considerations

Theories explaining interstate warfare abound (see for example, Sorokin, 1937; Richardson, 1960; Wright, 1965; Beer, 1981; Small and Singer, 1982). Almost all emphasize specific causes that correlate with the initiation of interstate warfare. If instead we look at why particular social formations are more war prone than others, we find two quite opposite theoretical points of view. Both views can be found in the last century and both predict the probability of interstate warfare on the basis of industrialization. They differ, however, in that one predicts that as industrialization increases, war proneness increases. The other claims the reverse: that as industrialization increases, the probability of warfare decreases.

The more pessimistic point of view is the best known and, I believe, the most widely accepted position on the war proneness of industrialized states. Well before the war of 1914, writers like Nietzsche, Burkhart, and Spengler saw industrialization, urbanism, and popular democracy as background causes for unwise, pugnacious government and increased violence. The reasons for this lay in the unregulated, inexperienced, yet increasingly more powerful regimes associated with the enormous increase in productivity, and in the democratization of the postindustrialized societies. They further believed that such increased power would lead to conflicts over extraterritorial claims on other parts of the globe and over trade and its international control. Industrialization was thus seen as increasing power and decreasing internal discipline while leading to greater external conflict, more wars, and more civil strife (Aron, 1958:5–6).

This intellectual trend was refined and embellished in the Marxian tradition. Marx saw industrial capitalism as freeing the worker from feudal domination only to enslave him under the liberal capitalist ideology of individualism. Thus, productivity increased under the false veneer of democratization. Warfare and industrial capitalism are, according to this theory, mutually stimulating because "capitalism implies imperialist expansion, and this in turn culminates inevitably in war between empires . . ." (Aron, 1958:23). As long as nations practicing industrial capitalism hold and require a dominant place in world affairs, because of their need for resources, market and control, they will breed violence within their own borders and between themselves and other polities. In contemporary times, therefore, this view holds the greatest danger to world peace to be Western dominance and the built-in attempt by "late" capitalism to maintain this position.[1] This it does by an accelerating search for increased warfare capability and a global foreign policy oriented towards Western dominance of the international system.

This widely known viewpoint is dourly pessimistic. Industrial capitalism is seen as increasingly powerful militarily, and increasingly threatened by noncapitalist nations who challenge its hegemony. This leads ipso facto to more war as "late" capitalist countries try ever more desperately to stem the tide of anticapitalist revolution while the scope of their empires crumbles in the face of a desire for independent progress on the part of the world's peoples. If war is the enemy, then from this point of view the Western writer must say, with Pogo, "We have met the enemy, and he is us."

The optimistic view is quite poorly known or understood today, rarely heard, and even more rarely discussed. It was first formulated by Saint Simon in the early nineteenth century, later expanded by Auguste Comte, and resuscitated by Raymond Aron (1958) in his Auguste Comte Memorial Lecture at the London School of Economics. Simon and Comte were writing during the transition from the pre- to postindustrial social and economic form of the European way of life. Where pessimists drew attention to emerging class differences, urban poverty and squalor, exploitation at home and abroad amidst imperial wars, these more optimistic commentators saw a future of peace and prosperity for ever increasing numbers of people freed by the hitherto unheard of productivity of industrialization. In this conception, war was seen as antithetical to industrialization; it wasted the new-found productivity, but more importantly, war was for these writers a characteristic par excellence of preindustrial society, of societies whose aristocratic rulers were trained specialists in warfare, and whose regimes were measured in terms of territorial expansion, success in war, conquest, and heroic battlefield exploits. Identification with the nation by all classes was promoted by martial victory over, and the successful defense against, the inevitable aggression of other states. In this view, then, militaristic regimes were more characteristic of preindustrial states than those based on the new mode of production. New elites were made up of business managers, bankers, scientists, engineers, and others who created and directed the new productivity, rather than the warrior aristocrats who had up to this time dominated the leadership roles in state systems. In preindustrial systems productive work was the task of commoners, serfs, and slaves, while freemen who aspired to leadership in society were trained in warfare. They might specialize in other occupations but leadership and warrior status were closely intertwined.

> There was no other means, in the early stages [of society] to bring the indispensable expansion of human society, and to restore within society, a sterile war-like ardor incompatible with an adequate growth of productive work, except the gradual incorporation of civilized populations into one conquering nation [Comte, cited in Aron, 1958:8]

Comte saw in industrial work relations and in factory production the very opposite of the Marxian critique. For him the change from serf to free worker was not a conspiracy to befuddle and exploit, but real emancipation. This change brought with it the potential for social mobility previously undreamt of in hereditary class society and for the substitution as the most prestigious and highly valued form of human activity of productive work for warfare. Comte believed that the American revolution spelled the end of colonial adventures for Europe. He saw, however, that some extension of expansionist goals would occur between more advanced and less advanced societies precipitating conflicts between nations of "unequal progress."

Later, both Veblen (1919) and Schumpeter (1919) compared the social development of England and Germany. In effect, they agreed with Comte. Imperialist wars of expansion were really extensions of preindustrial policies and values into the more pacific social formations of industrialized societies. Given the hindsight and experience of nineteenth and early twentieth-century European expansionism, they added the notion that industrialization did not create a sharp break. Instead, linkages and continuities in values, and even in personnel, appeared between the new capitalist class and the older ideals of a more militaristic aristocratic preindustrial society. Looking at it from a contemporary vantage point we can now see that the scramble for Africa of the 1980s was played out in a context of debates between Tories who represented more of these continuities, and Whigs whose laissez faire goals represented the desire to cut ties with expansionist goals of the earlier society. However, Schumpeter (1919) saw the continuity very clearly:

> Imbued with the spirit of the old autocracy, trained by it, the bourgeoisie often takes over its ideology, even where, as in France, the sovereign is eliminated and the official power of the nobility has been broken. . . . Because the (preindustrial) sovereign was in a position to exploit conquests, needed them to be a victorious warlord, the bourgeoisie thirsts for national glory. . . . Because pugnacious sovereigns stood in constant fear of attack by their equally pugnacious neighbours, the modern bourgeoisie attribute aggressive designs to neighbouring peoples. All such modes of thought are essentially noncapitalist. Indeed they vanish most quickly wherever capitalism fully prevails. They are survivals of the autocratic alignment of interests, and they endure wherever the autocratic state endures on the old basis and with the old orientation. . . . They bear witness to the extent to which essentially imperialist absolutism has patterned not only the economy of the bourgeoisie but also its mind [Schumpeter, 1951:124].

Reviewing these ideas Raymond Aron (1958) concluded that Comte was indeed correct in at least one respect. It is in the rational self-interest of industrial societies, whether they be pluralist democracies or planned socialist ones, to remain at peace. However, Comte, he says, did not see that these two kinds of industrial societies were to be led by competing ideologies into conflict and competition. And should the poverty of the third world become stable, (i.e., hopeless), it would perforce produce constant conflict. I take this to mean conflict between the poorer states themselves, as well as conflict between the rich and the poor nations.

Another closely related issue is duration. Given a particular degree of bellicosity at one time, can we predict that a state society will continue this level? Is this a variable that responds to influences producing greater or lesser war proneness in response to selective pressures operating on the conduct of its foreign relations? In cultural terms, it can be argued that peaceful or warlike qualities will be part of the shared, learned, attitudes, values, and symbols passed down from one generation to the next. In this sense culture theory predicts constancy. Societies that exhibit high levels of belligerency should be expected to continue to display such high levels over time. Similarly, peaceable societies should retain such features. One of the ways of containing war, therefore, would be to understand the cultural conditioning and conditions that give rise to warlike rather than pacific cultural configurations.

It is this type of theorizing that led to studies such as Benedict's *Chrysanthemum and the Sword* (1946) and to Fromm's classic *Escape from Freedom* (1941). In each of these, cultural analysis led to an interpretation and explanation of national state levels of bellicosity. The culture as a set of expectable national character traits was a knowledge claim for the understanding of the warlike quality of particular nations. If, therefore, the explanation for war can be located in a tradition, then expert analysis of traditions will uncover those roots as well as reveal the means by which such roots are culturally sustained and reproduced.

In summary, there are two contradictory intellectual streams of thought concerning warfare in the modern interstate system and its longer-term place in social evolution. One, the more pessimistic view, sees the latest form of technological development—industrial society—producing more conflict within and between nations because of bitterness between groups over inequities of wealth and power. The other views interstate warfare as a form of international relations that reached its peak of influence and frequency in preindustrial society. This is because war is inimical to the growth and welfare of the most important elements of such societies—those who produce its goods and services.

Warfare Data

The most comprehensive database on warfare available to social scientists is that of the Correlates of War Project at the University of Michigan.[2] The second edition of these materials plus some preliminary analysis is now in print (Small and Singer, 1982). The appendix to the report includes specific mention of hundreds of armed conflicts reported for the period 1816 to 1980. Given the comprehensiveness of information retrieval from books, articles, and newspapers, I assume that this is the most inclusive listing of armed conflicts between and within nations now available. Esoteric wars that I am aware of, such as the defeat of the Borno Emirate by a plundering Sudanese brigand and his troops in 1893 are included in the list, giving me confidence that almost any war mentioned by historians or newspapers is included. On the other hand wars between Sudanic States listed in local chronicles are not given. I shall add some of these typical examples of preindustrial wars.

One other caveat on the use of these data is important. The authors of the report and their colleagues count wars only if they involve a minimum level of battlefield deaths and the movement of a minimal number of troops. This limits the number and kinds of conflict included in their analyses. I have reported some of their findings below using their definition. For my own purposes I have had to change this count to one in which the decision to send troops is seen as war, in order to compare these data with African preindustrial materials not included in the list.

Using as a cut off point 1,000 battlefield deaths, the Correlates of War Project (COWP) finds that the last 165 years has on average seen one such conflict every two-and-one-half years. They find only twenty single year periods during this time in which no one such conflict was going on. This involved over 6,000 nation-months of active combat, by far the most intensive being the years 1917 and 1943, with 170 and 179 nation-months of war respectively. Not surprisingly these two wars saw the heaviest toll of total battle deaths in the period. However, and this is surprising, even with these two great conflicts biasing the totals, there is no clear evidence, using their definitions, that international wars per year or per decade are on the increase. It is well worth quoting the authors of the report on this point:

> Is war on the increase, as many scholars as well as laymen of our generation have been inclined to believe? The answer would seem to be an unambiguous negative. Whether we look at the number of wars, their severity [numbers of battle deaths], or magnitude [numbers of nation-months of conflict], there is no significant trend upward or down over the past 165 years. Even if we examine their intensities [battle deaths per nation-months, and battle deaths per prewar population of all nations involved], we find that later wars are by and large no different from those of earlier periods. Likewise, even if we differentiate among different types of war, there appears to be no appreciable change in their frequency, when we control for their statistical probability as a function of the number of national units available to fight. . . . That is, the number of interstate wars per decade has risen no faster than the number of nations in the interstate system. (Small and Singer, 1982:141)

Major powers are however differentiated in important ways. Using the COWP definitions of wars, most conflicts lump at the low end of severity, that is, they involve less than 31,000 battle deaths. Of those over this level of severity, major powers account for 70 percent of all instances. These materials taken directly from Small and Singer (1982) are summarized in Table 1.

Duration data from the study tell the same story. The majority of wars in the period last fewer than four years (82 percent). However, for major powers, 40 percent of their admittedly fewer wars lasted longer than four

TABLE 1
Severity of Interstate Wars, 1816–1980

	Battle Deaths per War	
	1,000–31,000	31,000–3 million
All interstate wars (n = 110)	77%	23%
Major-power wars (n = 10)	30%	70%

years, whereas this figure is 18 percent for the sample as a whole. Not surprisingly, therefore, major-power wars are more deadly, they last longer, and they involve more nation-months of active conflict.

Interesting as these materials are, they do not answer the question: Do industrialization and its related social and political development lead to more or to less warfare, to more or less war proneness?

To get at these issues I used data from several sources, somewhat opportunistically, but with an eye toward representing early states from around the world. The data come from sources on Sudanic states in West Africa, Europe, and India. I do not know if all wars for the early periods of these states have been recorded, but for the industrial periods the recording procedures are probably in general reliable and accurate. Warfare among preindustrial European polities is well documented. I therefore randomly drew the fourteenth century from the period of the eleventh through the fifteenth centuries, and considered all cases of war during that one-hundred-year period. Thus, there is a greater chance that data are missing about war in the early periods than that the data about war among industrial states is incomplete. This should bias the results of my analysis against the Simon-Comte-Aron thesis. To be included in the University of Michigan materials as a full-scale war, a conflict must meet a criterion measure of a minimal number of battlefield deaths. This is necessary if the research includes questions about the severity, intensity, or magnitude of war as does Michigan's COWP. However, here I am concerned solely with war proneness which I take to be indexed by the frequency of war. Therefore I define warfare as the sending of troops into situations ready for combat. I take it that even if no casualties result, if the campaign is a brief one, if the enemy sues for peace and surrenders without a fight, that a state's bellicosity is evidenced by the warlike act of committing its troops. Through its leaders a society has resorted to deadly violence, or its potential use, against another polity. This means that I have included in the analysis of data from the Michigan sample wars that they published but excluded from their own analyses because numbers of battlefield deaths were too low. It also means that my count of wars is in general higher for both industrialized and preindustrialized polities.

A problem emerges when several polities are allied. If the war or wars are part of a tightly linked antagonism so that countries A and B always join against polity X, then A's and B's attack is counted as one war. If, however, A attacks X and is only sometimes joined by B, I counted A's and B's attacks on X as two wars, since the decisions seem not to be obligatory.

The problem of entailed decisions is not just a matter of allies who must join forces. There is also the issue of one engagement entailing others. In such instances I counted an entire set of battles and skirmishes as a single war. Thus, in eighteenth-century India, one Salabat Jang invaded the territory of the Moratha soon after the death of the latter's leader. There took place a number of battles followed by a decisive encounter in January 1762. All of the separate engagements I counted as one war.

For preindustrial states, battles are more often of historical importance than troop movements, but the latter are mentioned frequently enough so that they increase the count of wars even when no battle deaths occurred. Thus in fourteenth-century Europe the King of Portugal and the Duke of Lancaster joined forces to war against Castile. The countryside ahead of them had been laid to waste and the English soldiers suffered greatly from illness. The King of Castile refused to fight and eventually the English simply went home (Bourchier, 1895:369). I counted this as a war. Troops were moved, battle preparations completed. The English were ready to fight, and if need be to die, and they moved resolutely toward that end.

In general the quality of data in this study is quite high, but I add one further caveat. Those materials I know best—on Borno—are not as reliable as I had hoped they would be. In this case I have a number of chronicles and fieldnotes to supplement the data. I am relatively confident that the early and later nineteenth-century frequencies of over ten wars per decade for the early period, and of less than ten wars per decade for the later period are correct. However, I do not have the detailed knowledge of other sites that would enable me to be as confident in those data as I am for the Borno data.

The material on early and late periodicity are clearest for Sokoto and Borno. Both of these had new governments in the early nineteenth century. Sokoto was founded at the beginning of the century and Borno's second dynastic rule began. For the industrial societies "early" and "late" refer to the ninteenth and twentieth centuries respectively. For India and for fourteenth-century France, it was impossible to make a judgment of early or late periods. The adequacy of the data for this analysis, then, is not very high except for the Sokoto and Borno cases.

Although not definitive, the data in Table 2 are strongly supportive of the Simon-Comte-Aron thesis that industrialization decreases the war proneness of state societies.[3] Except for later Sokoto all of the preindustrial states have frequencies of war at least twice that of industrialized state systems. If we transform these data to means for the entire period, and assign Borno the value of 7.5 wars per decade, the preindustrial states have an overall mean of 10.6 wars per decade, while for the entire 164 years the industrial polities average no more than 2.7 wars per decade. Because the Borno data are constructed and are the lowest, it is probable that more accurate measurements would *increase* the observed frequency of wars among preindustrial state societies.

TABLE 2
Frequence of Wars per Decade in Selected State Societies

	Preindustrial				Industrial				
Country	Sokoto	Borno	India 1707–71	France 14th cent.	France	U.K.	USSR	U.S.	Germany
Wars per decade	13.6	7.5	12.7	8.5	3.5	5.6	2.8	.86	.74
Mean wars per decade		10.6					2.7		

TABLE 3
Wars per Decade over Time in Selected State Societies[a]

	Preindustrial				Industrial (1816–1980)					
Country	Sokoto 19th cent.	Borno 19th cent.	India[b] 1707–71	France 14th cent.	France	U.K.	USSR	USA	Germany	
Early[c]	23.0	more than 10 per decade	12.7	8.5	4.4	6.1	1.7	.83	.83	1816 to 1900
Late	4.1	less than 10 per decade			2.5	4.6	1.8	.88	.63	1901 to 1980

[a]Sources for these data are given in the bibliography.
[b]The early/late distinction could not reliably be made.
[c]Early for Sokoto and Borno is defined as the time of the first two monarchs of the nineteenth century, and late is defined as the last two months before the colonial conquest in 1900–1901.

Table 3 displays these data by early and later periods. Here the Sudanic preindustrial states decrease wars per decade in the early periods of new regimes when these are compared to later periods. Data on the other preindustrial states were not available, at least to the nonexpert, and the material on industrial states does show a decline for France and the United Kingdom, but not for Russia (the Soviet Union), United States, or Germany. The data suggest, but not strongly, that preindustrial states are more war prone in their early periods, and that there is a tendency for this bellicosity to wane as time goes on. Industrial states do not follow a pattern that is easily discernible with this small a sample, although the United Kingdom and France tend to follow the predicted pattern.

Discussion

The inception of industrial society in the nineteenth century brought out two contradictory reactions among social theorists. Both positions accepted the notion that the new mode of production was a form of "progress" which would provide humankind with vast new wealth, more control over the environment, and a better life for peoples of all classes and races. One point of view says that these improvements are immanent, the other believed that they would result from an inevitable conflict whose root cause would be the increased inequity, suffering, exploitation, and growing anger of the poor, whose labor would produce the new wealth and power of the industrializing society. The first more optimistic view saw warfare as primarily preindustrial, the latter, more pessimistic one, viewed the new society as leading to increased conflict and more war, until those who produce the wealth by their own efforts unite to take over the reins of power from those who had perpetuated their power through control of property.

The data presented here show that simple theories correlating warfare to a particular type of society or evolutionary level of development depict an oversimplified world. Certainly early preindustrial society was more war oriented than later social formations. One to several active military campaigns per year was normal for such societies. Whatever else they were, preindustrial states in their early dynastic periods, at the beginnings of ruling regimes, were organized into effective war-making bodies. Warfare and its demands affected how these states were administered, and how they related to other societies (Rosenfeld, 1965; Smaldone, 1978).

In the Western Sudan, the dry season was synonymous with warfare. In capital towns, large numbers of craftsmen and their slaves engaged in war-related production of such items as weapons—swords, spears, arrows, quivers, flintlocks and shot, as well as horse trappings, tents, chain armor, and tons of provisions in leather bags for the army on the march. Taxation and other kinds of revenue collections such as fees were much influenced by the need to pay these annual war expenditures. New settlers, new ethnic groups, and other incorporated peoples were welcomed and then compelled to contribute contingents for the state armies in their annual dry season campaigns. Booty was a reward for victorious participants; paradise awaited those who fell.

As a group, the nobility was especially trained in military pursuits and all able-bodied men were required to bear arms for the state through their relations to local nobles. Whether it was Tokugawa Japan, early China, preindustrial Europe, Inca, or the Sudanic states of Africa, military glory, military training, and armed conflict were seen as normal parts of everyday life. The early state was a war machine.

At their beginnings such regimes carved out their position in the interstate system and their internal relations by force of arms. Borno's second dynasty was formed by a religious leader and his followers who took up arms to defend the failing kingdom against external enemies threatening to subdue it completely. This led to enormously expanded military activities which reestablished the power of Borno in the Chad basin. Sokoto's rule began during this same period as a *jihad* (holy war) led by a religious leader who mobilized oppressed rural nomads and other exploited groups against local monarchs. Again he increased the scope and frequency of warfare in the area and founded a new and powerful state in the process.

In both these cases, however, the original bellicosity seems to have died down after a few decades. Monarchs became much less keen on going to war and allowed their nobles to fight for them. Mobilizing for war was much less frequent, and a general decline in the power and influence of the state can be seen in its relation to neighbors and its own subjects. At this point the regime is ripe for internal revolts, civil wars over succession to the throne, or a successful assault by external enemies. In other words, military capacity, and strong involvement by the leadership in frequent military campaigns was a necessary feature of the preindustrial state. In this sense, the early state was really a warfare oriented polity.

Comte was right. Preindustrial society is strongly oriented towards militarism, expansionism and the use of warfare to achieve national purposes. He was wrong in not coping with the enormous military variability and its rise and fall within any one regime.

The early optimists were also right in seeing industrial states as less warlike. However, here too variations are important. The most active colonialist states, Britain and France, account for a large portion of the interstate wars in which a government actually sent in military forces. Nevertheless, these decline in war frequency from their early to their later industrialization. On the other hand, other industrial states, such as the

United States, Germany, or the Soviet Union, have a comparatively low incidence of interstate warfare throughout the same period.

The culturological theory that some societies have more bellicose cultures than do other societies is not supported by these data. Instead, preindustrial regimes seem to follow an entropic pattern of declining frequency of war when we compare their early periods to later periods in their history. Because the data are not entirely clear regarding the early/late division for industrial states (the United Kingdom and France might more accurately reflect this division than do the data for Germany, Russia, or the United States), further study of this question is needed before it can be answered with confidence. Nevertheless, the data are sufficient, it seems to me, to say that in some instances at least war proneness varies, but this variation is not the result of cultural factors. *War proneness cannot be predicted from only a knowledge of cultural ideology.*

But Small and Singer's (1982) data show that frequency is only one small part of the interstate warfare picture. Other measures show little increase or decrease of war in the total interstate system. At the same time, major-power wars are clearly more terrible, costly, severe and include more people.

Marvin Harris (personal communication) points out that the industrial states are generally larger than preindustrial ones, there are fewer of them, and therefore the same *rate* of interstate conflict will result in fewer wars per state than it would for preindustrial systems. Harris's point is well taken and must be investigated by controlling for scale at the same time that warfare is examined in a number of states with different modes of production. The inclusion of pre- and of postindustrial France does, however, help to allay this problem, albeit not completely. France was roughly the same size in the two time periods but was surrounded by more state entities than it is today. Still, it is encouraging that early and later France follow the same pattern as that predicted for all pre- and postindustrial state systems.

Aron (1958) points out that the most severe wars of the twentieth century (the 1914 and 1939 World Wars) were primarily caused by industrialized states whose mode of production gave a means of furthering early-state preindustrial values and cultural nationalism in a world whose major industrial powers were abandoning such ideology.

Putting these ideas and data together we can, I believe, look at current trends in warfare proneness from an evolutionary perspective. As societies become more industrialized, their proneness to warfare decreases. Conflict does not increase as technology and mode of production increase the capacity for higher standards of living. Theories used to explain this trend may need more refinement, but the trend is unmistakable. Warfare among contemporary states is a correlate of colonial expansionism and preindustrial political culture that equate political success and survival with militarism and warfare. The enormous increase in severity of warfare among major industrial powers is a growing deterrence to its occurrence. The most likely venue for wars is therefore among newly industrializing nations whose conflicts and expansionist thrusts are still partly determined by their preindustrial cultural background and the inability of major powers to conduct wars against one another because of the excessively high costs in life and property.

These results are not particularly surprising but they are clear. The remedy for war lies only partially in deterrence, the longer-lasting and more important control is the growth of fully industrialized and prosperous nations among the poor of the world.

Notes

An earlier version of this paper was presented at the Faculty Colloquium, University of Florida. It elaborates and tests a theory set out in Cohen (1984). I am grateful to Robert A. Rubinstein, Marvin Harris, and H. Russell Bernard for comments and criticisms on an earlier draft. I acknowledge with thanks the help of Christopher Rippel with the collection and coding of data for fourteenth-century France and eighteenth-century India.

1. The adjective "late" for capitalism implies a basis for understanding phases and direction in the evolution of a social form the pathway of which has not yet been charted. Elsewhere I indicated why basing the concept of directionality in futurological prediction upon it is untenable. Contemporary capitalism may be classified as "industrial" but not as "late." Early capitalism has already occurred and is therefore identifiable. Whether we are still within that period (which I suspect is the case), beyond it, or whatever, cannot be established.
2. This is the latest presentation of these materials. Publication of such a body of data goes back to Wright (1942).
3. I derived this number by estimating 10 wars per decade in the first half of the nineteenth century and 5 per decade for the second half of that century. The average is then 7.5 wars per decade. My reading of the records suggests that this is the lowest possible estimate that is reasonable. Taking a low estimate makes my analysis conservative in the sense that it is then biased against the Simon-Comte-Aron thesis. Omitting these estimates increases the preindustrial mean.

References

Alexander, R.D. 1980. *Darwinism and Human Affairs*. Seattle, Wash.: University of Washington Press.

Aron, R. 1958. *War and Industrial Society*. London: Oxford University Press (Reprinted in 1980 by Greenwood Press, Westport, Conn.).

Beer, F.A. 1981. *Peace against War: The Ecology of International Violence*. San Francisco, Cal.: W.H. Freeman.

Benedict, R. 1946. *The Chrysanthemum and the Sword.* Boston, Mass.: Houghton Mifflin.

Bourchier, J. 1895. *The Chronicles of Froissart.* Edited, translated, and reduced by G.C. Macaulay. London: Macmillan. 6 volumes.

Cohen, R. 1983. "The End of the Early State." Paper presented at the Eleventh International Congress of Anthropological and Ethnological Sciences, Quebec.

———. 1984. "Warfare and State Formation." In *The Anthropology of War*, edited by B. Ferguson, pp. 329–820. New York: Academic Press.

Fromm, E. 1941. *Escape from Freedom.* New York: Farrar and Rinehart.

Harris, M. 1980. *Culture, People and Nature.* New York: Harper and Row.

Koch, K.F. 1974. *War and Peace in Jalemo.* Cambridge, Mass.: Harvard University Press.

Richardson, L.F. 1960. *Statistics of Deadly Quarrels.* Pittsburgh, Pa.: Boxwood.

Rosenfeld, H. 1965. "The Social Cooperation of the Military in the Process of State Formation in the Arabian Desert." *Journal of the Royal Anthroplogical Institute* 95(1):75–86; (2):174–94.

Schumpeter, J.A. 1919. *Imperialism and Social Classes.* Translated version, 1951. London: Oxford University Press.

Smaldone, J.P. 1970. "Historical and Sociological Aspects of Warfare in the Sokoto Caliphate." Ph.D. dissertation, Northwestern University.

Small, M., and Singer, J.D. 1982. *Resort to Arms: International and Civil Wars, 1816–1980.* Beverly Hills, Cal.: Sage.

Sorokin, P. 1937. *Social and Cultural Dynamics. Volume 3. Fluctuations of Social Relationships, War and Revolution.* New York: American Book.

Veblen, T. 1919. *An Inquiry into the Nature of Peace and the Terms of Its Perpetuation.* New York: B.W. Huebsch.

Wright, Q. 1942. *A Study of War.* Rev. ed., 1965. Chicago, Ill.: University of Chicago Press. 2 vols.

20

The Developmental Dynamics of Peace

Rik Pinxten

The topics of development and armament/disarmament are so complexly interrelated that it is difficult to say much about them in a short paper. Nevertheless, my conviction that we must do research on this combined topic or perish (see also Cooper, 1975) compels me to explore this relationship. My conclusions and suggestions must necessarily be tentative and conditional. I hope they are thought provoking.

Scholars concerned with the relationship between armament and development will probably despair when they first examine the issue and take note of its history. One way for an anthropologist to avoid this despair is to focus most intensely on subproblems of greatest anthropological familiarity.

It is disappointing that anthropologists have done so little work in the anthropology of war. Otterbein's (1967, 1977) and Feest's (1980) work are probably the most thorough studies in the anthropology of war. A few anthropological readers (e.g., Fried, et al., 1968; and Nettleship, et al., 1975) also present insights on particular aspects of war. I have tried to get a more substantial picture of the phenomena involved by looking in addition at literature from other disciplines. My conclusions, of course, depend in part on the miscellaneous nature of this selection.

We all know slogans such as: "armament means underdevelopment," but (apart from *UNESCO Courier*, 1982) a scientific analysis of the mechanisms underlying such a statement is lacking.

In an analysis of the compensatory relationships of competition and cooperation in human evolution, the biologist, Bigelow, postulates an evolutionary pressure principle to explain the gradual and progressive enlargement of social units throughout human history, postulating that intergroup competition placed a high selective value on intragroup cooperation (Bigelow, 1975:235). Just as the combination of intragroup cooperation and external competition led to the eventual elimination of predators and other rivals to the human species, the same process leads to a situation where the entire species becomes, in effect, a single social group with some control over its own evolution (Bigelow, 1975:254).

At present, as the world is divided into only a few political blocs, we may be close to the final phase of the trend to unification. We must now begin to regulate the delicate interplay of competition and cooperation within and between blocs if we are to avoid nuclear war. Bigelow's analysis makes clearer that competition and cooperation interact to further political cohesion. Some mechanisms are nationalism, ethnocentrism, or even racism, as well as an image of a threatening outside enemy who must be defended against, and, perhaps actually fought. (See Foster, this volume.)

Otterbein (1977) notes that ethnocentrism and the enhancement of intragroup cohesion are well documented effects of warfare, as well as factors bringing it about through military preparedness. If we keep in mind that ethnocentrism always implies hostile feelings for the outsider (Levine and Campbell, 1972), it becomes clear that the three factors—ethnocentrism, intragroup cohesion and military preparedness—relevant in tribal warfare are also features of the Cold-War speeches one hears today (see Gittings, 1982 on this point).

Barnet (1972:51) provides the following description of the perspective of United States diplomats:

> The President spends about 90 percent of his time building and, to use the State Department term, projecting America's military power around the world. Increasingly, the civilian managers have come to see the world through military eyes. They plan for what are called "greater than expected threats."

This kind of planning certainly stems from the need of American politicians to develop a sense of "military preparedness." Almost certainly a similar case can be made about the USSR, where a tremendous amount of money and energy is spent to find an adequate response to the eventuality of an American "first strike" (Coolsaet, 1982; Steele, 1982). It is equally true of China (Gittings, 1982).

Approaching the problem of the relationship between disarmament and development from Bigelow's framework, I focus on processes resulting from cooperation and competition in order to discover the means to defuse competition and conflict and to enhance cooperation. In brief, development slows when warfare becomes a major political focus and armament leaves fewer resources for development. (See Melman, this volume.)

It follows that disarmament leads to development. Much of the world is underdeveloped—a condition that the present focus on armament exacerbates rather than relieves.

The Shift to War

Some anthropological studies of tribal communication have shown psychological and social changes within a community preoccupied with an "enemy" and working toward a violent solution to a problem. This process is well worth examining, for there are structural similarities between such processes in tribal contexts and those in the political arena of the modern state. For example, in the turn towards war as a solution of conflict, there is the shift to persuasive arguments of a certain kind intended by the political leaders of a community to prepare its members for the taking of armed action. This is discoverable both in discourses of tribal leaders and in present-day political talk. Other documented processes in the shift to war are also instructive.

Focusing on the mental and social preparation for armed deeds among Jibaro Indians, Karsten (1967) describes a range of processes designed to promote the shift to warlike attitudes and actions: houses are constructed in strategic places and are surrounded by high fences; the young Jibaro is instructed "in all kinds of manly business, but first of all in warlike deeds;" chiefs are nonexistent in times of peace, but, with the threat of armed conflicts, those men reputed for their killing of enemies are appointed chief; and blood revenge (as an armed solution of conflict) is seen as "an expression of justice," when armed conflicts are expected.

While Jibaro warfare differs in kind and in detail from most other types of warfare and especially those of technologically highly developed states, the general strategy of preparation has parallels in other communities.

Laughlin and Brady (1978) point out that societies coping with disaster experience striking changes in patterns at the level of ideological and cognitive adaptive infrastructures. Although their focus is on disasters rather than war, they describe political and cognitive changes that seem to characterize any type of abrupt change. Thus "leaders tend to have more influence during periods of crisis than they do under other circumstances" (1978:38). They review studies by Schroder and his colleagues which reveal that at times of stress individuals and groups become more hierarchical in structure (see also Rubinstein, this volume). They cite Sioux myths which prescribe certain coercive rule-bound behavior for bad times. These are sometimes held to be necessary as a way of minimizing the effects of earlier mistakes made by individuals or the group. They also cite examples from Tikopia, Yap and Samoa which, taken together, show a pattern that includes the following elements: there is a cognitive shift towards a more concrete and direct phrasing of problems; and,

> Both the perception of the problem and the generation of solutions to the problem become increasingly simplified, progressively reducing the number and type of creative or novel solutions that might otherwise be applied [Laughlin and Brady, 1978:45–46].

A serious shrinkage in cognitive exploration is noted and tradition becomes more important for decisionmaking.

Features revealed by anthropological studies of simpler societies are useful as a heuristic means for diagnosing the processes of social and mental regimentation taking place in more complex societies at the present time, notwithstanding obvious differences in size and in cultural tradition between the two. Derksen (1981) points to a regularly recurring feature of "political childishness" during periods of difficulty: some Other is seen either as a threat, as an inferior being or as both. The image of oneself is colored by nationalism and by a positive attitude towards a law-and-order mentality. Derksen cites genetic psychologist Kohlberg as viewing these attitudes as typical for those who will not reach political or moral adulthood, and summarizes them by speaking of a belief in one's own "exquisiteness" as a community characteristic in times of crisis.

Chomsky argues that during the past few years the classic Cold-War speeches have been constructed to overcome "the growing unwillingness of a large part of the [American] population to support aggression and subversion" (1982:32) resulting from the Vietnam experience. In the West such speeches use a human rights jargon. In the Soviet Union, a deepening distrust of the United States has weakened the belief in detente and promoted similarly hostile feelings (Steele, 1982). Gradually, the 1970 ideal of detente as a global solution healthy for Planet Earth has given way to isolationism and distrust.

Gittings (1982a) says that following the Decade of Detente came the Dangerous Decade. As this shift from world to national scale of bloc politics development occurred, problems of the Third World gradually disappeared from speeches and programs of politicians so that there was room for military doctrine, and important resource areas in the Third World are increasingly seen as possible targets for military intervention (Economics Club of Chicago, 1980). Meanwhile, development problems such as hunger and overpopulation increase in size and intensity at the same time that their political relevance for politicians of the rich countries of the North decreases dramatically. (Beeman, this volume, also sees world politics as polarizing North and South.)

Although the shift towards nationalism and isolationism has been gradual, it is possible to see characteristic political events which mark it. In 1974, the possibility of a small and controllable nuclear conflict was first suggested in the United States. By 1979, this idea became the President's official policy, and the Cruise and Pershing missiles were developed as a way of implementing this idea. Finally, President Carter's 1980 State of the Union Address denounced Soviet intervention in Afghanistan, thus marking the official reorientation to a North-South focus in the old East-West opposition. Commenting on a sober and unoffensive memorandum by the British Foreign Office in 1980, Gittings (1982a:18) says, "It is significant that this sort of low-key proposition is only put forward when the diplomats and strategists speak among themselves, and is not to be found in the public speeches of Mrs.Thatcher or Mr. Reagan."

Roling (1964) and Derksen (1981) both point to the following mechanism: at some point states build up the image of an enemy by stressing their own military preparedness, and this leads the other party to reinforce its own defense. Eventually, the cycle of mutual distrust and the expectations of attack work as a self-fulfilling prophesy. The *expectation* of war can thus become a *cause* of war.

Some war-associated processes and attitudes observable in modern states are strikingly similar to those noted in simpler societies by anthropologists: a social reorganization of some kind may precede a decision to go to war (for example, Jibaro appointment of a chief). An intense military build-up is such a social (and economic) reorganization (see, especially, Melman, this volume).

A cognitive narrowing of options occurs when military preparedness intensifies. This is reflected in the pronouncements of political leaders. A side-effect of this shrinkage of perspective is that attention to development and international cooperation diminishes proportionately (Gittings and Steele, 1982:99).

Decreasing Development

Development has diminished with the sharp increase in armaments during the last ten years. As Gittings and Steele (1982:98) note: "The 1970s was not only the Decade of Detente but of Development, when the Third World . . . seemed to be mobilizing so much more effectively on the economic front."

The evolution of the inverse relationship between development and armament during the last part of the 1970s was sketched dramatically in the September 1980 issue of *Scientific American*, devoted to development. Dadzie (1980) sets the stage for the discussion by summing up the raw data: since the Second World War the "flow of financial assistance has diminished from 1 percent of the G.N.P. to a now officially estimated .35 percent." He reports that the condition of the poorest countries deteriorated in the 1970s (Dadzie, 1980:58), that those developing countries which jumped to considerably enhanced economic positions over the last decades more often than not are now in deep financial trouble (Argentina, Brazil, Mexico, the Philippines are cited as examples). Over the years the arms race has increasingly required money and resources for military purposes. Even the developing countries participate in that race. The recent conflict between Britain and Argentina over the Malvinas was followed by bankrupt Argentina entering into contracts for new arms. Moreover, over the last decades the annual population increase of the seventy-three poorest countries was more than twice that of the average annual increase in the rich countries. Dadzie calculates that this leads to more severe nutritional problems in the poorer countries.

Leeds places the tension between development and disarmament in historical perspective. He points out that the capitalist (developed) systems "must expand to maintain themselves. They must, therefore, be transferred into the system through a boundary from one or more external political-economic systems (capitalist or not)" (Leeds, 1975:488). Chomsky, et al. (1982) note that now access to cheap resources can only be safeguarded by either military occupation or payment of concession rights. The costs of administering these resource facilities are rising continuously, threatening the competitive position of the developed country because infrastructural costs increase, and health and educational services in the resource countries must also increase to secure easy access to the resources. The growing competition among developed countries thus leads to more and more (small) wars and a growing tendency to military control in the underdeveloped countries where major economic resources sometimes lie (see Leontief, 1980 for a list). Thus, the tendency to install and support more and more military regimes in these countries can be seen as a historical confirmation of Leeds's description. Here again, as budgets are devoted more fully to armament, development is given lesser priority.

Some recent economic data substantiate this. N.C.O.S. (1982, summarizing the W. Brandt report and the 1981 United Nations report on development) states that: Each year $550 billion is spent on a worldwide scale for armament, while only $33.5 billion is reserved for development; increasing armament in Third-World countries leads to a growing dependence of these countries on the private bank concerns in the North; Third World countries are spending more and more on arms and less on development (for example, in 1980, Africa imported $15 billion worth of arms, and spent only $9.9 billion on development, and Asia spent $85 billion for arms import and only $12 billion for development); a tightly intertwined group of military industries and armed regimes is becoming a new elite with power on a worldwide scale.

Taking into account the facts of the arms race, the demographic explosion, and the real decrease in development funds over the past decades, the simultaneous increase in armament expenditures on a worldwide scale tends to suck up more and more of the funds. Thus, at this macrolevel, an increase in resources used for armament goes hand in hand with the decrease in resources used for development.

How does this relationship articulate itself on the microlevel, of each tribe or each community about which the anthropologist is concerned? Is it useful to extrapolate to developing nations the few insights we have about the effects on people of warfare and the effects on subsistence of arming for war?

Note that "development" can be used in two senses. In the first sense it refers to the gradual enhancement of conditions of survival and of the quality of life on a worldwide scale, judged according to the value system the North imposes on the South. In this use it is primarily a socioeconomic concept with some political connotations. In the second sense "development" can denote changes over time in the subsistence patterns of a community and the eventual expansion of that community according to the traditional standards of living and the native values of good, happy, healthy or proper ways of living. This is what has usually concerned anthropologists.

When development is used in the second sense, studies show that warfare and preparation for war are disruptive to the development of tribal societies. For example, Mair (1977) summarizes some British anthropological studies which show how warfare is destructive of traditional patterns. Otterbein (1977) reaches a similar conclusion. An ecological anthropological perspective can provide perhaps deeper understanding of how this happens. Morey and Marwitt (1975) show that war within a tribal setting can be interpreted as an equilibrating response to better fit the tribe to the ecological limits of a territory. Traditional development is clearly dependent on variables of ecological fit and demographic patterns, with war and preparation for war a useful feedback system. Harris (1974:56) generalizes this by speaking of tribal armament and war as a safety valve for ecological equilibrium in which "growth cutoff institutions" accompany the build-up of armies and the engagement in war.

Thus, while war and preparation for war disrupt the subsistence economy but still may have an equilibrating ecological effect at the microlevel of many anthropological studies, the present world situation indicates that the situation on the macrolevel of global confrontation may be very different. The possible level of destruction has increased to such a point that other means of global equilibration must be sought—a task in which anthropological studies may be helpful.

Increasing Development through Disarmament

It is clear in the context of the foregoing that the armament-development complex as well as the war mentality seem to be governed by rules at the subconscious level and not primarily by rational decisions. It is thus even more important that anthropologists find a role through which they can aid conscious and serious efforts at disarmament in order to guarantee worldwide development necessary to the fulfilment of the basic needs of even the poorest peoples of the world.

Cooper (1975) likens the inequality of the present world situation to a pressure cooker. He calculates that the earth can house and feed up to 12 billion people and projects that the global population will reach this size by the end of next century. The ever growing world population will necessitate an absolutely equal distribution of food in order to avoid mass starvation and large, violent riots. A vast reorientation of policy is needed to reach the goal of equal distribution. This will involve the thorough rethinking of the whole system of inequality, competition, markets, and the laws of success as they have been recognized in the capitalist system. Development is essential to guarantee a more balanced distribution of resources and food. In what he calls "scenario I" Cooper (1975:467) notes that the United States continues "to have unequal and privileged access to the world's resources." This is true of the Soviet Union to a lesser extent. Because of this, Third World countries are politically dependent (Steele, 1982), since the rich countries in general acquire more and more resources from the poor countries.[1] In a relatively short time this can lead to disaster because of a general shortage of basic resources (Cooper, 1975). The consequences of this policy are greater military control of the resources of the southern hemisphere and a growing pressure from the developing countries to control the resources themselves. Cooper (1975:469) concludes: "Both of these growing pressure trends are on collision course—against each other and within themselves." The direct historical results of this pattern are clear today: since the Second World War practically all wars have been fought in resource areas. Thus, current conflicts are taking place in Central America, the Middle East, West Sahara, Eritrea, Somalia, and the Philippines, and several South Asian, South American and African countries are headed by military governments. In all of these cases important resources are at stake. (For an exposition of the systemics of this development since World War II, see Chomsky, 1982.)

The important point noted by Cooper is that the policy of exploitation and underdevelopment (inequality) leads to armament and armed conflicts. This is precisely the sort of mechanism to which I have been pointing in previous sections, and for which anthropological foundations should be found. Cooper (1975:468), in line with such development theorists as Heilbroner and Galbraith, suggests a single alternative: to focus on an economics system that emphasizes services rather than material consumer goods in the rich countries.

The armament industry is notoriously more wasteful of energy and creates more employment inequality than peacetime industry. (For a thorough discussion of the military economy see Melman, this volume.) Barnet (1972) says that a growing amount of economic activity and resources is being invested in products that have only imaginary use: they cannot be consumed and have no service value. Thus they are, economically speaking, "wasted." The strategy to invest in arms and military facilities that will never be used is simply unconscionable in a world where millions will die of starvation before the end of this century.

A second economic point is that employment decreases sharply as more is invested in armament. United Nations Report 81-25177 is very instructive in this regard: $1 billion provides only 76,000 jobs in military industry, against not less than 100,000 jobs in the civilian sector. Military spending in 1980 can be seen as representing unemployment for more than 13 million people. ($550 billion with a loss of 24,000 jobs per billion dollars). In a recent Belgian governmental debate about the costs of jobs in the assembling of F-16 fighters, an even more dramatic figure was agreed upon: each job in this branch of military industry was estimated to cost a half million dollars, about twice the cost of an average civilian job. Moreover, as indicated in the U.N. report, reconversion of space, missile, tank, and other military industries is rather easy, since each of these uses materials which can also be used without loss of value for genuine civilian development purposes.

The Nobel laureate and economist, Leontief (1980), uses similar reasoning in discussing development. Using an input-output model of global economic development until the year 2000, he points to the untenability of the present economic order. He suggests an optimistic "new economic order" with vast gifts of surplus from the rich to the poor countries, and an "arms-limitation scenario" in which the tremendous amount of money spent currently on the maintenance of military establishments throughout the world every year provides the largest existing economic reserve that might be utilized to accelerate the growth of the resource-poor, less developed countries (Leontief, 1980:180). Keeping expenditures for arms at 1970 levels and safeguarding a balance between the major political blocks, Leontief calculates that, although the expense gap between rich and poor will remain in the year 2000, the poorest countries will be able to have a 2.5 times greater income and consumption pattern than in 1980. Under the present economic order (with increasing expenses in the arms race), this level would at best be about 50 percent more than it is in 1980, with the gap between rich and poor continuing to widen (Leontief, 1980:81). The intriguing part of Leontief's analysis is that even moderate disarmament can guarantee development in the poorest countries and limit mass starvation.

Conclusion

Anthropological study of warlike talk reveals principles that apply equally to simple and complex societies. These principles may serve as political manipulation of people's perception of events. This promotes growing conservatism, simplification and the avoidance of new and creative solutions; the Other either as enemy (e.g., East-West opposition) or excluded from political discourse (e.g., North-South relationship); more power given to leaders; and an expansion of regimentation and hierarchization with enhanced military preparedness to meet a greater expectancy of threat and attack.

It can be further hypothesized that armament and development are inversely related in that increase in one means decrease in the other. To increase development, expenses for arms should be kept at low or declining levels. And the spiral of military expenses and attendant dangers should be controlled. Such a policy would greatly enhance development in the next decades. Furthermore, positive evolution on a worldwide scale will only be possible when the traditional political-economic model of competition and inequality in consumption is given up.

Principles derived from anthropological research can be used in the effort to modify disarmament-development relationships. A shift to more rational political and economic decisions concerning development-disarmament might be brought about by a shift in attitudes, mental dispositions and sociocultural patterns. It is precisely at this level that anthropologists can offer expertise in active support of a development-based strategy.

Anthropologists (and social scicntists in general) might engage in a campaign to popularize broader global perspectives to counter the conceptual narrowness induced by militarization. The cross-cultural perspective of anthropology constitutes a useful vantage point for such a campaign, and the communication media can be a useful tool in extending it. Anthropologists can stress the necessity of global cooperation and provide insight into the culture of the Other, so that fear of him may be reduced. Such information should also be provided to politicians.

Finally, education should focus more on cross-cultural perspectives, and on global and interdisciplinary views. Other societies should be treated as less exotic and more human, with lessons to be learned from cultural differences. For example, my university (Ghent, Belgium), has initiated programs in anthropology as training for development programs in industry and government and to provide guidance for intercultural contacts. Growing racism and xenophobia in rich countries and the unthinking acceptance of economic disparity can be countered by making more available the insights of anthropologists and development specialists. Systematic interchange of ideas between scientists of different political blocks can also be a simple but beneficial first step in reducing tension and stimulating informed, peaceful solutions to global problems.

Note

1. A dramatic example of this trend, widely reported in the newspapers in mid February of 1983, was that Great Britain—like the United States and France before it—is buying huge stocks of basic materials from mines in the South, especially for industrial and military production.

References

Barnet, R. 1972. "Conversion and a Military Society." In *Conversion from War to Peace: Social, Economic and Political Problems*, edited by W. Meyers and M. Hayes. New York: Gordon & Breach.

Bigelow, R. 1975. "The Role of Competition and Cooperation in Human Evolution." In *War, Its Causes and Correlates*, edited by M. Nettleship, R. Dale Givens and A. Nettleship, pp. 235–61. The Hague: Mouton.

Bohannan, P., ed. 1967. *Law and Warfare*. New York: Natural History Press.

Chomsky, N. 1982. "The United States: From Greece to El Salvador." In *Superpowers in Collision*, edited by N. Chomsky, J. Steele and J. Gittings, pp. 20–42. London: Penguin.

Chomsky, N.; Steele, J.; and Gittings, J., eds. 1982. *Superpowers in Collision*. London: Penguin.

Coolsaet, R. 1982. "Europese Defensie: Retoriek tegen Realiteit." *De Nieuwe Maand* 25:323–45.

Cooper, K. 1975. "Life in a Pressure Cooker: Man at the Turn of the Century, 2001." In *War, Its Causes and Correlates*, edited by M. Nettleship, R. Dale Givens and A. Nettleship, pp. 463–71. The Hague: Mouton.

Dadzie, K. S. 1980. "Economic Development." *Scientific American* 243:55–61.

Derksen, Q. C. 1981. *Wapenen voor de Vrede*. Zutphen: Thieme.

Economics Club of Chicago. 1980. *The Nation* March 8.

Feest, C. 1980. *The Art of War*. London: Thames and Hudson.

Fried, M. H.; Harris, M.; and Murphy, R., eds. 1968. *War, the Anthropology of Armed Conflicts*. New York: Natural History Press.

Gittings, J. 1982a. "Introduction: What the Superpowers Say." In *Superpowers in Collision*, edited by N. Chomsky, J. Steele, and J. Gittings, pp. 9–19. London: Penguin.

______. 1982b. "China: Half a Superpower." In *Superpowers in Collision*, edited by N. Chomsky, J. Steele, and J. Gittings, pp. 65–96. London: Penguin.

Gittings, J. and Steele, J. 1982. "Conclusion." In *Superpowers in Collision*, edited by N. Chomsky, J. Steele, and J. Gittings, pp. 97–103. London: Penguin.
Harris, M. 1974. *Cows, Pigs, Wars and Witches*. New York: Vintage.
Karsten, R. 1967. "Blood Revenge and War among the Jibaro Indians." In *Law and Warfare*, edited by P. Bohannan, pp. 303–26. New York: Natural History Press.
Laughlin, C. and Brady, I., eds. 1978. *Extinction and Survival in Human Populations*. New York: Columbia University Press.
Leeds, A. 1975. "Capitalism, Colonialism and War: An Evolutionary Perspective." In *War, Its Causes and Correlates*, edited by M. Nettleship, R. Dale Givens, and A. Nettleship, pp. 483–513. The Hague: Mouton.
Leontief, W. W. 1980. "The World Economy of the Year 2000." *Scientific American* 243:166–81.
Levine, R. and Campbell, D. 1972. *Ethnocentrism: Theories of Conflict, Ethnic Attitudes, and Group Behavior*. New York: Wiley.
Mair, L. 1977. *African Kingdoms*. Oxford, England: Oxford University Press.
Morey, R. V. and Marwitt, J.P. 1975. "Ecology, Economy and Warfare in Lowland South America." In *War, Its Causes and Correlates*, edited by M. Nettleship, R. Dale Givens, and A. Nettleship, pp. 439–50. The Hague: Mouton.
Nettleship, M.A., R. Dale Givens, and A. Nettleship, eds. 1975. *War, Its Causes and Correlates*. The Hague: Mouton.
N.C.O.S. 1982. *Over Vrede en Ontwikkeling*. Brussels: De Vereld Morgen.
Otterbein, K. F. 1967. "The Evolution of Zulu Warfare." In *Law and Warfare*, edited by P. Bohannan, pp. 351–57. New York: Natural History Press.
_____. 1977. "The Anthropology of War." In *Handbook of Social and Cultural Anthropology*, edited by J. Honigmann, pp. 923–58. New York: Columbia University Press.
Pinxten, R. 1983. "Cognitive Anthropological Analysis and Genuine Development." In *North American Indian Studies*, edited by P. Hovens. Gottingen: Edition Herodot.
Roling, T. 1964. *Over Oorlog en Vrede*. Amsterdam: Bezige Bij.
Steele, J. 1982. "The Soviet Union: What Happened to Detente?" In *Superpowers in Collision*, edited by N. Chomsky, J. Steele, and J. Gittings, pp. 43–64. London: Penguin.
UNESCO Courier. 1982. "From Swords to Ploughs." Edited by A.M. M'Bow. Paris: UNESCO.
United Nations. 1981. *Studies on the Relationship between Disarmament and Development. Report of the Secretary General*. Report 81–25177. New York: United Nations Organization.

21

The Anthropology of Global Integration: Some Grounds for Optimism about World Peace

James Silverberg

Integration and Conflict

Our concern in this book is with the politics of human survival in a threatened world. Are we able to draw any comfort from anthropology to suggest that humanity may survive the threats? I believe so.

First, though, I need to define some terms so that my frame of reference will be understood. I see politics as the interplay of two processes, integration and conflict. Within and between human aggregates, in relation to the adaptive problems they face, coalition, coexistence, or combat occurs. Politics, in other words, is simply war carried out by nonviolent means (to reverse von Clausewitz).

Integration is built on shared adaptive needs. Conflict reflects contradictory or competitive adaptive needs. Integration is likely to occur where shared adaptive problems are most critical. When organization occurs at any social level, it does so at the expense of potential organization at some higher, more inclusive level and by preventing or minimizing conflict at lower, less inclusive levels.

It is useful to make certain terminological distinctions when we refer to aggregates of people.[1] People who are not yet, or who are no longer, organized may comprise a *social category*. A category is an *un*organized aggregate. It is composed of people who are identified (by themselves or by others) in terms of some shared attribute(s). Only in recent decades have anthropologists begun to give due attention to the structural and processual importance of social categories (Silverberg, 1978). Our introductory anthropology texts still largely ignore them.

Once the whole or some part of a category is integrated, the result is an *organization*. It will be an *association* to the extent that it emphasizes a single primary status, the *member* whose occupants play duplicatory or supplementary roles. If, on the other hand, there are two or more member statuses, with differentiated dovetailing or complementary roles, I call the organization a *group*.

Three topics of anthropological study point up the way part or all of a social category organizes to become an association or a group, or even to become an association that contains within itself action-taking groups. I refer to studies of segmentary *lineages*, of *network* sets, and of *factions*.

The dialectical approach to *politics*, suggested above, turns out to be a generalization, a universalization of the segmentary *lineage* picture that has been clearly described and explained for the Nuer and the Tiv (Sahlins, 1961). We see an organization with flexible boundaries. It expands (*massing*) within a social category or it contracts, in accordion fashion, in response to its adaptive problems. Of course, in Sahlins' description there are specific features which are not necessary to my more general model. For example, Sahlins points to shared agnatic descent, but category-defining critera can be quite different. The Tiv link between organizational segments and spatial or territorial segments is also not necessary to the general model. A governmentless tribal system is not a necessary context. Above all, it is not necessary for the most pressing adaptive problem to be one that is lodged in the *societal* rather than the geographical environment. Sahlins (1961:333) argued that "without opposition the higher segments do not exist," because "predatory expansion" against other human groups is facilitated by "complementary opposition." It is true that an external human enemy group is frequently an adaptive problem. Thus Sahlins recognized that "segmentation and complementary opposition are . . . nearly universal features of human social organization" (1961:322). Some group-theory political scientists, pluralists and corporatists (notably Arthur Bentley), have also emphasized this group-organizing-against-group view (Olson 1965:120). But external human opposition is not the only environmental pressure that stimulates part or all of a social category to transform itself into an organization.

Network analysis states that under certain adaptive pressures, a categorical set, made up of links between people who share some attribute(s), will develop into an organized set, an *action set*, in which these links become the roles appropriate to collective action (Mayer, 1966; Wolfe, 1970).

The analysis of factions shows how within a broader organization, a category of people who have some common identity, will organize in response to their shared adaptive problem(s) and will do so despite the illegitimacy with which their new organization may be viewed by other members of the old, broader organization (Nicholas, 1965).[2] Here, organization takes the form of a partial contraction, so to speak, in contrast with the expansion phase that is usually emphasized for the segmentary lineage.

In each of these lines of anthropological analysis we see the organization of a social category either into a higher and more inclusive level of integration, or into a lower and less inclusive one, to cope with adaptive problems. *Ceteris paribus*, organization will be maintained at a *given* level as long as the benefits derived thereby supercede the benefits of integrating at a lower level (autonomy) or at a higher level (strength through centralization).

Particularly striking in complex societies during recent decades is the readiness of people in diverse social categories to organize themselves: the Blacks, Hispanics, and Native Americans; the aged, gays, the handicapped, the poor, women, and youth; categories based on general lifestyle, occupation, mode of production-structured class; categories based on issue awareness such as environmental deterioration, world peace, and so on. (We hear a great deal about consciousness raising in the process of organizing such categories. I shall discuss this briefly later on.)

Another feature of complex societies bears on the potential for social categories to organize. Complex societies are characterized by the existence of many categories, many lines of identification, pulling people in different directions. Category identifications crosscut and intersect to such an extent that people hesitate to organize exclusively along the lines of any single category and ruthlessly to pursue its interests to the exclusion of others. This usually makes organization of a category incomplete relative to the category's scope. Besides, individuals with multiple interests and roles often participate in more than one organization. The fact that organizations are thus incomplete and crosscutting helps to maintain the integration of the broader sociopolitical system in which they are found.

Social Adaptation

In a discussion of peace and war, what is the significance of such anthropological analysis of social categories and their potential for organizing, in whole or in part?

I think there are two present-day phenomena—one concerning categories, the other concerning adaptive problems—that offer some encouragement about the prospects for human survival in our increasingly threatened world. The first is the already mentioned striking trend of recent decades for all kinds of social categories to develop networks, movements and organizations (see Hirschman, 1970:42 on "the participation explosion"). These problems crosscut each other. Furthermore, the news media suggest that many of them are becoming increasingly global in their reach. In keeping with the analysis of complex social systems suggested above, further development along these lines can provide a people-based support structure for global integration and may weaken the nation-state both as a focus of identity and unchecked power, and as the principle vehicle of adaptation. I say people-based and use terms like "global" and "world-wide," deliberately eschewing the term "inter*national*," as a small contribution toward undermining nation-state sovereignty. This was the spirit with which *Current Anthropology* was founded and why individuals rather than nations were its members (Associates, Sol Tax, personal communication).

The other present-day phenomenon is the global nature of the adaptive stresses favoring social integration. I argued earlier that integration develops to cope with problems of survival at the very level where those problems are most critical. Humans today face threats to survival on a world-encompassing level, as Jonathan Schell (1982) so movingly expounds in *The Fate of the Earth*. These threats confront us whether we live in the capitalist or the socialist worlds, or in the Third World, or in the ethnic communities that are sometimes called the Fourth World. These survival threats are sources for the emergence of issue-awareness categories such as those mentioned earlier. I shall cite four such threats. Nuclear annihilation and the possible extinction of our species if not of all life on earth (Schell, 1982) is the most crucial. Then there is the threat of waste disposal (nuclear, toxic nonbiodegradable) and other forms of air, soil and water pollution, including acid rain and threats to the ozone layer, that drift uncontrollably across national frontiers. We also confront the exhaustion of nonrenewable resources, especially energy resources, as well as ecologically vital portions of our biota. Finally, there is widespread poverty in the face of a population explosion that outstrips the growth of food supplies. We do well to remember the wisdom of nutrition expert, Josue de-Castro, one-time president of the World Health Organization. As he said, our world is divided into two sectors. One goes to bed hungry while the other dopes itself with tranquilizers since it can't sleep for fear of what those who can't eat may do (de Castro, 1961:408). With such threats to survival confronting us on a global scale, there is a strong and growing adaptive pressure for worldwide sociopolitical integration to take place. We are all in the social category of threatened humans.

Is Collective Action an Illusory Myth?

Two strong counternotes should be discussed. One is the *decision theory* or *rational choice* analysis of organized collective action, which has questioned the likelihood of its occurrence and, if it does occur, of its effectiveness.[3] The other is the insistence of "political realists" on the inevitablity and permanence of the nation-state and its sovereignty.

First I discuss the doubts about the frequency and effectiveness of collective action. Anthropologists everywhere have had to take as given phenomena of their field experience such organizations as households, lineages, clans, ramages, age sodalities, secret clubs, and common-interest associations of many sorts. We have sometimes gone further: we often explain the occurrence of these diverse forms of collective action in functional and ecological-evolutionary terms. This approach, like that of any presociobiology evolutionist (e.g., Darwin himself), makes no attempt to equate adaptation or social function with individual motivations or with the decisions of conscious strategists.

By contrast, in economics—particularly, *public choice, public goods* and *welfare economics*—and, to some extent also in political science, an interesting and sophisticated form of social psychology developed in the early 1960s which threw considerable doubt on the effectiveness and extent of large-scale collective action (Olson, 1965). That this research is pertinent here may be seen from the following quotes: "There is no reason to suppose . . . that as problems that small primary groups cannot handle begin to emerge, large voluntary associations will arise to deal with those problems (1965:27). . . . Large latent groups [i.e., categories][4]will not always organize effectively to counter the strong effective action of small vested interest groups" (p. 128). "There are multitudes with an interest in peace, but they have no lobby to match those of the 'special interests' that may on occasion have an interest in war" (p. 166). (Armament production and sales organizations.)

The public-choice analysts relied not only on the rational self-interest view of market economics but also on the game-theory strategies that became so prominent during and after World War II (especially the artificially isolated, two-person, one-play Prisoner's Dilemma). Accordingly, they emphasized and explained their expectation that voluntary participation in large-scale collective action would be meager (because of what is known as the "free-rider" problem) or else rather deviously recruited through compulsion or as a by-product of self-interest, and so on (Olson, 1965).[5] (Russell Hardin has recently noted the irony of Olson's publishing date "at the height of the civil rights movement . . . [initiating a period when] successful collective actions seem to have become commonplace" [1982:xiv].) The prime mover, then, is the clash of self-interest against special-interest organizations, or, even more, against public-interest organizations (Hardin, 1982:101). The successful use of apathy to obtain widely desired collective benefits (playing the role of free-rider) rather than that of activist in some collective action—is seen as a triumph of self-interest over public interest. The analysis assumes that the actor is Economic Man, a person motivated by self-interest, and "narrow rationality" (Hardin, 1982:9). A critic of this theory has labelled its actor "the rational fool" and "the social moron" (Sen, 1979:102). Hardin recently described the actor as a cynic (1982:xiv-xv) and, indeed, he would fit Oscar Wilde's definition: "a person who knows the price of everything and the value of nothing."

The most recent work in collective-action analysis—perhaps given a midcourse correction by the phenomenal growth of collective-action movements themselves (Hardin, 1982:101; Hirschman, 1970:42)—has made far greater allowance for successful collective action based on motivations other than self-interest. Reference is now made not only to compulsion and by-product motivation (Olson, 1965; Hardin, 1982:17, 31–35), but to loyalty and "voice" (Hirschman, 1970); also to "commitment . . . [which] drives a wedge between personal choice and personal welfare" (Sen, 1979:97), to the activity of political entrepreneurs (Hardin, 1982:36), to the ease of organizing against a "collective bad" (Hardin, 1982:61–65, 120–21), and finally to extrarational motivations (morality, misunderstandings), contract by convention (something like what anthropologists mean by custom), sanctions, and norms (Hardin, 1982). Times certainly have changed since Olson's original work when such social incentives were overlooked or dismissed as individual goods, not collective goods, and thus disqualified in testing the efficacy of collective action in securing public benefits (Olson, 1965:61).

It is possible to unite today's modified collective-action approach with the anthropological analysis of social categories I discussed earlier, but first, three further observations about collective action: (1) An organization may draw its membership only from some persons in a category and still obtain the adaptive benefits for all persons identified in that category, organized and unorganized (free-riders, from the narrowly rational viewpoint, as well as activists). Olson had discounted this possibility (1965:182). (2) Success in obtaining benefits may not be an appropriate test of what Sen called "commitment" (1979:108). Olson's disparagement of lost causes (1965:161) sounds, to me, like faulting a citizen for voting in favor of a preferred candidate rather than voting for a winner. (3) Many collective actions are powerful because they act as the spearheads for a much larger category—for instance, as reflected in public opinion polls—and thereby they can secure continuous and extensive benefits through government action. For example, United States environmental lobbyists spend $10 million a year to secure $20 billion a year in environmental and conservation benefits (pre-Reagan administration information). (This is known as the Baumol solution, named after the author of *Welfare Economics and the Theory of the State*, 1952; see Hardin, 1982:52, 84, 110).

We may link the decision theorist's concern with motivation to our analysis of social categories by insisting on the importance of consciousness in the process by which any unorganized aggregate gets organized. Accordingly, before people organize and take action, they must become aware of their category identification (their identity) and thus be motivated by their shared interests. This, of course, is the commonly accepted wisdom of Karl Marx. However, Marx seems not to have been unwaveringly committed to such a cognitive approach. He is frequently cited for characterizing the nineteenth-century French peasantry as ". . . incapable of enforcing their class interests in their own name." However, Marx does not cite a lack of consciousness as the reason. Rather he refers to the absence of "manifold relations with one another," adding, with characteristic Marxian vividness, that they remain "like potatoes in a sack," an unorganized class (Marx, quoted in Hardin, 1982:189). Unfortunately, Marx does not consistently stick to this view of a class as an unorganized category. For example, in another passage, he says that unless "the identity of their interests produce(s) a community, national association, and political organizations—they do not constitute a class" (Marx, quoted from Dahrendorf in Olson, 1965:107). In any case, Marx will be forever remembered for the concept of "class consciousness."

Quite aside from Marx (or more likely borrowing from him), we have heard the call for consciousness raising from the organizing members of one category after another ever since the time of the civil rights and black power movements in the United States. The apparently felt need for consciousness raising seems to accompany a rejection of individual mobility (*exit*) and an affirmation of commitment to collective action (*voice*) (see Hirschman, 1970:109–12 on *exit, voice*, and *loyalty*.) When we hear young people in the United States speaking of "finding my identity," "finding myself," or "getting my head together," they may well be referring to their choice of a category identification and to their commitment to category consciousness.

An understanding of collective-action analysis may be useful for the anthropologist who wishes to study the organization of a social category such as survival-threatened humanity. Apparently the contribution can be reciprocated by anthropologists. In the closing passage of his recent work, *Collective Action*, Hardin (1982) hints at this: "Occasional issues are broadly enough defined to support enduring movements, and within these movements contract by convention may motivate a high level of activity, especially . . . if the activity can be partly localized, as in the American civil rights, antiwar, women's, and environmental movements. Alas, to understand such activity in a particular case might require the patience of an anthropologist" (pp. 229–30).

Is the Nation-State an Inevitable Obstacle?

The sovereign nation-state seems to be here to stay, at least for the present, regardless of whether it is a vehicle for a dictatorship of capital or for a dictatorship of the proletariat. Thus, many of us feel that international anarchy is inevitable, though we may feel this uncomfortably. The sovereign nation-state is taken for granted by realists, especially by political scientists (perhaps when their role as normative instructors in national and international civics affects their role as social scientists). Whether they espouse deterrence theory or the spiral theory, their point of departure as they try to pierce "the fog of foreign policy making" is the sovereign nation-state (Jervis, 1976:58–113). Opponents of the view are naive visionaries, even for the political scientist who concedes that "for nuclear weapons to be abolished, sovereignty would have to be abolished" (Mandelbaum, 1979:15, 6). (For a more complete and forceful case on this point, see Schell, 1982.)

On the other hand, anthropologists do not generally accept metaphysical explanations for the nation-state that refer to "the primordial quality [of its] resilience," or the "tendency of people to sort themselves into national groupings . . . [that has] a force of almost Newtonian power and regularity" (Mandelbaum, 1979:7). We give greater recognition to the evolution of sociopolitical integration. Accordingly, we anthropologists note that the nation-state and even its predecessor, the city-state, are relatively recent phenomena—probably less than 7,000 years old, the most recent .01 percent of human evolution as a separated lineage of primates. We are, thus, quite prepared to see a higher, more inclusive form of sociopolitical integration emerge. (See Beeman, this volume.)

The forms of such a global integration are not clearly apparent.[6] While present-day international agencies (e.g., the United Nations), arms control initiatives (e.g., Charles Osgood's Graduated and Reciprocated Initiatives in Tension Reduction (GRIT), Hardin, 1982:209–11), and the like must be preserved, increased and strengthened, they are self-defeating to the extent that they emphasize nation-state sovereignty. Sooner or later nation-state sovereignties can frustrate global collective action to cope with world-scale survival threats. On the other hand, multinational corporations—supranational networks and organizations—even though they are wealthier and more powerful than many nation-states, are too confined in their goal of making profits to help integrate humankind against its survival threats. In fact, they are part of the problem rather than a solution to it.

As for ethnocentrism, ethnicity, and nationalism, they present a challenge to any tight and comprehensive integration on a global scale. But they also challenge the present integration of each of our three major

Worlds—capitalist, socialist, and Third—just as they challenge even the integration of the nation-states within each of these Worlds. Perhaps the most difficult task will be not simply to secure the world against threats to human survival, but in doing so to retain considerable freedom of action for ethnic communites. This is indeed a problem area to which anthropologists can usefully devote themselves.[7]

As Jonathan Schell (1982) eloquently reminds us, we now have at our disposal the means to end our world. We are certain to do that if we pursue our own isolated and transient goals. Yet, the pressing adaptive problems faced by the whole of humanity should force us to create criss-crossing global people-based movements as well as some global sociopolitical organization(s) through which we can avoid nuclear and other disasters.[8]

Notes

I thank J. Patrick Gray and my wife, Donna Silverberg, for reading an earlier draft of this paper and making helpful suggestions. I am also grateful to David Garnham, Gene Muehlbauer, Seymour Priestley, George Ulrich, Alvin W. Wolfe, and John H. Dowling for productive discussions, some of them several years ago. I also appreciate the assistance of the Office of International Studies and Programs, the College of Letters and Science and my Department, all at the University of Wisconsin-Milwaukee, and that of the Ford Foundation, which made it possible for me to attend the Congress.

1. The collective action literature that I will refer to later on, would be immensely clarified if it didn't employ the term *group* for every kind of social aggregate, organized and unorganized, "action-taking," and "latent."
2. Nicholas does not find unacceptable the liberties I have taken with his 1965 analysis (personal communication).
3. See Margaret Clark's paper in this volume for a discussion of how rational-choice theory, as risk-benefit analysis, has become important to the build-up of arms and the continuation of confrontational styles in international relations.
4. See note 1, above.
5. Marshall D. Sahlins (1976) points out the close correspondence in certain approaches of capitalist economics and sociobiology that emphasize the self-interest pursuit strategies of individuals. I would add an additional similarity: their common fascination with "cheating in reciprocatory arrangements" (e.g., Axelrod and Hamilton, 1981:1391). As yet a further contribution to this excursion into the sociology of knowledge, I call attention to the striking simultaneity of Olson's publication (1965) with the writings of the trailblazing heroes of the oft-repeated origin tale of sociobiology, Hamilton (1964) and Williams (1966).
6. Wolfe (1982) offers an excellent review of the academic programs and publications since 1962 that evidence a growing interest in phenomena relating to sociocultural integration at a supranational level. Wolfe emphasizes the new interrelationships and new systems on the part of multinational corporates vis-á-vis cities and nation-states since the time of his own 1962 reports on the African mining interests, and he sees the electronic revolution as a significant ingredient of the supranational level of integration (as also an instrument for studying it).

Preston (1983) depicts a sweeping apocalyptic vision of a somewhat acephalous world civilization whose emergence we are in fact witnessing. He sees it as born of a "synthetic transformation" (in contrast to traditional organic change), one that is symptomized by the "culture of consumption" and the "hollow men of the Wasteland." His gloomy image of despair is partially relieved by the possibility that as resources diminish we may also witness a "world order less prone to conflict between the superpowers . . . and more conducive to mutual cooperation." Kurth-Schai (1983) discusses the necessity, prospect and difficulties of attaining a workable "global citizenship" that successfully addresses discrepant cultural and political images of humanity and of social responsibility.

7. On the general subject discussed in this section, see "The Future of Nationalism" in Gellner (1983). Concerning the degree of sovereignty which national states will retain, Gellner writes, "It would seem overwhelmingly likely that differences between cultural style of life and communication, despite a similar economic base, will remain large enough to require separate servicing, and hence distinct cultural-political units, whether or not they will be wholly sovereign" (p. 119).
8. This prediction can be subjected to the ultimate test. If it is confirmed its validity can strengthen an anthropological theory of politics. If it is negated, no one will be around to say so.

References

Axelrod, Robert, and Hamilton, William D. 1981. "The Evolution of Cooperation." *Science* 211:1390–96.

Baumol, William J. 1952. *Welfare Economics and the Theory of the State*. New York: Longmans, Green.

de Castro, Josue 1961. "Aspectos Socio-culturales de la Nutricion." In *Memoria, Vol. 2, VI Congreso Latinoamericano de Sociologia*, pp. 393–408. Caracas: Imprenta Nacional.

Gellner, Ernest. 1983. *Nations and Nationalism*. Oxford, England: Basil Blackwell.

Hamilton, William D. 1964. "The Genetical Evolution of Social Behavior, I, II." *Journal of Theoretical Biology* 7:1–52.

Hardin, Russell. 1982. *Collective Action*. Baltimore, Md.: Johns Hopkins Press.

Hirschman, Albert O. 1970. *Exit, Voice and Loyalty: Responses to Decline in Firms, Organizations and States*. Cambridge, Mass.: Harvard University Press.

Jervis, Robert. 1976. *Perception and Misperception in International Politics*. Princeton, N.J.: Princeton University Press.

Kurth-Schai, Ruthanne. 1983. "Unity in Diversity: A Cross-cultural Approach to the Study of Global Citizenship." *Cultural Futures Research* 7:4 (publication delayed).

Mandelbaum, Michael. 1979. *The Nuclear Question: The United States and Nuclear Weapons, 1946–1976*. Cambridge, England: Cambridge University Press.

Mayer, Adrian. 1966. "Significance of Quasi-groups in the Study of Complex Societies." In *The Social Anthropology of Complex Societies*, edited by Michael Banton, pp. 97–122. London: Tavistock.

Nicholas, Ralph. 1965. "Factions: A Comparative Analysis." In *Political Systems and the Distribution of Power*. ASA Monograph No. 2, edited by Michael Banton, pp. 21–61. New York: Praeger.

Olson, Mancur Jr. 1965. *The Logic of Collective Action: Public Goods and the Theory of Groups*. Cambridge, Mass.: Harvard University Press.

Preston, James J. 1983. "World Civilization: An Anthropological Perspective." *Cultural Futures Research* 7:4 (publication delayed).

Sahlins, Marshall D. 1961. "The Segmentary Lineage: An Organization of Predatory Expansion." *American Anthropologist* 63:322–45.

———. 1976. *The Use and Abuse of Biology*. Ann Arbor, Mich.: University of Michigan Press.

Schell, Jonathan. 1982. *The Fate of the Earth*. New York: Alfred A. Knopf.

Sen, Amartya K. 1979. "Rational Fools: A Critique of the Behavioral Foundations of Economic Theory." In *Philosophy and Economic Theory*, edited by Frank Hahn and Martin Hollis, pp. 87–109. Oxford, England: Oxford University Press.

Silverberg, James. 1978. "Social Categories vs. Organizations: Class-conflict in a Caste-structured System." In *Main Currents in Indian Sociology, Vol. III: Cohesion and Conflict in Modern India*, edited by Girl Raj Gupta, pp. 1–32. New Delhi, India: Vikas Publishing House and Durham, N.C.: Carolina Academic Press.

Williams, George C. 1966. *Adaptation and Natural Selection*. Princeton, N.J.: Princeton University Press.

Wolfe, Alvin W. 1970. "On the Structural Composition of Networks." *Canadian Review of Sociology and Anthropology* 7:226–44.

———. 1982. "Sociocultural Integration above the Level of the State." *Cultural Futures Research* 7(1):9–22.

22

The Superpowers and the Tribes

Peter Worsley

The major object of this paper is to examine the relevance and usefulness of anthropology, not in order to improve our understanding of warfare among Them but to find ways to peace for Us. To change the world we need to understand it.

I begin by rejecting the traditional binary opposition between American "cultural" anthropology and British "structural" or social anthropology. My first point is therefore, a cultural one: politics is always, immanently, about ideas, and not simply about force. Power, as Weber (1947:152) wrote is "the capacity to carry out one's will despite resistance." But as he showed more clearly than many, force is never "force-in-itself". Rather, force is always used to achieve social ends and to express cultural values. And, compliance usually entails a rational calculation of self-interest on the part of those who comply or else the belief that nothing can be done to resist or change things.

But rulers generally try to foster more positive attitudes than these. They try to persuade people that they have a *right* to rule and the people *ought* to obey them, and thereby transform mere power into authority (Gerth and Mills, 1953:195). They thus add a moral dimension to an otherwise precarious reliance on the monopoly of the means of violence. No one was more aware of the limits to that kind of power than Weber's contemporary, Bismarck, who, though usually seen simply as the man of "blood and iron" or the "Iron Chancellor," knew that "you can do anything with bayonets except sit on them." His struggle to contain the rising socialist movement within Germany therefore included not merely the antisocialist laws but the later more imaginative and flexible introduction of wide-ranging welfare legislation in order to win popular support.

At the state level of modern industrialized societies legitimating ideologies are rarely explicitly religious. In the First World, church and state have long been formally separated and religion a matter of private conscience. In the Second World, atheism is the official creed of many states. Hence modern writers, imbued with the values and cast of thought of secularized societies and *Realpolitik* political theory, forget that before the "Great Watershed" of the capitalist Industrial Revolution and the French political Revolution, the medieval papacy not only claimed preeminence over secular rulers, but was actually powerful enough, by making an English king go to Canossa and fall upon his knees, to make that claim reality.

In many societies authority is internally divided among religious and secular competitors for preeminence, and though the religious are often equally ready to resort to force in order to buttress their institutional power, they are also able to appeal to further, immaterial values which confer a very special kind of legitimacy. Likewise, secular rulers commonly invoke the "divine rights of kings."

Stalin's famous materialist question: "And how many battalions has the Pope?" which expresses most pithily this modern dismissal of religion as a factor in international relations, has therefore much in common with the thinking of many otherwise opposed to everything he stood for, notably American *Realpolitik* theorists who see politics in narrow, "pork-barrel" terms: simply as a matter of "who gets what, when, how" (Lasswell, 1936).

These theorists would have great difficulty explaining the revival of Islam as a political force, or the persistence of Catholicism in Poland. But the danger with this perspective is not its underestimation of religion—which, globally, has indeed given way to secular ideologies—but its underestimation of the power of ideas in general.

My second point is a structural one: there is something to be learned from studying warfare and peacemaking among acephalous polities, since what is increasingly called the world system is, in fact an acephalous political field.[1]

The antinomy between stateless and state polities, moreover, though central to the theory of modern political anthropology (Evans-Pritchard and Fortes, 1940) and to Marxist political theory (Krader, 1968), is not absolute but rather an ideal-type distinction. Many political systems fit neatly into neither category, either because centralized authority is often ambiguous, contingent or impermanent, because there is no legitimate or effective monopoly of the means of violence, or because, while there may be a dominant class, what permanent apparatus there may be for decision-making and for implementing decisions is often meager. Thus the so-called "Paramount" Chief of the Trobriand Islands (a title invented by Sir William MacGregogor in 1896 and uncritically accepted by Malinowski) has been called the "Piltdown Man" of social anthropology (Singh Uberoi, 1962). Among the Anuak, three noble houses competed for the sacred emblems of kingship (Evans-Pritchard, 1940a).

Authority, in this kind of polity, is not an absolute, but must constantly be achieved. This may happen in a Renan-type *plebescite de tous les jours*, perhaps by using wealth to reward supporters and to help those in need (who may then become supporters), by carrying out ritual functions such as rain making, by preserving internal peace through settling disputes, or by providing effective leadership when war cannot be avoided. *Pace* theories which attribute the emergence of the state to the conquest of one group by another, it was the *resolution* of conflicts that gave Alur nobles prestige, the more successful being actually sought out and invited (even kidnapped, according to some accounts) to come and rule (Southall, 1956).

Nor is the establishment of the state irreversible. The existence of centralized state machinery may be only a phase in an ongoing oscillation, in which the attempt to imitate more stable systems, without the economic resources with which to sustain such institutions, periodically collapses, ushering in another period of statelessness. Leach's (1954) study of the fluctuations between *gumsa* and *gumlao* in Highland Burma is the most famous instance of this process.

Even where centralized political institutions have become more permanent and specialized, and decisive political power restricted to a ruling class, the control over centralized institutions is situational and contingent. Gluckman (1963a) demonstrated how the claims of rivals from different noble houses to the kingship in southern Africa were settled by wars of succession in which the capacity to mobilize a sufficient number of followers was the ultimate test.

Politics in Acephalous Societies

In some acephalous societies authoritative political status is taken by occupants of one preeminent role such as lineage head and is not embodied in specialized roles. Such a preeminent role "includes many duties other than (and sometimes more important than) making and implementing political decisions" (Swartz, et al. 1966:12). In yet other kinds of acephalous societies there is only an overlapping, plural set of groups, categories, and statuses no one of which is preeminent. Political leadership then depends upon the ability to muster a following by drawing on available clusters of potential followers (members of extended kin networks, of residential communities, or of ritual associations, and so on). These would not necessarily cohere were they not brought together via the entrepreneurship of "big men" endowed with what Pareto called "residues of combination" (Pareto, 1935), who persuade, cajole, induce, exhort, reward and browbeat others into following them, particularly in emulative competition with their neighbours (see e.g., Strathern, 1979).

Relationships between acephalous polities, though unconstrained by any superior power, are not unstructured. With immediately neighbouring societies ambiguity is normal; conflict is most likely with those who are nearby and who are therefore, paradoxically, more likely than not to be culturally similar. These are also the people with whom there will be trade relationships, whether in basics, luxuries, or valuables (Salisbury, 1962), with whom ties of kinship created by intermarriage are likely, and who are sometimes allies as against third parties.

However centralized power may be internally, relationships between states are no more regulated by any supranational, overarching authority than are relationships between acephalous societies. There is no agency analogous to the state able to monopolize the means of violence or to claim "transcendent" authority.

Rules of War

Despite the absence of such an agency, relations between societies at war never take place in an anomic social vacuum. They are constrained, first, by the necessity of interdependence, by the realization that, though peaceful relationships may be suspended "for the duration" of hostilities, they will eventually have to be resumed after peace has been reestablished, whether there is withdrawal or permanent occupation. Second, warfare always takes place according to rules which define what may and may not be done. These may be more honored in the breach than the observance, and may even permit quite brutal behaviour. "Every Nuer tribe," Evans-Pritchard (1940b:126, 128) wrote, "raided Dinka at least every two or three years and some parts . . . annually. . . . Older women and babies were clubbed." People further outside the range of known neighbours may be classed as virtually nonhuman and designated witches or cannibals, to whom the normal considerations of enmity do not apply. However, the likelihood of fighting them is also not very high.

The rules of intergroup war vary greatly, according to whether there is competition for scarce resources—among agriculturalists, for land, and for land and animals among pastoralists. Under these conditions, war becomes a mode of appropriation. Where resources are perceived as unlimited "armed conflict between groups is more often an opportunity for expressing emulative competition *within* the group. . . . Death, destruction or subjugation of the enemy [are] not major aims" (Richards, 1975:104). Under these very different conditions, warfare develops norms in which heroism becomes a value in itself. Thus North American Indian warriors achieved their greatest prestige not by actually killing their opponents, but by "counting coup"—by hitting their enemies with the hand or with a small stick—in the thick of the fight. Defeat, too, had its code of manners, which included the right to torture and the expectation that the tortured would endure his fate unflinchingly.

The Ends of War

The ends of war, then, as anthropologists have shown, are not universal: human propensities to aggression or structural imperatives for conflict, drives to expansion or the acquisition of material goods. They are cultural. "War," Rapoport (1968:17) writes,

> has at times been viewed as a pastime or an adventure, as the only proper occupation of a nobleman, as an affair of honour (e.g. in the days of chivalry), as a ceremony (among the Aztecs).

Geertz (1980:134) argues that in Bali politics is "finally . . . about mastery: Women and Horses and Power and War"; in short, about coercion. But the "motor" of state and society—the end for which peasants were made to pay taxes and fight for their lords—was the attempt to bring the state closer to a cultural ideal. This was the "exemplary center" located in the fourteenth-century Majapahit kingdom in comparison to which all subsequent kingdoms were only ever-inferior imitations. Both the structure and the culture of the state were therefore modeled upon this ideal in highly ritualized ways and even war itself was conducted as "theatre."

This is not, he argues, a commitment to idealism in analysis. It is a recognition that the central preoccupations of Balinese culture—genealogies, clientship, spatial arrangements, cremations—were not just "*ultimate* ends," but shaped everyday relationships and actions (Geertz, 1980).

This kind of analysis, in which culture is the central determinant, is at the opposite end of the theoretical continuum from formal sociology. Formal sociology concentrates on factors such as number, size, mode of organization, and technological equipment, as in *themselves* determining both how one's own society—including its military organization—has to be structured, and, dialectically, obliges the enemy to respond in similar ways (e.g., Simmel, 1955). Modern counterinsurgency responds to the strategies evolved by the guerrillas being fought. It replaces large-scale positional warfare by a war of small group movement in which the support of the civilian population, not the destruction of enemy troops, is the fundamental requirement for victory. What formal sociology does not capture is the vastly different social content of the respective protagonists. Guerrillas, who lack both sophisticated weaponry and the economic resources with which to reward compliance and the political legitimacy that the government can claim must win "hearts and minds" if they are to survive and expand, as MaoTse-Tung (1954:150) classically enunciated:

> We must go to the masses, arouse them to activity; concern ourselves with their weal and woe; and work earnestly and sincerely in their interests and solve their problems of salt, rice, shelter, clothing and childbirth . . . If we do so, the broad masses will certainly give us their support.

That kind of local-level development is only possible in areas under effective guerrilla control. Elsewhere, the alternative to life as it is now is necessarily restricted to a vision of a better future society, notably the promise of land-distribution. For their opponents, it is precisely these social objectives that are precluded, for they are struggling to prevent not just radical political change, but radical social change. (For a discussion of this problem, see also Doughty, this volume.) Hence compliance can usually only be achieved by resorting to force, including random, brutal terror, and even genocide, and by the selective use of economic rewards, rather than by holding out utopian prospects of an alternative society: by dependence upon what Etzioni (1964) has called coercive and remunerative sanctions rather than normative ones.

Relations between contending parties, then, are by no means limited to the kinds of factors emphasized in formal sociology. Cultural norms, moreover, include *supra* societal understandings—conventions as to what may and may not be done—which are shared *with the enemy*. Self-interest is one source of these, since whatever you do is likely to be done to you in turn.

In examining the conduct of warfare, the value of the absolute distinction between state and stateless societies is limited. The professionalization of modern war, it is often argued, results in a sharp distinction between the military and the civilian population which has no counterpart in societies where wars are waged by men who simply drop their normal everyday roles in field and village and pick up arms, often little different in kind (bows, arrows, bills, forks) from the tools they use in hunting or cultivating.

Professional soldiers indeed constitute a separate occupational group who are likely—especially foreigners and mercenaries—to be unconcerned about the fate of civilians to whom they have no ties, and to be preoccupied with their own subcultural ends (loot, pay, promotion). But modern war is usually fought by conscripts. And even in acephalous societies, war making is sometimes allocated to a quite specialized segment of the population, such as the warrior age grades of the Masai. In New Guinea warfare, raping women, destroying crops, and burning houses were normal practices in part precisely because there *were* no "specifically military" targets (Strathern, 1979). And when competition for land and other scarce goods becomes severe, war can become so endemic that, as in many small-scale Amazonian Indian societies under pressure from colonists, there are few families that have not lost at least one adult male in intertribal warfare.

Sources and Resolutions of Conflict

Warfare is thus not a phenomenon which emerges with the state, and older anthropological and popular notions that societies like the Eskimo were free from murder and other kinds of physical violence can safely be dismissed as pastoral myth. The resolution of disputes both within the group (which Radcliffe-Brown designated "law"), and in state societies, has as its ultimate sanction the possibility of resort to the use of violence. Though there is no specialized apparatus of law enforcement for carrying out political decisions, as in state societies armed intergroup conflict (which Radcliffe-Brown calls "war") is quite normal among hunters and gatherers (Evans-Pritchard and Fortes, 1940:Preface). As Sahlins (1961) showed for the predatory Nuer lineage, expansion by conquest does occur in acephalous societies.

But the more usual end state of war in acephalous society is reversion to the status quo. The limits upon what may be done therefore derive from the awareness that war is an episode, not some Hobbesian endemic state, and that peace is the norm to which society will return, at which point relationships of many kinds will have to be resumed, an awareness summed up in the saying "We marry our enemies" (Gluckman, 1963b).

That paradox derives from the fact that immediately neighbouring groups are both the most likely competitors (and therefore potential and traditional enemies) and those with whom the most frequent social contacts and closest ties exist. These ties may even be deliberately fostered in collective form, such as institutionalized ritual exchanges or competitive feasts.[2] But ties of various kinds also exist dyadically, between individuals, notably kinship ties and trade relationships. Marriages between leading families or houses are of special importance since they bring political units into closer relationship. Single-stranded relationships, such as those between trading partners, include not only most-favoured economic treatment (privileged or fixed prices, guaranteed supplies, exclusivity, and so on) but are often elaborated by creating extra-economic social ties, such as the contracting of marriages between children or other relatives, or the establishment of godparenthood relationships and other forms of ritual association from blood-brotherhood to membership of the same secret society.

Technical considerations—among agriculturalists, the need for access to different kinds of soil for different crops, as well as access to woodland, pasture and water—result in the dispersal of holdings, often in the form of strips in different areas. Pastoralists likewise lend out animals so as to minimize the loss of all of them in a localized epidemic. These animals may remain with those to whom they are lent virtually permanently, and only recalled on occasions of abnormal necessity such as famines or feasts or when needed for bridewealth payments. More normally, the loans remain in force, and only interest in the form of some of the offspring is handed over periodically. The capital remains with the borrower. As with shopkeeping in rural Ireland, debt is a permanent relationship tying both partners together (Arensberg, 1937).

The dispersal of people rather than of animals similarly provides ready-made ties which can be activated for the purpose of making peace. Within any Nuer village or cattle camp, there are people belonging to different lineages and age sets, and related by different kinds of kinship ties (Evans-Pritchard, 1940b). Fighting within the local community would make social life impossible, since all of these ties would be disrupted. Hence violent conflict, at this level, is limited to using clubs only, and elders are readily able to settle the issue by arranging for the payment of compensation.

But in Nuer intervillage conflicts, spears are used, and homicide results. Though only the lineage which has lost a member is in a state of direct feud with the killer's lineage, others in the two communities are again likely to get drawn in, since they have ties of many kinds not only with the aggrieved person in their own community but also with members of the village with which he is in conflict. "A feud," Evans-Pritchard remarks, "has little significance unless there are social relations of some kind which can be broken off and resumed. . . . At the same time, these relations necessitate eventual settlement if there is not to be complete cleavage" (Evans-Pritchard, 1940b:159).

Disputes between members of different Nuer villages are therefore ultimately settled by resort to external mediation in the shape of the famous "leopardskin chief," whose authority transcends any parochial, secular limits, because it is based on his sacred association with the earth.

The most difficult disputes to settle are those between tribes, which cannot be resolved by paying compensation. Fighting is therefore likely to be more difficult to bring to an end the more distant the relationship, since there are few social contacts and little interdependence in everyday life.

Direct relationships, then, do not prevent intergroup conflicts from arising, even in acephalous societies. But they do mean that many, if not most, people will have personal reasons for wanting to bring conflict with close neighbours to an end as soon as possible. Individuals with ties of kinship to the other side are therefore ready-made intermediaries.

But those mechanisms become less effective the further away one moves from close-range association. Conflicts that arise at more remote ranges are likely to be perceived not just as defense of specific aggrieved kinsmen, but, more abstractly, as an affront or threat to the collective interests or status of the group as a whole: as *political* disputes, "concerned with the determination of *public* goals" at the level of the community (Swartz, et al., 1966).

The resolution of such conflicts, even in acephalous societies, is therefore less likely to come about simply via the initiative of individuals with a personal interest in restoring harmony. Unfortunately, this is the level which conflicts between modern nation-states most clearly resemble. Interpersonal ties and contacts do exist in the modern world, of course. Businessmen, professionals, politicians, entertainers and sportsmen and women and innumerable others, move around the world on a scale never known before the epoch of the jet plane. In open societies, foreign tourism is a mass phenomenon. All this has its positive aspects: it prevents us from thinking of the Chinese in the same way as those nineteenth-century African societies which recognised their neighbours as human beings (however inferior or misguided) but believed that people further afield were witches or cannibals. The limits of interpersonal contact in the modern world, of course, are obvious. People take abroad with them stereotypes which are not likely to be seriously disturbed by a brief stay—and may often be confirmed. Most tourism consists in lying on beaches, or in confinement to the ghettoes of hotels, historic sites and artistic centers, insulated from any significant contact with the indigenous population, and often cut off from them by language barriers or interpreters. It does not entail ongoing, multiplex association and the constant adaption of one's own behavior necessitated by living together face-to-face.

Getting to know foreigners, and even establishing more enduring personal links with them, moreover, is a process that governments can readily exploit in a way that reinforces political prejudices. They can thus argue that "we have no quarrel with the people of country X, only with their government," a view which ignores the fact that peoples may, especially under the influence of modern state propaganda, identify quite closely with the government of their country and see other states as a menace, whatever their personal experience (if any) of individuals from those states. Patriotism (especially abroad) has a powerful appeal whose effect is to increase rapport between government and people and to open a gap between one's own country and others. In this century, nationalism and chauvinism have proved to be far more powerful than internationalism both in capitalist and communist countries. Hence although the world is indeed a "global village" in terms of communication technology, it is not such in terms of the content of the media available to the masses. What is shown on a country's TV screens depends upon what governments allow to be shown or insist will be shown. Attempts to establish ties with other countries or even persons outside official channels are treated, in some countries, as treasonable.

Despite such barriers, exchanges and visits of all kinds are one major means of creating trust, insofar as, at the lowest level, they help dissolve negative images of the Other. We cannot, unfortunately, arrange for members of our society to be distributed around towns and cities in the countries of potential enemies just as Nuer lineages are. There is no way that relatives of the top decisionmakers in the United States can be made to live near Soviet missile bases or even in Soviet cities, and vice versa. But exchanges of other kinds: student exchanges, professional conferences and congresses, the "twinning" of cities, sport and other forms of "ping-pong diplomacy," educational programs about life in other countries seen as hostile, and discussions about how to achieve peace and reduce tensions rather than how to build up more defenses, all contribute towards building confidence —without which more positive practical action is unlikely.

Such interchange does nothing, however, to promote mutuality. It is education about remote countries, at best contact between members of *separate* societies. We need, therefore, to go beyond mere acquaintance, or that kind of coexistence that is little more than armed truce, to international *cooperation.* In this respect, trade relations constitute an intermediate category. The building of the massive natural-gas pipeline between Siberia and Western Europe is thus an important step towards peace because it increases *material* interdependency (which is why cold warriors tried to stop it). In medieval Europe, there were institutions that transcended the state, notably the Roman Catholic Church and the Roman law (Anderson, 1974a, 1974b). With the emergence of the modern nation-state in the epoch of absolutism and the dissolution of the spiritual monopoly of the Roman Catholic Church during the Reformation, new supranational institutions had to be devised to regulate relations between states—the invention of modern diplomacy and new forms of international law which provided rules and mechanisms for dealing with disputes. But a supranational *agency* empowered to impose majority decisions on rule breakers did not emerge until the twentieth century with the establishment, first, of the League of Nations, and then of the United Nations. The limits of the power of the latter scarcely needs spelling out. Yet it is still the major forum for the expression of world opinion, especially of those voices that would otherwise never be heard, and however often it may be ignored now, its powers could be strengthened.

The major limitation on the power of the United Nations is that it is not the apex of a hierarchical international system, but a relatively powerless institution operating within an acephalous field of forces in which the camps headed by the USSR and the United States are the major wielders of military power, and the multinational corporations dispose of more economic resources than most governments. Yet gigantic material strength did not prevent the effective defeat of the greatest power in world history at the hands of a small peasant country. And in the modern world, what used to be referred to as the ultimate sanction, resort to violence, has become meaningless in the epoch of nuclear weapons, since their use would entail not merely the destruction of one's own military forces, but the entire society and human civilization as a whole. War is no longer an episode but a terminus.

One of the United Nation's chief functions has been to provide buffer forces in zones where the Superpowers agree to limit direct or surrogate conflict. The United Nation's authority in such situations, is only a moral one like that of the leopardskin chief; it cannot impose a solution, it can only defuse and mediate.

In the defusing of conflicts between the superpowers third parties of all kinds have a part to play: the older neutrals such as Sweden and Switzerland and the newer nonaligned grouping, which, though its individual members are now often de facto very much aligned with either the First or the Second World, is strongly critical of the economic domination of the West and by now representative of the great majority of underdeveloped countries.

In Western Europe, increasing numbers of people believe that there can be no freedom or security as long as all issues are immediately translated into the confrontational, totalitarian language of the superpowers. Further, this confrontation breeds enforced conformity *within* each of the blocs, since repression is visited upon those who reject the hegemony of "their" superpower: in Hungary, Czechoslovakia, Poland and Afghanistan; in Korea, Vietnam, the Dominican Republic and El Salvador. This mutual paranoia is particularly acute, naturally, around the borders of these giant countries. Hence it is precisely these zones that need to be converted into zones of peace, by denuclearizing Western Europe and by recognizing that wars such as those now being fought in Central America are genuine, indigenous struggles for liberation from genocidal dictators and oligarchies and not operations masterminded from Moscow.

Perhaps the most famous remark ever made about war is Clausewitz's dictum that war is "the continuation of peace by other means." To him, it was a rational means of defending the sovereign state, even a "fundamental condition of human existence" (Rapoport, 1968:22). Nuclear war, however, renders both of these cardinal assumptions invalid, for *both* sides lose, and postnuclear society would be far removed from anything most of us would wish to describe as *human* existence.

Perhaps the second most famous remark made about war is Clemenceau's wry observation that it is "too important a matter to be left to generals." It has now become too important a matter to be left to politicians. Generals, it has been observed, are always preparing for the previous war, a phenomenon anthropologists have designated cultural lag. Today, words such as "defense" and "survival," in the nuclear epoch, have become outmoded concepts fit only for the museum of intellectual history.

New ones need to be put in their place. The most important of these is coexistence, which at present connotes little more than living with a mutual balance of terror. That kind of coexistence has to be transformed into positive cooperation (which would enable us to wipe out world poverty overnight). The alternative, otherwise, is the probability, not the possibility, of the ultimate holocaust.

The unifying theme of the famous "Disappearing World" series of anthropological films was that the survival of the simpler societies—the so-called Fourth World—was under threat. Those societies are, indeed, going to have to come to terms with the infinitely more powerful world around them; missionaries, government officials, multinational corporations, and soldiers are not going to go away.

Some of these smaller societies still face genocide, and many will lose their cultural autonomy and identity altogether. But others will survive as distinct cultural enclaves within wider societies. They will have to learn to coexist and cooperate with powerful and numerous outsiders, however painful this may be. If we do not want to disappear, so will we.

Notes

1. "We stress the relative quality of the concept 'field' to offset the absolute or rigid quality imputed to concepts that have often dominated political thinking hitherto: 'political system', 'political structure', and the 'governmental process'" (Swartz, et al., 1966:27).
2. Malinowski likened the *kula* exchanges to a stage in the "evolution of primitive international law" (Malinowski, 1922:515).

References

Anderson, Perry. 1974a. *Passages from Antiquity to Feudalism; Lineages of the Absolute State.* London: New Left Books.

———. 1947b. *Lineages of the Absolute State*. London: New Left Books.
Arensberg, Conrad M. 1937. *The Irish Countryman: An Anthropological Study*. London: Macmillan.
Etzioni, Amitai. 1964. *Modern Organizations*. Englewood Cliffs, N.J.: Prentice-Hall.
Evans-Pritchard, E.E. 1940a. *The Political System of the Anuak of the Anglo-Egyptian Sudan*. London: London School of Economics.
———. 1940b. *The Nuer: A Description of the Modes of Livelihood and Political Institutions of a Nilotic People*. Oxford, England: Clarendon Press.
Evans-Pritchard, E.E. and Fortes, M., eds. 1940. *African Political Systems*. Oxford, England: Oxford University Press.
Geertz, Clifford. 1980. *Negara: The Theatre State in Nineteenth-century Bali*. Princeton, N.J.: Princeton University Press.
Gerth, Hans and Mills, C. Wright. 1953. *Character and Social Structure: The Psychology of Social Institutions*. New York: Harcourt, Brace.
Gluckman, Max. 1963a. *Custom and Conflict in Africa*. Oxford, England: Blackwell.
———. 1963b. "Rituals of Rebellion in South-East Africa." In *Order and Rebellion in Tribal Africa*, pp. 110–36. London: Cohen and West.
Krader, Lawrence. 1968. *Formation of the State*. Englewood Cliffs, N.J.: Prentice-Hall.
Lasswell, Harold. 1936. *Politics: Who Gets What, When, How*. New York: McGraw-Hill.
Leach, Edmund. 1954. *Political Systems of Highland Burma: A Study of Kachin Social Structure*. London: Athlone Press.
Malinowski, Bronislaw. 1922. *Argonauts of the Western Pacific: An Account of Native Enterprise and Adventure in the Archipelagos of Melanesia and New Guinea*. London: Routledge & Kegan Paul.
Mao, Tse-Tung. 1954. "Take Care of the Living Conditions of the Masses and Attend to the Methods of Work." In *Selected Works*. Vol. 1, pp. 147–52. London: Lawrence and Wishart.
Pareto, Vilfredo. 1935. *The Mind and Society*. Edited by Arthur Livingston; translated by Andrew Bongiotno and Arthur Livingston. 4 vols. New York: Harcourt, Brace.
Rapoport, Anatol, ed. 1968. *Clausewitz on War*. Harmondsworth, England: Penguin.
Richards, Cara. 1975. "The Concepts and Forms of Competition." In *War: Its Causes and Correlates*, edited by Martin A. Nettleship, R. Dale Givens, and Anderson Nettleship, pp. 95–108. The Hague: Mouton.
Sahlins, Marshall. 1961. "The Segmentary Lineage: An Organization of Predatory Expansion." *American Anthropologist* 63(2):332–45.
Salisbury, Richard. 1962. *From Stone to Steel: Economic Consequences of a Technological Change in New Guinea*. Melbourne, Australia: Melbourne University Press.
Simmel, Georg. 1955. *Conflict*. Glencoe, Ill.: Free Press.
Singh Uberoi, J. P. 1962. *Politics of the Kula King: An Analysis of the Findings of B. Malinowski*. Manchester, England: Manchester University Press.
Southall, Aidan. 1956. *Alur Society: A Study in Processes and Types of Domination*. Cambridge, England: Heffer.
Strathern, Andrew, ed. 1979. *Ongka: A Self-account by a New Guinea Big-man*. London: Duckworth.

Swartz, Marc; Turner, Victor W.; and Tuden, Arthur, eds. 1966. *Political Anthropology*. Chicago, Ill.: Aldine.
Weber, Max. 1947. *The Theory of Social and Economic Organization*. Edited by A.M. Henderson and Talcott Parsons. Glencoe, Ill.: Free Press.

PART V
ANTHROPOLOGY AND POLICY

23

Anthropology for the Second Stage of the Nuclear Age

David G. Mandelbaum

In the life of a nation, as of a person, critical turnings may occur—times and experiences that usher in new perspectives, new endeavors, new goals, new partners. Once that sort of turning is experienced, whether it be a divorce or a revolution, neither person nor nation can quite return to the previous condition or restore the earlier stage.

Such turnings have also occurred in the career of the human species. The acquisition of language, the development of agriculture, the formation of states and of the other appurtenances of civilization, the consequent stage of industrial and scientific revolutions, these and other profound shifts have affected humankind in ways from which there has been no turning back. The band of scientists at Los Alamos initiated what was quickly recognized as a turning of great potential for the whole species, the production of nuclear weapons.

When we consider nuclear developments since Hiroshima—technological, social, political—as unfolding within a first stage of the nuclear age, the turning toward a second stage could come about in three principal ways. One would be a nuclear exchange between the superpowers. Even if "limited," it would surely be followed by sizeable alterations in social assumptions and political organization. If full salvoes were to be exchanged, the second could be the terminal phase. As has often been told, civilization might well be extinguished, the species imperiled, an end brought to the liturgical world without end.

A second possibility is the steady continuation of negotiations through small, incremental steps until firm agreement among nuclear powers for effective controls was reached and implemented. Technological advances, as through greatly improved means of surveillance, might help in this process. The transfer of some elements of national sovereignty to a supranational agency would eventually be accomplished. That would mark a next stage of the nuclear age in which powers and peoples became more confident than they were before that the nuclear spectre was adequately contained.

More likely than either of these outcomes is one that may well happen sooner, perhaps within the average lifespan of young children now alive in industrialized countries. This turning would come after a jolting occurrence, such as a large nuclear accident or an act of nuclear terrorism, or a nuclear attack among states other than the superpowers. Any one such event could precipitate the passage to stage two in which political perceptions would be widely and sharply revised. While the potential of such accidents, terrorism, and attacks have been discussed separately, they have seldom been considered together. To do so we begin with a brief review of each.

Accidental casualties and contamination on a large scale have already taken place in the USSR, although the numbers and extent of these have not been made publicly known. A study of the event, done at Los Alamos long after the time it happened, is reported to conclude "that a large area near the city of Kyshtym in the Soviet Union was contaminated in the 1950s because of incredibly sloppy practices at a nuclear weapons plant" (Norman, 1982; 1983). Sloppy practices in nuclear procedures have been revealed from other countries, not excluding the United States. While the mishaps at the Three Mile Island plant did not result in casualties and the large contamination was contained, the consciousness of the potential danger of nuclear installations was considerably heightened in the vicinity and far beyond.

At the Salem 1 reactor in New Jersey on 22 February 1983 there was a failure of the automatic shutoff system. Such failures had been estimated by the nuclear industry as having a chance of occurring on the order of once in a million operating years. Yet it happened again at the same plant three days later on 25 February 1983. In both cases the reactor was shut down manually by operators within 30 seconds of the need for this action. Calculations by the Nuclear Regulatory Commission indicate that a delay of 100 seconds could have led to serious damage. Similar close calls had previously occurred at two civilian plants and in military reactors as well. An account of the incident asks, "The one-in-a-million event happened twice in three days at Salem. Why?" One of the members of the Nuclear Regulatory Commission gave part of the answer when he said that the investigation of the Salem failures reveals an intolerable degree of carelessness (Marshall, 1983:280–81).

Given the hundreds of civilian and military reactors in daily operation around the world, maintained by operators of diverse cultural traditions in the handling of sophisticated machinery, of varying predilection for drink and drugs, subject to differing social and domestic stresses, it seems not unreasonable to consider that a nuclear accident, more lethal than any so far, may well occur within the experience of the present generation of young children. Such a mishap could take many lives on the instant and waft deadly danger to thousands downstream and downwind.

To the chances for nuclear accidents may be added the chances of deliberate detonations. A panel convened by Congressman Edward Markey on the possibilities of nuclear terrorism was held in Washington in 1982 (Holden, 1982). Transcripts of the proceedings are not available, but a report of the presentations tells that one of the three experts who spoke was R.M. Sayre, Director of the State Department's Office for Combatting Terrorism. He minimized the danger as other authorities on the subject have done. The expert on weaponry, Theodore Taylor, testified that it is relatively easy to make a crude nuclear device using information that is publicly available. The expert on terrorism, R.H. Kupperman, formerly Chief Scientist at the U.S. Arms Control and Disarmament Agency, foresaw a possible use by terrorists of biological as well as radioactive agents.

While terrorist attacks by groups in the Middle East and Northern Ireland have gained world attention, it is well to recall that such attacks have also been perpetrated by groups drawn from a good many other nationalities. According to one informed estimate, it would take about a half-dozen technically trained and mechanically adept people to make a nuclear weapon. They would need diverted bomb materials, some high explosive, plus sufficient time, space, and money (Kupperman and Trent, 1979:60). And, of course, a degree of desperate commitment. If all the components for this combination have not yet been assembled, there are some students of the subject who believe that "if present trends continue, it seems only a question of time before some terrorist organization exploits the possibilities for coercion which are latent in nuclear fuel" (Willrich and Taylor, 1974:115; see also Laqueur, 1977:229–30; Wilkinson, 1977:205–6).

A third set of possibilities rises from states that are close to having nuclear bomb capabilities and either confront immediate enemies or face serious internal disruptions. If or when such a government acquires nuclear weapons, its leaders might sooner or later find themselves constrained to launch an atomic attack. Among such states are South Africa, Argentina, Taiwan, Pakistan, Israel, Iran, and Iraq. Iraq was apparently only a year or two away from attaining nuclear bomb capability when the Israeli air strike of 1981 seriously damaged its nuclear development facility. If that facility does produce a nuclear bomb, the Iraqi ruling group will have to decide whether and how to use it. A demonstration strike would be an option, perhaps against Israel rather than on their Muslim enemies. Each of these governments vigorously denies any intention to make and use nuclear weapons. But should the leaders of an oligarchy feel that their power and their lives were at stake, earlier denials could readily be brushed aside. Or a rebellious faction within a state might seize the nuclear-weapons facilities and, having secured the help of the relevant technicians, utilize them for purposes of their own.

Taken together, the parts of this triad pose portentous possibilities. To be sure, the forestalling of a total nuclear outbreak between the superpowers must command priority, since that catastrophe would wipe out other possibilities. Yet a passage to stage two through small, incremental steps negotiated between the superpowers can only be achieved over a long time, through generations or perhaps centuries rather than decades. Any one of the many potential sources of accident, terrorism, or third-country attack could explode any year now.

The political and social consequences of such an event will depend partly on its physical magnitude, partly on people's perception of their own danger. An incident that resulted in a few fatalities within a limited zone of contamination, coming at a time when international negotiations seem promising, might have relatively little impact other than accelerating negotiations already in progress. At the other pole of possibility, an event that snuffed thousands of lives on the instant, that destroyed or contaminated densely populated areas, and that spread lethal radiation downwind across international boundaries, would surely alter previous perceptions of the nuclear problem and ways of trying to cope with it.

An event between these extremes would be one in which there were perhaps only hundreds of immediate casualties, a zone of direct contamination that could be cordoned off, and some serious downwind radioactive effect. The latter may be the most persuasive threat of all. A good many of the world's people have heard about nuclear casualties and contamination. They do not usually translate distant tragedies into sensibility of peril to self and family. But when mortal danger is adrift in the winds, their minds are likely to be wonderfully concentrated, assumptions altered, priorities rearranged.

An assessment of the possible consequences of a serious incident of nuclear terrorism has been published by M.B. Jenkins of the Rand Corporation (1980). Jenkins says that because so many variables could be involved, it is extremely difficult to predict what would happen in the aftermath of an act of nuclear terrorism. But one obvious consequence would be the increase of security precautions at nuclear facilities everywhere. Governments would be likely to become "a bit more repressive in an age of nuclear terrorism." Such an act, Jenkins continues, would undoubtedly increase demands for greater international cooperation to prevent another occurrence. Yet, this expert concludes, "It is difficult to foresee greater cooperation than that which exists now in the terrorist area or on the issue of nuclear proliferation. Sovereignty probably will prevail" (1980:10–13).

Perhaps so, but the possibility of yet more occurrences of nuclear terrorism and of major accidents and attacks will still remain. With each succeeding episode, consciousness of the danger will surely heighten and more support for antinuclear movements will accrue until a critical mass of world reaction develops. Then the very strong attachments to complete national sovereignty may well be overborne by stronger emotions about the common peril.

At that juncture, not all peoples will be equally shaken or similarly informed. Some governments will try to slog on as before, and some groups within each nation will be inclined to respond by strengthening previous assumptions about, say, the focus of evil and the primacy of military power. But for many, the greatest evil will be aloft in the sky, and refuge will scarcely be found in armaments. It may even fall out that those who would stand fast on their previous platform may go the way of isolationist America Firsters after Pearl Harbor.

What may seem out of reach now may be quite feasible then. In assessing proposals for a nuclear freeze, the report of the Harvard Nuclear Study Group points out the practical difficulties involved. Accomplishing a freeze would require extensive and elaborate negotiations over a good many years "unless the arms-control budgets of the superpowers were raised a hundredfold or more, and many teams negotiated simultaneously and were convinced that both nations wanted a comprehensive agreement. . . ." (Carnesdale, et al., 1983:208). A hundredfold increase in the sum for the total U.S. arms control and disarmament activities in the President's budget for fiscal year 1985 ($24.4 million), comes to less than one percent (.76 percent) of the 1985 amount requested for defense ($313.4 billion).

Previous concerns, as with limiting new weapons systems or bargaining about a few hundred warheads, would fade before an overriding interest, shared by people of many nations, to diminish sharply the nuclear danger. Authorities and legislators will want to do something new, different, more effective, and will be pressed to do so quickly. The new measures will have to be based on the then existing repertoire of ideas and options. Hence the time when that repertoire should be developed is during the current stage, before an imperative push into stage two. Such studies cannot have much general impact if their results become known only in professional journals and to scholarly meetings. If they are to have broad influence their results will have to be widely discussed, perhaps hotly debated. That will require some concerted effort by the engaged social scientists and their professional associations.

All intellectual resources will have to be drawn upon for that effort; we note here some of the preparatory studies to which anthropology can contribute. Even more than is true for other research bearing on public policies, the studies for stage two will gain greatly in relevance and credibility if they can be done cooperatively by workers from different countries, of different disciplines and professions.

Not many studies of war and peace in modern societies have as yet been undertaken by anthropologists. In one of the relevant books in this field, the editors note that, despite its unique strengths, anthropology ". . . has been strangely inarticulate on the subject of war" (Fried, et al., 1968:xiii). The editors of a major interdisciplinary volume on the subject state that, "In spite of the great promise anthropology holds in store for peace research, however, the performance of anthropologists has been on the whole insignificant" (Falk and Kim, 1980:160).

One reason for this may be reflected in the comments by the senior editor of the volume, Richard Falk, about Jenkins's article on nuclear terrorism. Falk, a political scientist, does not disagree with the details of Jenkins's cool assessment but finds the tone of detached analysis morally deficient. "It is this pervasive tone of amorality, this thoroughly technicist stance, that is likely to make us as a polity capable of doing anything, and as such is a civilizational, and hence, a world historical menace" (1980:19).

Most anthropologists recognize that while no human observers can shake themselves completely free of the biases inherent in their own culture and language, they are generally committed to giving as "objective" a descriptive account as is possible for them of the behavior they study. In Kluckhohn's phrase, we try to give preliminary amnesty to the data. It has not been particularly difficult to do reasonably dispassionate accounts of warfare among say, New Guinea tribesmen or American Indians. But to do so about war in one's own society, particularly about substrates, prospects, and preparations for nuclear war, is more difficult. This is partly because an anthropologist who is enough interested in the subject to work seriously on it will already have some moral judgment that will affect whatever he or she writes. Partly also it is because the presentation of a presumably detached account lays the writer open to the kind of charge that Falk makes against Jenkins, of moral numbness. Yet Falk and others have perceived that the anthropologists' approach holds great promise for peace research and have regretted that they have as yet made relatively small contributions to it. So despite the difficulties, it is a field well worth cultivating.

What anthropologists can particularly impart to such studies is the capacity to take into account a people's inside views of the world and the issues, to articulate them with outside observers' findings, and to relate both to comparisons among cultures. Such comparisons are essential for an understanding of any institution as widely maintained among societies as is war. Historical accounts of particular wars, useful and necessary as they are, cannot help explain the phenomenon of war any more than an account of a particular divorce can explain the institution of divorce.

The broad perspective of culture helps, among its other uses, to correct some popular notions about war. The belief that making war is an inevitable characteristic of all societies is belied by the example of a number of war-free societies. In my own field studies I have worked in the Nilgiri Hills, a geographically isolated enclave in South India where live indigenous people of four culturally and socially distinct groups who have neither memory nor myth of war among themselves. There are other societies in the world who knew not war (Fabbro, 1980).

An anthropological approach should be useful for at least three kinds of preparatory studies, those concerning measures for institutional changes among nations, those relating to changes within particular nations, and those dealing with underlying cultural and social forces.

Institutional changes are likely to be in the forefront of public attention at a turning into stage two, changes designed to augment institutions for peace and to redirect those for war. One requirement will be the restructuring of international organizations as was done after each World War.

That task is commonly described as a movement from a present condition of anarchy among nations to some form of world government, complete with legislative, judicial, and administrative branches. Neither assumption is correct or necessary. Relations among states have been regulated by customary procedures or formal agreements since at least the Olympic truces of ancient Greece. Though the present structure of international relations falls far short of what will be desired by many at a turning to stage two, it is also far from being a condition of anarchy. It provides a base on which more effective international structures can be built. These will require new agreements, perhaps establishing international officials equipped with some degree of enforcing power. That should entail only limited transfer of national sovereignties, not a world government, at least not for the second stage of the nuclear age.

If the experiences in creating the United Nations are relevant precedents, much of the previous organization will be considerably revised although some key components, such as an international civil service, will undoubtedly be kept. To take the example of verification teams, there will have to be stricter, more efficient patrolling of nuclear agreements than now exists under the aegis of the International Atomic Energy Agency. Studies of the present inspectors and inspection teams may provide ideas useful for shaping a stronger verification agency under the conditions of stage two.

No less important than the strengthening of institutions for peace will be the redirection of institutions now committed to defense and war. The large part of the world's wealth and human energy that is now allotted to military forces is not only a huge economic investment that diverts from the physical well-being of much of the species, but is also a vast political investment in a security systems that a good many find increasingly insecure. The response of governments to growing feelings of insecurity has been the common human reaction of reinforcing what has been done before, especially the enlarging of military and military-industrial establishments. But should the traditional modes for national security become unacceptable following a general turning of public feeling, these institutions will have to be redirected. Millions of people, among them some of the most able and vigorous in each society, find in these institutions their metier, their self-identity, their principal and principled personal justification. It may be less difficult in stage two to transfer economic appropriations and alter political forms than to shift these personal commitments and their cultural roots. Effective redirection of military institutions will have to be done through planning based on pertinent, realistic information. While writings on matters military continue to mushroom, there has not been much on the actual conditions of military society or on the real world of military professionals. Some studies of this kind were published by anthropologists in the decade after World War II but very few have since appeared. More has been done by sociologists but it has not been a major focus of sociological attention. Any redirection of military institutions will benefit from some redirection of anthropological and sociological research in that field.

One avenue for such research might be to inquire whether military people of different nations share certain values and attitudes, by reason of their profession, and to compare their assumptions with those held by civilian groups. That difference is noted by the physicist Freeman Dyson in contrasting the views of the military officers, American and British, with whom he has worked, with the perspectives of the peace activists whom he knows. The officers share a common language and style, give allegiance to the same values of their profession, quite in contrast with the perspectives of the activitists (Dyson, 1984a:53, 57). Dyson concludes that the arguments between them are sterile, because the two do not have enough assumptions and language in common for useful discourse. Because the judgments of serving officers carry very great weight in matters of nuclear armaments, studies of their outlook and experiences may be of considerable help to those who will be thinking about honorable, worthy new directions for military people in stage two.

All the people of a nation-state are creatures and carriers of its prevailing culture and of one of its various subcultures. Effective redirection of military and other insitutions internationally will have to be guided by appreciation of the conditions for such change nationally.

There is no lack of writings about the national characteristics of each major state in the nuclear array. Often enough one analysis seems to be quite at odds with some of the others. Freeman Dyson, for example, has compared the views of two eminent students of Soviet polity and society, the historian Richard Pipes and the diplomat-author George Kennan. Both recognize the great difficulties, from the point of view of each superpower, in dealing with its counterpart. But while Pipes' assessment is largely adverse, critical, cautionary, Kennan's is more comprehensive, comprehending, forward-looking. Dyson shows that there is nonetheless considerable agreement between the two. The caustic appraisal becomes less foreboding when placed in Kennan's broader perspective that takes in the general cultural background as well as the more menacing military posture (Dyson, 1984b:87–89).

Anthropological research, too, tries to show the general culture patterns of a society and to find out how the people express themselves in contemporary events. In the case of Soviet society, there are some excellent studies by Western as well as by Soviet students, but as yet this field has not attracted the degree of anthropological attention that has been devoted to, say, Spain or India. A major hindrance has been the bar to long, intensive periods of field work. But there are thaws as well as freezes in the relations between the superpowers, and a future period of easement may allow for reciprocal field research in each country by students of society from the other.

In a comedy record of the 1960s, *The Two-Thousand-Year-Old Man*, the ancient one is asked, "What were your means of transportation in the olden time?" "Fear," is the instant reply. And fear propels the nuclear arms race, fear upon fear. In his account of the decision to deploy Cruise and Pershing II missiles on land rather than at sea, R. Jeffrey Smith quotes a British official who was involved in the decision. "The fear was not that America would actually be apprehensive about the use of its weapons on ships; the fear was that the Soviets would think that America would be apprehensive—in short, we fear what the Soviets think the Americans will think" (Smith, 1984:375).

The apprehensions raised by the realities of targeted missiles are viewed by each side from differing cultural perspectives and placed within differing social expectations. Anthropological studies of these differences will scarcely alter the circumstances of nations in confrontation, but when the circumstances and public opinions are altered during a major turning, such studies may be of considerable use, especially if they have already been widely discussed.

The studies should not only formulate general principles, as of conflict resolution, but should also transpose them into culturally specific concepts about particular kinds of conflict. Similarly, modes of communication should be examined within their cultural contexts. Discussions of nuclear issues in the West frequently mention signs and signals that one superpower sends to the other. There is small recognition that symbols and symbol systems differ among cultures and that one side's potent symbol may be quite incomprehensible to people of the other side. Since the most potent symbols are usually manifest in a people's religion, whether it is sacred or secular, an understanding of the civic faith as well as of a traditional religion is relevant.

Because no nation is a cultural monolith, preparatory studies have to take into account the major groupings—class, religious, regional, ethnic—that affect a country's political parties and processes. One way of beginning the preparatory studies can be the writing of a series of country guides that would discuss the resources and capacities of particular nations for coping with the conditions of stage two.

A third category of preparatory studies can deal with global forces. One such force is that of population increase. Not all nations have the problem of diminishing levels of living because of increasing numbers of people. But all nations are affected by the pressure of too many people among most of humankind. These pressures put at risk concord among nations as well as stability within a nation. Population planning programs have foundered in some countries partly because they took too little account of cultural and social factors among the masses. While there is now an able company of anthropologists at work on population problems, there are very few anthropological studies of the relations between population growth and social tensions.

Finally, the preparatory studies will later have to be revised to address the new circumstances that will arise after the turning into stage two. The nuclear problem may then be altered but it will not be ended (Mandelbaum, 1983:121–23). Humankind will continue to have need of knowledge useful for the next following stage of the nuclear age.

References

Carnesdale, Albert; Doty, P.; Hoffman, S.; Huntington, S.; and Nye, J. 1983. "The Harvard Nuclear Studies Group." In *Living with Nuclear Weapons*. New York: Bantam.

Dyson, Freeman. 1984a. "Reflections: Weapons and Hope. I. Questions." *The New Yorker* 59(51):50–73.
_____. 1984b. "Reflections: Weapons and Hope. III . People." *The New Yorker* 60(1):52–103.
Fabbro, David. 1980. "Peaceful Societies." In *The War System: An Interdisciplinary Approach*, edited by R.A. Falk and S.S. Kim, pp. 180–203. Boulder, Colo.: Westview Press.
Falk, Richard. 1980. "Inquiry and Morality." *Society* 17:18–20.
Falk, Richard A. and Kim, S.S., eds. 1980. *The War System: An Interdisciplinary Approach*. Boulder, Colorado: Westview Press.
Fried, M., M. Harris, and R. Murphy (eds.). 1968. *War: The Anthropology of Armed Conflict and Aggression*. Garden City, N.Y.: Natural History Press.
Holden, Constance. 1982. "Age of Nuclear Terrorism." *Science* 217:913.
Jenkins, Brian Michael. 1980. "Nuclear Terrorism and its Consequences." *Society* 17:5–15.
Kupperman, Robert H. and Trent, D.M. 1979. *Terrorism, Threat, Reality, Response*. Stanford, Cal.: Hoover Institution Press.
Laqueur, Walter. 1977. *Terrorism*. New York: Little, Brown.
Mandelbaum, Michael. 1983. *The Nuclear Future*. Ithaca, N.Y.: Cornell University Press.
Marshall, Eliot. 1983. "The Salem Case: A Failure of Nuclear Logic." *Science* 220:280–82.
Norman, Colin. 1982. "Soviet Radwaste Confirmed." *Science* 216:274.
_____. 1983. "The Kyshtym Mystery (Continued)." *Science* 221:138.
Smith, R. Jeffrey. 1984. "Missile Deployments Roil Europe." *Science* 223:371–76.
Wilkinson, Paul. 1977. *Terrorism and the Liberal State*. London: Macmillan.
Willrich, M. and Taylor, Theodore. 1974. *Nuclear Theft, Risks, and Safeguards*. Cambridge, Mass.: Ballinger.

24

Anthropology as a Nonpolicy Science

Bela C. Maday

Despite its considerable potential for assuming a prominent role in the formulation and implementation of policy in both public and private sectors of society, anthropology, for all practical purposes, is not a policy science. It is not so considered either by social scientists or by policymakers.

In a survey conducted by the Policy Studies Organization (PSO; 1979), a private nonprofit organization at the University of Illinois, Urbana, a list of 580 people involved in policy studies included not one with an anthropological background. Sixty-eight percent of the respondents were political scientists, and five percent was a mixed bag of social scientists that may or may not have included an anthropologist or two (Table 1).

Whatever the reasons for the absence of anthropologists from the PSO listing, difference in substantive areas of interest is not one of them (Table 2). Anthropologists, if asked, might have suggested different priorities for the various problem areas studied, but they would not have left out any of them in studying a culture in its totality. It is noteworthy, however, that anthropology is nowhere mentioned in the column of "most interested disciplines."

Slicing the pie in another way, the same survey inquired into the most frequently mentioned general approaches in policy studies. Here the overlap between anthropology and policy science is similarly modest; of 1,051 respondents, only 10 mentioned a cross-cultural approach and none referred to communication or cognition, though 233 alluded to "comparative public policy" (Table 3).

Academic and applied centers in the United States conduct policy research with no evidence of any anthropological contribution. Only four out of fifty-four university policy study centers reported having an anthropologist on the staff or as a consultant, and only one out of forty-five non-university-affiliated centers reported such input (Policy Studies Organization, 1978).[1]

Table 1
Background Characteristics of Policy Studies Personnel

Background Characteristics	Number of Respondents	Percent of Respondents
Disciplinary Background (N = 634)		
Political Science	435	68
Economics and Business Administration	43	7
Sociology and Social Work	32	5
Miscellaneous Social Science	29	5
Psychology and Education	23	4
Planning and Urban Affairs	20	3
Natural Science and Engineering	19	3
Interdisciplinary Policy Studies	13	3
Humanities	10	2
Law	10	2
Highest Degree Mentioned (N = 705)		
Ph.D. or Other Doctorate	536	76
M.A. or Other Masters Degree	168	24
B.A. or Other Bachelors Degree	1	0
Years Between B.A. and Ph.D. (N = 423)		
5 and Under	99	23
6–10	229	54
11–15	60	14
16–20	17	4
Over 20	18	4
Region Where Currently From (N = 1039)		
South	261	25
Northeast	239	23
Midwest	211	20
Far West	188	18
Washington, D.C.	71	7
Foreign	69	7
Sex (N = 979)		
Male	834	86
Female	145	14
Age (N = 570)		
Under 30	88	15
30–39	299	52
40–49	115	20
50–59	49	20
60 and Over	19	3

Source: Policy Studies Personnel Directory, p. 16.

What about the attitudes of anthropologists toward policy scientists? There is not much information on the topic. A letter written by the executive officer of the American Anthropological Association in response to a PSO survey inquiring about possible cooperation is vague and non-committal: "The Association's interest in public policy relates to areas

Table 2
The Most Frequently Mentioned Specific Policy Problems

Specific Problem	Number of Respondents (N = 1051)	Percent of Respondents	Most Interested Discipline
1. Environment	261	25	Planning
2. Health	230	22	Econ. & Soc.
3. Education	192	18	Ed.
4. Economic Regulation	186	18	Econ.
5. Poverty & Welfare	143	14	Soc.
6. Energy	130	12	Econ.
7. Criminal Justice	124	11	Law
8. Science & Technology	117	11	Nat. Sci.
9. Human Services	116	11	Soc.
10. Foreign Policy	112	11	Poli. Sci.
11. Taxing & Spending	108	10	Econ.
12. Manpower & Labor	81	8	Soc.
13. Transportation	60	6	—
14. Housing	54	5	Planning
15. Defense & Military	53	5	Poli. Sci.
16. Minorities	46	4	Psych.
17. Aging	45	4	Psych.
18. Land Use	42	4	Planning
19. Agriculture	33	3	—
20. Civil Rights	30	3	Poli Sci. & Soc.
21. Civil Liberties	29	3	Poli. Sci.
22. Population	29	3	Soc.
23. Women	28	3	—
24. Communication	27	3	—
25. Electoral	26	3	Poli. Sci.
26. Family Policy	24	2	Soc.
27. Government Labor	23	2	—
28. Water Resources	22	2	—
29. Mental Health	17	2	—
30. Consumer Protection	17	2	Econ.
31. Rural Policy	17	2	—
32. Legislative Reform	13	1	Poli. Sci.
33. Court Administration	12	1	—
34. Government Organization	8	1	—
35. Law Enforcement	7	1	—
36. Arts & Leisure	7	1	—

Source: Policy Studies Personnel Directory, p. 8.

where anthropology has a useful application. These include but are not limited to cultural resources management, health and education program planning and evaluation, and domestic and international socio-economic development" (Policy Studies Organization ,1980:33). As to potential co-operation:

Table 3
The Most Frequently Mentioned General Approaches to Policy Studies

General Approach	Number of Respondents (N = 1051)	Percent of Respondents
1. Policy Formation	475	45
2. Administering Public Policy	351	34
3. Empirical Research Methods	256	24
4. Evaluation	241	23
5. Comparative Public Policy	233	22
6. Urban Policy Problems	199	19
7. Policy Implementation	177	17
8. Research Utilization	172	16
9. Policy Studies in General	97	9
10. Planning	88	8
11. Intergovernmental Regulations	80	8
12. Analysis of Policy Impact	79	7
13. Local Government	65	6
14. Social Values and Public Policy	65	6
15. State Government Policy	58	6
16. Theory of Public Policy	56	5
17. Organization Theory	45	4
18. Citizen Participation	43	4
19. Modeling, Optimizing, Deduction	38	4
20. Decisionmaking Theory	35	3
21. Community Development	33	3
22. Service Delivery	31	3
23. Systems Analysis & Theory	25	2
24. Bureaucratic Politics	24	2
25. Regional Policy	24	2
26. Political Economy	23	2
27. General Policy Science	21	2
28. Futuristics and Forecasting	21	2
29. Management	19	2
30. Ethics in Policy	18	2
31. Diffusion of Innovation	15	2
32. Social Indicators	12	1
33. Cross-Cultural	10	1
34. Teaching Policy Studies	8	1
35. Determinants of Public Policies	6	1

Source: Policy Studies Personnel Directory, p. 11.

The Association is not interested in participating in a consortium to exchange data, subscriptions, and mailing lists. We would be interested in participating in collective action to communicate social sciences information to governmental bodies. We would also be interested in participating in an effort to establish or expand centers to bring academics and practitioners together.

There are, to be sure, signs of budding interest among anthropologists in an increased number of publications and symposia at annual meetings, but one swallow does not make a summer, and these efforts have so far had no measurable impact on either policymakers or anthropologists at large.

Policymakers in business and government have no use for anthropology or anthropologists except for culture-specific technical data. Few policymakers are aware of the absence from their consideration of policy issues of cultural factors, though they sometimes wonder why their policies do not work. On the other hand, anthropologists in business and government are like babes in the woods, slowly recognizing the differences between anthropological and nonanthropological frames of reference.

When twenty-one government executives at the branch-chief level and higher (grade 15 and above) were asked if they had ever used anthropological concepts in their daily policymaking activities or if they contemplated doing so in the future, most of them (twelve) took anthropologists for archaeologists and didn't know what a relevant anthropological concept would be. When reminded of the culture concept, they felt more at ease and pointed to the need for anthropological knowledge in a cross-cultural context, principally in the area of communication with members of other cultures or domestic subcultures. More of those interviewed at the National Institute of Mental Health than elsewhere pointed to the need for considering cultural factors—in communication between policymakers and policy targets. Yet the principal agency charged with devising sound mental health policies has only one anthropologist on its staff, and he is not involved in policy formulation as an anthropologist. Consequently, no anthropological contribution is apparent either in the structure of the institute or in its policy recommendations to higher echelons of the government.

Having said all this, one must be ready for the question: Why this state of affairs? Several answers suggest themselves.

One is historical. The development of anthropology is characterized by a holistic approach to culture, mainly focusing on simple, preindustrial societies and on descriptive ethnographies which include the study of power and policy among other factors but rarely single them out for special study. It is basic to anthropology to consider problems in the context of the total culture in which they occur.

Another answer has to do with theoretical and methodological approach. Anthropologists rely heavily on empirical data and are discovery oriented, contemplative in their style, while other social scientists are becoming more manipulative in their orientation, aiming at acquiring knowledge of immediate use in policy formulation and implementation. No anthropologist, I think, would venture to predict the consequences of instituting one-way traffic at a certain location, or to explain why Johnny can't read or to project whether employment will rise or fall in the next six months (Lindblom, 1980:21). Anthropologists as a rule are willing to say what a certain culture or society is and how it functions, but not what it should be.

Leslie E. Wildesen (1983), a Congressional Fellow for the American Anthropological Association in 1982–83, expressed her observations in regard to anthropology's policymaking role as follows: "The AAA has sponsored at least one Congressional Fellow each year since 1976," yet "to walk around the Hill, you would think that anthropology did not exist. Anthropologists of various kinds abound in the executive branch: linguists, social-change experts, archaeologists, and social statisticians. But the place where policy is made, the legislature, is bereft of anthropological expertise. I think this is a tragedy, not only for the profession but for the quality of the public policy that results from lack of anthropological perspective on issues," including those on peace and war.

In sum: since the demand for anthropological input into policy research is virtually nil and the supply is meager, I do not see any basis for speaking of anthropology as a policy science, other than as a desideratum. A massive educational effort seems to be needed on the part of anthropologists to alter the image they have acquired while confined to the university campus and to clarify for policymakers the importance of culture in individual and collective human behavior and the potential of anthropology for contributing to the solution of human problems.

Note

1. The four centers reported were: Duke University, University of Kentucky, University of Michigan, and the University of Southern California. The non-university center which listed an anthropologist on its staff was the Resources for the Future, Washington, D.C.

References

Lindblom, C.E. 1980. *The Policy Making Process.* Englewood Cliffs, N.J.: Prentice-Hall.

Policy Studies Organization. 1978. *Policy Research Centers Directory.* Urbana, Ill.: University of Illinois.

_____. 1979. *Policy Studies Personnel Directory.* Urbana. Ill.: University of Illinois.

_____. 1980. *Policy Publishers and Associations Directory.* Urbana, Ill.: University of Illinois.

Wildesen, Leslie E. 1983. "Anthropology Visits but Does Not Live on Capitol Hill." *Anthropology Newsletter* 24:9 (December):12.

25

Global Policy and Revolution in Social Sciences

Silviu Brucan

As we approach the end of the twentieth century, the rapid globalization of the phenomena, processes, and problems besetting our world poses before social scientists the totally new task of global policy formulation—for which they are neither theoretically prepared nor institutionally organized.

Indeed, national limitations combine with ideological prejudices to make social sciences a highly restricted field of activity, mirroring the larger political system within which they operate. In most countries, the growth of social sciences since World War II has been nationally institutionalized with the government being the main source of funds, national institutions the principal consumer of research, and national research councils the administrator of developmental resources. Large and wealthy countries offer so many opportunities for teaching and research projects that social scientists need not be professionally concerned with the outside world. And even when they are, the parochial national spirit is pervasive in their work. In small countries it is a matter of geographic, cultural, linguistic, or ideological isolation.

Ideology, which is so strong in social sciences, has also been affected by the political system of nation-states. Thus, bourgeois ideology in the United States is somewhat distinct from that in France or Japan as is Marxist ideology in the USSR distinct from that of China or Romania, as I pointed out in my earlier paper (this volume). Because of the prevalent ideology within which their discipline is formed, social scientists are mentally nation shaped, and therefore ill-prepared to deal with what is fashionably called the "world problematique." This is particularly painful at a time when changes on the global scene are so rapid that decisions made today must be necessarily conceived in terms of tomorrow.

Economic Problems

The world of the next decades will be a "small world" in which the per capita gross national product (GNP) of the developed nations will still be twelve times that of the developing nations, even if the growth rates set by the United Nations for the year 2000 were achieved. The population of the developing nations, however, will be five times that of the developed world. Anyone who puts these two sets of figures together must realize that the explosion will not be limited to population. We will live in a world in which it will take two or three hours to fly from Caracas to New York or from Lagos to London, a world in which the Bolivian or the Pakistani will see on television every night how people live in the affluent societies, a world in which there will be no suburbia for the rich to insulate themselves from the poor.

While the insane nuclear race will go on, generating its own perilous moments in the drive for first-strike capability and military superiority (whatever that means in overkill terms), the world of the 1990s will live and sleep with a balance of terror in the hands of twenty or so ambitious nations armed with atomic weapons, not to mention terrorist groups using atomic bombs for blackmail or ransom. With the shift of superpower confrontation to the battlefields of the Third World, the arms race will continue to be exported to Africa, Asia, and Latin America, infecting a growing number of nations with militarism, dominance appetites, and regional policeman roles. As the pillars of the old order crumble one after the other, the world of coming decades will look like New York, Tokyo, or Paris without traffic regulations and policemen.

The current dislocations in the world market and the recurring disruptions in the monetary system, compounded by "stagflation," are but signals of a long period of instability ahead for the world economy. We can thus expect an equally long period in world affairs that will involve great dangers of military adventurism and neofascism caused by the desperate attempts of finance and corporate capital to hold on to its challenged positions of dominance. It is my belief writer that the remaining two decades of this century may go down in history as its most critical and explosive period. For never before have so many social and political contradictions requiring structural change converged in a world so small and so capable of destroying itself.

Recently, international U.N. conferences have called attention to the enormity of such world problems as the human habitat, population growth, transfer of science and technology, ecological deterioration, food, and pollution. They all point in the same direction: the need for global planning and management. To cite but one area of concern, merely to build the physical infrastructure of the human habitat—houses, schools, hospitals, utilities—required before the end of the century, will entail a construction job similar in scope to that accomplished since the Middle Ages. And what about the task of providing the one billion jobs that will be needed throughout the world by the year 2000?

Surely the United Nations is not equipped to deal with problems of such nature and magnitude as face us today. A decisionmaking system with more than 150 independent participants is in itself a prescription for ineffectiveness in dealing with global problems.

The Method

Whereas anthropological research has an almost inherent inclination to use the traditional scientific method of going from simple elements to more complex ones, and to theorize on the basis of close studies of small human groups, global policy requires a totally different methodology—from the whole to its parts. Indeed, we cannot make an intelligent analysis of policies of individual nation-states taken separately without placing their activities in the context of the world economy and the international system.

I believe that the convergence in time of global problems and the commonality of their nature and scope, are not accidental. Although they seem to be products of a chaotic amalgamation of factors and processes, there is a certain logic in their appearance, manifestations, and magnitude. I think they actually inform us about something fundamental taking place in the very system of international relations and that is the transition from the interstate system to the emerging world system. Whereas in the former, the nation-state is the prime mover and its inputs are predominant in shaping the system and determining its behavior, in the latter it is the reverse effect of the world system that is beginning to prevail over its subsystems, adjusting them all to its own motion. No longer is the nation-state functioning as a self-contained social system whose decisions are determined inside; now outside factors increasingly participate in national decisions and governments are totally inept in coping with them.

The effect of the world system upon the military policy of nation-states is apparent in the active participation in the nuclear arms race of all great powers, irrespective of their domestic regime, and in the tendency it generates in other ambitious nations—some of which are still in a preindustrial stage—to go nuclear.

The current economic and financial disorder is truly worldwide with all nations, including socialist ones, feeling its effect. Attempts to plan our way out of the crisis have ended in complete failure, proving that the industrial nations cannot overcome inflation and unemployment by planning in a closed circuit. Protectionist measures dictated by narrow national interests are self-defeating, while U.S. policy directed against East-West trade is primarily hurting American farmers and industries. Only global planning could help overcome the present crises.

The impact of the world system is thus felt in all major areas of national foreign policy and, as far as we can tell, the tendency of the external stimuli to influence the behavior of nations is going to grow.

Apparently, international and transnational activities are growing so interdependent and so systemic that the world system acquires a drive of its own. And since such a drive has no conscious direction and rationality, it is the task of social scientists to formulate the ways and means whereby the whole process can be controlled and directed. There can be no more urgent and important use of "anthropological knowledge."

The Revolution in Social Sciences

Natural and technical sciences have had their revolution. It is time for social sciences to have a revolution of their own.

Its premise has already been set as the discovery of computers, cybernetics, and systems theory which have produced a new scientific methodology that can be well applied to social systems, particularly complex and hypercomplex ones. Now, a conceptual breakthrough is required, namely a theory that explains the world system and its workings.

In fact, what I am talking about is *world modeling*—a new and fascinating field of scientific inquiry that was initiated only a decade ago with the controversial study "The Limits to Growth." That Forrester-Meadows model was built upon five key variables—population, capital investment, natural resources, fraction of capital devoted to agriculture, and pollution; it ended up with the rash forecast of the world's collapse in the early 2000s. But the reduction of our world to physical and economic parameters was rightly criticized and so was the model's treatment of the planet as if it were homogeneous in resources, wealth, technology, and power.

Indeed, while a model is not supposed to reflect all the features of reality, it must nevertheless include the essential ones, namely those variables or forces which make the world function as a system. And it is *social* and *political* forces that manage (or mismanage) distribution and use of physical and economic resources. To cite but one case: one can hardly assess the impact of a resource like oil without considering the Arab embargo and OPEC policies.

Other authors of world models viewed *technology* as the prime mover. However, as one looks deeper into the matter one notes that their projections into the future are very long on technological change and very short on social change.

Finally, a series of world models focuses on development economics and strategies dealing with the issue of the new international economic order. The field of global models has been dominated thus far by two groups: economists/econometrists and systems engineers. While recognizing the importance of physical and economic variables in world modeling, I propose to attack the problem from a different perspective: the fulcrum of politics and decisionmaking in a global setting.

Let me add here that I view integrated global models as a multidisciplinary effort toward a symbiosis between economic-system engineering and world politics. Indeed, all global models based solely on economic or technological considerations suggest that to avoid the undesirable consequences of approaching the physical limits of our planet, and to overcome the eternal "widening gap" of economic development, the only course for our global future lies in social and political change.

But how does this social and political change come about at the global level?

What are the forces that determine the "laws of motion" of that global sphere?

These are the questions social scientists must answer before the end of the century.

26

Conflict and Belief in American Foreign Policy

William O. Beeman

Recent foreign conflict throughout the world has shown an unusually coherent and powerful belief system operating in the exercise of United States foreign policy. Like most belief systems, that of the United States foreign policy community is highly coherent, and extraordinarily rigid in its exercise. It continues to be pursued despite extraordinary, repeated evidence of its fallaciousness.

After outlining the broad structures of this belief system, and some of the questions about it that have been raised by recent foreign crises, I will suggest that it maintains its strength in the conduct of foreign policy, becausc, as with most belief systems, its abandonment threatens more danger to the internal order of the United States government than the actual crises which challenge its validity.

The Five Principles of Belief

There may be more principles of belief concerned with American foreign policy than the five provided here, but these form a cohesive whole and reinforce each other. It is a set of beliefs for our place and age—post-World War II United States. Those who have memories of earlier periods in United States history will be able to see how the current belief system differs from some earlier version.

The five principles of belief are these:

1. The world consists of nation-states.

It is not surprising that the United States should come to believe that the world consists entirely of nation-states with basically homogeneous populations whose primary identity (and homogeneity) derives from identification with their common nationhood. The United States was the first great nation founded on this principle.

Of course, there are very few nation-states in the world. One can think of a few European countries, Japan perhaps, or a few of the new Pacific island states, but that is about the extent of it. The majority of the people of the world do not identify primarily with their nation, and certainly not with the central governments that rule the nations in which they happen to live. The notion that one would sacrifice one's life for one's president or prime minister is a patent absurdity in virtually every nation on earth.

2. The East-West power struggle is the most important event in world politics. All other political relationships must be ranked in terms of it.

Before World War II, even the United States accepted the belief in a multipolar world structure. Now the United States has accepted a basically bipolar model, and tends to structure its foreign policy perception of the entire world order within this framework.

Of course, for most nations on earth the East-West struggle is very nearly irrelevant for the conduct of everyday life, except as an enormously bothersome obstacle which they must confront at every turn. The possibility of nuclear destruction is of course a paramount concern for thinking people everywhere, but it is the height of bitter irony that the bulk of the people who would be destroyed and suffer in a nuclear holocaust have absolutely no interest in the ideological struggle that would be the basis for that holocaust.

Few nations would accept the American belief that all nations must eventually assign themselves to one camp or another, and some, like India, have had to work very hard to stake out an independent position.

3. Economics and power are the bases of relations between nations.

Power politics as a philosophy has been with the United States only a short time. It was articulated in an extremely effective way by Hans Morgenthau, perhaps the principal teacher of the current crop of United States politicians currently exercising executive power in the United States foreign policy community.

For anthropologists of all shades it is particularly galling to see that in the United States' conduct of foreign policy, almost no attention is paid to cultural differences between nations. It is assumed that wealth and military might are universal levelers, and that little else matters. Occasionally it is recognized that pride, greed, and altruism may be factors in the course of human events, but such matters are often dismissed as unpredictable factors.

Nowhere is the structure of this belief so clear as in the composition of United States embassy staffs. There are always economic attachés, and political attachés, but in no embassy in the world is there a single officer whose primary duty is to interpret cultural differences which could cause misunderstandings between nations. This lack is reflected in mistake after mistake made by U.S. diplomatic personnel everywhere—mistakes that hardly need to be detailed here, since virtually everyone has heard hundreds of "howlers" about United States diplomats and their outrageously inept behavior throughout the world.

As an aside, I should mention that the United States is not alone in having unskillful diplomats or in being unable to analyze cultural differences. I think the world could use many more anthropologists in diplomatic staffs everywhere to compensate for those who believe that money and guns are the only basis for international understanding.

4. Nations are ruled by a small group of elite individuals.

It is difficult to understand why the United States, with a strong internal ethic-supporting democracy and broad-based, grassroots participation in public affairs finds it so difficult to take these same broad-based processes seriously in other nations.

Yet again and again the conduct of United States foreign policy is based on identification and support of narrow elite political structures with their elite elected officials, elite dictators, elite religious officials.

Clearly, power is thought to inhere in these narrow structures. An office becomes the the chief sign of this power, perhaps reflecting the earlier stated belief that the world consists of nation-states. Thus the United States cannot easily see underlying cultural processes which contribute to social change, or, where it sees such processes, it automatically assesses them negatively because they threaten the established order.

As the world knows, if broad social movements prove to be important in terms of thc United States' interpretation of the East-West struggle, they assume great global significance.

5. The normal conduct of foreign policy thus consists of the elite leaders of nation-states meeting in seclusion discussing matters of power and economics, presumably in the context of the East-West conflict.

This final point is not a separate belief but rather a fusion of the preceding beliefs into an image—a scenario which in fact describes much of the conduct of foreign policy carried out by the United States in recent years.

My own, perhaps iconoclastic, belief is that this conduct rarely yields anything productive or lasting, because it is not based on reality, but rather based on the mythic structure of the United States' idiosyncratic view of what the nations of the world are, and how their peoples are motivated to act in their own interests.

The Iranian Hostage Crisis: A Challenge to Belief

The Iranian hostage crisis (perhaps better called the Iranian-American hostage crisis) lasted from November 1979 to January 1981. During this period a number of people, myself included, had the opportunity to observe the United States policy process in action. We served as informal advisors to the State Department and to the White House during this time.

The hostage crisis was remarkable in the degree to which it successfully challenged the basic foreign-policy beliefs outlined above, and literally threw the American foreign-policy community into a panic.

State Department and White House officials frequently exhibited behavior recognizable as typical of culture shock. One State Department official was most articulate:

> They just don't play by the rules, these Iranians. We can't figure out who is in charge. Nothing they tell us seems to have any basis in fact. They promise to do something and then they do something completely different. How do you work with people as irrational as this?

Of course, many individuals were far more vivid than this in speaking about Iranian political behavior during this period.

Taking the points in the belief system cited above one by one, it is possible to see how the Iranian situation caused severe cognitive dissonance for American policymakers.

Iran and the Nation-State Model.

In the Middle East, Iran comes closest to being a nation-state, but it is not such in the Western sense of the word. It is more properly an empire where a monarch (the late shah) was able to subjugate a vast number of disparate groups who for many centuries had had only the loosest allegiance to his, or any central authority's rule.

Until the twentieth century Iran had permeable boundaries and no clear sense of sovereignty of territory except as defined by conquest. There was great identification with Persian culture throughout the area of Iran's sphere of influence, but little sense of identification with Iran as a nation. The sense of Iran as a nation-state is really an invention of the Pahlavi era.

After the revolution, the Khomeini regime was faced with the same old difficulties of keeping the nation together. Tribal groups throughout the country moved swiftly to reestablish the semiautonomous rule that they enjoyed in past decades, which had been usurped by the strong-handed tactics of the Pahlavis. Religious divisions were strong and led to great turmoil. Clashes between religious and secular forces made consolidation of power in the country very difficult.

United States negotiators assumed that because officials of the newly formed revolutionary government had the normal titles of heads of governments, they actually were nation-state leaders in some normative sense. During this turbulent period, however, it was impossible for anyone to fill this role: to have the authority to speak with the voice of the nation as a whole. More importantly, anyone who presumed to do so and made an error was likely to be toppled from power rather quickly.

Thus there was never a single voice or voices which could speak authoritatively for the Iranian nation during the entire period of the hostage crisis. Indeed, even the settlement of the crisis was never attributed to one person or group of persons. In Iran no one wanted to be associated with the event.

The Irrelevancy of the East-West Power Struggle.

There were no normal models that provided the United States with useful means for dealing with the hostage crisis. The crisis had nothing whatsoever to do with United States–Soviet confrontation, despite many feeble attempts to demonstrate that the Soviet Union might have had a hand in the proceedings.

The result for the foreign-policy community was that they were forced to deal with Iran as Iran and not as a projection of the global chess game. Sadly, the policy community was almost totally unprepared to do this. The number of Iranian experts in government posts was (and continues to be) woefully small.

With no automatic responses available, the foreign policy community found itself in a frantic search for ideas. The White House, in particular, made a number of amateurish attempts to contact "fixers" to get hostages released. An ill-planned military rescue ended in fiasco. It was only when a solution was found which perforce touched Iranian cultural sensibilities that the release was effected.

Power and Money as Irrelevancies.

The hostage crisis was a true confrontation of cultural values, played brilliantly for internal consumption in Iran by Ayatollah Khomeini and his supporters.

The United States had no economic or military force capable of securing the release of the hostages. This was clear from the beginning. The Iranians were able to withstand a long economic boycott, ignore threats, and turn the United States' abortive rescue mission into positive support for the Islamic Republic. The United States failed to realize that by addressing its concerns primarily to questions of power and money, it was playing directly into the hands of clerical leaders bent on establishing an Islamic Republic with themselves in control.

The clerics set up an internal moral dialogue in Iran with the United States at one pole of morality and Iran at the other. The United States was characterized as "the Great Satan" concerned with the material world and providing a corrupting influence. The revolutionary leaders, by contrast, were portrayed as spiritual men concerned with morality and righteousness. The moral questionableness of taking the hostages was subsumed under the greater moral directive (actually a tenet of Shi'a Islamic doctrine) of "resisting the Wrong and promoting the Right."

Thus the crisis from an Iranian standpoint was not seen as a differential struggle for power, but was rather portrayed as a moral struggle. The more the United States blustered and postured during this period, the more it reinforced the picture painted of it by the clerics.

The Iranians suffered considerable financial losses in the final settlement. Some oppositionist politicians attempted to use this fact as a means of discrediting the officials of the regime, but the fact that the nation lost financially was taken by many as demonstration that Iran was not after material gain in the hostage takeover, but was truly concerned with the moral and spiritual questions involved.[1]

The Irrelevance of Elite Actors.

In keeping with the United States' projection of nation-statehood on the new Iranian revolutionary government, it also attempted to project an elite power structure on the new regime. Thus it was assumed from the beginning that somewhere there must be somebody with the authority to push a button and get the hostages released.

Iran's leadership, as stated above, was highly diffuse at this time. Leaders were conscious of the fragility of their situation and the need to curry public favor at all times. Thus, though often posturing as though they had power, individuals such as Sadeq Qotbzadeh or even Abol-Hassan Bani-Sadr had almost no ability to control day-to-day governmental affairs. Indeed, Qotbzadeh was quite skillful in increasing his own influence in Iran by manipulating the American public and government officials.

Still the White House continued an unceasing search for a "plumber" who would carry out the United States' bidding on this matter. Hamilton Jordan went to Paris wearing a wig and false moustache in search of an Argentine businessman connected with a French lawyer who could reach the Iranian officials. Even the president's own brother, Billy, hardly a diplomat, was dispatched to Libya to tap some secret pipeline to Khomeini.

These attempts were pitiful and ludicrous, and demonstrated how sadly U.S. officials were in the grip of their own myths about how governments operate. Not able to see the reality of the Iranian situation, they persisted in running after chimeras of their own making.

The clearest instance of firm belief in elite government power during the crisis was shown in the behavior of United States officials themselves. Despite the fact that the State Department and other government agencies had after a year accumulated considerable knowledge concerning Iran, its motives and probable reactions to United States overtures, hostage crisis negotiating was centered exclusively in the White House and delegated to individuals who had little or no experience in dealing with the Middle East or with Iran.

Zbigniew Brzezinski, the president's national security advisor, filtered all reports coming in from the State Department and other agencies, letting President Carter see only those things which accorded with his ideas of how the situation was proceeding. The Secretary of State, Cyrus Vance, was effectively cut out of the negotiations. He was not told of the abortive rescue mission (which he opposed) until it was underway, prompting his resignation.[2]

Unexpected Diplomacy.

Clearly the normal, expected patterns of diplomacy anticipated by United States officials were not found in the hostage crisis. Iranian officials were not able to speak for their nation as a whole during this period, they were not swayed by considerations of economics and force, and they were not elite leaders in any sense understood in the United States. Moreover, because this problem could not be construed in the context of East-West confrontation, there were no easy responses available for United States leaders in dealing with the situation.

The worst problem of all for United States leaders was that they could not make contact with Iranian officials at all. Rhetoric against the United States was so virulent and potent that officials who could be associated with the United States in any way were "tainted" by the contact. Their own enemies could then use this against them to destroy them.

Thus "secret" messages sent by President Carter and others were revealed publicly almost as soon as they were received. Often they would be read to the masses during Friday prayers. For the United States, diplomacy as an elite operation is carried out in secret. For the Iranians at this time, secrecy in dealing with the Americans was the kiss of death.

The eventual release of the hostages came when Brzezinski relinquished control of the hostage release operation and it was taken over by the new Secretary of State, Edmund Muskie, and his team of advisors.

The eventual solution was culturally correct both for Iran and the United States. It involved a mediator, Algeria; no face-to-face contact between American and Iranian officials; and a combination of ideological and economic agreements. More to the point, it involved bargaining, something that both nations understand in certain specific contexts.

Hope for Cultural Solutions to Crisis

Unfortunately the United States did not reevaluate its belief system concerning foreign affairs following the hostage crisis. For most members of the foreign-policy community, Iran was an aberrant state which refused to play by the rules. Thus the basic belief in what the rules are remained unchanged.

The United States has employed the same basic belief system in other international events since the hostage crisis. Lebanon is a case in point.

Lebanon is of all Middle Eastern nations the least qualified to be called a nation-state. Indeed, the various religious groups in Lebanon think of themselves as primary in terms of personal and social identification. One is a Maronite Christian, or a Shi'a Moslem, Druze or Armenian long before one considers oneself Lebanese. For this reason, treating the government of Lebanon as representative of the people of the whole of Lebanon and expecting that government to carry authority on the basis of its constitutional legitimacy alone is entirely unrealistic.

Despite this, the United States government persisted from 1980 to 1984 in insisting that the Maronite leaders of Lebanon had to be supported solely on the basis that they were "constitutionally elected" officials.

The majority of Lebanese are Muslim, and the largest single religious group in the country is Shi'a Muslims. The Lebanese constitution under which Maronite leaders continued to dominate the government was established under the influence of the French in the 1930s when Maronites formed a larger share of the population. Demographics have changed radically since then, and the Maronites no longer constitute even a plurality in the government. In 1984, in fact, they constituted barely more than 20 percent of the total population of the country. Thus, constitutional legitimacy—a nation-state concept—became totally irrelevant for the powerless Muslim majority in the country.

The decision of the United States government to send in Marine troops to protect the "legitimate government" made Washington look like the protector of illegitimate power. It was hardly any wonder that those same Marines became subject to the same kinds of guerrilla attacks levied against the Christian troops.

Syria, which had a long-standing claim to Lebanon as an integral part of its own territory also had an alliance with the Soviet Union which involved the stationing of several thousand Soviet military advisors on Syrian soil in 1983. In addition, Syrian troops occupied parts of Lebanon continually during this period. Nevertheless, internal strife in Lebanon was never an East-West issue, as was claimed repeatedly by the Reagan administration. The Lebanese opposition had excellent reasons for opposing the Maronite ruling minority with no need for external aid from the Soviets, the Syrians or any other external group (Iranians were also widely blamed for fomenting trouble).

Nevertheless, Soviet advisors in Syria were continually pointed out as a prime danger to stability in the region, and as prime inciters of strife in Lebanon. Their presence was also cited as a prime legitimization for the stationing of U.S. and other Western troops in Lebanon.

The United States seemed almost entirely blind to the cultural, religious and ideological issues involved in the Lebanese crisis. In seeking to impose a military solution on the situation, the United States government underscored its belief in military and economic issues as primary in international crises.

Finally, in continually backing the officials of an essentially illegitimate government simply because they held titles, Washington demonstrated its continual need to seek out a narrow group of elite actors to address in finding solutions to conflict. In fact, the solution to internal conflict lay in establishing a broad-based coalition among a large number of groups. Continuing to appeal to a narrow group of elite elected officials only made the situation worse.

Thus, as in Iran, U.S. involvement in Lebanon was rendered almost totally ineffective through rigid adherence to principles of a belief system which was utterly inappropriate for meeting the immediate policy needs of the situation.

The Middle East is not the only place where U.S. beliefs inappropriately reflect cultural realities on the ground. Central America is yet another place where close understanding of the real issues (local broad-based discontent based on several centuries of social and cultural conflict) is blocked by a dogged belief that Soviet-U.S. confrontation is the only real issue one needs to understand in assessing the policy requirements of the region. Washington's somewhat futile pursuit of narrowly based elite "elected" leaders to support in Central America likewise indicates extraordinary myopia. Any visitor to the region can readily see that the true axis of power lies outside of the capital cities with warring groups in the countryside. Providing additional funds to U.S. backed officials to "win elections" is almost totally irrelevant.

The end result of the application of these principles of belief is repeated miscalculation about the course of world events and the United States' proper role in them. The U.S. government continues to ignore the broad social and cultural processes which motivate the vast majority of humans in the conduct of their day-to-day affairs. Because it believes these processes irrelevant in foreign relations, it gives them no place in its own calculations. The result: The United States ends up on the wrong side of the fence almost every time. This is not the result of bad luck; it is the result of an inaccurate system of belief.

In a world growing rapidly interdependent, those who can reform their mythology to accord with the actual course of observed events will have a better chance of survival. The present rigid mythology which governs United States foreign relations does not, unfortunately, bode well for the future survival of that nation.

Notes

1. Cf., Beeman, 1982, 1983a, 1983b, for additional discussion of Iranian leaders' moral characterization of the United States and its political uses in establishing the Islamic Republic.
2. Cf., Beeman, 1981, on negotiation problems during the hostage crisis.

References

Beeman, William O. 1983a. "Images of the Great Satan: Symbolic Conceptions of the United States in the Iranian Revolution." In *Religion and Politics*, edited by Nikkie Keddie. New Haven, Conn.: Yale University Press.

_____. 1983b. "Patterns of Religion and Development in Iran from the Qajar Period to the Revolution of 1978–1979." In *Religion and Economic Development*, edited by James Finn. New Brunswick, N.J.: Transaction.

_____. 1982. *Performance, Culture and Communication in Iran*. Tokyo: ILCAA.

_____. 1981. "How not to Negotiate: Crossed Signals on the Hostages." *The Nation* 232(2):42–44.

27

The Collapse of Strategy: Understanding Ideological Bias in Policy Decisions

Robert A. Rubinstein

The premise of this paper is that anthropologists can contribute directly and importantly to the processes of policy formulation and implementation in international relations. In my view, anthropological data, methods, and approaches can all be used in ways that will help us to avoid or to resolve conflict at both the local and international levels. Before anthropologists will be able to put their work to such uses, however, we need first to overcome the widely held misconception that anthropologists are mostly interested in esoterica, and that they have little of immediate value to offer in the process of strategic thinking. We need to offer specific suggestions about the roles that anthropologists are especially prepared to play in the development and evaluation of policy alternatives. The purpose of this paper is to sketch one of several such roles. To do this, I describe briefly some of what anthropologists and others have learned about decision making. I indicate how this is especially applicable to understanding some situations in which conflict and fighting occur, and indicate why I see anthropological input to policy development as useful for such situations.

Decision Making and Strategy

Schroder and his associates (1967) show that the strategic decisions taken by a group can be characterized according to whether they result from group processes that are relatively more complex or relatively more concrete in the way information is evaluated and used. On the one hand, high-level strategies are those that result from group processes that take account of a wide variety of information and use that information in flexible ways to define a range of options. On the other hand, low-level strategies are those that result from processes wherein only a limited range of information is taken account of, and the information is used in limited, rigid ways, usually in response to immediately observable situational factors.

Whether a group adopts a low-level or high-level strategy depends on the skills and abilities of its members, most especially the group's leaders. But, it also depends upon some of the aspects of the environment in which the decisions are taken. The environment is called more or less noxious depending upon (1) how severe the adverse consequences of a decision might be, (2) the amount of reward that appears to be available to a group, (3) the amount of interest group members have in a particular outcome, and (4) the degree to which the situation in which a decision is to be taken is consistent or not with the beliefs held by the group. When the adverse consequences are severe, the available rewards great, the group's attention focused with interest on a particular outcome, and the situation dissonant with the group's views, the environment can be stressful or noxious. An additional factor is the amount of ambiguity in the environment, such as the number of alternative paths that might be followed, conflicting information from different sources, uncertainty about one or more aspects of the environment, and the like.

A group which adopts a high-level strategy at one time may at another time use low-level strategies to try to reach some desired outcome. Such shifts from high-level to low-level strategies may result from a change in the skills and abilities of the group's leaders. But such a shift can also happen as a result of an increase in the stressful complexity of a group's decision-making environment. (See Mandelbaum, this volume, for predictions of future shifts of this kind.) In fact, the general relationship between the level of strategy used by a group and the stressfulness of the group's environment can be characterized by an inverted U-curve (see, Figure 1). Thus, as the amount of ambiguity in, or the stressfulness of, the environment in which group decisions are taken increases, the levels of strategy used by the group also increases (as long as there exist in the group skills and abilities to support that increase), but only up to a point. Beyond this point (which Schroder et al. call the point of optimal complexity) increasing environmental stress or ambiguity is dealt with by the group's using lower, and lower level strategies. That is, once the environment becomes more complex than can be handled by the group's strategy, attempts at maintaining the group's position are made using increasingly more concrete and integratively simple responses. (See Frank, this volume, on use of such strategy by national leaders.) Those responses are made to immediate factors in the environment.

The point at which the environment becomes overcomplex is reached more quickly for low-level strategies than for higher-level strategies (see Figure 2). Hence, lower-level strategic responses will start to collapse to options that are even more anchored in immediate situational factors sooner than will higher-level strategies.

Figure 1
General Relationship between Strategy Level and Environmental Complexity*

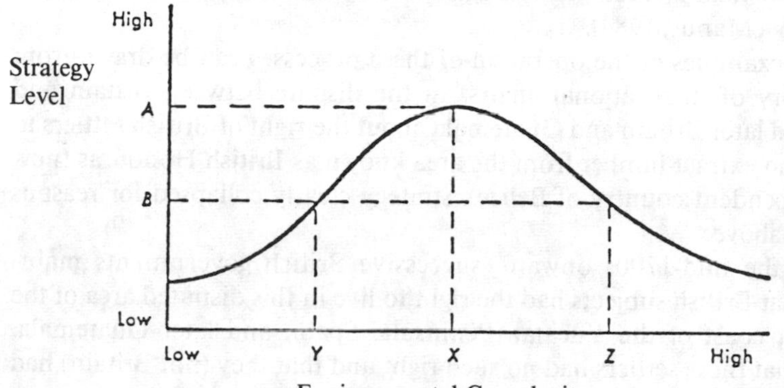

*Adapted from Schroder, et al., 1967.

This general relationship found by Schroder and his associates between the complexity of response and the stressfulness of the environment has been documented in numerous settings. In addition to simulations of international negotiations carried out by Schroder, et al. (1967) anthropologists have discovered it in relation to stress induced by environmental deprivation and disaster (Laughlin and Brady, 1978), in

Figure 2
Relationship between Environmental and Response Complexity for Different Strategy Levels*

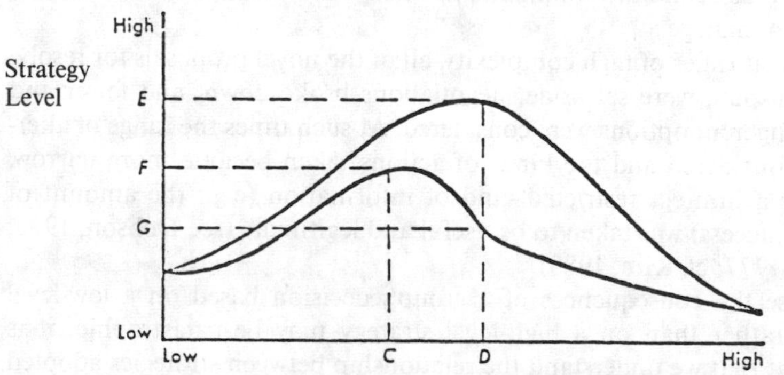

*Adapted from Schroder, et al., 1967.

human and animal ritual behavior (d'Aquili, et al., 1979), in the development of language and thinking ability (Rubinstein, 1979), and in the way scientists defend favored theories against falsification (Rubinstein, Laughlin, and McManus, 1984).

Many examples of the operation of these processes can be drawn from the history of international affairs. In the dispute between Britain and Spain and later Britain and Guatemala about the right of British settlers to live in and extract lumber from the area known as British Honduras (now the independent country of Belize), strategy clearly collapsed for reasons outlined above.

From the mid-1700s onward, successive British governments maintained that British subjects had the right to live in this disputed area of the southeast coast of the Yucatan Peninsula. Spain, and later Guatemala, argued that these settlers had no such right and that they (not Britain) had sovereign control of that area. Periodically, elaborate negotiations (first with Spain and later with Guatemala) were conducted in attempts to resolve the dispute peacefully. These negotiations sometimes resulted in formal treaties. Yet during this time there were several episodes of war between the British Hondurans and Spaniards or Guatemalans.

Armed conflict between Britain and these other countries occurred when economic difficulties or political unrest within these countries was particularly severe. During times when there was a relatively less complex international or home environment, the negotiators entertained a wider range of options than when conditions were more complex.

For instance, there were a number of proposals in the mid and late 1800s to settle the dispute by building a railroad or submarine cable to connect Guatemala to the Atlantic Coast. Yet these potential solutions ceased to be considered as economic conditions in Britain became more complex and difficult to manage.

Indeed, at times of high complexity, all of the novel proposals for resolving the disputc were set aside, negotiations broke down, and fewer and more belligerent options were considered. At such times the range of alternatives considered and the kinds of actions taken became more narrow, and only a limited, restricted kind of information (e.g., the amount of military success) was taken to be useful and legitimate (see Dobson, 1973; Bolland, 1977; cf. Kim, 1983).

Because the consequences of a group's decision based on a low-level strategy rather than on a high-level strategy may be catastrophic, it is important that we understand the relationship between strategies adopted and conditions triggering them. As in the case cited, groups acting on the basis of low-level strategy will turn to aggressive, violent acting sooner than will groups acting on the basis of high-level strategy. Equally important, if not more so, is the observation by Schroder, et al., that the use of "last resort responses" by low-level strategy groups is irrational—it occurs whether or not it is likely to result in the desired outcome. (See also Frank, this volume, on the means selected by national leaders.) For groups functioning with high-level strategies the "last resort response" is likely to occur only when it would lead to the desired goal. Thus strategies that are based upon concrete situational factors (what might be called positional bargaining) are more likely to lead to conflict and failure in international relations than are higher level strategic decisions (Schroder, et al., 1967).

Bias in Strategic Decisions

Understanding this general relationship between levels of strategy and the complexity of the environment obviously can be helpful in a general way. For instance, it makes it possible to differentiate among strategies in international relations and to understand why some strategies are dangerous and ought to be avoided. Further, when it turns out that low-level strategies are part of an ongoing exchange, the dangers resulting from this can better be avoided. We can act to change the environment within which intergroup relations are conducted so as to make it less stressful or less ambiguous. But understanding this general relationship tells us little about the dynamics of the high-level to low-level shift, and is therefore of little help in finding ways to avoid a high- to low-level strategic collapse. For reasons that will become clearer later, I believe it is to the understanding of the processes which are part of this shift and to the monitoring of those processes that anthropologists are especially prepared to contribute.

Each time we make a decision to pursue one policy alternative rather than some other, our choice is made on the basis of incomplete information. This is so for many reasons. An important one is that when we consider the wealth of information upon which we might base our decisions we pay attention selectively to some of that information and ignore other parts of it. This selective attention to information is not a random process. Rather, it is based on the use of heuristic principles to help us choose what it is that is important to take into account. This is helpful; the time needed for and the difficulty of evaluating alternatives is decreased. But, the use of heuristics necessarily entails that we also accept some biases, and these direct our attention systematically away from some kinds of information (Rubinstein, 1984).

For instance, Tversky and Kahneman (1974) describe studies which show that people often use three general heuristic principles as aids in making judgments under conditions of uncertainty. (1) The likelihood that something is a member of a particular class is assessed by the degree to which it is similar to, or has characteristics representative of, members of the class in question. They call this the *representativeness heuristic.* (2) The likelihood of an event, or the frequency of a class, is estimated by how easily occurrences or instances are recalled. This they call the *availability heuristic.* (3) Estimates of the likelihood of particular outcomes are often based upon some initial value or view which, during the process of estimation, is adjusted to give the final answer. The source of this starting point may be arbitrary, suggested by the way the problem is asked, or it may be the result of some other estimation. This third heuristic they call the *adjustment and anchoring heuristic.*

Used judiciously, each of these heuristics can be helpful guides for decisionmaking. But in conditions of uncertainty, or at times when for other reasons like the stressfulness of the environment their limitations are not kept in mind, they may lead to systematic errors. Tversky and Kahneman point out several such errors for each heuristic. A few brief examples illustrate the point.

Associated with the representativeness heuristic is a bias, which they call the *illusion of validity.* People frequently expect to find an outcome that is representative of the information which they have. Finding a good fit between the outcome they observe and their input information leads them to develop confidence in the prediction even if the input information is scanty, unreliable, or outdated. This confidence persists even when it is misplaced, and the factors limiting the value of the input information are known.

Biases to which the heuristic of availability may lead are due to the ease of retrievability, the effectiveness of our search for, or the imaginability of instances of a particular situation occurring. In addition, bias due to a tendency to assume a relationship between two situations that often cooccur is frequently found. That is, the heuristic of availability can lead to mistaken conclusions because of such factors as how familiar, salient, or frequent in our experience one sort of outcome is in relation to others, how thorough (for whatever reason) our search for alternatives is, or whether we can imagine a particular situation happening. Since each of these is affected by many different factors, conclusions reached using the availability heuristic can easily be in error.

The predicament in which we now find ourselves is in part the result of the operation of such heuristics. Kim (1983), for example, shows that strategists most frequently approach the task of international negotiation from a perspective he calls *political realism.* Kim (1983:9) argues that this approach depends upon a "concept of 'power' in mainstream realism that is excessively narrow and limited. This realism respects only material, and physical power. . ." As well as a specific and general narrowness of perspective, Kim (1983:10) sees in this realism a mistaken assumption that there is a continuity between our past and the present circumstances. These assumptions and shortsightedness lead directly to the failure of many world leaders, as described by Jerome Frank earlier in this volume, to recognize that the possibility of nuclear war is a problem of a different order than that posed by conventional warfare. Thus "deterrence" continues to be discussed as a practical "solution" while other approaches such as disarmament are dismissed as unworkable and not worthy of consideration (see Foster in this volume; Mandelbaum, 1983; Rubinstein and Tax, 1985).

The process of collapse in the level of strategic decision making under conditions of excessive stress observed by Schroder and his associates probably takes place, in part at least, because of an increased reliance on the use of heuristics without proper caution in monitoring for the errors that these might introduce. There is ample evidence that even very sophisticated thinkers among scientists and policy analysts are not immune from the kind of systematic error that results from this process of increasing reliance on heuristic aids. Thus, for example, scientists faced with disconfirming evidence about a widely held theory (Rubinstein, Laughlin, and McManus, 1984) and policy analysts seeking information on which to base the design of their programs (Rubinstein, 1984), display a tendency to rely heavily on favored heuristics and to incorporate systematic errors into their work. Moreover, many instances of dispute in international relations that erupt into violent confrontations appear to conform to this analysis. In these cases it is not when high-level strategies are used, but at times when strategic decisions revealing low-level group processes are taken, that conflicts escalate and violence occurs.

Cultural Knowledge and Strategy

Understanding how the shift from high-level strategies to low-level strategies in overcomplex environments takes place is in part provided by seeing that heuristics and the biases that accompany them play a role in the development and evaluation of policy alternatives. In addition to being aware that uncritical use of heuristic aids for decision making can lead to systematic errors, it must be further recognized that the heuristics that guide policy formulation and evaluation are made up of systems of symbolic material with cultural and ideological content (Beeman, this volume).

Identification of information that is possibly being left out of account, or the options that are real but unconsidered by particular policy initiatives, requires the careful description of both the explicit and tacit meanings and commitments of the symbolic material guiding the development of that policy. It is to this task that anthropologists come with particular expertise and understandings and which they are especially prepared to carry out.

Description of the way in which particular groups adapt to their social and physical environments is a major focus for anthropological work. Anthropologists also have been concerned to understand the ways in which different political, ideological, and, in general, cultural groups selectively use information. In a very real and important sense, anthropologists have long experience in discovering and describing the heuristics used by the people with whom they work. For these reasons anthropologists have been very successful in showing why particular local-level policies failed to bring about the particular changes or effects for which they were intended (Spicer, 1952). It is now important that anthropologists begin to use these understandings in prospective as well as retrospective studies (Cohen, 1984; Rubinstein, 1984).

Similarly, anthropologists might participate in the policy process for international relations by exploring social and cultural heuristics guiding that policy process. They would then be in a position to help prevent the collapse of higher-level strategies to lower-level strategies by offering for consideration alternatives not recognizable under certain heuristics, by monitoring assertions about the likelihood that policy alternatives will have specific results (to insure that supposed results do not depend upon self-fulfilling processes) and, in general, by offering information that will help policy discussions take account of a wider variety of information. Anthropology thus has the potential to insure that information is used in flexible ways, and that a range of conceivable options is available so that policymaking may remain a high-level strategy.

References

Bolland, O. Nigel. 1977. *The Formation of Colonial Society: Belize, from Conquest to Crown Colony*. Baltimore, Md.: Johns Hopkins University Press.

Cohen, R. 1984. "Approaches to Applied Anthropology." *Communication and Cognition* 17:135–62.

d'Aquili, E.; Laughlin, C.; and McManus, J. 1979. *The Spectrum of Ritual*. New York: Columbia University Press.

Dobson, Narda. 1973. *A History of Belize*. Trinidad and Jamaica: Longman Caribbean Limited.

Kim, Samuel S. 1983. *The Quest for a Just World Order*. Boulder, Colo.: Westview Press.

Laughlin, C. and Brady, I. 1978. *Extinction and Survival in Human Populations*. New York: Columbia University Press.

Mandelbaum, Michael. 1983. *The Nuclear Future*. Ithaca, N.Y.: Cornell University Press.

Rubinstein, R.A. 1979. "The Cognitive Consequences of Bilingual Education in Northern Belize." *American Ethnologist* 6:583–601.

———. 1984. "Epidemiology and Anthropology: Notes on Science and Scientism." *Communication and Cognition* 17:163–85.

Rubinstein, R.A.; Laughlin, C.; and McManus, J. 1984. *Science as Cognitive Process*. Philadelphia, Pa.: University of Pennsylvania Press.

Rubinstein, R.A. and Tax, S. 1985. "Power, Powerlessness and the Failure of 'Political Realism.'" In *Native Power: The Quest for Autonomy and Nationhood of Indigenous Peoples*, ed. J. Brøsted et al., pp. 301-8. Bergen: Universitetsforlagetas.

Schroder, H.; Driver, M.; and Streufert, S. 1967. *Human Information Processing*. New York: Holt, Rinehart and Winston.

Spicer, E. 1952. *Human Problems in Technological Change*. New York: Wiley.

Tversky, A.and Kahneman, D. 1974. "Judgements under Uncertainty: Heuristics and Biases." *Science* 185:1124–30.

Conclusion: Toward an Anthropology of Peace and War

Mary LeCron Foster

Anthropology, for the most part, has not been a problem-solving discipline. Although an applied dimension in anthropology has been recognized for about fifty years, most anthropologists still view their science as exploratory and explanatory. They have been concerned to bring to light the biological steps in human evolution that have led from the first protohominids to modern human beings. They have also been concerned to trace the cultural development of the world's societies, from the earliest technologically simple forms to the technologically complex forms of today, and to describe the processes underlying and molding social structures in all of their global variety.

As the discipline has developed beyond the mere ethnographic description of its early days into an analytic science of human social behavior, common ground has increasingly been discovered among what initially seemed very disparate practices. The underlying unity of human social behavior, whether the groups in which it is practiced are technologically complex or not, has come to seem at least as characteristic as its variation.

Culture is the central concept in anthropology. It has been defined in many ways, but always it must be viewed as an adaptive or coping device. Any society, in order to survive, must solve a series of problems, including technological adaptation to the physical environment, social adaptation within the community, and adaptation to friendly or hostile communities outside. The technical, social, and cultural repertoires that have been developed as coping devices are almost unlimited. One thing that they have in common is that they must prove workable or the society in question will disappear. Some institutions are better than others, and any may become outmoded in the face of rapid change or readjusted in response to the slower change that, in the past, technologically simple and fairly isolated societies have experienced.

New technologies have brought major readjustment in their wake and have quickly spread from society to society. Inventions such as settled agriculture, metalurgy, new means of transportation, and mechanization of industry have required a great deal of social readjustment, as have ecological pressures such as increases in population or shortages of economic resources, as well as aspects of the social readjustments themselves, such as the emergence of social classes or the formation of larger social and political groups.

Anthropologists have found that, however repugnant the idea may seem, warfare has often been a successful coping device. Warfare has been a major implement in uniting social groups into larger and economically more viable bodies. At least up to the level of a gunpowder technology, warfare has resolved conflicts, rarely forever, but long enough to allow participants to rebuild their resources and reformulate allegiances. Anthropologists have also found that most societies have developed (or borrowed from other societies) social and other strategies that have reduced intercommunity tensions and hence the likelihood of armed conflict. In the Balkans, for example, the institution of godparenthood, by cutting across Christian-Moslem boundaries, reduces interethnic tensions.

Many anthropologists view the conflict-resolving and stress-reducing mechanisms found in societies that have been the object of anthropological investigation as potential sources of policy leads that can be useful in the attempt to develop long-term strategies at high political levels capable of reducing the threat of nuclear annihilation. Unfortunately, in most cases, anthropologists are not trained either to think or to do research at the macrolevel. Their object of study, at least until very recently, has been the small community, which they have tended to interpret as an isolate. They are only now beginning to learn to relate the insights they have developed in their microlevel studies to the realities of the macrolevel world.

But this apparent weakness may be a strength. The breadth of their cross-cultural examinations provides anthropologists with unique insights into the wide range of solutions that human groups have found to problems that are common to all. They have also developed theories about the nature of change and human resistance to change, and for the task of finding strategies to reduce the nuclear threat, these insights can be very useful to policymakers.

This book is a first attempt to test the value of an anthropological viewpoint in the context of improving international security and peace policy decisions. The authors of these papers seek to discover whether, guided by their anthropological training and experience, they can ask the right questions about human behavior in relation to the problems of reformulation of national and international policy. These questions have not yet been answered, but so far the questions that have been asked have been often narrow and misdirected. Answers to the wrong questions are worse than no answers at all, while answers to the right questions can be pursued, often with productive results. The authors believe that the questions which they have raised *are* pertinent to the discovery of fruitful strategies for reducing international tensions, and that answers which they begin to discover simply by asking the question can be helpful to policymakers. They also believe that anthropologists should participate at the level of designing long-term international policy and that their unique knowledge about human behavior in diverse social situations should be utilized alongside the economic, psychological, diplomatic, and technical expertise that forms the usual base for formulation of policy. By participating in this book, and by expressing their thoughts on the crucial problem of establishing an enduring peace, they hope to stimulate other anthropologists to apply their science to this problem and to stimulate policymakers to draw upon the largely neglected resource of anthropology.

About the Contributors

William O. Beeman is associate professor of anthropology at Brown University.

Silviu Brucan is professor of political science at the University of Bucharest, Romania. He was formerly Romanian ambassador to the United States and then to the United Nations.

M. Margaret Clark is professor of medical anthropology at the University of California in San Francisco. She is past president of the American Anthropological Association.

Ronald Cohen is professor of anthropology and African Studies at the University of Florida, Gainesville.

Paul L. Doughty is professor of anthropology at the University of Florida, Gainesville.

Mary LeCron Foster is research associate in the Department of Anthropology, University of California, Berkeley.

Jerome D. Frank is emeritus professor of psychiatry at the Johns Hopkins School of Medicine.

Jill Leslie Furst is adjunct associate professor of anthropology at the State University of New York, Albany.

Frederick C. Gamst is professor of anthropology at the University of Massachusetts, Boston.

Walter Goldschmidt is professor of anthropology at the University of California, Los Angeles. He is past president of the American Anthropological Association.

Nancie L. Gonzalez is professor of anthropology at the University of Maryland.

Carol J. Greenhouse is associate professor of anthropology at Cornell University.

Bernard Huyghe is a research assistant in anthropology at the Katholieke Universiteit, Leuven, Belgium, and a practicing psychiatrist.

Alice B. Kehoe is professor of anthropology at Marquette University, Milwaukee.

Larissa Lomnitz is an anthropology professor in the interdisciplinary Instituto de Investigaciones en Matematicas Aplicadas y en Sistemas at the Universidad Nacional Autonoma de Mexico.

Bela C. Maday is professor in the Department of Anthropology at American University.

David G. Mandelbaum is emeritus professor of anthropology at the University of California, Berkeley.

Seymour Melman is professor of industrial engineering at Columbia University.

Laura Nader is professor of anthropology at the University of California, Berkeley.

Rik Pinxten is professor in the Seminarie voor Antropologie, Rijksuniversiteit, Ghent.

Alexander Randall 5th is a freelance consultant trained in anthropology and education.

Robert A. Rubinstein is acting director, Program in Ethnography and Public Policy, Department of Anthropology, Northwestern University.

Sam C. Sarkesian is professor of political science at Loyola University, Chicago.

James Silverberg is professor of anthropology at the University of Wisconsin, Milwaukee.

Valery A. Tishkov is Head, Department of American Ethnic Studies in the Institute of Ethnography at the Academy of Sciences of the Union of Soviet Socialist Republics.

Peter Worsley is emeritus professor of comparative sociology at the University of Manchester, England.

Index